Praise for Bowie

"Perceptively written, this excellent life is refreshingly short on fanzine eulogy and tabloid censure."   —*Daily Telegraph* (London)

"Illuminating, thoughtful, and provocative."   —*Financial Times*

"To decipher some tangible kind of reality behind a monumentally enigmatic figure such as Bowie is surely a daunting task for any biographer. . . . Sandford ultimately digs deeper [than others] and includes some authoritative musical analysis."   —*Vox*

"[An] exhaustive biography. . . . Sandford shows how, despite early mistakes, Bowie's grip on his career has always been extremely sure."   —*Times Literary Supplement*

"*Bowie* gives a clear, thoughtful picture, which suggests that, with the fading of the chameleon rock artist, something like a human being has emerged."   —*Sunday Telegraph* (London)

BOWIE
LOVING THE ALIEN

CHRISTOPHER SANDFORD

DA CAPO PRESS • NEW YORK

Library of Congress Cataloging-in-Publication Data
Sandford, Christopher.
  Bowie: loving the alien / Christopher Sandford.
      p.   cm.
  Originally published: London: Little Brown, 1996.
  Includes bibliographical references and index.
  ISBN 0-306-80854-4 (alk. paper)
  1. Bowie, David. 2. Rock musicians—England—Biography. I. Title.
ML420.B754S26   1998
782.42166′092—dc21   98-19603
[b]   CIP
                                                                 MN

First Da Capo Press edition 1998

This Da Capo Press paperback edition of *Bowie* is an unabridged
republication of the revised and updated edition published in
England in 1997, with one minor textual emendation. It is reprinted
by arrangement with Little, Brown and Company (UK).

Published by Da Capo Press, Inc.
A Subsidiary of Plenum Publishing Corporation
233 Spring Street, New York, N.Y. 10013

For Johnny Johnson
1921–1996

CONTENTS

ACKNOWLEDGEMENTS

Coincidentally, another man whose initials are D.B. got me started on this project. Don Bates, an old friend from the early seventies, first played me a copy of *Hunky Dory*. Overnight my interest in Bowie became what it is not extravagant to call fascination. I'm grateful to Don for the introduction.

For insights into Bowie and his music, I should thank: Kevin Armstrong, Candy Atcheson, Edith Baldry, Stuart Belsham, Ross Benson, Pete Brown, William Burroughs, Lesley Buzan, John Cambridge, Malcolm Carr, Edith Cearns, Keith Christmas, Ray Connolly, Neil Conti, Margaret Cooper, Terry Cox, Chris Farlowe, Herbie Flowers, Gitta Fuchs, James Grauerholz, Nigel Green, Jeff Griffin, Uwe Herz, Cheryl Hise, John Hutchinson, Brian James, Tom Keylock, Edith Kohl, Linda Kreal, Chuck Leavell, Patrick MacDonald, Stuart Mackenzie, Marcus Maclaine, Dave Markee, the late Steve Marriott, Phil May, Nick Miles, Bela Molnar, Alan Motz, Pat Mountford, John Murray, Eric Myren, Tony Newman, Alan Parker, Mary Parr, Julie Anne Paull, Andy Peebles, John Peel, Peter Perchard, Anthony Phillips, Kenneth Pitt, Len Price, Maggie Riepl, Tim Renwick, Tim Rice, Keith Richards, the late Mick Ronson, Matthew Seligman, Eric Smith, Dick Taylor, Rick Wakeman, Ryan Ward, Willie Weeks, Horst Wendt and Graham Wright.

On an institutional note, source material on Bowie and his family was provided by: *Berliner Morgenpost*, the British Library, British Newspaper Library, Burnt Ash Primary School, Companies House, David Bowie Information Service, the *Evening Standard*, General Register Office, the *Mail on Sunday*, *Melody Maker*, Performing Rights Society, Ripple Productions, Seattle

Public Library, *Seattle Times*, University of Washington and the Warwick Group.

I also interviewed a number of people who prefer not to be named. Where sources asked for anonymity – usually citing friendship with Bowie or Corinne Schwab – every effort was made to persuade them to go on the record. Where this was not possible, I have used the words 'a friend' or 'a musician', as usual. I apologize for the frequency with which I have had to resort to this formula.

Finally, a doffed hat to: American Speedy, Kathleen Anderson, Peter Barnes, Terry Bland, Robert Bruce, the Camlin Hotel, Noel Chelberg, Albert Clinton, Monty Dennison, Milan Drdoš, Nicole Drdoš, Godfrey Evans, Focus Fine Arts, Malcolm Galfe, Tim Holman, the Gay Hussar, Joan Lambert, Terry Lambert, Belinda Lawson, Borghild Lee, Vincent Lorimer, Emma Lynch, Al Meyersahm, Jim Meyersahm, Sheila Mohn, Phillip Oppenheim, Robin Parish, John Prins III, John Prins IV, Bryan Richardson, Amanda Ripley, Nancy Roller, my father Sefton Sandford, Peter Scaramanga, Sue Sims-Hilditch, Fred and Cindy Smith, Jane Spalding, Hilary Stevens, Ti-fa, Tower 801 and Victoria Willis Fleming. Special thanks to Barbara Levy and Alan Samson.

C.S.
1996

LIST OF ILLUSTRATIONS

BOWIE
LOVING THE ALIEN

1
GOLDEN YEARS

Summer 1973

David Bowie was missing. Forty minutes away from his swansong as Ziggy Stardust, and he slipped through the mob into Hammersmith Broadway. He was wearing a check shirt and jeans and with his waxy, pale skin he looked like one of the teenage Bowie Boys posing hopefully at the stage door. Had anyone noticed him, they would have remembered only a bone-gaunt figure with dowdy clothes and elaborate hair, talking to a thirteen-year-old girl. No one noticed him.

Julie Anne Paull, a fan from the East End of London, knew that Bowie was growing tired of the Ziggy character and bored with the rock scene. Yet even that paled compared to what she heard in the deserted alley behind the Broadway. Bowie was in a state of collapse, induced, in part, by his fear of 'going mad'. He was bitter with anger at his manager. His marriage had gone wrong. He spoke of his homosexual affairs. According to a member of Bowie's group at the time:

> I think it was coke. Cocaine and demons. I think there was definitely demon power involved. He took all that dope that would give him a low in the morning and a high at night. That's when the paranoia came out.

Whatever the cause, it would be hard to argue with Paull's verdict that 'he was a man on a razor's edge', or that his reluctance to play that night would strike another fan as 'the mother of a Stephen Fry-like breakdown'. It was only after a

tearful, self-lacerating scene that he finally agreed to recross the
road to the Odeon, where a steward could be seen rolling around
in the gutter with Bowie's bodyguard, discussing his where-
abouts. The second girl remembers that 'David, who'd been so
low, seemed to brighten' at the sight. Bowie walked straight to the
back of the theatre, past a startled guard and into the building, up
the backstage stairs to the loft, then out on to the balcony that
looks over the street. He stood gazing silently at his fans for at
least five minutes. A musician who passed by claims he saw tears
in his eyes. As Bowie turned to go downstairs, he suddenly
stopped short, struck by a hoarse shout from his manager of
'Where's David?' According to Bowie's guitarist, his exact
response to the question was to mutter, 'You tell me', before
surrendering to the frantic cries from the dressing room.

The show that followed was vintage Bowie. Rock production
values, in 1973, may have been horizontal – the light show
seemed to have been borrowed from some school disco, and the
sound engineer achieved an authentically dreadful, Beatles-era
drone – but Bowie's winning mix of kabuki and *Clockwork Orange*,
welded to catchy suburban riffs, struck even *The Times* as an
'orgiastic triumph'. As 'Watch That Man' was followed by 'All the
Young Dudes', which gave way to 'Oh! You Pretty Things', fans
were reminded of why they liked this music in the first place:
Bowie, it seemed, was incapable of writing a tune that didn't stick.
It didn't hurt that his band – three pub rockers from Hull
squeezed into ship's cabin boys' breeches and tunics with bell-
bottom sleeves – backed him beautifully. Mick Ronson made a
particularly happy match, his Jeff Beck-style leads meshing with
Bowie's dramatic blurting. The long, power-chord solo in 'Moonage Daydream' came across not as swaggering but as genuine
give-and-take. It was striking, as Bowie returned from the
dressing room in a red-and-green jumpsuit and red platform
boots, that, in a colleague's words, 'he was having as much fun
as Bette Midler'. He didn't know that, an hour earlier, Bowie had
been crying on a teenage girl's shoulder and refusing to sing.

'Space Oddity' followed, a canny mix of semi-acoustic folk and
futuristic kitsch. Bowie's finest moment, it blueprinted his whole
later image, even while he fretted in and out of Ziggy Stardust.
After a merely melodramatic 'My Death', Bowie was back in an

off-the-shoulder wool catsuit for 'Cracked Actor', swooning to the floor under the nasally electric guitar and indulging in the same kind of theatrical, rock-star vanity the song was making fun of. The man of paradox had been obvious since his first tentative efforts at writing ten years before. But fame enormously magnified and engrained the oddities that were evident in Bowie's character from the earliest professional days. There was the folk singer and Bob Dylan *manqué* with a love for abrasively noisy, guitar-heavy rock. There was the androgynous beauty with, as his ex-wife writes, 'the morals of a bisexual alley-cat', who was strangely passive in bed. He had the ambition to shock and outrage – as when he knelt before Ronson, seized his thighs and sucked at the strings of his guitar – but could still insist in 1995, 'I was a very shy boy.'

All of these paradoxes were there when Bowie, now wearing a sheer black vest, black satin trousers and a diamond earring the size of a chandelier, tore through an anthemic version of 'White Light, White Heat'. At that point the band left the stage. After passing around a cigarette in the gloom behind the drum kit, Bowie turned to his old friend John Hutchinson, added to the group on twelve-string guitar.

'Don't start the encore yet,' he told him. 'I've got something to say.'

A white spot played on Bowie as he walked to the microphone. He stood gaping into the damp, upturned faces in front of him, knowing, he later said, that he had to make contact 'soul to soul'.

'Yeah!' he shouted into the mike.

'Bowie . . . Bowie,' chanted the fans.

'Everyone,' he panted, 'this has been . . . the greatest tour of our lives . . . Of all the shows on this tour, this particular show will remain the longest, because not only is it . . . not only is it the last show of the tour . . . it's the last show we'll ever do.'

Then Bowie nodded to Hutchinson, publicly sacked in front of an audience of thousands, to start the last number.

There were different views and different explanations of Bowie's retirement. To some, it was a strategy of Byzantine cunning. Bowie's manager, it later emerged, had his own reasons for withdrawing his star product. There were complicated discussions

with a record label and a publishing company. Advance negotiations for an American arena tour had broken down acrimoniously.
There were others who saw it as a general disintegration of Bowie's
personality. To Roy Carr in *New Musical Express* he was 'copping
out ... trotting out his ego ... an actor playing at being a star'.
Bowie, according to this reading, had increasingly become a
caricature of himself. The tricks and stagecraft that once helped
him stand out from the herd of singers equally talented but far less
colourful had become a curse. David Bowie the icon had overtaken
David Bowie the musician. To Julie Anne Paull, who talked her way
backstage after the show, Bowie complained about his audience –
'stupid little kids' – and being ill-treated by what he later described
as his 'staff'. This rankled and dramatized his already strong
tendency to see himself beset by enemies.

What followed – furious, pent-up and at times psychotic –
revealed in five minutes why Bowie in the past had been so intent
on never losing his temper: he had a deadly fear of what might
happen if he did. When Paull left the dressing room he slumped
forward on to his vanity table and cried. Then Bowie went on the
rampage. The table with its wine bottle and flowers, the walls,
chairs, lamp and windows were all kicked and spat on. But it was
against himself, finally, rather than his fans or staff, that Bowie
turned. When he emerged it was noticed that, as well as his
bloodshot eyes, he was scratched about his neck and face and
sported a red bruise the size of an apple on his cheek. The violence
showed again the volatile, nervy personality, but this time it was
followed by a reversal that shocked everyone who did not know
how habitually with Bowie fire gave way to ice.

While not only the musical and heavyweight press but his own
colleagues began to ponder the mystery of Bowie's retirement, a
celebratory party took place at the Café Royal. At some stage in
the evening John Hutchinson found himself dancing with Nina
Van Pallandt. As they passed by a buffet table groaning with
luxury, Hutchinson became aware of a satin-suited figure gliding
towards them. 'David looked over,' he remembers, 'said, "All
right?", nodded, and then waltzed off.

'That nod was when I knew it was all over.'

Winter 1995

Twenty-two years ago, David Bowie had said he would never do another tour. This is it.

Bowie and his opening act, Nine Inch Nails, settle for the fate of co-headliners. The strategy may make more sense to them than to their audiences: some in suits and ties, others who chart NIN's progress via a parade of torn T-shirts. The two camps mingle uneasily in the frigid vat of the Tacoma Dome. The older crowd, men and women in their forties, sit, belted and shivering, clutching their opera glasses. In the mid-distance a mob dances itself dizzy and rushes the stage. After their idols leave, a few thousand NIN fans also make their way out. Respectful applause greets the slender pale figure who lopes unannounced on stage.

At first glance he looks miraculously unchanged. Bowie's weight, as he approaches fifty, has been gradually falling until, reed-thin, gaunt about the cheeks, with a shock of spiked hair, and clad in baggy, tie-dyed work clothes, he seems ghostly and lost and forbidding. He wears a slender silver crucifix and a wedding ring. The middle two fingernails of his left hand are painted black. The stage décor is kept to a minimum – a bare-floored room hung with mannequins and torn window blinds, lit by klieg lights, like a Hollywood idea of an artist's garret. An illuminated sign reads STRANGE HAND NOISE. Later in the set Bowie will sing sitting slumped at a kitchen table while smoke jets pour on him from above.

The first number, played at ear-ringing volume, is 'Scary Monsters (and Super Creeps)'. Raucous in the best sense of the word, the song ends with Bowie's cryptic announcement, 'Never, *never* tell the truth,' and the dreaded words, 'Here's one off the new album.' The next hour is a virtual recital of *Outside*. Somewhere in the jumble of pneumatic guitars, pounding drums and lyrics about an 'art-ritual' *fin de siècle* murder, pop songs signal wildly to be let out. When Bowie covers his twenty-five-year-old 'Andy Warhol', a sense of relief from the furiously dispatched salvo of tales of slaughter and dismemberment fills the upper tiers: here is a tune you can *hum*. As though embarrassed, Bowie sings in a gruff cockney accent and skewers the fans' ovation with a wry 'Ta.'

Can this really be the man who once performed in a dress? One of Bowie's achievements has been the distance his music goes both forward and back, linking folk with grunge, the fifties and the nineties. Now that connection seems to have been broken. 'Warhol' aside, Bowie's repertoire is relentlessly modern. Dim frowns greet the stripped-down sound and unheard cuts from *Outside*. Even Bowie has to use a lyric sheet for the words to one song. On 'The Man Who Sold the World' he stoops to imitating his imitators, revamping the tune which Nirvana brought to its own fans on *Unplugged*. 'Thru' These Architects Eyes' follows – another slab of brooding melodrama, the band creating a downbeat mood not even a storming 'Night Flights' can lift. This is Bowie pleasing himself, not the audience. The mute applause, typically, emboldens him. Pressure brings out his intransigence. As another barrage starts up, Bowie seems not so much to be ignoring his past as wilfully killing it. Somewhere in the solid wall of art-noise, a single brick survives from the forgotten night in Hammersmith: Bowie's old pianist Mike Garson, looking vaguely bemused in his bulging shirt and black hat, still sounding exactly as he did on *Aladdin Sane*.

The next three numbers need no introduction. Bowie sings a gut-wrenching 'Under Pressure', stalking the stage like a caged animal, then 'Jump They Say' and 'Look back in Anger'. The final half-hour is a hoarse medley of mid-career classics. Bowie may have disowned the user-friendly *Let's Dance*-era hits, but these are songs that share that album's virtues: the fat, rocking guitar and breakneck riffs, the noise, energy and quirky, free-form verses wrapped around danceable choruses. In the last number Bowie rocks to and fro, a curious way of swaying on the balls of his feet. On the final bar he flings out his arms and drops into a Ziggy-like pose. He gives an extravagant bow. Rock may have produced its share of ironies, but none as curious as this – a forty-eight-year-old millionaire from the London suburbs, dressed like a mechanic, suspended under a huge green-and-yellow scroll, being wildly applauded for singing songs about mutilation.

Bowie, swaddled like a boxer, disappears down a flight of steps to his trailer, An assistant of gigantic proportion, whose jacket bulges significantly by one armpit, hands him a lit cigarette and a glass of wine. It was one of the legends of his Ziggy persona that

Bowie enjoyed total privacy when relaxing backstage, and many were the rumours swirling around his dressing room door. Now a few nervous, Nosferatu-pale VIPs are nudged into a holding area inside the compound gate. 'Who's Kingsley Amis?' asks one epicene man, scanning a rain-soaked newspaper. 'Whoever he is, he's dead.' After twenty minutes of monumental patience, looking nonchalant as they remove the *Outside* posters nailed to the walls, the VIPs are rewarded by a stir at the trailer door. Two assistants walk down the steps. Behind them comes Bowie. Up close you notice, again, the wolf's teeth and the matter of his left eye. With his heavy mascara and his milk-pale skin he almost exactly resembles an animal, a favourite of his family's which they could never see without recalling the likeness – a panda. Bowie is wearing a pair of jeans that sag away from his non-existent waist and a black leather jacket that seems to swamp him. He talks in a voice quite unlike that he uses on stage.

'Excuse me,' he says as he coughs behind a hand.

'David . . . That was great, really . . . *wonderful*.'

'Thank you.'

'Loved it.'

'Ta.'

'You know, Dave, there's this *bookish* strain in some of your songs.'

'Oh yes, there is. I'm glad you realized it. There is.'

'Sort of like William Burroughs.'

'More like that other writer,' someone says. 'You know. Amis.'

A pause; of definite awkwardness.

'Amis, eh?'

'You know – *Lord Jim*.'

'It's sweet of you,' says Bowie, 'to come see an old hack like me on a wet Tuesday night. Good God,' he lowers his voice to mutter, '*Lord Jim*.' On cue, the black-rimmed eyes of one of the handlers turn towards a row of lights in the rain. 'If you'll brook me now, a car should be waiting.'

An accurate prognosis. With a flip of his hand, Bowie drops into a white boatlike limousine which coasts off on a sea of spray and dust. Its licence plate reads simply: CHOICE ONE.

2
BUDDHA OF SUBURBIA

'Pop stars are capable of growing old,' said Bowie at thirty-two. 'Mick Jagger at fifty will be marvellous – a battered old roué. An ageing rock star doesn't have to opt out of life. When I'm fifty, I'll prove it.'

Pop psychiatrists will dismiss Jagger, but will still pay court to the middle-aged Bowie. Actual Ph.D. theses have been accumulating for years, several of them written on the artist formerly known as Davy Jones as he nears his half-century. Part of Bowie's appeal lies in symbolizing a rock culture that, though hoary itself, still seems weak and insecure; as Robert Sandall writes, 'He embodies that uncertainty with style and wit, puts it in quotation marks and gives it a consistently good haircut.' Then again, there are not many artists whose clothes, hair, habits, moods, even their moments of blindness and self-pity, so perfectly evoke their times. Nostalgia for Bowie's golden years is in order. You could rent an Edwardian mansion flat in Beckenham for £8 a week, pose for record sleeves wearing a dress and start to reflect youth styles so fast that you became one. To others, Bowie today is a kind of Renaissance Man, a respected artiste who has struggled heroically to be an actor-writer, whose misfortune it is to be famous for singing songs about a pop star from Mars. No other modern performer has so ruthlessly killed off one image after another in order to extend his shelf life. Bowie's career has included a folk fixation, psychedelia, mime, blues, cabaret, forays into disco and Eurorock, other-worldly camp, soul, grunge, forties nostalgia and perverse avant-gardism. Aside from his stage personae, he has acted in TV and films, patronized artists from

Duchamp to his friend Damien Hirst, exhibited his own work in Cork Street, embraced fads from near-fascism to total anarchy, married twice, been idolized as a gay icon, dabbled in satanism and fallen to his knees to read the Lord's Prayer in front of an audience of seventy thousand. It is one thing to keep a fresh artistic standpoint, another to make a virtue of fickleness, and quite another to claim that in the process you are mapping out a new kind of moral versatility. David Bowie has pulled off all three. Even the name is a hybrid.

He was born, illegitimately, David Robert Jones on 8 January 1947. His father Haywood Stenton ('John') Jones, a promotions officer at Dr Barnardo's, would marry the boy's mother Margaret Mary ('Peggy') Burns eight months later. The family lived in Stansfield Road on the edge of Brixton and Stockwell. There are ugly houses and ugly houses, but number 40 is a brute, a pock-marked leper which has blundered into the south London streets from another world and somehow been preserved, dead but completely intact. Its dark bricks and flaking white window frames suggest something gloomily Victorian. The identical terraced houses to left and right give it a claustrophobic feel, and it is hard to think of more dreary surroundings for a small boy. Almost from the start David seems to have withdrawn, acting out the 'only child' tradition. The introversion that followed him through life began early.

The news on the Wednesday morning he was born was about the nationalization of the coal industry; the nationalization of electricity and oil; the setting up of a Transport Commission to manage all privately owned railways and canals; and the further cutting of the food ration. In Washington it was announced that General Marshall would replace James Byrnes as US Secretary of State, ushering in a new era of subsidies for countries, like Britain, threatened with economic collapse. A Senate committee heard the first references to civil unrest in Vietnam, drawing the promise from Marshall that 'this is not our fight'. In Memphis, a boy named Elvis Presley celebrated his twelfth birthday.

This was a world still agonizing from the war, where the British, in particular, were faced with bankruptcy until they could secure a loan from Washington, and would find it hard, even then, to hold their country together. On 8 January 1947

18,000 transport workers rejected the advice of their union and remained on strike. Main-line and suburban train services closed down. A crowd marched on Downing Street to protest against the cutting of food quotas. Meanwhile, Britain suffered its worst winter in living memory. By day fog descended, leaving spectacular rime deposits on streets and houses. At night the sea froze solid. On 8 January the snow and slush in Stansfield Road was knee-deep. Coalless grates, reduced gas pressure in south London and extensive cuts in electric power made conditions in many homes almost as cold and cheerless as they were outside. According to a neighbour named Edith Kohl, 'London in the forties was the worst possible place, and the worst possible time for a child to grow up in.'

Such was David's lot. His father in fact was a Yorkshireman, from Doncaster. After a raffish career in the 1930s and a failed marriage to a nightclub singer, John Jones settled in Brixton in 1946. His work with Barnardo's took him to Tunbridge Wells, where he met Peggy Burns, a waitress in the café at the Ritz cinema. David's mother appears as one of those dominant, slightly dowdy women beloved in British humour. With two previous illegitimate children, a political flirtation with Oswald Mosley and a reputation as a sexual predator, it was inevitable that gossip would accumulate around the serial seductress in Stansfield Road. It did accumulate. From his mother David inherited his curious mind, the sense of being aloof or apart, and a set of physical characteristics that included his canine teeth. The other peculiarity he shared with Peggy was a growing tendency to depression and, later, schizophrenia.

From his father's side David took his two first names (Jones itself translates as 'son of John'), a dry wit and a capacity for self-containment at odds with Peggy's volatility. Where John was cautious she was flamboyant. Where he was mild she was demonstrative and given to alternating fits of passion and violent rejection. She was extrovert, opinionated and unpredictable. He was kindly, contained, and quietly concerned with his son's life. John was enchanted when the midwife attending David's birth told his parents, 'He's been here before', since he had such 'knowing eyes'. Edith Kohl remembers that Jones cut out and kept a horoscope for his son in which, as a typical Capricorn, he was expected to be 'single-minded, determined and dedicated', though with 'repressed emotions' and a tendency to fret.

David Jones lived in Brixton for six years. As David Bowie he emphasized the exotic, dangerous world of his youth, and credited Brixton for making him 'very butch ... I was in street brawls and everything.' He would also remember how he was raised in a 'houseful of blacks', and how the streets around Stansfield Road were 'like Harlem'.

It was true that Brixton, in 1947, had been reduced to a miserable level of poverty. A quarter of the population were illiterate, there was no work, and the Fuel Order meant that shopkeepers kept their lights doused even in the evening. It was also true that south London would, in the 1950s, become home to a large Caribbean community. Tens of thousands of immigrants settled in Clapham and the neighbouring boroughs. By the early part of the decade aspects of West Indian culture had filtered as far east as Brixton, rousing its drab streets into life overnight. 'Everything went from black-and-white to technicolour,' says Edith Kohl. Atlantic Road took on the look of a bustling North African souk. On summer nights the carts of barbequed chicken patties and spiced Jamaican cofta sent up a relay of ethnic smells and the clubs around Granville Arcade were among the first to feature Ska and bluebeat. This was the tough, romantic place, full of desperadoes drinking away the afternoon, that fixed itself in David's imagination.

The truth, as so often with Bowie, was different. There was no 'houseful of blacks' and no immigrants in Stansfield Road. The first sizeable West Indian presence in Brixton was not until 1952, shortly before the Joneses left the area. Their own home, though unlovely, stood on the fringe of surburban Stockwell, a social no-man's-land in which the immediate neighbours were not gangsters and thugs but a corner shop and the Anglican chapel. It was a world of shabby bourgeois gentility, held in check by the grip of national bankruptcy. The Brixton *Mercury* for January 1947 bristles with news of bingo and whist drives, church services and advertisements for Dr Cassell's Tablets, halibut oil, Ribena and other remedies for the London winter. The only mention of crime records a sorry fall from grace: on 31 December 1946 the Brixton Cage Bird Society admitted purchasing 12lb of canary seed knowing it to have been stolen. Although John Jones was a member of the society, there was no suggestion that he was tied up in this scandal.

In later years Bowie would talk privately about 'the ball-and-chain of middle-classness' he was doomed to lug around. He frequently distorted the story of his childhood for public consumption. Often he was simply opaque. In 1976 he told an American reporter that he lived in south London for eleven years and that he walked to school 'past the gates of Brixton Prison', actually more than a mile to the south. The fact that Bowie struggled so hard to make his youth colourful and exotic is the surest sign that, in reality, it wasn't. There were few frivolities at Stansfield Road – the pride of place was a painting Kohl describes as 'like a Woolworth's chocolate box' – but the boy was never deprived. Peggy's sister would recall him as 'clean and tidy and spotless', spoilt within the limits of the family budget. When David was a baby his mother used to carry him around on a silk pillow. On successive birthdays there was a gramophone cranked up by a handle and a flickering black-and-white television set. The whole house came to a stop when David watched *The Flowerpot Men*.

The cossetted, pampered infant did not become less surly and aloof as a boy. 'He made enemies,' says one of the Joneses' friends, Trevor Gaar. 'You weren't right. He was right.' 'Other kids were shy of him,' adds Edith Kohl. David's aunt would recall him as 'a vain child' who learnt early on how to tyrannize his parents. But he also learnt that a boy who is cleverer than others in getting what he wants may be despised by them for his very success. Gaar remembers him as 'a loner who came across as odd and effeminate'. Bowie himself would later say that 'I've always been camp since I was seven ... I was outrageous then, only because my interests weren't centred around obvious seven-year-old interests, like cowboys and Indians. My things were far more mysterious.' Even in 1951, the Joneses' neighbours would routinely be startled by the arrival of the borough ambulance, summoned by the boy's plausible, yet always unfounded, claim to be 'dying'. Despite the money shortage, number 40 was among the first houses in the street to boast a telephone. As he grew older, David grew more ambitious in his efforts to draw attention to himself. Kohl remembers a winter's night when 'two fire engines – half the local brigade' arrived at Stansfield Road on a false alarm. Even then, she says, 'both parents just smiled'.

Perhaps John Jones's most important legacy was his contribution to his son's belief that *laissez-faire* morals could be welded to extreme emotional caution. His own story reads like a feat of upward assimilation. On his twenty-first birthday John received an inheritance of £3,000. He took the money and opened a piano bar named Boop-A-Doop in the West End of London. After the club folded he became a gambler, an alcoholic and a sick man. He began to suffer attacks of liver trouble so severe that his doctor had to dull the pain with morphine. After a life-saving operation Jones swore off drink and took a job as a clerk at Dr Barnardo's, eventually rising to chief publicist. Edith Kohl is among those who think that 'John spent the second half of his life making up for the first.' Since the 1970s a wealth of material has accumulated on Bowie's father. We know that he was soft-spoken, irrepressibly proud of his son, responsible and honest, but also dour, taciturn and tight-fisted – a cold man, an unresponsive man. According to Trevor Gaar, 'John had a stream of unhappy affairs behind Peggy's back.' Jones's first wife Hilda would call him bitter and 'very prejudiced towards coloured people – *very*'. Bowie himself recalled his father as 'a compassionate man, and I think he had a lot of love in him, but he couldn't express it. I can't remember him ever touching me.' The shyness he claimed for himself as a star was 'John's doing'.

While Bowie's father's life became more settled, his mother refused to stoop to middle-class convention. Extravagant and an obsessive spendthrift, she often went on shopping sprees to the West End, then complained that her husband made her 'beg for every penny'. Peggy was loud, fractious and given to bewildering mood swings. A neighbour remembers 'the whole street freezing when she tore into John, screaming at him at all hours'. The police once called at Stansfield Road in response to complaints about a domestic disturbance. Gaar recalls a 'really violent, nasty row' one night at the Joneses', then hearing a Nat King Cole record 'being blasted at top volume through the open window'. Yet Peggy, for all her volatility, could also be inhibiting and aloof.

'A compliment from her was very hard to come by,' says David Bowie. 'I would get my paints out and all she could say was, "I hope you're not going to make a mess."'

There was a lesson here in human relations and he seemed both willing and able to learn it.

Peggy, with a streak of mental illness in her background, brought lifelong complications into her son's thinking. The impact of the family disease was of vital significance for Bowie. He often spoke of his inherited 'nuttiness', and it was in that light that he interpreted the whole point of his career. The Burns history was chilling enough. Peggy's younger sister Una suffered from depression and schizophrenia, underwent electric shock and finally confinement at a Victorian asylum named Park Prewett, and died in her late thirties. A second sister, Vivienne, suffered a schizophrenic attack, and a third girl, Nora, was lobotomized in an effort to cure what her mother described as 'bad nerves'. Of Peggy's two remaining siblings, a brother won a Military Medal for 'utter disregard of his own life' in the African desert, and a fourth sister, Pat (described by Bowie as a 'frightful aunt', and later to appear regularly in the *News of the World*), was cast as the family rabble-rouser. Peggy's parents, Margaret and Jimmy, were, respectively, a frustrated poet and self-confessed 'mad-woman', and a fantasist who concocted a fictional career as a war hero.

With no fewer than three aunts clinically diagnosed as mentally ill and two eccentric grandparents it was hardly surprising that Bowie would return to the theme of insanity throughout his career, channelling it into his finest work and insisting to one startled interviewer, 'Everybody says, "Oh, yes, my family is quite mad." Mine really is.'

In 1937 Peggy had given birth to a son after an affair with a bartender. Ten years later Terry Burns would move into Stansfield Road, where he slept in the bed next to the newborn baby. 'My family is quite mad' may be harsher than Bowie meant, but there is no denying the shadow cast by his schizophrenic half-brother. Over the next fifteen years Terry, the good-looking boy with a taste for jazz and Beat authors like Jack Kerouac, became a role model and virtual tutor. As Peggy's sister Pat said, 'David worshipped Terry, and Terry idolized him.' Bowie's obsession with madness in the abstract remained a constant, but he drifted apart from its flesh-and-blood archetype. By the time Burns was diagnosed as a manic depressive and schizophrenic his half-brother was already on the slopes of commercial success: 'Space Oddity' was released in the same month that Terry was institutionalized. In 1971 Bowie's 'The Bewlay Brothers' (later used as the name of his music publishing company) was widely interpreted as an autobiographical nod. It would be another fourteen years before self-destruction finally caught at Terry's heels, and a further eight before Bowie would write about the story. 'It scared me that my own [mind] was in question,' he said in 1993. 'I often wondered at the time how near the line I was going ... how far I should push myself.' Ziggy and the other characters, explained Bowie, had been 'alternative egos', a form of madness through which he had meant to save his sanity.

David Bowie never crossed the divide into full mental illness. He did, though, both as a boy and later, share a number of the quirks shown by his maternal family. He would suddenly burst into tears. He cried when he was happy and he cried when he was angry; when he was admiring his looks, and when he was ruing his left-handedness. It was a thing he could always do for maximum effect, just like an actor. That Bowie was conscious of his heritage is obvious in the number of songs he wrote touching on lunacy or schizophrenia: 'Rubber Band' and 'Little Bombardier' (with their references to his grandfather Jimmy Burns), 'The Wild Eyed Boy From Freecloud', 'Cygnet Committee', 'All the Madmen', 'The Bewlay Brothers', 'Aladdin Sane', 'Big Brother', 'Sound and Vision', 'Beauty and the Beast', 'Jump They Say' and most of *Outside*. Explaining the lyric of 'Oh! You Pretty Things' (one that cut deeper than the bubblegum version by Peter Noone), Bowie would tell a reporter: 'I hadn't been to an analyst ... my parents went, my brothers and sisters and my aunts and uncles and cousins, they did that, they ended up in a much worse state, so I stayed away. I thought I'd write my problems out.'

Brittle emotions, role-playing and the therapy of art – all three came to David Jones at an early age. The last lesson of his youth, and the one he practised longest, was to suppress his own feelings. The warping in his capacity to love, later remarked on by his first wife, was interwoven with his fear of madness and the need to carry protective masks. A show of indifference, to Bowie, was neither illogical nor anti-social. Rather, it was a way to preserve his own ego. It is a plausible and fair explanation of his shyness that he never fully trusted in his response to others. On this reading, Peggy Burns's family resulted in her son growing up emotionally stunted.

In November 1951 David entered Stockwell Infants School, an event he marked by losing control of his bladder in his first class. The baby who struck Edith Kohl as almost 'unnaturally clean' became a spirited brawler in the playground. The fastidious child who would not wear a vest unless it was freshly laundered now won fame as what Kohl calls 'a devil in kid's clothing'. Though he struck his teachers as gifted, a pattern of defiance was already emerging in David. His single-mindedness and boredom with academic discipline were obvious.

Aside from a developing strife with his mother, his home life appears to have been – within the Joneses' vast definition of the word – normal, though dramatized by a changing cast of characters at Stansfield Road. The five-year-old continued to share a room with his teenage half-brother, a boy who self-admittedly 'hated' John Jones. From the mid-1950s Terry Burns would start to display the characteristics of violence and paranoid self-loathing that led to his confinement and eventual suicide. Into the home, meanwhile, came David's eleven-year-old cousin Kristine (abandoned by her schizophrenic mother) and his half-sister Annette, John Jones's daughter from a pre-war affair. The subsequent myth of the frothing, carpet-biting madness of the household, a lie Bowie himself helped propagate in the scramble for plausible scapegoats for his adult behaviour, is hardly borne out by Kohl's memory of a 'mildly loopy but unremarkable' family. David's privileged position as his parents' only shared child added to his overwhelming faith in his own abilities and a reputation as a bully at school. Kohl thinks his problem was precisely that he had so many acolytes, yet no real friends. He was totally incapable of personal love.

In 1953 the Joneses made the short journey south to suburbia, buying a semi-detached house at 106 Canon Road in Bromley. A year later they moved to a home in nearby Clarence Road, before settling in 1955 at 4 Plaistow Grove, a tiny working-man's cottage perched on a bluff over Sundridge Park station. It was to be David Jones's permanent address for the next decade. As late as 1969 he was staying at Plaistow Grove while working professionally as a musician. His claims to be a child of the Brixton ghetto are refuted by the long years spent in the leafy Edwardian outpost. His need to be different, so obsessive later, began with his rejection of his own roots.

In 1993, in an interview promoting *Black Tie White Noise*, Bowie would refer scathingly to his experience at Plaistow Grove. He recoiled from the 'meanness' of his surroundings, with their sense of utter conformity, and the endless double rows of identical houses. The confusion and mythology came in the 1970s, when Bowie spoke of 'seeing visions' and UFOs landing in Bromley, and the spate of stories which then mushroomed served to underline the hazards of the pop biographer. In any case, one can be sure that the monotony of the place was total. That it served to make the restless child rebellious and refractory, a family member thinks 'certain'.

Bromley, in fact, is such a drab, featureless dormitory town as grew up close to any large city between the wars. Until the 1950s it had only one claim to fame. H. G. Wells wrote *The War of the Worlds* there, a book which Bowie himself later admired. The village Bromley had once been was still visible in its bay-windowed villas, narrow streets and olde-world tearooms, evolved today into housing estates, dual carriageways and the unisex hair salon at Sundridge Park. For David Jones, who now entered the local council school, Raglan Infants, it was an almost friendless existence. Neither his cousin nor his half-sister lived regularly at Plaistow Grove. Terry Burns, meanwhile, had left school at fifteen and been abandoned to his own desires in London. After an unsuccessful experiment of moving to Bromley, he would not reappear until the late 1950s, and only then as a hollow-eyed vagrant turned away by his mother.

Throughout his life Bowie would be in deep conflict over his roots. He valued and to some extent came to share his father's self-portrayal as 'the sane Englishman with his pipe'. He spoke warmly of his love of British art and history. He protested frequently at the shallowness of 'abroad', particularly of America.

John Jones's suspicion of foreigners was open; his son's was hidden. As a rock star, Bowie would also be volatile, unpredictable and callous in dealing with friends, traits his family more commonly associate with Peggy. In this view, David's mother represents the turbulent, chaotic world of Brixton, while the emollient commuter belt is expressed by John.

Some of this conflict spoke in the cottage at Plaistow Grove. Clearly, on one level it was a model of middle-class sobriety. There was a low front wall, a miniature paved terrace and a garden gnome. The house itself was of dirty brown brick and, once inside, the dark walls bulged out with ridges and lumps. There was a downstairs kitchenette and a cramped front room with net curtains. The singer Dana Gillespie would tell an interviewer that 'the chairs had all those crocheted things to soak up the Brylcreem and those little arm-rests and it was a very cosy little room – absolutely tiny'. Up the stairs were a bathroom, two small bedrooms and a boxroom. From where David lay at night he could hear the rattle of the railway and look down onto the coaching-lamp of the Crown pub. A neighbour remembers how romantic was the old lantern at dusk, and how David used to stand theatrically in its glow, anticipating his pose as Ziggy Stardust nearly twenty years later.

On 20 June 1955 David Jones became admission number 603 at Burnt Ash Junior School, cycling up Rangefield Road in his uniform of brown blazer, orange and brown tie and brown shorts. According to contemporaries, his three years there were neither distinguished nor the reverse. They were anonymous. His form mistress Edith Baldry remembers him as 'a leader not a follower', yet 'not very brainy' and uncommunicative in class. His recorder playing showed him to possess above average, but not startling, musical ability. Though in the school choir, he had merely an 'adequate' voice.

Burnt Ash's principal, George Lloyd, an otherwise utterly conventional figure, brought one innovation to the school curriculum. He was a pioneer of 'music and motion' classes, in which small groups of children were instructed to move to the beat of a drum or tambourine. For someone who slouched through most of his schooldays, David came startlingly alive on the dance floor. A teacher named Pat Mountford remembers him as 'quite vividly artistic' in the way he interpreted music. Lloyd himself would call his star pupil sensitive and imaginative, with an inbred poise 'astonishing' in a nine-year-old.

In 1956 rock and roll happened. It reached England, specifically the wind-up gramophone in Plaistow Grove, in the form of a heavy wax disc, a foot wide, bearing the titles 'Houn' Dog' and 'All Shook Up'. David was transfixed, though even that understates a process bordering on reincarnation. According to an interview he gave in 1972, 'I saw a cousin of mine dance to ... "Hound Dog" and I had never seen her get up and be moved so much by anything. It really impressed me, the power of the music. I started getting records immediately after that. My mother bought me Fats Domino's "Blueberry Hill" the next day.' His claim to have met Tommy Steele backstage after a concert that Christmas is hard to prove since Steele has no recollection of the event, but it is clear that the die of David's career, and the whole direction of his life, was cast by 1957. At age ten, when he trudged off to maths class, he was also astonishing a contemporary named Eric Smith by telling him why Buddy Holly 'had a better act than Elvis'. Later, when Holly was killed in an air crash, David broke down in tears at school. A relative remembered how he had bought the boy a ukelele and then helped him build a string bass out of a tea-chest:

> One day in Clarence Road David was watching *The Flowerpot Men*, and the next it was *6.5 Special*. When he was just nine he stood up against the door of his bedroom and said, 'I can play guitar just like the Shads.' And he did.

Actually the Shadows' first appearance was not until 1958, when David was eleven not nine, and when he was living in Plaistow Grove, not Clarence Road. If the relative's memory was fragile, the story was sturdy, and found its way into the early Bowie fiction.

Before school returned on 24 September 1956 David Jones had listened to 'Hound Dog' a hundred times. He talked music on equal terms with his cousin Kristine. He could, after a fashion, strum the ukelele. In his second year at Burnt Ash he fell in with a ten-year-old named Dudley Chapman, who remembers David

BOWIE

for two things: his interest in martial arts and things oriental, and his enthusiastic effort to copy the R&B hits of the day. Chapman's house in Lake Avenue became home to a series of skiffle sessions, impromptu singalongs in which David scrubbed at the tea-chest and Dudley pounded the piano to the same raucous result. Although later on Bowie was to show extraordinary skill in imbuing his voice with personality, as well as raw power, he did not instantly proclaim himself a vocal genius. 'He had no inbuilt talent,' Chapman would tell the authors Peter and Leni Gillman; while Edith Baldry insists he was 'strictly average' in the school choir. From a technical standpoint, it is hard to think of a single area in which he was a genuine prodigy. His singing and ukelele playing were merely adequate. He was an original mover, but even then he never mastered the popular dance steps of the day. It was the same with the string bass, the same with the piano, the same even with the tambourine. Only in putting himself across to an audience did he rely entirely on his own carefully guarded expertise. By 1957 he was performing Elvis and Chuck Berry numbers to a stunned audience of Bromley Wolf Cub boy scouts. Eric Smith remembers him as 'mesmerizing' in the way he emulated the very gyrations of the originals, and carried on 'like someone from another planet'.

David's appearance was striking. He was a thin, bony, double-jointed boy whose legs, according to Smith, 'he used to braid rather than cross'. After his time in the Stockwell playground he again became forbiddingly clean. As an adolescent he was fussy about how his shirts were ironed and was greeted in the local chemist's as 'Mr Shampoo'. His custard-yellow hair was neatly parted. David's chief peculiarity was a set of protuberant front teeth which the school dentist, Graeme King, took the trouble to X-ray on 11 May 1956. 'There was some talk about them being written up in a journal,' says Eric Smith. 'They were so canine we actually used to call him Rover. You can imagine how it set him apart.' When he was fifteen David was treated in hospital for a damaged left eye, both paralysed and doomed to remain open, thus permanently affecting his sight. Not only that, it left him with strikingly different-coloured irises. In the seventies there were outlandish explanations for this: it proved his alien origins, and neatly symbolized his other-worldly alter ego. The truth is that he was punched in the face during a fight over a girl.

David's father was untroubled by the fact that his son leant more to the artistic than the academic. In his post at Barnardo's, John forged links in the entertainment world and listed his recreations for the company newsletter as 'music, cinema and the stage, always happiest in greenrooms'. It is not stretching belief to suggest his theatrical dreams came to be inherited by David. On 17 December 1957 a conjuror and ventriloquist entertained the children at Burnt Ash. Smith still remembers the effect of the performance on his schoolfriend, who now gave it as his ambition to break into show business. 'I'm not sure Peggy was entirely comfortable when Dave told her. John was.'

In January 1958 David was confronted with the eleven plus. It is perhaps difficult today to convey the significance of the ordeal: for those passing there was the promise of grammar school, university and a white-collar career. The alternative was the secondary modern, and a likely unqualified exit at sixteen. David failed the exam. Horrified, Peggy went to Burnt Ash and asked George Lloyd to write a letter of recommendation to Bromley Technical School. Lloyd, hesitant, told her he 'wasn't sure he could do that', whereupon Peggy put her hands firmly on the headmaster's shoulders, sat him down and handed him a pen. Lloyd sent the letter.

Records show that David had been accepted to Bromley Tech by early June, and that the Borough Education Officer interviewed him on 14 July. If David had fantasies about breaking into show business he kept them to himself. 'It just never entered the conversation,' the officer says, 'that he would make a career in music.' David did, however, take a new guitar – a gift from John – on a Wolf Cub outing to the Isle of Wight, where he performed his medley of Elvis and Chuck Berry hits.

David already had enthusiasm and a curious mind. Now experience was filling out his education as fast as he could get it. Later that summer a girl named Liza Fisk, thirteen but with looks three years older, met him in Brook Lane, a narrow tree-lined footpath leading to Burnt Ash. The episode that followed, which she describes as 'a bit of wickedness on my part ... I stuck his hand in my pants and told him I loved him', is worth noting if only to correct the impression that the 'camp' child was the forerunner of the gay adolescent. 'For a twelve-year-old [sic] he was quite passionate,' says Fisk. 'He knew what he was doing.'

Bromley Technical High School, a red-brick complex rising up behind an iron fence, lay in the authentic Kent countryside to the south. Despite its status it was, by the time David arrived in 1958, as rich in arcane ritual as any public school. There were houses, named after eighteenth-century statesmen like Pitt and Wilberforce. There was a uniform, and an elaborate system of rewards and punishments. There was also an accent on languages, science and particularly design, where a collegiate atmosphere flourished under the tutorship of Owen Frampton. In David's account, Frampton led through force of personality, not intellect; his colleagues at Bromley Tech were famous for neither, and yielded the school's most gifted pupils to the arts, a regime so liberal that Frampton actively encouraged his own son, Peter, to pursue a musical career with David, a partnership briefly intact thirty years later.

At the Tech David saw the intimate workings of both art and music. He watched Frampton and other students like Colin Clark and Lesley Buzan at work. He learnt something of technical skills like lay-out and typesetting. Whether, in the depths of his soul, he was a committed artist would always be open to doubt. But certain aspects of his character were not. He was aloof, clever and brilliantly organized, with what a classmate calls 'a superb flair for standing out'. He was thin, verging on emaciated. In place of his grey flannels he acquired black drainpipe trousers which he wore in the school photograph, to even Frampton's annoyance. He was left-handed. Above all, he brought a touch of lurid drama in his home life. At the end of 1958, in the middle of David's first year at Bromley Tech, his half-brother returned home, unkempt, from his service in the RAF. Peggy Jones turned him away. When David appeared at school the next morning he spoke of Terry having 'run off, crying, down the street'.

The story was true. But it was not good enough. David also added a violent, knife-wielding scene between mother and son. In this version a family feud had become a wild, near-murderous brawl. It also made David Jones a legend at Bromley Tech: an odd-looking, intelligent misfit, and a scion of real madness.

It was now that a streak of true eccentricity began to show. David was unable to sleep more than three or four hours a night. He started to hold imaginary conversations with foreign statesmen 'in order to warn them about the world'. A relative estimated that around this time he was writing five letters a week to General Eisenhower. He was fascinated with guns and, not coincidentally, all things American.

David's strangeness was very real. In the next three years his parents frequently worried that he had inherited the Burns curse. But he was also an intelligent boy, unusually aware of the number of masks he carried around. Like many shy youngsters, he turned to acting, seeking for any identity other than the one he wanted to escape. As a fantasist, David could easily give in to what he couldn't express in real life: love, or hate, or simple foolishness. The make-believe in these years was satisfying, even cathartic. But the acting became more hazardous as an adult. The 'alternative egos' of the 1970s had their origins in the thirteen-year-old dreamer.

Even as a child, when his friends pursued normal hobbies, he seldom failed to strike a singular note. He was precociously well read. David later credited John Jones for exposing him to the world of Thackeray, Wilde and Shaw, as well as Voltaire, Rousseau and other political thinkers 'mostly in the original French'. In due course he discovered Sartre and Genet. Through Kerouac's influence he would become interested in meditation and yoga. At age seventeen David was spending his weekends in the Bromley Wimpy Bar; a year later he was a fixture at the Tibetan Buddhist Institute. His interest in eastern philosophy was real enough. After meeting a refugee priest named Chime Rimpoche he became involved in organizing a Buddhist monastery in Scotland. A number of his earliest songs show a fascination for Buddhist ritual. He could, according to a colleague, go into a 'meditative trance' when composing. The prospect of monastic life – with its threat of seclusion and self-denial – would, however, prove too great. When Chime Rimpoche began to urge David to become a novice monk, his response was a characteristic reversal, in which he seemed to change not just in body but in soul as well. 'I ran out,' he told William Burroughs, 'and got drunk and never looked back.'

Terry Burns, though banned from Plaistow Grove, continued to exert his own influence. For a suburban teenager like David, the greatest opportunities for rebellion lay in the coffee bars and cellars of the West End. These Terry helped him trawl. At fourteen the younger brother was an enthusiastic commuter to Charing Cross and the world of free-form jazz, Italian bistros, cappuccino and Beat 'happenings' in the square mile around Wardour Street. He began to emulate the late James Dean. David would darken his hair with shoe polish, and curl his lip into a snarl as he sat sipping his Coca-Cola. The renewal of his friendship with Terry helped to catapult the eccentric-but-shy choirboy into leering adolescence. From this time on David Jones was busy either as a rebel or a rock-based pluralist.

The notion of the deranged elder brother as a Svengali figure has proved attractive, and been seized on by Bowie's biographers. One actually went as far to write that 'Terry stamped the iron into David's soul.' His classmate's account of a 'self-promoter' hardly supports this claim, though David certainly enjoyed the patronage of an older friend during his visits to London. Adolescence would be a stormy period for both brothers. But whereas Terry saw rebellion as a personal crusade, one of David's greatest strengths was his gift for detachment – not from the values of those he admired, whom he often imitated, but from himself. A friend is convinced 'there was nothing half as fanatical about him as you read'. A boy named Eric Myren met David one evening on the return journey to Sundridge Park, 'where he told me he thought Soho was crude. He used those words. Sitting there with his hands clasped, he looked like someone from the Temperance League.'

What Myren and others were witnessing was the empty canvas that constitutes the basic fabric of David's life. He had nothing resembling a moral centre. For every imaginary conference with General Eisenhower there was a discussion with quiet, austere John Jones about finding a job. For every night of mild debauchery in Shaftesbury Avenue there was a family evening over the tiny bluish television set. Even as a fourteen-year-old, Myren remembers, he had a strangely remote, alien quality – a sense of reconciling things in his mind. To another boy at Bromley Tech, David gave it as his ambition to 'go on a quiz show and answer questions on theatre, music, books, the lot. He wanted to be the Brain of Britain.'

David did, in fact, enjoy a wide education. Like his half-brother, he admired the avant-garde and outlandish, but unlike him he had a selective mind. He was as capable of living in John Jones's world as he was in Terry's. He could read *The Picture of Dorian Gray* in the same week as a jazz potboiler. A year or two later he would sit happily through revues by Frankie Howerd and Leslie Crowther. He saw *Oliver!* and Cliff Richard in *Aladdin*. His manager Ken Pitt would remember how much 'David admired *The Taming of the Shrew*' and emerged from *Cabaret* 'fascinated by the use of stark white light as a dramatic effect'. That he harboured theatrical dreams of his own was obvious when Pitt applied for Equity membership on his behalf; he joined without ever having set foot on the legitimate stage. All of these influences – pantomime, theatre, film, books and art, as well as mundane pleasures like Madame Tussaud's and the football ground, would co-exist in David's mind and eventually achieve a composite in David Bowie.

That left the question of music. Here, at least, supply hugely outstripped his demand. From the moment he first heard 'Purple People Eater' in his parents' front room, through to his discovery, via Elvis and Buddy Holly, of the guitar, David sailed into adolescence at the exact moment a world sprang up to meet him. The key here, as with his taste in film and art, is versatility. David's stories about his Brixton childhood show a severely defective or almost nonexistent memory; it is certain though, that he heard reggae and Ska as a young boy, and Edith Kohl remembers him 'clicking his wooden rattle' to a Stanley Motta calypso. With his discovery of 'Hound Dog' he acquired, successively, a ukelele, a string bass and finally a cheap toy guitar. By 1961, in vague homage to Charlie Parker, David had persuaded his father to buy him a plastic alto saxophone. The following spring he took lessons from a local musician named Ronnie Ross, who remembered him for his volume rather than the purity of his technique. Thereafter David's enthusiasm, first fired by Elvis and the stirrings from America, followed down a direct line to jazz, blues and the awakening of British R&B.

The Yardbirds, above all, won his admiration. These suburban

Chuck Berry mimics had their faults, David granted, but in the mustard-haired lead singer they boasted a recognizable role model – 'someone I physically related to'. Accordingly, he stood far closer to Keith Relf than he did to a Lennon or McCartney. On 3 November 1963 David was present as a package tour comprising Little Richard, the Everly Brothers, Bo Diddley and the Rolling Stones wound down at the Hammersmith Odeon. Relf was immediately replaced in his affection by yet another bouffant blond. 'I *am* Brian Jones,' he told a girlfriend that winter. Yet Brian Jones, despite his oft-expressed desire for musical growth, had no basic need of change. The young David made room for change, for reform, as an organic force, and his next conversion was no more drastic than a switch of emphasis. By 1965 his unqualified love was for the dramatic ballads and epic production style of the Walker Brothers; a year later for the back-to-the-roots raveup of 'Wild Thing'; while in 1967 Flower Power became the irresistible backdrop to influences as sundry as Scott McKenzie, Hendrix, Dylan and the cabaret-tinged melodrama of Anthony Newley. The last's *Stop the World, I Want To Get Off!* had the same seismic impact of an Elvis or Buddy Holly. Not just on the young David, either: well into the 1970s Bowie was mimicking Newley's histrionic delivery and striking even Bing Crosby as a 'crooner type' who sang 'old songs, Tony-newly arranged'.

Newley's singing style, rooted in natural charm and cannily dramatic phrasing, rarely varied over forty years. By comparison Bowie's technique, with its shrill impatience and desire to touch bases, seems like a nervous tic. Late in his career he agreed privately that his problem had been 'to try to do justice to all sides'. He gave a list of his five best-loved records: 'Alley Oop' by the Hollywood Argyles*; *Oh Yeah* by Charlie Mingus; and three very different out-takes from the summer of love: the Velvet Underground's 'Waiting for the Man', Frank Zappa's *We're Only in It for the Money* and the near-feckless 'Summer in the City' by the Lovin' Spoonful. It was a tortuous path that took Bowie to

---

*In 1971 Bowie would appropriate a line from the song – 'Oh man! Look at those cavemen go' – for his 'Life on Mars?'.

stardom. He held a sneaking admiration for men like Crosby and Sinatra, though he strove to be outlandish and avant-garde. He admitted freely that after ten years' singing he had yet to find his own voice. One result of his long musical apprenticeship was an unusually wide repertoire and a willingness to experiment. Another was that Bowie took a decade to achieve what a more single-minded performer might have done in a year.

In 1962 David's classmate George Underwood punched him in the eye over a girl called Deirdre. (He and Underwood were still friendly, and casually collaborating on a number of projects years later.) After treatment in Farnborough Hospital it was found that David's pupil was permanently damaged. Already he was gathering a reputation as someone who enjoyed a singular home life, and American imports like baseball, basketball, Coca-Cola and rock and roll. Now, with a left eye totally different from the right one, he progressed from being merely odd to full freakishness. 'People noticed him,' says a classmate. 'He looked like someone from Mars.'

Not only did David's friendship with Underwood survive: the latter, who played guitar and boasted membership of a group, welcomed even as modest a novelty as an acrylic sax, and Underwood's quartet remained a prominent feature of Bromley night-life for a month afterwards. Sometimes they played impromptu on the school grounds; sometimes they would have migrated to the high street. Of the four members, David was thought the least innately musical, though with a compensatory drive one friend thought 'scary'. A local woman remembers the group 'under the spell' of the blond boy who sang his own material in a thin, reedy voice among the cover hits. This was the first recorded instance of David's songwriting.

Among those whose afternoons were spent sloping between Bromley's coffee bars and clothes shops were Dave Hadfield, Neville Wills and Alan Dodds, three youths who brushed their hair alike, wore matching corduroy jackets and varied their routine only by walking across the square to Furlong's record shop to listen to the latest hits from America. By autumn 1962 the trio had been joined by David Jones. The new group, named the Kon-rads, eked out a living, playing at youth halls and the occasional wedding and splitting or re-forming on a weekly basis. By Christmas the line-up had grown to include two female singers, a guitarist named Rocky Shahan and George Underwood on miscellaneous noises. Within their limited terms of reference, the Kon-rads proved an adequate copy of the Shadows, identically dressed in their corduroys or grey lounge suits, lurching from side to side with their guitars in tandem. Like their role models, the group's primary interest in rock and roll was a romantic and visual one. A member recalls them as 'passionately wanting to create our own image'. In so far as they achieved their modest objectives, the Kon-rads were a success. Its ex-members refer to the group with nostalgic respect. But it was clear that, even at fifteen, David's ambitions already vastly outstripped the world of dances and church fêtes. Within weeks he was lodging complaints about the group's name, looks and, above all, material. Thereafter the Kon-rads became both David's friends and his servants. By early 1963 a silent coup had taken place in the group's leadership, and a steady diet of American cover songs had given way to David's quiet insistence on his 'own thing'.

Despite pressure on him by Owen Frampton, David left school that summer. Nearly thirty years later Bowie would tell a reporter,'I got two O Levels, in English and woodwork ... I would have got three, but they don't award them for imagination.' Yet even this low figure proved an embellishment. He left Bromley Tech with a single exam pass, in art. After informing his housemaster of his intention to become a pop idol, David passed through the iron gate on to Bromley Common, strapped on his saxophone and laid out his school blazer on the ground in front of him. When the afternoon was over he had collected a total of two pounds. Thrilled at his success, David took the bus home to Plaistow Grove, where he repeated his career plans to John and Peggy. His mother's response was to find him work as an electrician's mate in Beckenham.

Len Price remembers a morning that August when 'a tall, thin, ginger-haired kid named Dave' arrived to help him rewire a local children's home. Price's impression of his apprentice was favour-able: he was inventive, clever and a firm believer in his own ability to achieve the seemingly impossible. The songs David sang while he worked were, like himself, invigoratingly different – yet so catchy, Price remembers, 'they sounded like the Beatles'. David also had a vivid imagination. He told Price that John Jones had had a career as a war hero. There were other yarns that a second colleague saw as 'a desperate effort to build up a fantasy life'. None of these attributes, however, specifically qualified David as an electrician. He left after only eight weeks, telling a friend that his mother was 'desperately ill' at home. It was another small bid for affection.

David then endured a month of manual labour around Bromley before finding work as a tea-boy–trainee artist in a Bond Street advertising agency. He hated the job instantly. It was, however, a significant step nearer the maze of West End R&B clubs and a five-minute walk to the stylists and boutiques, as barbers and tailors were now known, around Carnaby Street. If, on his earlier forays to London, David had discovered jazz, bistros and subterranean Beat readings, from 1963 his love of music would meet a matching obsession with clothes. 'I lived out of the dustbins on the back streets of Carnaby,' he recalled. 'The very best young designers were down there and because they were very expensive Italian, if any of the shirts had a button off, it would be [thrown away]. We'd go around and nick all the stuff out of the dustbins. Entire wardrobes for nothing.'

Meanwhile, despite polite interest from Eric Easton, the man who co-managed the Rolling Stones, the Kon-rads never progressed beyond the suburban club circuit. David left the group that winter. Within a few weeks – after having nearly severed his thumb with a scalpel – his career as an advertising executive had also failed. At Plaistow Grove he now gave it as his ambition to go into pop full time. Peggy was appalled; John Jones's attitude of tolerant support for his son was one he maintained for the rest of his life. At his father's urging David wrote to the washing-machine mogul John Bloom – a new, media-friendly tycoon widely said to be 'with it' – with the provocative claim: 'With your money you could do for us what Brian Epstein has done for the Beatles – and make another million.'

Bloom resisted the offer. He did, however, pass on David Jones's name to Leslie Conn, a record plugger and publisher who, with his partner Dick James, came to epitomize that corner of London around Denmark and Flitcroft Streets known as Tin Pan Alley. When Conn met David he was already working in his second semi-professional group since leaving Bromley Tech. The King Bees, with a name filched from the blues wailer Slim Harpo, and a repertoire of Willie Dixon and Howlin' Wolf, contained the contradiction of five white boys from Kent singing about wayward women and freight trains, and a fastidious vocalist who bit his lip in embarrassment when anyone cheered. The King Bees' first engagement, Bloom's wedding anniversary at the Jack of Clubs in Soho, gave little such problem. As they ran through their primitive set, the Bees found themselves playing to a stunned audience of dinner-jacketed businessmen, quaffing champagne and calling for 'Born Free'. Despite this unhappy start, Conn signed David to a personal management contract, after visiting Plaistow Grove and winning over no less a cynic than Peggy with his talk of launching 'another Cliff Richard'. At this, remembering the calamity of their first performance, there would be titters of amusement from some of the King Bees.

They did little better on their début recording session. Seven hours in the Decca studio in West Hampstead produced 'Liza Jane', in point of unashamed rawness little more than a carbon of the Rolling Stones and striking one of its few reviewers as stooping to 'copy the copy-cats'. The single was released on 5 June 1964 and featured, after ruthless plugging by Conn, on the next day's *Juke Box Jury*: of the four panellists only one, the comic Charlie Drake, voted the record a hit. Within a month David had left the King Bees. Dick James's memory was that 'he quite simply outgrew the band'. Though his hopes of finding 'another Cliff' or another Tommy Steele had swiftly flopped, Conn persevered with his new protégé. By August he had introduced him to yet another Kentish R&B group, once again taking their name from a blues idol – this time Muddy Waters – the Manish Boys.

The band was vital to David. With tastes that ran from folk to blues to soul, and a stage act that incorporated a parody of James Brown's patent lurches and twists, the Manish Boys were a definite step up on the show-business ladder. 'I used to dream of becoming their Mick Jagger,' David told Dick James. It was rare for him to allow anyone a glimpse of his fantasy life, but there was no doubt among his family and friends that, from 1964, David's desire to be a pop star was no mere dream, but a consuming ambition which stamped itself powerfully on his colleagues. 'We all fell under his influence,' said the Manish Boys' Paul Rodriguez. Not only did David launch the same kind of silent coup remembered by the Kon-rads, he instigated reforms in the way the group acted and looked. By autumn of 1964 the Boys uniformly sported shoulder-length hair. They began to join their singer on clothes-foraging excursions to the Soho dustbins. They experimented with make-up and American accents. David himself, meanwhile, on the basis of his near-nightly attendance at the Marquee Club (an era he would recall nostalgically on *Pin-Ups*) and the exaggerated flamboyance of his new stage act, began to speak of himself as one of 'a scene', and R&B's most ambiguous sexual enigma.

It was true that, by late 1964, David Jones occupied a lowly niche in the pop hierarchy. Through Conn he had met up-and-coming figures like Mark Feld (later Marc Bolan), as well as established stars like Hank Marvin and Adam Faith. As frontman for a brassily theatrical R&B group he was rapidly gathering fame for his fragile but effective voice and the way he moved on stage. David also had a manager whose tireless pursuit of an 'angle' matched his own. On 2 November 1964 Conn persuaded his friend Leslie Thomas to report in the *Evening News* on the formation of the International League for the Preservation of Animal Filament. 'It's really for the protection of pop musicians, and those who wear their hair long,' explained the founder and president, one Davy Jones of Bromley. 'Anyone who has the courage to wear hair down to his shoulders has to go through hell. It's time we united and stood up for our curls.' Ten days later Conn managed to insinuate his client on to the BBC's *Tonight*, where David told Cliff Michelmore: 'For the last two years we've had comments like "Darling" and "Can I carry your handbag?" thrown at us and I think it has to stop now.'

David also enjoyed, as he loftily informed Conn, a reputation as a sexual outlaw. His comment during a lost weekend in 1976 that 'Sex suddenly became all-important to me. It didn't really matter who or what it was with ... [whether] it was some pretty boy that I took home and neatly fucked on my bed upstairs' aimed to shock; the intended note of decadence rang false. His androgynous stage act, on the other hand, was very real. Here, some discrepancy exists between David's own assessment of his role ('Weaving a new romantic vision ... a pre-gender dream') and a close colleague's ('Poncing around'). His stage persona would lead some to question whether life had become intertwined with art. A musician David met in 1966 was startled to be greeted by 'a wet kiss, full on the mouth'. Two years later, Ken Pitt would remember his client's habit of 'loping around the flat, naked, his long, weighty penis swaying from side to side like a pendulum of a grandfather clock'. Pitt, a long-time friend and confidant, was not alone in finding something unnerving in the way David went from 'rock and roller' to 'drama queen' in the course of a minute. The actor-director Michael Armstrong remembered him 'always playing a cat-and-mouse game with you ... He flirted, he really did.' Dick James believed 'David used every trick in the book to get what he wanted. If that meant coming on to you, he did.'

There was the closet homosexual who, aged eleven, 'knew what he was doing' with an older girl. There was the self-professed 'poof' scarred for life in a fight over a woman. There was the camp teenager who befriended a schoolgirl named Dana Gillespie, with whom he spent the night and on whose 'Zeppelin tits' he commented favourably to the Manish Boys. There was the fastidious, shy adolescent who shouted outside another woman's bedroom window, 'You don't know what you're missing. I'm a pop star! I have a big cock!' All of these paradoxes suggest a man divided, a man at odds with himself; a man with a wavering sense of identity. There are clues, buried deep in his mother's past, to the evolution of major parts of David's life, his loneliness, his sense of being an outsider, his shyness, his delight in acting, and his narcissism. In sex, as in these other areas, says an ex-lover, 'David was schizo.'

The Manish Boys' dormobile ploughed the motorways from Scotland to Southampton, carrying the group on their first package tour, headlined by Gerry and the Pacemakers and Marianne Faithfull (whose friend Tom Keylock believes 'she definitely had it off with David'.) There was also a single, 'I Pity the Fool'. Previously an R&B hit for Bobby Bland, the raucous interplay of the original was lost in an inanimate mix: despite David's relentless promotion, both it and the B-side 'Take My Tip' sank without trace. It depressed the other members of the group to see how their vocalist inevitably took star billing. 'When we did one gig,' says a colleague, 'the poster said "Davie Jones and his Boys". When we asked him about it, he left at a run.' A second musician remembers the tour as combining 'a business trip and an ego trip'.

Here, following in the ground-breaking role of Andrew Oldham, Conn once again turned to a press now teeming with stories about Nehru jackets, miniskirts, bells, beads, love-ins and the other new regalia of Swinging London. On 4 March the *Daily Mail* reported that David had been banned from the pop programme *Gadzooks! It's All Happening* because of his long hair. 'I won't have it cut for the Prime Minister, let alone the BBC,' he replied dramatically. (Evidently the BBC weren't the only ones who took offence at David's looks. 'Even my girlfriend doesn't like it,' he added, hoisting his voice above the sniggers. 'I get asked out for more dates than she does.') Within days the *People* and the *Daily Mirror* had taken up the saga. Lost in the ensuing fracas was Conn's smile, the look of a man who couldn't believe his luck. The group duly made their appearance – though even that failed to revive 'I Pity the Fool', or to halt the break-up one member recalls as 'running out of money and things to say to each other'.

Unemployed, and owing his parents six months' back rent, David spent his days at the Giaconda in Dean Street, sitting for hours over one cold coffee mug, scanning the 'Musicians Wanted' column in *Melody Maker*. An R&B shouter named Chris Farlowe, shortly to find fame with six UK chart hits, remembers him 'hunched there, all emaciated, with hair dangling down onto the table'. From time to time David would break off from his reading to suggest the two singers invest in a 'frothy coffee', and then deftly mine ninepence from Farlowe's pocket. A version of the same tactic would gain him nightly entry to the Marquee Club, where David formed a particular – some thought unnatural – attachment to the Pretty Things. 'He was always there, wanting to talk music,' says the group's Phil May. 'I remember a funny incident when Dave came backstage and asked for my home phone number. I didn't want everyone to hear it, so I took the address book out of his hand to write it down. I couldn't help noticing that in the left-hand column, where my name should have been, he'd written in "God".'

Among those whose days were spent wedged between the Giaconda's greasy tables and Wurlitzer jukebox were three teenagers billed majestically as 'South-east Kent's Best Rhythm-and-Blues Group'. The members of the Lower Third met David at an audition – where he led the band through Little Richard's 'Rip It Up' – that spring. The singer-guitarist Steve Marriott, at the same session, would remember how 'the others hero-worshipped Dave. He seemed about ten years older than them.' With a Who-fixation that verged on plagiarism and a second-hand ambulance doubling as a dressing room, the Lower Third were never in danger of setting the pop world alight. They did, however, learn what dozens of musicians would find out later. With David Jones, the need to play was scarcely more important than the need to dominate. Even at the first meeting, Marriott recalled, 'They thought they were getting a singer. Dave thought he was getting a band.' A week later a press release headed 'TRUTH SHOWS', and bearing an address in Plaistow Grove, landed on the desks of Britain's pop writers:

> This is to inform you of the existence of DAVIE JONES and THE LOWER THIRD
>
> Reputation-wise, Davie has a spotless chart. Having picked up the gauntlet in the now-legendary 'Banned Hair' tale, he stormed into BBC2's *Gadzooks*, leaving such an impression that he has been contracted for yet another appearance this month.

It was another small fantasy. There was no follow-up appearance. Nor would Fleet Street's interest be much stirred by the Lower Third. In a circular letter in July 1965 David catalogued the virtues of (as he now called them) his sidemen: they were mean, they were moody, they were maximum R&B; they were full of ideas. Yet nothing happened. Their two singles flopped and they never progressed beyond the club and cabaret circuit.

Among the reasons were the problems the Lower Third faced with their manager. When, that summer, the group recorded their first single – a slogging, Who-style raver called 'You've Got a Habit of Leaving' – Conn's failure to plug the record spelt the end of his deal with Davie Jones, who announced he was leaving pop 'to study mime at Sadler's Wells'. The five-year contract was quietly torn up. Using his corner table at the Giaconda as an office, David next considered applications for the job of Conn's successor, eventually settling on an unemployed booker-cum-Moody Blues roadie named Ralph Horton. Horton tolerated and even encouraged David's Mod obsession. Within days the Lower Third had traded their corduroys and jeans for a wardrobe of pin-collar shirts, trousers with creases and two-tone Italian winkle-picker shoes. For the full Who effect, Horton had the group's hair teased into elaborate bouffants. The Lower Third's regular Saturday-afternoon performances at the Marquee took on a more sexual mien. What the audience saw on these occasions was a frenzy of tightly played pop in which the lank, pale singer swayed and shook his bony posterior in between rasping toots on his saxophone. By September of 1965 David had a small but fanatical following and the trappings of stardom. His reputation did not, however, extend to making serious money.

Here Horton's entrepreneurial flair would founder the moment his protégé first asked for a wage of £50 a week. After the laughter had died down, it was pointed out to David that not even the Who earned that. A fight ensued and for a week manager and client split. Horton did, however, make the rounds of the Denmark Street song-pluggers and persuaded a company director named Ray Cook to part with £1,500 in return for 10 per cent of David's monthly earnings above £100. It was a desperate, though vital stopgap bid to relieve the financial pressure: Cook's first payments went to settling the various court actions brought against David and the Lower Third for hire-purchase debt.

The still relatively obscure and uneasy teenager thus found himself yoked to a real-live backer. It was Horton's inspired idea to push David as a solo artist, and the group as merely talented also-rans; but it squared with the singer's equally fixed image of himself as aloof. It showed in the way he referred to the Third as his 'backing', insisting that his name appear above theirs; or somehow always shirked mundane jobs like carrying his own equipment. (Dick Taylor of the Pretty Things remembers the group 'lugging a piano into the ambulance while David watched the proceedings sitting on a folding chair'.) Acting was also David's *métier*, and it was not always easy to tell when he was motivated by simple opportunism – putting on a show for the fans – or by conflict rooted in his identity problems. Dick James was among the first to note him 'not just mimicking, but turning himself inside out and *becoming* Tony Newley'. Ken Pitt recalls him 'switching a cockney persona on and off . . . He liked to shock people into thinking he was a yob.' There was no focal point even to David's 'normal' voice: clipped and effete one minute, blokish and lewd the next. James would remember him doing a hilarious but irrevocable parody of Michael Caine, 'the accent, the whole delivery, everything'.

From an early age, David had been dissatisfied with his own name. At Bromley Tech he once insisted on the sobriquet Luther, later modified to Lou, before emerging a year later as Cal or Calvin. Horton would listen to him agitate for 'a name like Crockett – something American'. By late 1965 the emergence of a young English actor called Davy Jones had brought David's problem to a crisis. Egged on by Horton and his search for a truism about 'cutting through the lies', he came up with the name Bowie. It combined terseness with a threat and was also American, a homage to the Texan hero who gave his name to a double-edged knife. The other Davy Jones went on to join the Monkees.

By February 1966 *Melody Maker* would run a column head-lined 'A message to London from Dave', with the gratifying lead, 'Without doubt, David Bowie has talent.' And versatility: under his baton, the Lower Third rehearsed a repertoire that included a Kinks medley, Rodgers and Hammerstein's 'You'll Never Walk Alone', and snatches from the *Planet Suite*. The drummer Tony Newman remembers Bowie in a sound-check at the Marquee. 'His head may have been up in the clouds, but his feet – and sense of rhythm – were planted on terra firma. He led the band like a drill-sergeant.' The journalist Peter Perchard received a visit from Bowie early in the new year. 'He gave me a hand-drawn advertisement which he wanted run, and a copy of his new record . . . Good self-promotion.' To another reporter, 'there was a tendency to push himself forward, but always with a surface shyness'. The critic Don Gunn calls him 'torpedo-like in his ambition, with an unshakable belief that everything he touched would be crowned with final glory'.

Vying with the Third's repertoire of fuzzy rock-guitar hooks and classical noodlings was a well-tailored pop tune called 'The London Boys'. Bowie wrote the song about himself. The lyric, parodying every teen melodrama of its day, spoke of an adolescent lost in a world of bright lights and pill addiction. It took the Third an hour to record it at Pye's Marble Arch studio, and the label less than half that time to reject it. Bowie's response was another angst-ridden anthem, 'Can't Help Thinking About Me', dealing with a wayward son leaving home. It was his first release as a solo artist. Despite occasional pirate-radio airplay, the single was a commercial and critical flop. With Bowie's patron Ray Cook already looking askance at his investment, the Lower Third's days were numbered. After Horton announced that the group's wages would be more sparingly paid in future, they took the hint and disbanded. The actual parting took place in a club in – of all poignant places – Bromley. One by one the Lower Third unstrapped their instruments, hurriedly repossessed by Horton, under the silent and impassive stare of their singer. When the drummer walked over and said, 'Ta-ta, Dave,' and extended his hand, Bowie refused to answer him. Another member of the group then accused him of being 'twisted' by ambition. Bowie's glacial reply was that it was the Lower Third who had been twisted, precisely by their sloth. On that note he turned his back and left.

Moving rapidly in his smoky brown glasses and cap, Horton next advertised for musicians to join an R&B group under Bowie's leadership. The first to rely was a twenty-six-year-old bass player named Derek Fearnley. He was followed by John Hutchinson, a guitarist who remembers 'David telling me to "play like Bo Diddley",' and, that done, Horton's assistant Spike Palmer informing him, 'Your application has been accepted.' Over the next week, Derek Boyes and John Eager also auditioned to Bowie's satisfaction. After the familiar visit to Carnaby Street and the unisex salon, the new group was christened the Buzz.

The next month was a whirlwind of activity and of rising enthusiasm, Bowie for the Buzz, the Buzz for Bowie. 'He had all these quirky songs, an off-centre way of looking at things,' says

Hutchinson, 'and the first thing that struck me was that he was so *grounded*. David had an unshakeable belief in himself.' A curious incident at this period shows how Bowie's imagination was at work on his future career. One night Horton received a phone message that an 'international recording star' was about to call on him. Soon there was a ring at the bell and a dusky woman in a chauffeuse's uniform announced, 'Miss Garland is here.' At the door was Bowie in a ballgown and feather boa masquerading as his heroine. He was already identifying himself with the diva and gay icon, already playing the game of make-believe.

The reality was considerably more banal. On 1 April 1966 Bowie's first single with the Buzz, 'Do Anything You Say', was released to an indifferent world. It was his fifth consecutive flop. The truth is that, for all their quirkiness, Bowie's early songs rarely had much going for them except his own personality. All that he had achieved up to now had been a clever variation on the kind of Mod anthem best left to the Who and Small Faces. Even Bowie's producer Tony Hatch later admitted, 'I thought he wrote too much about London dustbins.'

By Easter 1966 he was reduced to hosting a Sunday afternoon series at the Marquee that became known as the Bowie Show-boat. Reciting a litany of complaints, he wrote Horton a 1,500-word letter on the subject of money, his lack of it, and Ray Cook's 'panicky' withholding of it. The harangue had been triggered by Cook's refusal to buy the Buzz new stage clothes. According to a close friend, Bowie got 'all emotional' and burst into tears. Horton decided to use the episode as an occasion for challenging Cook's stewardship – which he had increasingly resented – over the group's purse. 'It was desperate,' says Hutchinson. 'There were literally guys pounding on the dressing room door asking for money.'

Horton's response was to turn to a forty-three-year-old show-business entrepreneur named Kenneth Pitt. Pitt does not always make a sympathetic character in Bowie biographies. Until 1966 he was known chiefly for his management of the lightweight R&B/pop group Manfred Mann, and an interest in interim figures like Mark Leeman and Crispian St Peters. In later years Pitt would be lampooned for his ambition to turn Bowie into a cabaret star, and his tolerance (some said encouragement) of his client's Anthony Newley fixation. 'People laughed a little behind Ken's back,' says Hutchinson. But they respected him as a decent and considerate manager, honest, well connected and with surprisingly eclectic tastes. It was Pitt who would take up Terry Burns's role as Bowie's tutor. There were renewed visits to the West End theatres and galleries. More pertinently, Pitt exposed Bowie to the world of Dylan, Andy Warhol and the Velvet Underground – strangely, all artists he knew or had represented. Nor did he explicitly encourage a watering-down of Bowie's music. 'Contrary to popular opinion,' says Pitt today, 'I *hated* cabaret. In the course of four years, I mentioned it to David once. That was when he was broke and unable to feed himself. Cabaret? Not likely. It *killed* Scott Walker.'

Pitt's first meeting with Bowie, on 17 April 1966, took place at the Marquee. A mutual friend recalls 'Ken coming in the stage door on Wardour Street. He had a tweed jacket on, and a cravat. Very smart. I remember him at the back, leaning against the wall with his arms crossed.'

What Pitt saw that Sunday was Bowie giving a routine Showboat performance. There was a medley of his own songs, covers of the Kinks and Yardbirds, and a rousing finale of 'When You Walk Through A Storm'. The number ended with Bowie, stage centre, in skin-tight trousers and a sweater, flinging out his arms like a vision of Garland herself. Then, as the applause started, he kissed the tips of his fingers and waved at the crowd.

By that evening Pitt had replaced Ray Cook as Bowie's Maginot Line against destitution. The Buzz's main problem remained survival. On 15 June Hutchinson, after a running feud with Horton, resigned. There were rumblings from Boyes and Eager. The group did, however, consent to accompany Bowie to the studio, where they were met by the professional session men quietly engaged by Hatch to 'tart up' the sound. The resulting single, 'I Dig Everything', suffered the same dismal fate as its predecessors. There was merit, though, to Hatch's view that 'David was so prolific, it was obvious he was going to make it', and a second man's: 'I told him he'd end up being a millionaire.' (Bowie was currently reading a letter from a hire-purchase company requesting the return of his microphone.) Within two months he was re-recording 'The London Boys' as well as two new songs, 'Rubber Band' and 'Please Mr Gravedigger', that replaced happy-go-lucky choruses with genuinely inventive, offbeat story-lines.

Marc Bolan would claim later, 'I never got the feeling from Dave that he was ambitious.' Bowie himself spoke of everything he did pre-1970 as 'fooling around' and a learning curve. Self-confidence – that was the quality that struck Hatch, Horton and others during the anxious months of planning, waiting and brooding during late 1966. 'David knew what he wanted, but his tactic was to coax, or burst into tears, rather than to rant,' says Terry Helm, a man who met him at Pye. Bowie now turned the full beam of his personal charm on to Pitt. The latter remembers him as someone who took 'everything in. He exuded magnetism and poise and charisma. He had the ... human touch. You know, you felt you could communicate with him. You wanted to do your best for him.' Not only did Pitt take over the previously chaotic management of Bowie's finances: by November he had sold 'Rubber Band' and 'The London Boys' to Decca (home of the Rolling Stones), and secured a £100 advance for a début album – virtually unheard of for an artist with six failed singles. Despite this windfall, Bowie then fired the Buzz. The same fate befell Horton, talented as a small-time booker and roadie, but unable to adjust to the commercial prospects now materializing on every side. For the rest of the decade Bowie would answer solely to Ken Pitt. The older man became not only a tutor, but a kind of father figure. When, in 1967, Bowie moved into Pitt's flat, some thought the relationship cut deeper still. In keeping with his Svengali role, Pitt took personal responsibility for honing his client's rough edges. He greatly favoured the romantic strain of Bowie's talent, and disapproved of the brash young producer Tony Visconti, who arrived with the idea of 'making Dave *rock*'. Paradoxically, Pitt also introduced Bowie to the music of John Cale and Lou Reed.

Having recently seemed tired, depressed and ready to give up, Bowie once again had spring in his step and his killer instinct for publicity. At all times of his career he was an artist, who observed himself in action. He told Helm how he felt that he split into two people on stage, one playing to the audience, the other anxiously watching him. As a result he worried more about his image than about the day-to-day management of his career. Here Pitt was able to impose order and stabilize a figure who had already been through five groups in as many years. Not only did he supervise sessions for Bowie's first album (for which the Buzz's Derek Fearnley was paid £50 to help with arrangements); he fired off letters, took advertisements, sent out press releases, negotiated with publishers and took over the crude accounts he inherited from Horton. On 9 March 1967 Pitt registered Bowie as member F2565 with the Performing Rights Society, listing twenty-nine of his client's songs, including the most recent, a novelty item called 'The Laughing Gnome' in which the vocals showed an alarming resemblance to a chipmunk's. Six weeks later, on 25 April, Pitt formally became Bowie's manager.

The *David Bowie* album was released on 1 June. Following in 'The Gnome's' bouncing-clean image, the first side of the record shunned teen drama in favour of upbeat vigour and melodies and words that dared to be childish. Bowie's homages to Jimmy Burns, 'Rubber Band' and 'Little Bombardier', were valiant efforts to tap the same vein of music-hall whimsy mined by *Small Faces* and *Well Respected Kinks*. But trite, warmed-over ballads like 'There Is a Happy Land' and 'When I Live My Dream' were a pale shadow of the allusive genius of *Sergeant Pepper*, released on that same day. *David Bowie* had its motley pleasures: 'Join the Gang' reprised the subtext of despair and isolation of 'The London Boys'; 'Please Mr Gravedigger' was a macabre dirge with sound effects; 'Silly Boy Blue' showed Bowie's familiarity with Buddhist jargon. At their best, the music and words of *David Bowie* were inseparable, as though they were conceived organically in the same breath. As the album progressed, so the lyrics became more proficient. The most powerful revelation was 'We Are Hungry Men', an apocalyptical view of famine and decay that anticipated both *Diamond Dogs* and *Outside*. Such reviews as *David Bowie* generated dwelt at length on the unconventional themes and cockney vocal affectations. (When Bowie's publisher sent Anthony Newley a copy of the record, he smashed it.) It bombed commercially.

Pitt was struck above all by Bowie's personal frustration. He felt 'unappreciated', anguished at having won recognition from

neither his friends nor family. Although John Jones was support-
ive (a neighbour remembers him rushing down the high street
waving a copy of the album), Peggy 'never said a word about it'.
One of Bowie's maternal cousins wrote to say she was ashamed
to hear him singing such 'muck'. A second relative who visited
Plaistow Grove and argued with David daubed a nearby wall with
graffiti: BOWIE IS A SODDING POOF. By morning the adjective
had been erased by an unknown passer-by who still agreed with
the main thesis. Even Terry Burns proved unsympathetic. After
another row in the home with Peggy Jones, he walked in a rage
into the Kent farmland around Maidstone, sleeping rough and
living off stolen food which he told one protesting shopkeeper his
'smart-arse brother' would pay for.

Behind the disappointment rose a new David Bowie, one who
would decisively quit Bromley, to proceed now boldly, now
cautiously, towards greater ends. Nineteen sixty-seven was the
year his Buddhist dabblings crept to their peak. He redoubled his
interest in avant-garde theatre and art. He also left Plaistow
Grove to move into his manager's London flat at 39 Manchester
Street, Marylebone. Pitt now became the latest in a long line of
benefactors to support Bowie financially through his apprenticeship. Like Conn, Cook and Horton before him, he was motivated
by a belief that he possessed genuine quality. But he was also
enticed by Bowie's looks and by the latter's clear understanding
that his career worked through people, and thus required a
personal commitment as well as loyalty to ideas.

Partly as a result of Pitt's subtle press-agentry, the word about
Bowie (in Bolan's words) 'cut more in the business than with the
kids'. Among those who bought and admired the first album was
the mime artist Lindsay Kemp. Hearing about this, Bowie enrolled
in Kemp's class at the Dance Centre in Floral Street. Both men
had a striking affinity for the stage, for play-acting and vanity.
But the similarities did not end there. While passing the long
afternoons in Soho, Helm remembers, it was impossible not to
notice some of Kemp's favourite themes and phrases creeping into
David's speech. So began the last act of Bowie's own private
Pygmalion. Under Kemp's eye, he was exposed to names like
Genet and Cocteau, beyond even Pitt's wide tastes. He learnt
something of Herzog and Fellini, and the gay cabaret mentality

epitomized by Danny La Rue. Kemp, who recalls Bowie as 'a golden-haired swain' with 'the voice of an angel', lost no time in casting him in his new production, *Pierrot in Turquoise*, Bowie himself suggested the title, after the Buddhist symbolic colour of eternity.

Travelling as he did in artistic circles, Bowie had always known gay men and doyens of high camp, and counted a fair number among his friends. Both Pitt and his predecessor Ralph Horton had balanced their professional interest in their client with a more personal one. Danny La Rue, the exotic cabaret artiste who watched Bowie perform at a charity show in London, wrote him a long letter asking if he would be free to collaborate with him on a future project. Even Rudolf Nureyev was seen to give the singer a sidelong glance when they met backstage at the Queen Elizabeth Hall. Bowie was also a sometime companion and lover to several women. A neighbour in Bromley recalls an explosive scene when Peggy Jones returned home to find her son and two 'darkies' together in the front bedroom. The ensuing row turned heads the length of Plaistow Grove. Lindsay Kemp ruefully recalled Bowie 'always in the coffee bar, chatting up the birds'.

All of these sides – the predatory seducer, the serious artist, the androgynous flirt – were in conflict when Bowie began a provincial tour with *Pierrot in Turquoise* late in 1967. He and Kemp had already become lovers. In the same month, Bowie started an affair with the company's set designer, Natasha Kornilof. One grey January morning in Moresby, Cumbria, a lovelorn Kemp cut his wrists. On stage that night the stitches broke and Kemp's white costume became soaked in blood. At this, Bowie wept so heavily that his tears shredded his cardboard mask. The audience, thinking he was illustrating his role as 'Cloud', applauded wildly. This aroused Bowie and Kemp to new transports of anguish and remorse. As the curtain fell both actors were in each other's arms, kissing passionately, while a third member of the cast traced a heart in the air above their heads. Later that night Natasha Kornilof swallowed a bottle of aspirin.

3
THE PRETTIEST STAR

Tony Visconti, a promising young producer and songwriter, was at work in his Richmond Organization office in New York one day when a friend dropped by to tell him he *had* to listen to this 'English fag' and his new album. Visconti bought a copy of *David Bowie* the next morning. Later in 1967 he moved to London and met Bowie himself, setting up a partnership that lasted into a fourth decade. 'He was very young and very wide-eyed,' Visconti would tell the Gillmans. 'David was a nice, well-mannered Englishman, not the bizarre person he was made out to be – or would later become. We became very close in a very short space of time.'

Bowie's last single before meeting Visconti was 'Love You Till Tuesday', a coy if mildly witty slice of flummery culled from the first album. Its failure not only proved the urgent need for a new producer; it brought Bowie to the brink of a demoralizing crisis. When Pitt took him his late-morning breakfast in Manchester Street, 'David frequently started the day by complaining how broke he was' – and how perplexed. 'His line of vision is as straight and sharp as a laser beam,' Pitt had written in the liner notes of *David Bowie*. Now, that vision seemed to have failed altogether. There was no throughline to his career. A reporter from *Melody Maker* who came to interview him about his plans found him talking about giving up. Visconti urged him to return to the rootsy world of R&B. Pitt, though never the doddering vaudevillian he was later stigmatized, lobbied from the other direction. Bowie's mistress, who had a great deal of influence on him, was well known to consider him primarily an actor, and had been against his singing career from the start. Her opposition intensified as the news grew worse. The unfortunate Bowie's nights were, therefore, as grim as his days.

Visconti's first session with Bowie produced 'Let Me Sleep Beside You', an effort to cash in on the current vogue for songs about horizontal activity, and unanimously vetoed for release by the Decca selection panel. At this point Bowie's fortunes, already apparently at their darkest, turned black. His record company let him know they considered him 'unsaleable'. In the face of such calamity Pitt continued to harbour a sense, not exactly of optimism, but, rather, of willed determination. His efforts to revive Bowie's career were as ingenious as they were unflagging. There were jingles, voice-overs and even translation work. A column in *Record Retailer* announced that Bowie was engaged in furnishing English lyrics for a catalogue of Israeli songs acquired by Essex Music. A French publisher asked him to perform the same task for a ballad called 'Comme d'Habitude'. Bowie duly submitted a lyric, 'Even a Fool Learns To Love', and proceeded to make a test recording. For a while, Pitt had hopes that this 'infectious melody' would pass even Decca's scrutiny to become Bowie's next single. Then he heard that the song had been sold to Frank Sinatra and given the title 'My Way'.

Bowie continued, intermittently, to tour with Kemp and Kornilof in *Pierrot in Turquoise*. At the urging of a producer named Günther Schneider, he set about writing his own mime adaption of Stravinsky's *Circus Polka*; he auditioned for the cast of *Hair*, as well as *Sunday, Bloody Sunday*. He actually landed a blink-of-the-eye cameo in *The Virgin Soldiers*. Early in 1968 Bowie applied for the compère's job on a new pop music series being planned by ABC Television. After a private screening of the pilot programme, the company forgot the project.

Bowie's contract with Decca expired on 22 April 1968. His violent explosion at the 'men in suits' produced no clear-cut alternative plans, but did dangerously increase his own anxiety level. After three days of brooding in a friend's house in Chelsea, Bowie broke down. Terror-stricken, sobbing, he heaved a huge chair through the plate-glass window of his bedroom and nearly threw himself after it. Later that afternoon he was seen in a café with his head on his chest, crying, 'Please help me.' In this, Pitt carried off with equal assurance his double role as a hard-talking businessman and Bowie's utterly devoted, good-natured friend. He not only provided board, lodging, career advice and touches of emotional guidance, he hawked Bowie's contract to Parlophone, Apple, Liberty, Atlantic and Rak – all of whom, with varying degrees of tact, declined it. Eventually, under these dire circumstances, Pitt proposed cabaret. This was the origin of one powerful Bowie legend: that for nearly a year his manager had tried to resurrect him as an all-round entertainer, someone in the winsome tradition of Tommy Steele. In fact, as he says, Pitt raised the subject just once, and only then 'because David was stone broke'. That Bowie himself recognized the crisis is shown by his taking a part-time job at a London printing firm called Legastat, and his appearance, six months later, in a television commercial for LUV, a new ice-cream.

In spite of the increasingly precarious state of his finances and a CV that led John and Peggy to conclude that he lacked drive, Bowie decided to give much of 1968 to the lover who had become his obsession. In August he moved out of the Manchester Street flat to live in a room at 22 Clareville Grove, South Kensington, with Hermione Farthingale. Since appearing together in the BBC play *The Pistol Shot*, the couple had become inseparable. Not only did Farthingale supplant Kemp and Kornilof in Bowie's affections, as a trained ballerina and singer she took over their role as his collaborator. There the similarity ended. Kemp and Kornilof had cast themselves in a melodrama, one in which their own parts were mannered and easily readable. Farthingale, by contrast, rarely tipped her hand. Her easygoing affability served to conceal the actual intricacy of her personality. According to a friend from 1968, 'David fell for the English-rose looks and the highbrow charm. She was a likeable girl who never really approved of Bowie as a pop singer. That's not to say she didn't have plans for him of her own.' Within a month Bowie and Farthingale had recruited a guitarist, Tony Hill, to form a multi-media trio called Turquoise. It lasted for one night. At the very moment Hill walked out the Clareville Grove door Bowie's old friend from the Buzz, John Hutchinson, arrived. 'David told me he was getting into poetry and dance, and needed a new band,' he recalls. After an audition in which Hutchinson played not Bo Diddley riffs but Leonard

Cohen, he duly joined the trio, now renamed Feathers.

Bowie's real ascension would come, three years later, when he merged the group's folk and cabaret-tinged tunes with loud guitar and a freakish stage act. He also dabbled in the old-fashioned realms of bruised romance and simplistic, fist-pumping slogans. Yet Bowie was always careful to measure the distance between himself and the music that inspired him in the first place. 'Whenever he rocked and rolled,' Pitt writes, 'he did so in the context of theatre, as an actor.' Bowie himself has said: 'Rock does not play an important part in my life. Music for me is something I use to put down my thoughts – like paint.' John Hutchinson is only the most compelling witness to the view that 'While some bands work up a repertoire of songs, what Dave developed were different sides of his personality': alternately turning on the charm or 'camp swagger' – enjoying the spectacle of confusion on the perplexed faces unable to decide if he was putting them on or putting them down. The first author of the Bowie enigma and the greatest of the Bowie dramatists was Bowie himself.

The words 'swishing' and 'queen' could have been invented for Bowie in his early years. Yet even Ziggy was only one link in the androgynous musical chain that stretched back from Liberace to Syd Barrett and, through Bowie, embraced Elton John, who dyed what was left of his hair blood red. He may have been, as he said, 'aiming to end gender'; but Bowie did so from a calculated theatrical stance, and with a sense of irony – all his best roles are, to some extent, anarchically funny – starkly at odds with the gay activists whose letters begging for support always went unanswered.

Bowie was an active heterosexual who also slept with men. His approach to lovemaking corresponded neatly with his view of women's mission in life, which seems to have been based on a mixture of biological theory and phobia. According to what he told a lover, he felt that women had charge of humanity. It was their business to ensure the continuity of the race and to look after men and children. Along with a rigidly orthodox view of female roles went a broad streak of old-fashioned chauvinism. Bowie 'went out of his nut', according to a girlfriend in 1969, if kept waiting for a clean shirt or a meal. He later earned a rebuke from John Lennon for barking at his fiancée to make breakfast after a long night of partying in New York. Angela Bowie recalls an incident when, angered by his wife's behaviour, 'David hurtled across the room, grabbed my throat in both hands, and started to throttle me.' Bowie not only relinquished those activities in middle age, but tried to compel others to give them up as well: thus 'Boys Keep Swinging' revised his former misogynist views, while 'Repetition' attacked domestic violence. He was less successful at overcoming his fear that women were essentially treacherous. Although, in later years, Bowie was rarely without an actress or an African model in tow, the relationships still acted out the rites, manners and forms of language he learnt as a lonely child. This meant a permanant apparatus of self-containment and a coldness widely remarked on by his partners. An ex-lover believes 'David had an inability – almost a pathological aversion – to open up to a woman.' It was doubtless this condition which caused Bowie to propose to his first wife with the words, 'Can you handle the fact that I'm not in love with you?'

David Bowie, then, was not one to make a play of passion. He slept with women because it appealed to him; he slept with men as trophies as he exerted control over them. A writer named Mary Finnigan, with whom Bowie had an affair in 1969, would tell the Gillmans, 'He was more into women than men. [Homosexuality] with him was more opportunist and contrived.' Androgyny was also an obvious way to put clear water between himself and the stultifying world of John and Peggy. A lot of it, Helm shrewdly guessed, was 'Dave up in arms against Bromley'. Bowie and his wife 'lived in a fantasy world', said Finnigan, 'and they created their bisexual fantasy'. Along with the experiments with make-up and perfume went Saturday-night cross-dressing parties: 'they used to turn up in the same clothes, his better-fitting than hers', says a mutual friend. Bowie laughed uproariously when a dinner guest once tapped him on the back and called him 'Angie'. In later years he made a positive fetish of repeating the quip that he and his wife had met while 'fucking the same bloke'.

Gay sex was always an anecdotal and laughing matter. That Bowie's actual tastes swung the other way is clear from even a partial tally of his affairs with women. During one short period in 1969 after breaking with Farthingale, he was bedding Mary Finnigan, Dana Gillespie, his future wife and a fourth person who prefers anonymity. Bowie's chaperon during his first trip to America remembered him 'grabbing girls right and left. He was picking up girls hitch-hiking in the street.' A female employee would recall Bowie ending a business meeting by asking her, 'Where do you like to crash out – a house or a hotel?' In 1973 a singer named Ava Cherry moved into the Bowies' London home, with the enthusiastic approval of both husband and wife. (He was 'fascinated by black chicks', she recalled. 'Any girls he slept with when I knew him were black.') Six months later Bowie began an affair with Amanda Lear, a leather-clad exotic who hovered between his bed and that of the artist Salvador Dali. He then entered into a brief, though intense liaison with his female assistant. By summer of 1974, according to the Gillmans, Michael Kamen, on tour with Bowie in America, would find 'groupies three deep in the hallways, waiting for a glimpse of David'. Sex was one thing: in the years ahead Bowie's emotional life also followed down a straight line, from divorce and a custody battle, through a failed engagement, to a second, apparently successful marriage in 1992.

In 1969 neither his career nor his finances fared as well as Bowie himself. Having been reduced to appearing in an ice-cream commercial, he was now turned down for a similar job by Kit-Kat. Bowie's publishers were unable even to place his new single with a record company. His total income for the year plummeted to £906. When he was offered two days' work at the Magician's Workshop in Falmouth, Bowie had to ask for a loan for the rail fare.

It was against this grim backdrop that Pitt hit on the equivalent idea to vanity publishing, a self-financed television film. Bowie, who underwent several hours of cosmetic dental work before shooting, was, a colleague says, 'not exactly aglow with enthusiasm' for the project, which had various teething problems of its own. Bowie spent several days dredging friends' wardrobes for 'with-it gear' like paisley shirts and flares to wear in front of the cameras. As a final indignity, he was forced to don a wig to cover his severe *Virgin Soldiers* haircut. Recruiting his ex-assistant Malcolm Thomson as director, Pitt finally agreed both a script and a budget: the first day of shooting took place on location in Hampstead on 26 January 1969.

Love You Till Tuesday, as the short became, was a well-meaning piece of Flower Power claptrap, chiefly notable for catching Bowie, sometimes accompanied by Hutchinson and Farthingale, at his turning-point from ancient to modern: an acoustic-bound folkie, yet also a performer of style and wit. Eventually released in 1984, its charm today lies in its historical *post facto* appeal, its homage to the vanished world of beads and loon pants, rather than in anything Bowie specifically sings or does. The all-round versatility of the star is *Tuesday*'s bristling subtext. To a sound-track lifted largely from his first album, Bowie agitates his guitar, croons his soft-focus ballads and mugs through the one mime piece. It was not that the film was actually bad, or even, by the modest standards of its day, technically flawed. Pitt's labour of love was well photographed and lavishly produced, but the meandering thirty-minute result was as fickle as the career it celebrated, with bravura touches in short supply.

Love You Till Tuesday did, however, include a song that came to epitomize Bowie's early output just as 'Heroes' or 'Let's Dance' would embody his later work. It was in mid-January – the same week as he was chirping a chorus of LUV LUV LUV for Lyons Maid – that Bowie approached Malcolm Thomson with the words, 'That film of yours – I've got a new song for it.' The pair then went to Manchester Street, where Bowie took out his guitar, settled in a chair and strummed the early chords of 'Space Oddity'. 'I remember it vividly,' says Pitt. 'The hairs actually *did* stand up on my neck.'

'Space Oddity' was recorded at Morgan Studios, Willesden, on 2 February 1969. Thomson shot the accompanying clip on the 6th, making the lyrics' denouement – with Bowie being caressed by two scantily clad sirens – cut less deep than the later version by Mick Rock. It was to Bowie's credit that the song's theme of utter, profound alienation survived even *Love You Till Tuesday*'s papery costumes and tin-can props. 'Space Oddity' was, of course, on one level a straightforward homage to *2001*. A friend remembers the 'seismic impact' the film had on Bowie, particularly the final, climactic images of the monolith doomed to float eternally in space. Nor did the song's subject-matter come about in a vacuum. It followed 'In the Year 2525' and preceded 'Rocket

Man' in taking its lead from both Kubrick and the Apollo moon-shots. But where Elton John and a host of novelty artists moved on, Bowie himself became obsessed with 'Space Oddity's' central message of withdrawal, of life closing down. He returned to it repeatedly later in his career, notably on *Low* and in the song's 1980 sequel 'Ashes to Ashes'.

Tony Visconti hated 'Space Oddity'. To his rock sensibility it was 'a cheap shot – a gimmick to cash in on the moon landing'. On the other hand, it was exactly this virtue that commended it to Mercury Records, a Chicago-based company represented in Britain by Philips. On the basis of the 'Space Oddity' audition tape, the label offered Bowie and Pitt an unprecedented advance of £1,250, plus a wage of £20 a week when Bowie was in the studio, in return for which he was to deliver one album and three singles a year. The contract was signed on 20 June 1969. 'David was over the moon,' says Pitt, in almost every sense of that satirical phrase. 'It seemed finally as if all the hard work had paid off.' That same day Bowie re-recorded 'Space Oddity' with Gus Dudgeon, the engineer on *David Bowie*, at the mixing desk. Dudgeon generously admits that the tune was 'so drop-dead great' his only job was to hire the backing musicians. (Among those recruited was a young keyboard player named Rick Wakeman.) The drummer Terry Cox remembers 'a pretty loose session, with David playing the basic riff and then telling us to get on with it. Other than the fact that he wanted to put a blanket on my drums, there wasn't a lot else said. By the end of the song I was making things up, adding little fills of my own.' Cox was paid the 'top money' of £9 10s. for his services. He remembers Bowie as 'a bit funny, but a nice guy. At the end of the session he shook my hand and told me to stay in touch.' When Cox wrote to Bowie ten years later there was no reply.

'It just sort of oozed out,' Bowie would say of 'Space Oddity'. A girlfriend remembers a more protracted process, in which the number evolved, via half a dozen failed choruses, over a week at Clareville Grove. Hutchinson, too, though hastening to join the consensus that 'the basic idea was Dave's', recalls adding a major-seventh chord and 'helping the song along'. Hutchinson was impressed how Bowie salvaged an old Lower Third riff and the bass line from 'There is a Happy Land' for the song's distinctive intro. There were touches, too, of both Simon and Garfunkel and the Bee Gees in 'Space Oddity's' folkish arrangement. Although Bowie never discussed the origins of 'Major Tom' with either Pitt or Hutchinson, a third man involved with Philips has an ingenious explanation: 'The name was suggested by the words on an old theatre bill David saw as a kid in Brixton, advertising the Prime Minister's father, Tom Major.'

'Space Oddity' was previewed at the Rolling Stones open-air concert on 5 July and released commercially six days later. In a rare excursion into pop's seamy side Pitt paid a chart-rigger £140 to guarantee the song a place in the *Record Retailer* top twenty. Two months later, it reached number 48. On 1 November 'Space Oddity' crested at number five. After nearly six years and at the tenth attempt, Bowie had a hit single – at least, as Pitt qualifies, in Britain. By late autumn, Bowie's manager had global ambitions for the record; what he lacked was a carefully conceived strategy to carry them out, given Mercury's lukewarm support. Despite frantic activity on the transatlantic phone, 'Space Oddity' died a lingering death in America.

In February 1969 Bowie, whose set was predominantly mime, began a short tour supporting Tyrannosaurus Rex. Marc Bolan would later remember a particularly striking night at Manchester's Free Trade Hall. 'David opened wearing a blouse and ballet pumps, and acted out a twenty-minute piece about Chinese troops' rape of Tibet. The first couple of minutes weren't easy. I mean, it was "What a poof", you know?' The hall was even more crowded than normal that night. In one corner, members of the T-Rex appreciation society sat in gold lurex suits calling for 'Pewter Suitor'. In another, skinheads watched silent and hard-eyed, making no attempt to conceal their dislike for the perm-haired queen wearing women's clothes. In the event Bolan made an early entrance and, with the faithful Hutchinson strumming in the wings, joined Bowie for an acoustic version of 'Space Oddity'.

It would be an eventful year at the Free Trade Hall, but even the most blasé rock fans would remember how it began: with two of the 1970s' most glittering icons singing a folk song about an astronaut deciding to leave earth's orbit.

*

'Space Oddity' was the end of Bowie's gruelling apprenticeship. The spring of 1969 was also the end of his affair with Farthingale. Within days of completing *Love You Till Tuesday*, Bowie had retreated to his old bedroom at Plaistow Grove and told his parents brokenly and tearfully that he and his lover were parting. The break-up was for reasons John and Peggy would not understand, he said, but painful as it was, it was best for both of them. Bowie also sought out Dana Gillespie, to whom he announced dramatically that he felt 'dead'. So far as a third woman could gather as they lay together in bed, 'Hermione had a problem with David, physical and otherwise.' John Hutchinson believes 'things had been going downhill, and when the film was finished, so were they'.

Within a month Bowie had moved in with Mary Finnigan in her flat in Foxgrove Road, Beckenham. 'He warned me that he had no money,' she recalled. 'I was doing nothing and was also broke. We were all broke. He turned up two days later.' As Bowie walked north from Beckenham Junction, he must have recalled what he dubbed the 'semi-death' – the identical red-brick suburban houses – of Bromley. Even the High Street was far too narrow to provide the kind of 'big feel' he told Finnigan he wanted. But things dramatically improved as Bowie entered Foxgrove Road, an avenue of high Gothic villas that had been converted into flats. There was something 'improper' about the crumbling stone façades overgrown with weeds and bushes; but impropriety of a forgotten, Edwardian kind. As Helm recalls, 'you could imagine kinky goings-on behind the lace curtains'. With one short break later that summer, Beckenham was to be Bowie's full-time home for nearly five years.

Without making any apology for abandoning rock and roll, Bowie set about re-inventing himself as a torch singer. He did reaffirm his love of 'spade music', and for individuals like Little Richard, but his own primary allegiance, he made clear, was to the protest tradition of Bob Dylan – to music as a direct act. To ease his perennial cash crisis, Bowie arranged with the landlord of the Three Tuns pub in Beckenham to stage a series of Sunday-night folk sessions. With Finnigan's energetic support, the programme became known as an Arts Lab. Fired with enthusiasm,

Bowie sat down to design a hand-drawn poster announcing the first night. Along with Finnigan, he also edited a weekly newsletter called *Growth*. 'Growth is people, Growth is revolution, Growth grows at its own speed, expands according to the energy input it receives, is open to all, but closed to old ideas, clichés, destructive elements and grey thoughts' ran the issue of 16 August. 'Come for the fun of it, and for instant identification with the vibrations.'

'It was always cool,' says Keith Christmas. 'It was always Sunday night.' Christmas was a local guitarist who became a staple at the Three Tuns. He remembers the strange hybrid of mime, poetry, art, Buddhist incantations, tie-dying classes and free-form jazz in the pub's back room, surrounded on one side by the beer garden and on the other by the clicking glasses and occasional belly laughter of the saloon bar. 'Dave was something of a twerp in those days,' he states. 'We had him down as a floor singer, someone who'd strum a few folk songs in between a lot of crap about changing the world.' This bleak assessment is modified by Christmas's view of Bowie personally. 'He was into arty stuff like mime and ballet, but there's no doubt he really meant it. One thing about Dave – he always believed in what he did when he was doing it.' Later that summer the disc jockey John Peel received a 'really elaborate' letter and drawing from Bowie, along with an appeal for funds for the Arts Lab. Finnigan, too, was utterly convinced of Bowie's good faith. 'We were all very sincere about being involved with the community,' she said, 'and David was too. He was very, *very* sincere.'

On 9 April 1969 Bowie was at the Speakeasy Club to see King Crimson, the art-rock group whose career would graze his own. At some stage in the proceedings he was introduced to a nineteen-year-old *ingénue* with a flat, boyish figure and a self-confident personality expressed, he remembered, in a high, singsong voice 'like Minnie Mouse's'. Within an hour he was accompanying Angela Barnett to her room in a rundown ghetto of Paddington. Not only did they become lovers; to the surprise and consternation of friends like Pitt, Bowie was soon talking up Angela as 'brilliant, well educated, kooky, sophisticated, knew the ways of the world' – and, yes, he said, 'determined to marry me'. Others, like Bolan, were startled at how Bowie's formidable reserve melted so quickly. By midsummer Angela had moved in to Finnigan's house in Foxgrove Road. By autumn she was advising Bowie (whom she addressed as 'Nama-Nama') on not only his clothes, hair and the choice of their mutual girlfriends, but the whole direction of his career. Keith Christmas offers a revealing portrait of the couple together at their next flat in Beckenham. He describes the ornate, *Gone With the Wind*-style staircase, the stained-glass window, the carved fireplace, the permanently drawn velvet curtains and the tenants whose waiflike appearance gave them the air of 'two kids left alone without a baby-sitter'. Within less than a year of his saying 'Never', Bowie would marry.

Angela Barnett was born, a US citizen, in Cyprus, where her father worked as a mining engineer. Her paternal family was Anglo-American; her mother's, Polish. As if not already exotic enough, Angela was educated in Montreux, Connecticut and finally London, where she studied marketing at Kingston Poly-technic. While there she met Lou Reizner, the head of Mercury in Britain, and, through him, Calvin Mark Lee. Lee was not a good-looking man in the classic sense, some acquaintances would sniff jealously, with his sallow skin and the odd polyester disc stuck to the centre of his forehead. But he was, nonetheless, stunningly attractive. With his drooping Chinese eyes, perfect hair and flowing Carnaby Street wardrobe, Lee was almost the epitome of Swinging London. It was inevitable that, sooner or later, he would gravitate to the music business. By 1969 Reizner had appointed Lee (whose background was in molecular chemistry) as a talent-spotter for Mercury. His first quarry was Bowie. Here Lee mounted a campaign of Machiavellian cunning, out-flanking his boss (who saw 'no potential for this artist in Britain or America') by appealing direct to head office in Chicago. With the lure of 'Space Oddity' and Lee's fanatical endorsement, a contract was duly signed that June. Pitt remembers this as 'not a great deal, but a good, solid one – a leg-up for David'. The industrious Lee, meanwhile, had embarked on affairs with Bowie and Angela Barnett. It was he who introduced them at the Speakeasy that April, thus fulfilling his role as 'the bloke they were both fucking'.

True to tradition, Bowie hedged his bets, keeping one foot in the new world and the other planted firmly in the old. Late that July he accompanied Pitt to two song festivals in Malta and Italy.

The first, within its banal limits, went well enough. Bowie sang 'When I Live My Dream' to a big-band arrangement, under the golden baton of Norrie Paramor. He placed second to Cristina, a child prodigy from Spain. Any illusions that Pitt may have had about his proprietorship of Bowie were shattered forever in Italy, where Angela appeared at the hotel. It was now that the full extent of her ambitions was revealed. Not only did she consider 'La Pitt' and his festival a waste of time: David, she announced, would forthwith move from his manager's suite into her own. A London businessman named Malcolm Carr, also staying at the Reale, was 'surprised but not shocked' by Bowie, Angela and a teenage girl ambling past him late that night in the corridor. (What was surprising was that the girl was topless.) According to his memoir, Pitt had a similar reaction when waiting for the couple to emerge the next evening:

> As we were all assembling in the foyer, waiting to leave for the theatre, David and Angela were seen slowly descending the wide curving staircase. It was the grandest of entrances and caused much excitement. David's hair was swept back and held by a black velvet bow. He wore a magnificent old-fashioned shirt, while she wore a diaphanous, full-length, see-through dress, so transparent that one immediately saw that she wore beneath it the briefest of panties and nothing else.

This time around, the organizers gave Bowie a special award for his 'unique contribution' to the festivals.

He returned to London to the news that John Jones was dying. Bowie and his girlfriend rushed to Plaistow Grove. His father was lying in the cramped front bedroom, morbid with pneumonia and emaciated. John managed a faint smile when Bowie brandished his Italian statuette and told him he was 'really famous'. Downstairs Peggy sat in uneasy silence with Angela, appraising her future daughter-in-law's smudged mascara and micro-skirt. A good case can be made for saying their meetings would never be so civil again. Two days later, on 5 August, Bowie was at work in Trident Studios on his new Mercury album. A session musician remembers 'a phone ringing in the control room . . . David walked up a long flight of stairs and answered it. I could see him

speaking. Then he came back down and said, "John's dead."'
'There were a few tears,' says Keith Christmas. 'But I don't
remember a big scene about it.'

Bowie's sensitive nature was vulnerable to the rebuke that he
had ignored both his parents in recent years, and he attended the
funeral at Elmers End Cemetery on 11 August. The next week the
Arts Lab, in keeping with the trend set at Woodstock and Hyde
Park, staged an open-air concert. Bowie performed an acoustic
set including 'Space Oddity', and later eulogized the event in
'Memory of a Free Festival', in which he sang 'I kissed a lot of
people that day'. The truth was more oblique. A friend clearly
remembers Bowie 'in a foul mood' after a violent row with Calvin
Mark Lee. That, in turn, induced various complaints about the
festival's sound system, which Bowie likened to that of a 'church-
hall bingo night'. From there, what remained of civility gave way.
Angela and Mary Finnigan approached Bowie with the news that
they had raised £400 from the sale of festival posters and fast
food. 'You materialistic arseholes,' he snapped. Another group on
the bill were derided as 'wankers – just in it for the bread'. In an
interview with Kate Simpson later in the year Bowie lashed out
at the 'hypocritical attitudes among the groups that haven't made
it. They're striving like mad for some kind of commercial success
… I've never seen so many dishonest people in my life.' His
co-performers at the festival were 'lethargic', 'apathetic' and 'the
laziest people I've met'.

Bowie never found it easy to reveal intimate feelings. John
Hutchinson, who worked with him in three different eras,
eventually left feeling that he 'hardly knew' him, although he had
travelled the world with him, co-writing his songs, appearing in
his films, staying in his home, sharing his daily life. 'He wasn't
inconsiderate,' Hutchinson recalls. 'He was just no good at
human relations – naturally aloof.' Bowie himself believed the
dark side really began with the blows he took in 1969. 'I was in
love once,' he recalled. 'It was an awful experience. It rotted me,
drained me, and it was a disease. Being in love is something that
breeds brute anger and jealousy.' To compound matters, his
father's loss led him to conclude that 'I didn't need anybody to
survive, because they always get taken away from you.' On this
reading, Farthingale's defection and John Jones's death resulted

in Bowie hardening his already flinty exterior. Because of his reserve, says Terry Helm, casual acquaintances found him 'a shit' and he made friends slowly, whether they were women or men. Jeff Griffin, a BBC producer who met Bowie in 1970, says, 'there was an edge to him even then. You couldn't talk to him, as you could to, say, Jagger, about things like cricket or football. It was strictly business.' Even his half-brother fell victim to Bowie's policy on affection. When Terry Burns arrived in Beckenham one afternoon in 1971 he was turned away with the words 'I'm sorry. I'm busy.' Angela herself, after the initial honeymoon, came to remark on Bowie as 'one of the most coldly calculating human beings I've ever met', an 'ice man' whose frigidity was based on his 'fear of feeling' and, specifically, his dread of madness. Marc Bolan, a friend of Bowie in the 1970s, vividly recalled his line, 'Love? I don't know what that word means.'

Paradoxically, Bowie was often emotional. Keith Christmas remembers him 'in floods' when the two of them listened to a playback of 'God Knows I'm Good', a melodramatic tale about an old woman caught shoplifting. Another Beckenham friend says it was 'weird, the way laughter gave way to tears. Dave was ten times more sensitive about himself than about others.' When Pitt came to express misgivings about the Dylan affectations of Bowie's second album, 'David let out a sob and ran upstairs to the bedroom.' Steve Marriott believed Bowie was 'quite potty' for a year, at which point he went insane.

That Bowie was obsessed by his two losses was clear from the parting salvos he aimed at Farthingale on his new album, as well as a curious scene recalled by John Cambridge, a drummer who met him in Beckenham and later that year playing in Scotland. One evening the two men found themselves at the bar of Edinburgh's Royal Ballroom. After the second drink, says Cambridge, 'David told me that, for a whole week, his phone had rung at the same time every afternoon. When he answered it, there was no one there. He was convinced it was his father, calling him from the beyond.'

Cambridge, along with Visconti and the guitarists Mick Wayne and Tim Renwick, accompanied Bowie on tour that autumn, both headlining and backing Humble Pie. Most of November was spent testing the unfamiliar waters of Kilmarnock, Dunfermline,

Glasgow and Dundee. In all four towns the public and critical response was mixed. Bowie's mingling of loud electric rock and whey-faced folk was confidentially described by Renwick to Cambridge as a 'cock-up'. 'I went on in front of these gum-chewing skinheads,' Bowie recalled. 'As soon as I appeared, looking a bit like Bob Dylan with this curly hair and denims, I was whistled and booed. At one point I had cigarettes thrown at me.' Worse was to come in London. Due to a demarcation dispute between Pitt and Calvin Mark Lee, only two journalists attended a gala concert at the Purcell Room on 20 November. With better coverage, Pitt believes, 'superstardom would have come two years earlier than it did'. Instead, Bowie stormed out of the stage door with the words 'Fuck it!', paused to slam his fist into a brick wall, and took the train home to Beckenham in tears.

Bowie's second album* was released the same week. Writing in her memoir *Backstage Passes*, Angela would recall a 'magical communication in the studio during the six weeks of recording ... The musicians showed up every morning ready and willing, worked all day until early evening, and quit in time for dinner. They didn't have to wait until darkness before emerging from their hideouts and venturing to the studio, and when they worked they didn't have to do so within a cocoon of bodyguards, drug dealers, sex providers, and assorted other sycophants and leeches.' Keith Christmas speaks of the aircraft-hangar dimensions of Trident, and a resulting cold, impersonal atmosphere more businesslike than creative. Some of this coldness came through in the music. Bowie told his group he wanted to 'sleaze it', and on one occasion during the six weeks he screamed, 'It's gotta *rock*.' Yet he aroused the suspicion of raucous R&B merchants like Wayne and Renwick that he didn't go far enough. He never disowned the Simon and Garfunkel affectations nor recaptured the off-centre nervous energy of his first songs, which was what they most wanted to hear.

---

*Although released in the UK as *David Bowie*, and in the US as *Man of Words, Man of Music*, the album was reissued in 1972 with the title *Space Oddity*.

Their doubts were justified. In Bowie's mouth 'It's gotta rock' expressed a hope, not a promise. Despite the wry theme of 'Space Oddity', the album itself struggled to find a voice. Bowie had hit the chart with a chorus that soared, well-crafted verses and a topical story. Homespun moral messages were laid over a seductive folk-rock beat and a hummable tune. But, stretched over forty-five minutes, the plot soon unravelled. *David Bowie* lacked clarity and punch. Songs lurched between the mundane ('Letter to Hermione', 'An Occasional Dream') and the mawkish ('God Knows I'm Good'). Bowie's post-hippie sensibility was at work in the nine-and-a-half-minute 'Cygnet Committee' – a critique of the peace-love generation also reprised in 'Memory of a Free Festival'. 'Wild Eyed Boy From Freecloud' conjured the same sub-Tolkien brew of an all-wise guru, madness, violence and mist-topped mountains of an early Led Zeppelin number. Like its predecessor, *David Bowie* had its moments: there was the hard-rock edge of 'Unwashed and Somewhat Slightly Dazed', where Bowie found new levels of self-awareness while maintaining his trademark mix of whimsy, paranoia and alienation. He included some numbers that managed to be upbeat and yet strangely touching, like the pseudo-love ode 'Janine'. The final, repeated chorus of 'Free Festival' recalled the Beatles' 'Hey Jude'. But while most of the album's nine tracks boasted at least one novel twist, they sounded as if they could all have done with less of Bowie's meandering philosophizing and more editing in the melody department. *David Bowie* was released to respectful reviews and dismal sales.

In the late autumn of 1969, bowing to Angela's wishes, willing to indulge her stylish fantasies if simultaneously they would serve to remove him from his recently widowed mother, Bowie agreed to move to a mansion flat at 42 Southend Road, Beckenham. Haddon Hall, as the Edwardian villa was known, lay a quarter-mile north of Foxgrove Road in a similar zone of sturdily built yet decaying houses with gravel courtyards and tall Gothic towers choked with weeds. Bowie and his lover furnished the ground-floor flat with Carnaby Street bric-à-brac and Art Deco lamps, hand-tooled chairs and oriental rugs trawled from Kensington Antique Market. Bowie located a Regency bed in a local junk shop. With its minstrels' gallery, full-length mirrors and heavy black drapes drawn at midday, the flat quickly assumed the look of a rock star lair, remembered by one visitor as 'like Dracula's living room'. The rent was £8 per week.

Haddon Hall also evolved into a commune. By early 1970 the minstrels' gallery housed a motley kibbutz of musicians like John Cambridge, and Arts Lab alumni such as Nita Bowes. Tony Visconti and his girlfriend occupied a separate wing. 'Thursday was gay night,' he later recalled. 'David would go to a gay club, Angie to a lesbian club, and they would both bring people home they found. We had to lock our bedroom doors because in the middle of the night these people would come looking for fresh blood.' Nita Bowes shared Bowie and Angela's bed on and off for a year. Dana Gillespie experienced the same fate. According to a neighbour, John Dalos, 'Angie pulled girls like a magnet pulls iron filings. She used to invite chicks back for a cup of tea and end up posing them stark naked for David and her to ogle. It was like *Satyricon*.'

Bowie's pattern of shuttling back and forth between his Beckenham demi-monde and the more seemly world of Pitt was to go on for six months, with the time spent at the flat lengthening during periods of career crisis – and also varying with Bowie's tolerance for being cooped up with Angela. Her unlimited presence was at times a major source of unease. Devoted to him she undoubtedly was, but it was devotion tinged with control. 'She was a storm trooper who yakked at David twenty-four hours a day,' Pitt recalled. Not surprisingly, his dudgeon rose as his own influence over Bowie dwindled. Pitt adds that 'looking back, I can see that my days were numbered once he moved to Haddon Hall. Suddenly there was a whole court swarming around David, all united against me as the man-in-the-grey-suit. *That's* hindsight. At the time it was just annoying.'

Bowie began the new decade by granting an audience to *Jeremy*, a magazine which, though couched in the furtive terms of its day, was aimed squarely at homosexuals. After watching Bowie rehearse 'Space Oddity' at the London Palladium, the interviewer visited Haddon Hall. He arrived in the rain to find the door open 'and no sign of David – he's popped down to the shops for paraffin, and meat for the night's stew'. Later, outside during the photo session, squirrels leapt through the branches and a fox hurried across the lawn. Bowie continued his familiar rant at his Arts Lab cohorts ('Every bloody hippie wants money to do their own non-capitalistic thing'); he confirmed he was a loner; the 'few friends' he had belonged to the period before the success of 'Space Oddity'. Later the interviewer watched Bowie perform at the Speakeasy. He noted the 'sprinkling of boys in bone-tight velvet pants' and 'hordes of girls with deader than deadpan faces'. When one of them groped Bowie in the dark he made the quick-witted retort: 'Who was it? I ought to get a fee for that.' The impression was of a good-natured, fey Renaissance figure with not only a fondness for George Formby and Gracie Fields, but discernible serious tastes like Kurt Weill and Jacques Brel – one who, above all, resisted the lure of the pigeonhole. 'I don't want to be a leader,' Bowie insisted. 'After all, who wants to be a cause?'

On 8 January 1970, his twenty-third birthday, just as *Jeremy* hit the newsstands, Bowie recorded a love song to Angela called 'The Prettiest Star'.

The guitarist on the session was Marc Bolan. His brooding presence in the studio reflected not only momentary jealousy of 'Space Oddity' but his stored-up rivalry with Bowie, a nature unravelling. After Bolan had stalked out into Wardour Street, a conference took place in the now darkened control room. According to a colleague, 'David began talking about wanting a full-time band for gigs and recording – people he could relate to personally.' John Cambridge was recruited on drums. Visconti resumed on bass. Over the next two weeks Bowie scoured the agencies and the back pages of *Melody Maker* for a guitarist. When these proved fruitless, Cambridge suggested a friend living in Hull, where, after a failed first visit to London, he was currently working as a municipal gardener. His name was Mick Ronson.

Ronson was one of 129 people present when Bowie and his group performed at the Marquee on 3 February. He remembered being 'not exactly floored' at the spectacle, particularly as Ronson viewed the music business generally, and London particularly, as a modern version of Sodom and Gomorrah. Bowie, on the other hand, was enchanted. Not only was Ronson's blond, ant-eater countenance visually striking, he could give a note-by-note facsimile of Jeff Beck. Moreover, Ronson and Cambridge, with their dry, opaque senses of humour, restored the Yorkshire connection in Bowie's life.

Two days later, just five weeks into the decade that made them icons, Bowie and Ronson worked together for the first time, on John Peel's *Sunday Show*. They made an immediate impact on Peel. 'What you had was the classic combination of the guitarist raunching up the singer's pop songs ... You never knew what to expect.' According to Cambridge, 'David and Mick were genetically made for each other.' Bowie had changed his means before, but in accepting an equal partner he was forced for the first time to turn his back on his cherished independence. Ronson's musicianship and quiet, wry wit – his habit of deflating pomposity – would be qualities in constant demand over the next four years. Bowie, meanwhile, in his own ironic protest against the pretentiousness and snobbery of the business, dubbed his new group the Hype. Their début appearance was at London's Roundhouse on 22 February. In a foreshadowing of the glam rock era he patented, Bowie became Rainbowman, in spandex tights, a cape and thigh-high Chelsea boots. Ronson's worst misgivings about the world he was joining must have been confirmed as he surveyed his colleagues' ruffled shirts, lurex and dripping eyeliner. The evening was a substantial disaster. The fans became apoplectic and jeered Bowie from the stage. 'We died a death,' he remembered. 'That's the period that broke me up. I just about stopped after that performance.' The same abject note was struck by the three group members. While Ronson and Cambridge walked to the pub to ponder their career prospects, Visconti, whose clothes had been stolen from the dressing room, had to go home on the bus in his luminous white Hypeman suit.

Despite this unpromising start, Ronson consented to stay both in the Hype and as Bowie's guest at Haddon Hall. (Bolan believed that the 'fucking-for-Britain' that went on there was a major factor in the decision.) Ronson moved into Beckenham on 1 March, and the next day Bowie summoned him to his bedroom. In a rambling, offhand conversation, he talked as though it had long been understood that Ronson would collaborate with him from now on. Bowie had few specific plans. The group re-recorded 'Memory of a Free Festival' for release in the US and began first-drafting a new album. These were isolated projects. Visitors to Haddon Hall in spring of 1970 invariably found Bowie depressed by his lack of recognition, pacing the floor and discoursing gloomily about Pitt. In the hope of improving his mood, a Mercury executive was able to take a small sheaf of favourable reviews of the second album out to Beckenham. But Bowie's reaction was not all that the executive had anticipated. The more he read the notices, the more agitated he became, until finally, he angrily got up and started sobbing about the demands being made on him. The executive returned to London puzzled and distressed by Bowie's abrupt mood swings, which he shrewdly guessed were caused 'from outside'.

On the evening of 19 March, Bowie gave his normal perform-ance at the Three Tuns. The next morning he woke up with Angela and Nita Bowes. After a leisurely breakfast the party set off with John Cambridge and two friends, Roger Fry and Clare Shenstone, to Bromley Register Office. There, among the stacked chairs, the dust that sifted down from the rafters and the green electric signs spelling GENTS and LADIES, Bowie and Angela were married. Uninvited but also present was Peggy Jones. Bowie had asked Cambridge to be a witness, but just as he was about to walk to the table to sign the register, Peggy bustled forward, picked up the pen and did so herself. Bowie turned to Cambridge and made a face. Outside the couple posed for photos for the *Beckenham and Penge Advertiser* and the *Beckenham Journal*, both alerted by Bowie's mother. Then they joined their guests in the pub, where Bowie struck Cambridge as 'just as casual as if he'd decided to wander in for a game of darts'.

Much the same nonchalance distinguished the marriage. Here some disparity exists between Angela's account ('I was truly in love and I knew that he was in love with me') and Bowie's ('The reason we got married was for her to get a work permit to stay in England'). A friend believes the arrangement worked to their mutual advantage. 'Everyone knew David was marrying Angie partly to get a Green Card. He wanted to be able to work in America.' He also benefited to the tune of £3,000, donated by Angela's parents. Finally there was a guest's view, widely circu-lated in Haddon Hall, that Bowie was marrying 'an arm-twister – she did literally everything he didn't want to do himself'.

That Bowie was relaxed, even, in the vast province of the words, 'in love' with Angela is certain. There were his own frequent claims to friends like Cambridge, and outpourings like 'The Prettiest Star'. Bowie once told Ronson she was 'the moon and the stars', rich for one so sparing of praise. To a Beckenham friend, it was 'typically narcissistic' of each to marry someone who looked just like they did. 'In those days, they went everywhere and did everything together. They were virtually the same sex. You couldn't tell them apart.' But the hectic round of events only papered over the underlying tensions. Within a year Bowie was complaining of having been 'shanghaied' by the woman dubbed the Cypriot Terrorist. He took to grumbling about Angela's extravagance and 'scheming' to Dana Gillespie and other friends. Both parties had welcomed the idea of children, so when Angela went to Bowie to tell him she was pregnant, she eagerly awaited his response. His only reaction was to wince and ask whether his wife was sure. To raise a child in Haddon Hall, he warned, might be 'awkward'.

The last gasp of Ken Pitt's world came early in April. Bowie collected an Ivor Novello award for 'Space Oddity'. Even as plans were being made for him to perform at the televised ceremony at the Talk of the Town, his manager became uneasily aware that 'my face no longer fitted' – that whereas Bowie anticipated the seventies, Pitt himself celebrated the fifties. Already the antique wardrobe at Haddon Hall bulged with crushed velvet flares, cheesecloth shirts, tie-dyes, tank tops, Isadora scarves, clogs and shoes with high rubber heels and straps. With Angela, Bowie's experiments at cross-dressing extended into feather boas, ball gowns and, it was whispered, lingerie. It would be a mistake to imply that the decade had already swung into life in its fourth month, but Bowie's preoccupation with novelty and style was already enough to put blue water between himself and the man who considered Mel Tormé 'a great singer'.

Bowie responded to his professional crisis by regrouping in Haddon Hall. He had no real reputation except that which his friends gave him by their support and flattery, but because they deferred to him so freely, he began to grow in confidence. Once a week, he called in Visconti, Ronson and the rest for a planning session; and like Gillespie they loved his private lack of pretension, his habit of calling everyone 'ducks' in his Liberace baritone, telling little stories, making irreverent jokes about Pitt, and his uncanny impressions of famous singers. Haddon Hall became the command post for Bowie's next offensive. The lights on Southend Road now blazed until the early hours of the morning, Angela's relentless phoning and letter-writing keeping them burning on nights when the couple was not entertaining. Slowly, over the course of a month, a new Bowie began to emerge. When the photographer Ray Stevenson visited Beckenham he felt 'real energy emanating from David for the first time'. The producer Jeff Griffin remembers taping a session with Bowie early one morning. 'He'd been up all night and looked like hell. David turned on the ritual charm and had everyone eating out of his palm. Then he played a killer set.' Griffin came away impressed by Bowie's ability to hover between the two roles: fey, effeminate troubadour, and the 'ice man' who expressed by a gesture, a nod or a look whether his musicians had interpreted his wishes.

However cold his natural reserve may have seemed, it was a veil for one strain in Bowie's total personality. While he basically trusted no one, he had, at the same time, a core belief in the decency of most people, and held to the sanguine view that they were potentially as affable, as aware and as decent as he was. Bowie had never learnt as a boy, as had almost all suburbanites in the 1950s, to deal in limited expectations. Treated in his own family like a god, he had met in the outside world a steady series of generous backers. With only a few notable exceptions, he never stopped believing that, with minimal hard work and luck, he could make it.

A woman named Mary Parr spent the first half of 1970 in Wardour House, a run-down block of flats a few doors from Trident Studios. She met Bowie on his way out of the building one evening. 'He had a delicate, spooky quality,' she says, one matched by a seam of Yorkshire grit. Over a glass of gin in the nearby pub, Bowie began outlining his plans for the next year, then apologized for 'sounding like bloody Ted Heath'. He accepted Parr's invitation to join her in Wardour House. After a night she describes as 'groupie heaven' she awoke to Bowie serenading her with his Martin guitar. Tom Keylock, the Rolling Stones' tour manager, met Bowie at the same time. 'He had a nice, laid-back way,' he says, 'but it was always in the context of his making it. He gave off about a million volts of self-confidence. It was something he always had, just like Jagger.'

Bowie was able to benefit from his colleagues' loyalty to him because of his success in concealing the extent of his own ambitions. John Cambridge says that Beckenham was like 'a co-op – everyone did literally everything'. Keith Christmas, too, remembers an air of, if not equality, invigorating give-and-take both in Haddon Hall and the studio. Yet beneath the benign façade, Bowie still played a waiting game, always leaving it to others to act first, and then exploiting their mistakes. Making whatever allowance one will, there was something odd about his constant protestations in 1970 to be 'one of the gang'. The implied note of humility rings false. Cambridge himself became a victim of Bowie's ego when, after a difficult session at Trident, the singer raged that 'You're fucking up my album'. Cambridge left the next day. His replacement, also from Yorkshire, was Mick Woodmansey, a steady timekeeper and unobtrusive personality who would never challenge Bowie's self-image.

Ambition, in Bowie's eyes, was a sovereign virtue, to be curbed only for the sake of expediency. Though he contained few of the conceits of the average rock star, the seeds of his egoism had been sown as a young boy, and these had blossomed by 1970 into an impressive ruthlessness. Now Pitt found what Conn and Horton had learnt before him. On 31 March Bowie appeared in Manchester Street and announced, after a long preamble, 'I want to have a go at managing myself.' He then asked for £200 and left the flat. After four weeks' uneasy silence Pitt received a letter in stilted, quasi-legal jargon informing him he was fired. The actual showdown came on 7 May, when Bowie arrived and introduced Pitt to his successor. Five years of litigation followed, at the end of which Pitt accepted an offer of £15,000 and costs. According to the settlement, Bowie's solicitor said, 'This is not one of those cases where management and artist had fallen out. Both sides hoped for an agreement of this kind.' Bowie would add later, 'Ken is a very nice man. I like him very much, but that's not enough in this business.'

Pitt's replacement was a twenty-six-year-old litigation clerk and would-be show-business agent named Tony Defries. The introduction was made through Olav Wyper, the general manager at Philips, who said Bowie approached him in March 1970 claiming to be the victim of a conspiracy – 'he wanted to make records and Ken wouldn't let him'. Bowie, says Pitt, knew perfectly well that this accusation was false, the scenario for which had been prepared by Angela and was constantly encouraged by the 'Beckenham mafia'. Yet on another level Bowie found no difficulty in believing that it was essentially true. His whole career had been an exercise in thwarted dreams. When Defries told him in his calm, measured tones, 'I'll make you a star,' Bowie broke down and wept.

It is a remarkable fact that, throughout the next five years, as he presided over an endless flow of firings, litigation and bitter disputes involving not just his business contacts but Bowie himself, Defries betrayed no sign of his morale or nerve being affected. Pity was unknown to him. He is remembered today as the seventies prototype of the aggressive rock manager – though, like Bowie, he was deceptively soft-spoken and rarely lost his temper – with an unquenchable belief in himself and his client, matched by a shrewd inherent grasp of the market. Defries' hero was Colonel Parker, the ex-carnival barker and Elvis Presley's manager, whose business maxim, 'I want everything bigger 'n everybody!', he enthusiastically echoed. According to John Hutchinson, who knew Defries in 1972–3, 'There were two possible reactions to Tony. Either you feared him and liked him, or feared him and didn't like him.' Those who met Defries in and around his office in Regent Street, and later in boardrooms in New York and Los Angeles, had no trouble recalling him. As well as his bushy dark hair, protuberant nose and impeccable seventies uniform of hip-hugging crushed velvets, unbuttoned shirt and bare chest, Defries was unblushingly frank in his own promotion. In June 1972 he bought up 99 per cent of an agency called MainMan to represent his clients' interests. 'David loved that at first,' says Pitt. 'Until he realized who the company name referred to. It was Tony.'

Part of Defries' new strategy was to earn enough money in the next two years to free Bowie and himself from financial worry, allowing more time for other projects. The plan was straightforward: a new Mercury album, then a renegotiated recording deal, a clutch of hit singles and a major tour of America. If all went well, Defries planned to make Bowie into a film star. Having 'made a fortune', they would then take a year off and re-emerge in 1975. Not everyone, however, was prepared to believe in Bowie's conversion to a global icon. To Ronson, the sessions at Trident were 'long-drawn-out, boring and a pain in the arse'. Pitt felt that 'David was giving his talent to become a star before he became a name.' The follow-up to 'Space Oddity', 'The Prettiest Star', sold just 798 copies in a month. 'Memory of a Free Festival' fared little better. Bowie's major coup in the summer of 1970, the Ivor Novello award, celebrated his past rather than his future. Defries' good intentions were embedded in hyperbolic promotion that lent them a certain verve, but at the cost of establishing his client on a steady footing.

Unsurprisingly, Bowie compensated for the frustrations of his career in frequent, intense gratification. As early as 1964–5 the King Bees and the Manish Boys had added amphetamines and period-pain pills to their relentless diet of cappuccino and cheap red wine. In 1968 Bowie confessed to having a 'silly flirtation' with heroin. Mary Finnigan remembered him as a fanatical user of marijuana: 'He used to do incredible amounts of hash and he used to drink a lot,' she told the Gillmans. By 1970 Bowie had graduated to LSD and a form of liquid cannabis he charmed from a dentist concerned at his chronic toothache. A man who should know claims the control room at Trident 'looked like the Scotland Yard narcotics lab'. Bowie later described the resulting album as 'the most drug-orientated record I've made ... That was when I was holding on to some kind of flag for hashish.' That he had acquired the surface trappings of a rock star without yet being one was clear from an aside Bowie made at Trident – 'without grass, you're an outsider looking in'. His burgeoning habit was all the more striking in a man who pestered Defries for pocket money, and whose policy on rent-paying would lead to a clash with Mr Hoy, the Haddon Hall landlord, four years after he moved out.

Many who played on the Trident sessions were also Bowie's lodgers in Beckenham, where he developed another obsession to go with the drugs. As Ronson recalled, 'David became convinced he was being stalked by men from Mars.' His lifelong fixation with

UFOs was not the ordinary weekend diversion of the science buff; rather, as Angela suggested, it was part of the couple's unshakable view that Bowie was one of the Light People – extraterrestrials from some other planet or dimension in whose ranks they counted Leonardo, Galileo, Newton, Gandhi, Churchill and, closer to home, Dylan, Lennon and Hendrix. As a twelve-year-old in Plaistow Grove Bowie had fantasized that aliens were visiting him at night to 'study my habits'. A thriving 1950s science-fiction culture egged him on: Bowie's favourite TV programme as a teenager had been *The Quatermass Experiment*; the main highlight of his week was the war and space travel hybrid of *Dan Dare*. By 1969 Bowie was contributing to a UFO magazine in London. 'I made sightings six, seven times a night for about a year,' he told *Creem*. 'We had regular cruises that came over. We knew the 6.15 was coming in and would meet up with another one. They would be stationary for about half an hour, and then after verifying what they'd been doing that day, they'd shoot off.' Bowie's star-gazing may have amounted to little more than buying a telescope and occasionally standing on the roof of Haddon Hall aiming a wire coat-hanger at the skies. (He came down one evening and complained to Ronson he felt like 'a pillock' when a golfer on the next-door course had shouted up at him, 'Do you get BBC2?') None of this diluted Bowie's interest in space travel, or his rising conviction that aliens were playing a sinister role in controlling his thoughts. On 20 July 1969, the day Neil Armstrong walked on the moon, Bowie claimed, quite seriously, to have seen a rocket land on the corner of Southend Road. On another occasion he ended a session at the Three Tuns by suddenly shouting that 'greenies' were leaping up at him. But it was when he was sober and talking about his own sanity that Bowie most grabbed. For years, whenever he walked home from Beckenham Junction, he complained of a 'buzzing in the head' caused by the Crystal Palace transmitter, whose pulsing red lights were 'fucking up my mind'.

Ironically for a man who cultivated a niche as a Martian rock star, Bowie would rarely even get on an aeroplane. In November 1969 he and Pitt were flying home from Zurich when Bowie grabbed his manager's arm and shouted, 'One of the engines is on fire.' ('It wasn't,' says Pitt.) Others date his much-publicized vertigo to two stormy flights he took in 1971, after the second of which Bowie claimed his father had come to him in a dream and told him never to fly again. Not only was Defries forced to resort to Jules Verne-like tactics to convey his client around the world by boat and train, he actively made a virtue of Bowie's phobia. 'David *was* frightened,' writes Angela, 'so that was worked into the promotional garbage.' The pictures of Bowie being chauf-feured through the American desert or posing jauntily on the boat-deck of the *QE2* would attain an almost iconographic quality in the mid-seventies. 'It was deliberately sold as a myth,' said Ronson. 'Elvis hadn't flown, so Tony decided that neither would David.' Even Bowie's fear of heights – his hotel suites were never above the eighth floor – was regularly worked into press releases.

It was Defries who played the principal part in erasing Visconti, although he made a point of consulting him as ostentatiously as possible in the studio. A colleague would remember 'sparks whenever those two talked money. They got on like a match and petrol.' According to Visconti, Defries had wanted him to sign a personal contract at the same time as Bowie. When the producer baulked, warning his old friend that 'it was either me or Tony', Bowie broke down in tears and accused Visconti of treachery. The two would not speak again for four years. Meanwhile, the moment recording ended at Trident, Ronson and Woodmansey took the return train to Hull. Bowie, without a producer and now effectively without a group, returned to playing for a few pounds a night in the clubs around Beckenham and south London. It was another low point in a career not untouched by shadow. Without Angela and Defries coming together in self-protective alliance, Bowie might yet again have pondered retirement. Instead, these two made clear they intended to carry on the war on his behalf. It suited them to do so. Both Bowie's manager and his wife viewed the winter of 1970–1 as a chance to put their vast ambition, tireless planning and undoubted enthusiasm to good use in promoting a career that would raise not only money but their own profiles. For Defries, the issue was a simple one: through his Gem Productions, he took a basic 20 per cent of Bowie's earnings, while two separate publishing deals ensured a healthy royalty flow even if actual record sales were puny. Angela, meanwhile, was given to understand that 'I was to concentrate on David's career for two years, after which he'd help mine.'

On 23 October Defries renegotiated Bowie's publishing contract, transferring it from Essex Music to Chrysalis for a £5,000 advance. It was an impressive coup. But Defries added a clause, if not secret then capitalizing on his client's lack of interest in business, setting up a second company, Titanic Music, to administer a uniquely generous royalty rate of 75 per cent. In theory – and, as it turned out, in practice – this could generate a sizeable fortune for both manager and artist. Bowie made no difficulty about signing the paper making him a potential millionaire. After shaking hands with Defries and the three Chrysalis directors, he walked back to Trident, where he blurted out to the first person he met (as it happened, the cleaner) that he was 'a star'. That night in Beckenham, realizing he was at least paper-rich, he broke down and cried.

His own father had realised that Bowie had a habit of moving by 'inner truth', had the ability to wait patiently until he felt his path was clear and then in a flash to sense it and seize his chance. With his meeting Defries and signing the Chrysalis deal, a doom seemed to have lifted. Freed of any obligation other than to write songs, Bowie did his best work since 'Space Oddity'. In the course of two months that winter and early spring he produced 'Moonage Daydream', 'Andy Warhol', 'Changes', 'Lady Stardust', 'Hang On to Yourself', 'Song for Bob Dylan', 'Queen Bitch' and (the night of his son's birth) 'Kooks'. Through Chrysalis and Mickie Most he sold 'Oh! You Pretty Things' to Peter Noone, who had a Top 20 hit with it. That was the first most of the world had heard of Bowie in eighteen months. Next, at remarkable speed, he wrote the raw material for his fourth album, *Hunky Dory* (this before the third, *The Man Who Sold the World*, had been released). Bowie also roused Ronson and Woodmansey from Hull, along with a new bass player, a local man named Trevor Bolder whose pale, craggy face was framed by a set of bristling black whiskers. When the three sidemen arrived at Haddon Hall they were told by Defries that 'David had all these great songs and, provided we toed the line, we were going to be huge.'

The opportunity to kick-start Bowie's career came when

Mercury agreed to pay for a coast-to-coast radio tour of the US. He landed in Washington late in January. Whatever impression his label had formed of Bowie from Pitt, nothing could have prepared them for the arrival of the milk-pale singer dressed in a purple maxi-coat and white chiffon scarf. As Bowie tripped into the customs hall he was greeted by a snarling dog and the snapping of rubber gloves. An hour later, Mercury's Ron Oberman was able to finally welcome him to America – 'a bit shaken up', he recalled, and muttering that one official had addressed him with the word 'fag'.

It had been Bowie's and Pitt's secret dream to have him cross the Atlantic in a fancy-dress costume, like a modern-day Oscar Wilde. With the Chrysalis contract, motive met with opportunity. Armed with the first instalment of the £5,000 advance, Angela had bought a wardrobe of six Mr Fish dresses: either (as Bowie insisted) as a parody of the artist Dante Gabriel Rossetti, or, in Angela's words, 'contemporary inspirations on the theme of garments worn by medieval kings'; but undeniably *dresses*. Two of these garments accompanied Bowie to America. Despite the mixed official reception, the critics made both him and his wardrobe a huge hit – and talking point. That is, the music critics. Many Americans who met Bowie on the street came away distinctly less enthusiastic. One woman in Los Angeles broke into shrill laughter at his appearance. Even that paled by comparison to the man who pulled out a gun and suggested Bowie 'kiss my ass'.

Mercury had wanted Bowie to talk up *The Man Who Sold the World* on radio stations and the influential Hollywood cocktail circuit. He did their bidding, on the surface. But his real interest lay in absorbing as much of America, swallowing as many pills and sleeping with as many women as he could lay hands on. Oberman's colleague would remember 'the lobby pulsing with girls' in Bowie's hotel. Insofar as he saw the country, renewed his drug habit and bedded, in his own words, 'everything that moved', the tour achieved its chief objectives. Bowie was rewarded with his first coverage in *Rolling Stone* (where John Mendelsohn wrote of him as 'ravishing, almost disconcertingly reminiscent of Lauren Bacall'); he also listened, for hours on end, to tales about Lou Reed and Iggy Pop, two seminal punk figures launching solo careers after abandoning their respective groups. Bowie would tell Oberman that a combination of Reed's song-writing and Iggy's cartoon stage persona – he routinely waded out into the crowd – would make 'the ultimate pop idol'. A girlfriend called Linda Kreal recalls 'David scrawling notes on a cocktail napkin about a crazy rock star named Iggy or Ziggy'. Within hours of returning to Beckenham, Bowie was raving – to the point of obsession when he was in the mood – about creating a fantasy character 'who looks like he's landed from Mars'.

The Man Who Sold the World, rush-released to tie in with Bowie's tour of America, appeared in Britain that spring. The album earned him the beginnings of a major following. It also virtually invented the term 'glam rock'.

Having become a small cult with 'Space Oddity' and his second album, Bowie now hosted a raucous heavy metal party at which his early fans clearly weren't welcome. No one could have confused the heavy-riffing guitar and pneumatic beat of *The Man* with the fey, folky affectations of *David Bowie*. Between them Visconti and Ronson produced a sound as abrasive as Bowie's angst-ridden lyrics. 'The world is doomed. We're not capable of making it any better,' he remarked at the time. The core message of the album is that redemption is possible only through a psychic journey – like that described in 'The Width of a Circle' – such as Bowie had embarked on with Buddhism. The vision he presents is one of unmitigated horror. 'Width of a Circle' aside, *The Man*, with its references to bombs, guns, blood, nightmares, 'gooks', 'cracked heads', lobotomies and supermen, marked a return to the basics, the jungle. The Bee Gees and Paul Simon impressions were replaced by an unbroken diet of terror and decay, compared to which, said one critic, 'Leonard Cohen sounds ballsy.'

'We had a commitment to make an album,' Visconti would say; yet Bowie hardly cared. Ronson's memory of 'David on a stool in Haddon Hall, going through all the arrangements' scarcely supports this view: but it is certain that Bowie pasted together the lyrics in one breathless race against the studio clock. Musically, *The Man* tapped into most of the varied themes incorporated through the years. There were touches of Dylan and Lou Reed and (on 'Black Country Rock') an almost actionable parody of Marc Bolan. Yet Bowie emerged as his own man. Almost uniquely among his contemporaries, he stopped short of affecting an American accent. The lyrics were delivered in his dry, ironic voice, as compelling as it was natural, and the album would be understood as wholly Bowie's even without his name on the cover. There were technical flourishes from the group – notably Ronson, whose guitar on 'She Shook Me Cold' climaxed by evolving into Jeff Beck – but overall the record burst with its creator's dark mood.

The album most famously came with a sleeve showing Bowie lying on a couch, listlessly scratching his head and dropping playing cards on the floor. He was wearing a dress. When he first saw the photograph, even the urbane Oberman paled. A Beckenham artist named Mike Weller hurriedly produced a new design, a drawing of Cane Hill Hospital (where Terry Burns was confined), for the American market. The original cover became the most talked-about image in the history of British pop that year.

Bowie impressed Ronson not only with his talent, but also with his dedication and perfectionism. He was no evanescent teen god, primping on *Top of the Pops* on the chance of exciting the romantic hopes of his female fans and the envy of the males. He was already, at twenty-four, a raw, half-formed but maturely dedicated artist with fixed plans. Bowie wanted to be known the way Marc Bolan was – or at least as several up-and-comers were: Rod Stewart, a pallid imitation of Sam Cooke until he released *Every Picture Tells a Story* in 1971; four pub rockers from the Wolverhampton suburbs who emerged as Slade; Elton John, who made The Top 5 US album chart; and Paul Gadd, reinvented as the Liberace of British pop, Gary Glitter.

Bowie had long been notorious for hidden ambition. Ronson himself found his friend 'a bit mental' after his American trip and, along with Woodmansey and Bolder, beat a hasty retreat from Haddon Hall. For the remainder of their time together, the group would live in a flat in nearby Penge. Terry Helm felt that 'you could see him *becoming* David Bowie, the way he acted under the surface charm'. A local man named Tom Dollery arrived one morning to offer Bowie a lift in his car to London. 'After fifteen minutes, David came out of the door, got in the back seat and began reading a paper. I drove him like that all the way to Wardour Street.' A man called Brian Leeson had a similar experience when he picked up Bowie as a favour to Ken Pitt. 'I thought I was driving royalty,' he recalled.

There were times when some of Bowie's faults worked to his advantage: his unpredictability, his coolness, his fickle policy on friendship. There were times when he struck even Defries with his vanity. But Bowie knew that ambition and talent were not the only means by which his career progressed. He was also a consummate professional. Jeff Griffin remembers that 'even in 1970–1, *nothing* was left to chance in the studio. If David felt something wasn't right, he thought nothing of spending a day fixing it.' No reviewer failed to notice how polished were Bowie's new songs. Night after night, in Haddon Hall or in a rehearsal room over the Thomas À Becket pub, the four musicians buffed 'Moonage Daydream' and 'Hang On to Yourself' and 'Andy Warhol' to a gloss. Bowie always regarded the first half of 1971 as a significant turning point in his career. In later years he gave full credit to Haddon Hall and the sweaty boxers' pub as the unlikely mangers in which Ziggy Stardust was born. Bowie also took outside lessons in judo and gymnastics while honing his mime skills with Kemp. Then there was voice projection: singing unamplified into the pit of an empty theatre while dancing a rapid sequence of crisply executed gavottes without panting.

The important moves were those Bowie was learning about play-acting. As early as 1966, Helm had seen how 'David yearned ... to bring a dramatic aspect to pop.' Now the times had come into alignment with Bowie's theatrical vision. A golden age of glam or pantomime rock was dawning – a half-decade in which the art form's greatest practitioners did their most glittering work. The lead given by Iggy and Lou Reed made Englishmen with names like Dwight and Jones feel they were at last able to make inroads into the public perception of male sexuality. Bowie, for one, responded like a dog fresh from the leash. Already seven years in the business, veteran of three albums, his enthusiasm struck even colleagues like Ronson. 'In '71, David felt he was just starting out,' he said. 'That's when the songs, the band and the big plans all came together.' All that Bowie lacked was a unique stage personality.

Within twelve months he was the world's most memorable vision of sexual ambiguity. Bowie's androgynous odyssey began, promisingly enough, with his six men's dresses. Shortly afterwards, Angela introduced him to a club in Kensington High Street named the Sombrero. This prototype disco, with a mainly male, ambisexual clientele, had an immediate impact on Bowie. He spent hours on the neon-lit dance floor, or sitting craning to appraise the most *outré* extremes of hair and make-up. Bowie was particularly drawn to one Sombrero *habitué*, Freddi Burretti. His devotion even extended to encouraging Burretti, posing as Arnold Corns, to record 'Moonage Daydream' as a single. In turn, Bowie began to shamelessly emulate his protégé's taste in eyeliner and mascara. The cross-dressing star of 1971 was already unrecognizable from the diffident poseur of 1970. Now, thanks to Burretti and Andy Warhol, Bowie was moving into fully fledged queendom. The latter's influence came about through the London opening of *Pork*, a play whose excesses made Joe Orton seem to possess plenipotential dignity. Its characters revelled in an unbroken diet of masturbation, menstruation, defecation, urination and every variant of sex, gay and straight. Bowie was enchanted. According to a cast member, the show's 'New Yorkness' and overall celebration of Warhol (whose life it loosely portrayed) 'shook David cold'. Both the Bowies told the same actor they were sexually turned on by the performance; its plot and, significantly, its 'look'. An extra sheen of glitter was now added to the androgynous experiments unveiled in Mr Fish and the Sombrero. Finally, Angela hired a Beckenham hairdresser named Suzi Fussey to give her husband the violent cockade that became his trademark. The effect was electric. Thus adorned, Bowie's look would reach beyond image, beyond theatre and into a visual expression of youthful defiance. Previously, his music had symbolized emotional liberation, and a kind of simplistic political realism to thousands. Now, sparkling with fancy dress and flashily staged, it became an anthem for millions.

Here came Ziggy Stardust. In a silver lurex catsuit, skin-tight and bulging below, and artfully padded above. It was a culminating expression of the futuristic garb of 'Space Oddity', with touches from the Sombrero and *Pork*. The shimmering garment ended at the cheeks in outsize earrings that looked like diamonds (the very rhinestones Bowie had bought Angela). His distinctive hair, cropped short at the crown but caressing his shoulders, was vivid red. Loosely draped around his neck was an oriental-print cape trimmed in yellow silk, which he used as a fan and which swept the floor behind him as he flounced on stage, shook his hips, and counted out time with his knee-length red plastic boots. The *ad hoc* style brought gasps as loud as the percussive assault of the music.

Bowie himself claimed that the ultimate British pop icon was based, ironically, on two American cults, Iggy and Lou Reed. Insofar as the character was a caricature there was a strong whiff of Warhol. On one level, clearly, Ziggy was the product of what Bowie would see in America in 1971. Even 'Stardust' was a tribute to the celebrity-struck world of Los Angeles. Into the mix, too, went a medley of H.P. Lovecraft and Robert Heinlein's *Stranger in a Strange Land*. Later, from the safe vantage of the 1980s, Bowie would argue that Ziggy was based on the 'French Elvis', Vince Taylor, whose career ended when he announced to his fans he was Jesus Christ. This same messianic quality was at work in the morality tale Bowie acted out in 1972–3. Here was a drama in which a great man shouldered the burden of a blundering and weak people, suffered for them and was destroyed at the peak of his powers.*

Rehearsals of Bowie's new songs, involving not just Ronson, Woodmansey and Bolder but a variable cast of Burretti, Dana Gillespie and Bowie's old friend George Underwood, continued at the Thomas À Becket and at Underhill Studios in south London. The first public outing was on John Peel's *In Concert* on 5 June. Bowie, for whom Ziggy lay six months ahead, appeared in his high-waisted jeans and his hair bleached bright yellow. (He 'stood out', says Peel.) Two weeks later the group made a triumphant appearance at Glastonbury. As Bowie sang 'Memory of a Free Festival', Gillespie remembered, 'the sun came over the hill and lit him up and everybody warmed to him'. The first, tentative

---

*Significantly, Bowie had admitted to being 'mesmerized' by a planned 1967 satire of *Orpheus*, in which the lead was a pop singer torn to pieces by his fans.

outbreak of Bowiemania brought a matching response at Haddon Hall. It was later that summer, Ronson recalled, that 'David said "Stop mucking about."' Within weeks, two albums' worth of material would be written and recorded; Defries would extricate Bowie from Mercury and, armed with a first pressing of *Hunky Dory*, sign a lucrative deal with RCA; Bowie himself would discover his alter ego. By the last weeks of 1971 and the first of 1972, Haddon Hall was a place of perpetual ferment. Protest and social comment were abandoned for the less vagarious world of glam rock. 'Let's not just be another band' was Ronson's memory of the words with which, one night, Bowie led his group downstairs. There, in a makeshift dressing room, attended by Angela and Suzi Fussey, the three sidemen were permed, dyed, squeezed and shoehorned into their new personae. Overnight, the donkey-jacketed corporation gardener and the two rockers from Hull were converted into Weird, Gilly and the Spiders from Mars. Now Bowie was ready to set the world on fire.

4

'MR BOWIE DOES SOMETHING NEW'

Duncan Zowie Haywood Jones was born in Bromley on 30 May 1971, cracking his mother's pelvis in the delivery. The baby was named not after his father, insists Angela, but as an Anglicized version of the Greek word 'zoë', or life. Bowie himself added 'Duncan Haywood' in case, as a grown-up, 'Zowie object[ed] to his kooky name'. (He did.) Immediately she recovered her health, Angela left for an Italian pursuit with Dana Gillespie. Such was Bowie's rage at his wife's departure that Ronson believed 'mentally, the divorce began that summer'. Angela herself would call it 'the beginning of the end ... I'd gained a son, but lost a husband.'

Bowie continued his whimsical promotion of friends like Burretti and George Underwood. He wrote a new song celebrating his son's birth. And he resumed work at Trident, replacing Visconti as producer with Ken Scott (the engineer on his Mercury albums), a man who later remarked, 'Everything I have to say about David, I said on vinyl.' Scott's cryptic utterance neatly summarized a relationship that, though never close, was both fruitful and rewarding. The studio also gave Bowie a chance to escape the pressures steadily accumulating from outside. Ronson remembered a scene one morning in Regent Street when Defries raged at his client for not working quickly enough on *Hunky Dory*. Bowie replied he wanted time with his son, and besides, he had 'plenty of bread in the bank'. Defries calmly pressed the button on his office speaker and said, 'Find out how much money Bowie has in the bank.' Five minutes later, the machine spoke back: 'Twenty-seven pounds.'

The journalist Steve Peacock found Bowie, at twenty-four, discoursing moodily about being 'washed-up – a disillusioned old rocker'. He saw the pop business as 'an art form of indifference'. Not for five years would there be another such admission. After his humiliation in Defries' office, Bowie began to lobby his manager for a new recording deal, and, critically, a first full American tour. Defries responded by drawing up two separate documents. The first bound Bowie to Gem Productions for six years. The second agreement was timeless. Defries then freed Bowie of his Mercury contract and flew to New York with an acetate of *Hunky Dory*. One of his first appointments was with Dennis Katz, head of A&R at RCA Records, a subdivision of what was mainly an electronics company, manufacturing TV sets, washing machines and prototype home computers. Katz had never heard of Bowie. He did, however, recognize the potential of the piano-based songs, full of hooks and melodies, that Defries played him. A deal was drawn up offering Bowie a modest $37,500 advance for each of three albums. Neither elated nor distraught, Defries rang Haddon Hall with the news. According to Ronson, the mood was stoical – 'We needed bread, and we've got it.' Bowie himself was struck by the coincidence of being signed to the same label as the very man who recorded 'Hound Dog'. As soon as he put the phone down on Defries, he called Peggy to tell her he was going to be 'bigger than Elvis'.

Defries returned to New York in September, accompanied by Bowie, Angela and Ronson. Operating from a suite at the Warwick Hotel, the four formed an assault party on midtown Manhattan. Bowie, in eyeliner, lipstick and a black fedora, signed his RCA contract; he had dinner with Lou Reed; and, in an interlude that fascinated him because 'nothing happened', he met Andy Warhol.

When Bowie and Defries arrived at The Factory on 9 September they rang a bell labelled 'Do Not Ring', clumped up the concrete steps and stared at the huge stuffed dog in the reception area. The door to the back room was opened by Warhol's assistant Paul Morrissey. Warhol himself appeared wearing high-laced boots, jodhpurs, and swishing a riding crop. He shook hands with an icy, reptilian grip. Then, slowly, he reached for his Polaroid camera and took several pictures of Bowie's feet. There was a pause. Bowie passed on greetings from a mutual friend in London, whom Warhol reproached as a 'sick boy'. There was another pause, then Bowie produced his *pièce de résistance*: the acetate of 'Andy Warhol', received by its subject with a quizzical shrug. There was a final pause, ended by Defries muttering 'It's been a gas.' He repeated it several times, while backing away towards the concrete stairs. 'Goodbye, David,' said Warhol. 'You have such nice shoes.'

There comes a moment in most aliens' lives when it suddenly bears in on them that they have infiltrated the host culture. Bowie's came as he entered his hotel suite that night. Piled on the bed, the wardrobe, the writing desk and every available surface were gifts from RCA: hundreds of albums, including the entire Elvis catalogue, clothes, perfume, jewellery and Bowie's own RCA promotional material. According to Angela, 'David and I looked at each other like little kids' as they surveyed the cornucopia of American hospitality.

'This is it, isn't it?' said Bowie.

Before leaving New York the party also met the punk magnifico Iggy Pop. Bowie had long been fascinated by the tales swirling around the author of *Fun House*, especially his penchant for self-laceration and carnage. The introduction was made one evening by Iggy's manager at Max's Kansas City, a dim, barnlike club close to the Factory, with a private room for visiting English pop stars. The reality matched up to even the substantial legend. Iggy was pale, intense, faultlessly manic, a hollow-eyed vagrant twenty pounds underweight. In his first hour at the club, he ate four full-scale breakfasts. Iggy's ways intrigued Bowie. His humour diverted him: the stories about Detroit and Ann Arbor, growing up in a trailer park, the clinical discussions about heroin and methadone. (Bowie was shocked.) The evening lengthened into morning, when Iggy, now three days without sleep, suggested 'the only good rocker [was] a dead rocker' and rendered himself insensible by smashing a beer bottle over his head. When Bowie returned to the studio the next week he told Ken Scott, 'You're not going to like the album. It's much more like Iggy Pop.' Ronson confirmed that 'David was just *taken* by that crap. I wasn't.'

It was Bowie's brainchild to have the best gags from Iggy come on stage red-nosed and tragic like the seedy vaudevillian of *The Entertainer*. Not only did he plan to see the vision first sketched out on a cocktail napkin to completion. He also needed the money. Of RCA's initial advance of $56,250, Bowie saw just £4,000. The rest was held by Defries, who possessed the knack of being constantly plausible as a banker. In late 1971 Bowie and his wife were living on £400 a month, enough to periodically pay the rent, but modest by the illusory standards of New York. Even when *Hunky Dory* was released just before Christmas, its first-quarter sales barely reached five thousand.

Six months later Defries's partner Laurence Myers, having played the same cheque-writing role as Ray Cook, though under greater stress, pulled out of Bowie's management. Defries then bought an off-the-shelf company called Minnie Bell Music and incorporated it as MainMan, with offices in Gunter Grove, Chelsea. Its principal held ninety-nine of the hundred available shares. In later years, Bowie always claimed to have been 'fucked, royally' by the company, and he proved not to be wrong. MainMan, according to its own rights document, existed as an investment manager for its artists' funds: 'all income arising is MainMan income until such time as they choose to distribute same, and all of the artists are investing in all of the other artists and/or the growth of the Company'. Simply put, MainMan would receive all Bowie's earnings, and deduct its vast expenses – a $500,000 settlement to Myers alone – before paying him the balance.

Numerous satellite projects were launched on the promise of MainMan cash. As a rule, these involved living expenses for FODs (Friends of David) such as Iggy, Dana Gillespie and *Pork*'s Wayne County, invariably charged to Bowie's account. MainMan itself expanded to New York, with a fourteen-room suite of offices on Park Avenue. Defries' empire included a twenty-room estate in Connecticut; eight separate Manhattan apartments; and a court, largely staffed by *Pork* refugees, of vice-presidents, consultants, agents, chauffeurs, cooks, maids and babysitters. In this financial twilight zone, the members of the 'MainMan family' considered Defries, not Bowie, to be the sugar-daddy. The stunning result was that the actual creator of the company wealth essentially lived on pocket money. In 1972–3, the year Bowie exploded into the charts, MainMan posted a loss, after expenses and bad debts, of £28,185. (Iggy alone was written off to the tune of £13,371.) Operating funds shrank proportionately. Bowie went 'fucking nearly out of his head', according to Ronson, at the economies forced on the group. The Spiders' shows followed the pattern of their wages: Defries was threatened with strike action by Bolder and Woodmansey over their *combined* salary of £35 per week. Bills to car hire companies, hotels, caterers and music supply shops went unpaid for months, leading to tense backstage scenes as bailiffs attempted to serve writs on Bowie at the door of his dressing room. At the height of its success, MainMan was losing some £1,000 a week to its myriad hangers-on, and Bowie was forced to borrow money in order to live. According to Ken Pitt, 'When David was quite big, he and Angela came back one night and found their door padlocked. Things were so bad that Zowie had to go up to Aberdeen, to his nanny's parents, to ensure he got fed.' In contrast to Pitt's 30 per cent, which included acting as Bowie's housekeeper and publicist, Defries' cut of his client's earnings rose to a full half.

In *Hunky Dory*, Bowie began his assault on the mainstream with a blatant roll-call of influences. There were tributes to Warhol, Reed and Dylan, echoes of 'Martha, My Dear' and the novelty hit 'Alley Oop', and even a chord structure lifted from 'My Way'. The very first song on the album used the ruse of a stuttering 'My Generation' chorus. As on *The Man Who Sold the World*, the words were complex and introspective, but the writing was sharper, the tunes were tighter, and the hooks grabbed harder. Ronson's guitar, for once, was almost inaudible behind the rippling piano. Numbers like 'Changes' and 'Life on Mars?' seemed to have been over-arranged, with a glossy, Lucite finish at odds with the dense, opaque lyrics. The distance between the songs' subject matter (madness, drugs, the occult, cross-dressing and the obsolescence of the human race) and their lavish production makes the tunes sound oddly disconnected – 'like a turd in a chocolate box', in Ronson's vivid simile.

The album opened with 'Changes', aptly a song of mixed tempos, and a turntable favourite which, to Bowie's dismay, became Tony Blackburn's Record of the Week. It segued into 'Oh! You Pretty Things', another foot-stamping melody, but with a joke that not everyone (Peter Noone, for instance) got. Bowie's reference to 'Homo Superior' was an early glimpse of the hero figure who dominated a portion of his later work. 'Eight Line Poem' struck no less a judge than William Burroughs as reminiscent of *The Waste Land*. (Within a year, even the *Times* would lose its proprietary brand of *sangfroid* and also compare Bowie to T. S. Eliot.) It was followed by 'Life On Mars?' This was the lush, orchestral arrangement – a lift from 'My Way' – for which many remember *Hunky Dory*. The lyric sets up a complex parallel world in which the cinema becomes life. Walking through her 'sunken dream', the heroine is 'hooked to the silver screen', but finds 'the film is a saddening bore – she's lived it ten times or more'. It was a neat, if well-worn trick, blurring the art–life divide. The rest of the song dissolves in surrealist-Nonsense blurting and an outro pilfered from *Also Sprach Zarathustra*. 'Life On Mars?' was released as a single eighteen months after *Hunky Dory*. It came with a startling video in which Bowie appeared in Burretti's turquoise suit, red hair and pink and blue make-up, looking, says Graham Wood, 'like an exotic bird that had flown into a freshly plastered wall'. It reached number three on the chart.

On 'Quicksand', Bowie moved beyond the tenuous first steps of pop writing for a tortuous slab of self-analysis. The song starts off as a biting satire on fascism, then ends up as a grim elegy for the human race. Bowie later called this a mix of 'narrative and surrealism', and a precursor to the songs on *Low*.

The album switched gears on side two: the nods to Warhol and Dylan were followed by an exhilarating Velvet Underground pastiche, 'Queen Bitch'. Bowie had always proudly celebrated the cult of street life, and 'Bitch' is rife with lowbrow pleasures. 'I dug it,' Lou Reed once muttered, high commendation from one so wary of praise. The album's last cut, 'The Bewlay Brothers', is Bowie's most oblique lyric. Twenty-five years on, no two critics agree about what it means. Bowie's uncanny sense of when to show his hand and when to be cryptic demonstrated his potential staying power. The song, in fact, dealt with the schizophrenic Terry Burns.

Hunky Dory contained the paradox of a set of upbeat, catchy tunes with impenetrable words. Bowie took themes like anarchy, bedlam and sexual ambiguity and made hit singles of them. The songs were characterized by the lush ambience established by Bowie's vocal and the piano, and marked a first step on the easy-listening continuum that led from Elton John to Phil Collins. Though not an immediate hit, *Hunky Dory* was subsequently discovered as a classic. In 1976, a *Melody Maker* journalist described how 'the first time I sat up and took notice of David Bowie was when a *Hunky Dory* ad quoted a New York critic as saying he was the most intelligent person to have chosen rock music as his medium of communication'. The New Yorker was ahead – but the rest of the pack was coming up behind, rapidly. Bowie had at a stroke established himself as one of pop's major talents. Even Marc Bolan would marvel at the way *Hunky Dory* 'easily matched' his best work. From then on he never hesitated to call on Bowie for advice.

'Changes' was released in January 1972. The song became a signature tune for Bowie, as he wove one version of himself after another, only to slough it off suddenly and go slithering into a new skin. Although he prided himself on the courage required to venture boldly through strange seas of thought, he was troubled by his growing awareness that he could never return comfortably to the harbour provided by being David Jones.

Like Peter Sellers, Bowie was a cypher; an innovative changeling; a blue screen; and, as he put it himself, a Xerox machine, somehow able to wander between images and come up with a composite no one else would have thought of. At his highest level, he was an original – 'art on legs', as the guitarist Adrian Belew calls him. To others, holding a different version of Bowie's talent, he was a clever plagiarist. 'You simply go and see everything, and you nick the good ideas,' Lindsay Kemp said of the craft he taught his protégé. 'Then you do it better simply by using Scotch tape, sawdust and a little imagination.' According to this view, Bowie was a cold-eyed, rootless operator, a scheming cowboy who sold his own soul to get what he wanted. From Burretti to the cast of *Pork*, through to William Burroughs and Iggy Pop, a roll-call of willing victims offered themselves to his vampire's bite. By the late 1970s, not all of Bowie's prey were so amenable. Angela, who spent much of the decade as a celebrity without portfolio, felt she never received credit for envisaging the Ziggy look or, later, for nudging her husband into films. 'He sucks what he can get and then he moves on,' Bowie's friend Ian Hunter told the Gillmans. Even Mick Jagger would make the wry dig: 'Never wear a new pair of shoes in front of David.'

While there were mumblings about the origins of Ziggy Stardust – a man even threatened a lawsuit for copyright infringement – such grumbles were either too obscurely positioned or appeared too late to halt Bowie's success. They also ignored his own role in bringing the character to life. Bowie would claim, convincingly, that 'I was young and I was full of life, and [Ziggy] seemed like a very positive artistic statement. I thought that was a grand kitsch painting ... a beautiful piece of art.' Twenty years after the event he offered the simple but telling comment, 'I was trying to make the music look like it sounded.' When Bowie took the Scotch tape and sawdust to other people's ideas, he was approaching them from that new angle of offering a space-invader Messiah to a generation weaned on a steady diet of denim-clad rockers, with little to add beyond the empty roar of the football terrace. Thus 'Starman', in some views an 'Over the Rainbow' steal, was in fact an anthem about salvation, black-hole jumping and the coming of an alien being to save the earth. 'It was trash, of course,' says a well-known author, to whom Bowie explained the song. 'But the point is, he really meant it.' 'I was there,' said Ronson, 'and ninety per cent of the whole vibe was David's.' The prime mover of the Ziggy legend, the greatest of the Ziggy publicists – and at least a partner in the Ziggy look – was Bowie himself.

Into the mix went red plastic boots, breathtakingly taut trousers, see-through blouses and glittering, sequined jackets. Angela's jewellery box was plundered for earrings, a necklace or, on one occasion, silk gloves for Bowie's bangly wrists. The whole was topped off by a red cockade that became Ziggy's best-known symbol, and that regularly led the list of great rock haircuts. Bowie himself would later dismiss the look as 'a cross between Nijinsky and Woolworth's', something cobbled together from whatever was lying about. In fact it was as carefully contrived as that other icon of seemingly random array – Chaplin's tramp – and as broad in appeal. Above all, Ziggy was sex without gender: sex with whatever gender one wanted to see, or Bowie wanted to project – something for everyone.

Ziggy began his pursuit of fame by drawing to his side an entourage of Elvis proportions. There was a bodyguard named Stuey George, first in a long line of bulwarks between Bowie and the rest of the world; a young and fanatically loyal publicist, Dai Davies, whose job became a variation on the same protective theme; the hairdresser Suzi Fussey; and a photographer named Mick Rock, whose collaboration with his subjects on creating their public image produced some of the classic album covers of the seventies. (Rock not only took the famous picture of Bowie miming sex with Ronson's guitar, he later directed four videos of Bowie's songs, still seen today, for a fee he recalls as 'cab fare'.) Bowie, at Defries' urging, thus learnt to act like a star before he actually was one. As early as Christmas 1971 Davies went on a safari of Fleet Street, while Rock's photographs achieved wide circulation among picture editors, bookers and ordinary fans. Weeks before 'Starman', Ziggy became a living pop legend in a sense that was certainly not true of other, doomed efforts to adopt alter egos, notably Bolan's half-baked *Zinc Alloy*. 'Mr Bowie,' the Beckenham paper stated, 'is doing something new for his next one or two moves.'

Many were Bowie's protests that he was not 'just a singer', but an actor playing a rock star. That was not to say he had no ambitions as a musician. Bowie wanted his group to be 'in the same sphere as the Who ... visually exciting ... but on a very solidly routined and rehearsed basis'. More pertinently, Bowie began to tease the press into its normal state, halfway between curiosity and shock, when pondering gay sex. 'I'm certainly not embarrassed by wearing a dress, or ashamed of it,' he told *NME*. 'The dresses were made for me. They didn't have big boobs or anything like that. They were men's dresses. I thought they were great.'

By 1972, acceptance of homosexuality had reached a fragile truce in Britain. At a distance it was fine, even expected. The public calmly forgave it in scout masters and ignored it in artists. But here was a married man, father of a young boy, who appeared as a leather-and-denim rocker one moment and a vision of Lauren Bacall the next. David Bowie was on his way to becoming the sexual outlaw of his times.

'OH YOU PRETTY THING' ran the headline – almost as much part of pop mythology as 'Would You Let Your Daughter Go with a Rolling Stone?' – in *Melody Maker*. In what he described (but much later) as his greatest mistake, Bowie told Michael Watts: 'I'm gay, and always have been, even when I was David Jones.' To anyone under twenty-five, the words became virtually a national catchphrase. In what seemed an instant, Bowie had made a breakthrough. When critics first heard the *Ziggy* LP that spring, much was made of the distance between the album's unthreatening campness and the fear and disgust, as *Melody Maker* put it, of Bowie himself. One was sunny, one was dark, but the music and the man had this in common: both were rallying points in the eternal struggle of one generation to be different from another. The 'I'm gay' interview was a defining moment in rock journalism. It also made a shy family man from the London suburbs into a bisexual fashion icon on two continents.

Ziggy Stardust and the Spiders from Mars first touched down in the modest setting of the Toby Jug pub in Tolworth, on the fringe of Surbiton, on 10 February 1972. They were a sensation. For seven months, from Guildford to Glasgow, from Redruth to London's Rainbow, and including such virgin territory as Worthing, Yeovil and Torbay, the group delivered a nightly fusion of guitar rock, pillow-soft pop, moody science fiction and camp drama. The critics suspended judgement. As with all genius moves, only in retrospect did Ziggy seem inevitable – the missing link between American punk and tight, Beatlesque melodies. It was mid April, when Bowie performed on *Top of the Pops*, before the media awoke to the phenomenon. To John Peel, 'Rock, in '72, had begun to take itself seriously. All that beards and backs-to-the-crowd stuff. Everyone was longing for something light, good-looking and, above all, colourful. Bowie's timing was perfect.' Less analytical minds spoke of the concerts as 'wild', 'crazy', 'amazing' and 'far-out – the rapport with the audience was fantastic'. By closing night Ziggy had become the heavyweight champion of glam rock, whose only other contenders were Gary Glitter and Alice Cooper. Bowie's stage presence already equalled both Glitter's and Cooper's combined. In *Gay News*'s perceptive view, 'He is the understudy who's been waiting in the wings for years. Finally his big day comes, and he's got every step, every note, every voice-warble right. A star is born.'

At the core of the show lay the classic rock relationship between singer and lead guitarist. Ronson would remember with what force Bowie advised all the Spiders on matters of stagecraft and make-up. There were some startling embellishments. But, try as they might, the two sidemen remained just that – the necessary dirt from which exquisite flowers grew. The eye never travelled to them as it did to Bowie and Ronson. 'No other combination, including Jagger–Richard, was as visually strong,' said Bolan. 'They were *riveting*.' Even that assessment understated the effect when, at Dunstable Civic Hall, Bowie dropped to his knees, seized Ronson's buttocks and engaged in the first lewd act on a Gibson Les Paul performed on the British stage: one captured by Rock's camera. That photograph took its place in the iconography of rock and roll and made Ziggy a talking point overnight. It also brought a startled reaction from Ronson's family, who, he remembered, 'never quite looked at me the same way again'.

Like 'Changes', 'Starman', released that April, was a forward-looking pop song that doffed its hat to the past. There were blatant steals in the melody, and the familiarity was key to the appeal. As well as the lifts from 'Over the Rainbow' and 'You Keep Me Hangin' On', the song came within a chord of Bolan's 'Telegram Sam'. The image of Bowie, in full Ziggy regalia, miming 'Starman' on *Top of the Pops* made headlines around the country. It also provided him with his first hit since 'Space Oddity'.

The *Ziggy* album followed in June. In later years certain critics, previously faithful, became tetchy about Bowie's breakthrough, making it a point to find fault. According to Lester Bangs, for one, Ziggy's success was no more than a kind of listless fluke. It was true that, though never so billed, *Ziggy* was a rock opera, with a lead, supporting parts and a satirically inane storyline: alien comes to earth, forms a band and warns humans they have five years before extinction. Yet because of the quality of the tunes (brimming with hooks, and quickly working their way into the subconscious) and the neat ruse of writing in the third person (making *Ziggy* a running joke, a sort of *Carry On Up Uranus*), Bowie kept, and greatly accelerated, the momentum of *Hunky Dory*.

Bowie's music was still laced with soaring guitars and layered, choirboy harmonies, only now dunked in a morass of surging bass and throbbing drums. The overall quality of the songs was impressive enough. But *Ziggy* bristled with unexpected touches, some good, some not so admirable. On the debit side were almost all the clever-but-oblique lyrics, replacing greeting-card pleas for world peace and vague Buddhist jargon with a song cycle of clichéd science-fiction slang. More engaging were the deft musical quirks: the shocking opening bolt of 'Moonage Daydream'; the wry, muttered outro to 'Star'; the mood and tempo swings of 'Rock 'n' Roll Suicide'. These were the flourishes of an extraordinarily self-confident songwriter.

Ziggy's tracks held their particular pleasures: 'Five Years', with its lyrical debt to Lou Reed; 'Star', in which Bowie and his alter ego met; 'Hang On to Yourself', with its whiff of 'Summertime Blues'; the title track, whose left-handed guitar god was thought to bear a resemblance to Bolan or, more plausibly, Jimi Hendrix; 'Suffragette City', which owes its manic feel to the droning 'Hey Man!' from the backing vocals, evoking the plight of someone endlessly distracted by lackeys and hangers-on; and the climactic 'Rock 'n' Roll Suicide', which effortlessly achieved anthem status as Bowie illustrated the song live by reaching out into the fans.

This was some of the most inspirational and ultimately timeless music of the seventies. When Bowie's vision triumphed over his foibles (such as the Anthony Newley crooning on half of the tracks), it triumphed so spectacularly that the disappointments of eight years seemed to melt away in its white-hot glare. From its faultless production to its quirky-but-danceable choruses, through to its enigmatic cover (shot one wet January night in Heddon Street, Piccadilly), *The Rise and Fall of Ziggy Stardust and the Spiders From Mars* was a classic: H. P. Lovecraft with memorable melodies and a foot-pumping beat.

Defries delivered the *Ziggy* acetate to RCA in mid-March. Three months later, he returned to New York with Bowie for a whirlwind weekend in a lull in the British tour. Barbara Fulk, an

RCA secretary, remembers being rushed to the Park Lane Hotel – 'it was like a medical alert' – to bring Bowie a hairdrier. She arrived to find Angela wearing a garment recalled as 'some kind of babydoll lace number' and no bra. A nude Bowie was asleep on top of the bed. Angela then made a pass at Fulk. A second woman, Edith Cearns, met the Bowies in a Manhattan restaurant. She liked his sensitivity and his musicianship and the shy, tentative way he had. She found it remarkable that a man who had 'hung around with so many groupies, in so many bands' did not project more feisty, extroverted chauvinism. She decided, like others before her, that 'Angie really wore the pants'. A source at RCA who prefers anonymity recalls the triangular relationship between Bowie, Angela and Defries as 'perfect in the way each one acted a different role. Tony had this habit of seeming ominously calm and almost *too* reasonable, like a man struggling to control himself. Angie was a thug. And Dave just wandered in and out of everyone's office looking engagingly lost and British.' Edith Cearns adds that 'all three of them had the morals of a cobra' – though even the group's combined efforts failed to secure tickets to a sold-out Elvis concert in New York, something Bowie rued for years to come.

By early summer the Ziggy tour was earning admiring notices from those, like *Sounds* and *Melody Maker*, for whom Bowie was 'a bitch', 'a vision', '*Vogue*'s idea of what the well-dressed astronaut should be wearing' and a 'darkling prophet'. After a Friends of the Earth benefit on 8 July, the media chorus became a giant band that played only one tune. Not only was Bowie 'probably the best rock musician in Britain today', 'the undisputed king', 'a deadly mixture of fragility and desperate intensity'; even heavyweights like the *Guardian* described him as 'a remarkable performer' and, in *The Times*' words, 'T. S. Eliot with a rock and roll beat'.

One of the first lessons Defries learned in show-business was to make friends with the media. Starting with the Beatles, most major papers had begun featuring 'beat' music – as it still appeared – while, in the US, *Rolling Stone* satisfied the nation's new mania for any chat about rock stars. Stacks of imitators followed. It was Defries' genius to turn the gaze of two continents' musical press on to his client. On the home front, Dai Davies began a campaign that led to reviews, and ultimately to headlines wherever Bowie went. (Almost every other story began in the same way: 'Lock up your sons – Ziggy is coming'.) Defries' own greatest coup was to fly a plane-load of American journalists to London (at a cost of £20,000) where they interviewed Bowie at the Dorchester Hotel after watching him perform. 'Ziggy Stardust' thus won more feature-length coverage in the US than any other character who had yet to actually play there. A sign of Bowie's mounting fame was his two sold-out concerts at the Rainbow Theatre, where he headlined over not only Lindsay Kemp's mime troupe, but a new entrant into the now burgeoning world of glam rock, Roxy Music, and their boa-clad keyboardist known simply as Eno.

To his credit, Bowie also found time to promote other musicians. Dana Gillespie, Freddi Burretti and George Underwood, whose careers remained frustratingly in chrysalis, were quietly shelved when Ziggymania took hold. Bowie did, however, arrange for Iggy Pop to fly to London, where, after a meeting recalled by one executive as 'like trying to dislodge a pit bull from one's windpipe', Defries persuaded CBS to pay Iggy a $25,000 advance for an album. That record, co-produced by Bowie, was *Raw Power*. Bowie and Ronson then collaborated with Lou Reed on *Transformer*, catapulting him from cult figure to rock star virtually overnight. Meanwhile, four albums along with rigorous touring had brought the Midlands group Mott the Hoople a club following but no real mainstream success. By spring of 1972 the band had been dropped by their record company. Bowie heard Mott and persuaded them to give it one more try. The result was 'All the Young Dudes', a song Bowie wrote and produced, and on the strength of which Defries obtained an advance – this time for $50,000 – from CBS. The single became an immediate hit, as did Mott's Bowie-produced album. All of these relationships soured to some extent in later years. There were dark mutterings by Mott's Ian Hunter about his mentor's 'genius for nicking other people's ideas'. Iggy and his friend would, he said, 'punch each other's buttons' during a mutual exile in Berlin. And Reed, too, commented disparagingly on Bowie after *Transformer*. But, in 1972, the man of genius was happy to help the men of talent. Bowie never lost his fan's awe of rock music, even for groups less exalted than himself, and years later a band member would remember that 'Dave was trembling' when he first knocked at Mott's dressing room door.

Ziggy's British tour ended at Stoke-on-Trent on 7 September. Bowie then released 'John, I'm Only Dancing', a single that, if not overtly gay, was not of the Tom Jones variety. It, too, was accompanied by a Mick Rock video, taking the whole concept of the 'short' into a higher, more provocative category. Visual interest was sustained by Bowie, as Ziggy, flanked by two epicene dancers clad as spiders. Lester Bangs called this 'the very moment the modern idea of a video was born' and ten years ahead of its time in offering a contentiously witty and surreal view of its subject.

Like a stagnant pond, motionless to the naked eye, MainMan, though portraying itself as a mere fund manager, was inwardly teeming with furious, invisible activity. In July Defries had flown his style gurus, including the correspondents of *Harper's* and *Playboy* to London (and been rewarded with the headline in *New York*, 'I went to England and saw the Queen'). Next he recruited two fugitives from *Pork*, Tony Zanetta and Leee Black Childers, as, respectively, president and vice-president of MainMan, with offices at 240 East 58th Street in Manhattan. Finally, by way of RCA and a California booker named Jim Rismiller, Defries made plans for a full-scale American tour. To anyone who would listen, Zanetta and Childers began to talk up the event as a second-wave British Invasion. By early September, Bowie's advance publicity was following the pattern of mid-sixties forays by the Beatles and the Stones. Trailers began to appear in trade titles like *Rolling Stone* and *Creem*, with the daily press dancing attendance. Advertisements loomed from billboards, and, less formally, on brick walls chalked with the words ZIGGY RULES. Dai Davies flew to America, along with Bowie's personal bodyguard, photographer, hairdresser and equipment manager. Defries instigated round-the-clock negotiations with local promoters, resulting in a 90–10 split of all concert takings in MainMan's favour, unprecedented for an artist whose current UK tour had begun in the back room of a Surrey pub. As Bowie himself rehearsed in the Stratford East Theatre, Defries arrived in New York and took up residence in the Plaza Hotel. By now press interest in the tour was not merely intense: it was feverish. With four phone calls Davies secured an equal number of feature stories, all dwelling on Ziggy's peculiar, camp mixture of make-up, science fiction, stagecraft and transvestism. To Defries' delight, even his client's sea voyage, coming at a time when rock stars had begun to cross the Atlantic by Concorde, made news. As a final flourish, MainMan provided Bowie and Angela with travelling companions, their Bromley friend George Underwood and his wife. The two couples stepped off the *QE2* in New York on 17 September 1972.

Bowie could not have wished for a more agreeable month than that which followed. The first half of the tour proceeded in a style wildly at odds with his modest American sales. By the time he reached the Beverly Hills Hotel on 16 October, Bowie had a travelling crew of forty-six: as well as the MainMan entourage there was Iggy Pop, sundry drug-dealers and groupies, a professional palmist, and others whose precise status was hard to define, all signing 'RCA Records & Tapes' to bills that, at that hotel alone, topped $20,000. Bowie travelled for the most part in chauffeured cars or private train compartments, ushered by Stuey George and George's own helper, Tony Frost. To the bodyguards' primary brief – discouraging all photographers and ensuring that no one without authority approach Bowie – was added a secondary role as procurers. A Marilyn Monroe-lookalike and MainMan secretary named Cyrinda Foxe would recall 'spying through those huge old Plaza Hotel keyholes, and watch[ing] the guards giving it to some groupie ... After they were through David would occasionally take over, and I would sit in a chair sometimes and talk to him while he was having sex. I'd watch television and sit in a chair, because he wanted somebody to talk to.' Foxe is only one witness to the lavish spending, as promiscuous in its way as the sex, that nearly bankrupted both RCA Records and MainMan. Despite gross receipts of $112,500, the reissuing of Bowie's two Mercury LPs and a new hit single, the seventy-one-day tour would lose $485,000, or nearly $7,000 for every day on the road.

The concerts brought Bowie up against audiences reared on a diet of denim rock, some of whom booed his frequent costume and set changes. In the first week, at least, the omens seemed promising. Opening nights at the Cleveland Music

Hall* was a triumph. All 3,500 seats were sold and the press was
everything that Davies could have hoped for. Six nights later, on
28 September, the party reached New York. It was the day Henry
Kissinger returned from the Vietnam peace talks in Paris with the
fell phrase 'Peace is at hand'. The slogan on the Carnegie Hall
marquee, picked out by a huge spotlight, read simply:

FALL IN LOVE
WITH
DAVID BOWIE

Outside, scalpers offered tickets for $50 apiece, while within, the
actors Alan Bates and Anthony Perkins mingled with Andy
Warhol, Truman Capote and the arts correspondent of the *New
York Times*. As the lights dimmed, the march from *Clockwork
Orange* surged through the hall, hitting its climax simultaneously
with three strobe lights that played on the entrance of the band,
and Bowie himself, in gold lamé, singing 'Changes'. After a neat
acoustic rendering of 'Space Oddity' and generous helpings of
Ziggy Stardust, all amplified to the pain threshold, the concert
ended with 'White Light, White Heat' and a five-minute standing
ovation. The show was 'as transcendent as rock and roll gets',
according to the *New Yorker*. In the *Times*'s view, Bowie gave a
performance of 'beautiful coordinated movements and well-
planned music'. Lilian Roxon, not one to overpraise, restricted
herself to the trite but effective, 'A star is born'.

Bowie's achievement was the greater in view of the fact that he
performed while suffering from flu. Other than attending several
adult films in Times Square he did not, therefore, indulge himself
in New York outside the privacy of his suite. He was now plainly
a being apart from the other musicians: screened by George, Frost
and yet a third man, Anton Jones, all dressed alike and with
faintly sinister, Maoist armbands reading BOWIE PASS. A sign of

---

*Cleveland also saw Mike Garson's first appearance as the Spiders' pianist.
Garson, a New York jazz virtuoso, had never heard of Ziggy Stardust. He was
recommended by a contact at RCA. Garson is still playing with Bowie today,
twenty-four years after his first audition.

the shifting equilibrium within the party came in Nashville. First Angela caused a minor scandal by falling to her knees and giving frottage to a female fan in the closed, but not deserted bar of the Bowies' hotel. Later that night she went skinny-dipping with Anton Jones. After Bowie mediated with the furious desk clerk, he retreated to his room with Defries and Zanetta. The next day Angela was told to leave the tour and fly to London. Jones survived.

If east-coast audiences had 'fallen in love with' Bowie, critics did no less. As well as the *New Yorker* and the *Times*, *Newsweek* ran a long feature hailing 'the Stardust Kid ... the dark, satanic majesty of David Bowie'. The other big-city titles followed in kind. Davies' greatest thematic coup was a *Rolling Stone* profile seamlessly building on the image of the singer as an actor – 'always playing roles, fragments of himself'. In his enthusiasm, Defries spoke, quite seriously, about launching a line of Bowie accessories in America: clockwork Ziggy dolls that said 'Wham Bam, Thank You Ma'am', and a range of 'exclusive MainMan merchandise' like red plastic platform shoes and lurex catsuits.

The second half of the tour did not always live up to the promise of the early dates. Only two hundred people showed up to see Bowie at an amusement park in Miami. He sagged visibly as he ran on stage surveying tier after tier of vacant seats. The San Francisco turnout was so disappointing that Bowie snubbed the city on his next US tour. In Seattle he played to an audience of four hundred. Defries was forced to cancel dates in Dallas and Houston because of weak advance sales. Bowie did, however, give two sold-out performances at the Santa Monica Civic Auditorium, the first of which was broadcast live on radio and released as an album twenty-three years later.

By the time the tour ended in Philadelphia on 2 December, poor ticket sales and mounting pressure from RCA – whose payment of the Beverly Hills bill would cause cancellation of the Christmas bonus – had forced a gesture towards sanity. The Underwoods had been sent home, and Davies replaced by Cherry Vanilla, the title player in *Pork*, whose promotional offensive included baring her breasts at press conferences, biting one female reporter in the buttocks and talking up Bowie as a 'sexual antichrist'. ('We peddled David's ass like Nathans sell hotdogs,'

she later told *Village Voice*, 'and I screwed disc jockeys across
America to get Bowie's records played on the radio.') There was
also a scaling-down in transportation to a chartered Greyhound
bus, though even here, Ronson noted, 'it was champagne and
fish eggs all the way'.

Most of the mixed responses to Bowie were on show at a
reception hosted by RCA before he boarded the RHMS *Ellinis* in
New York. The label had promised 'the ticker-tape party of the
year'. Yet the few journalists making their way to RCA's Studio
C were offered only a glass of cider and a Ziggy poster (for which
they were charged $5) before Bowie, resplendent in tight jeans
rolled up to the knee with silver lamé stockings and a paisley
quilted jacket with lapels the size of wings, walked in with Defries.
The first question was 'What made you start writing queer
songs?' A heated argument then took place as to whether or not
gays were 'accepted' fully in America. (They were, according to
Bowie.) At the end of the debate a respected rock writer told
Bowie he was 'full of crap' and directed a question to Defries. 'We
heard RCA underwrote this tour,' the critic said. 'How much did
they do that?' A few surprised gasps and a shuffling of feet made
it difficult to hear Defries' mumbled answer. But it sounded to
some that he had said that, strictly speaking, they were all
advances. Bowie then left the room looking ashen-faced and close
to tears.

Ziggy Stardust's first contact with America came as a mutual
jolt. In the key markets of New York and Los Angeles, at least, the
tour achieved its commercial aims. Bowie had been noticed by
style pundits on both coasts. He was greeted warmly by Truman
Capote and without insult by Warhol. Nobody still asked if he
could deliver. Sales of the *Ziggy* album doubled. Bowie described
his first weeks on the eastern seaboard as 'euphoric'. By the
second month of provincial dates, however, even Defries had
realized that middle America would not fall to an English
transvestite. Bowie learned the hard way that, in Kansas or
Indianapolis or St Louis, Ziggy was a cul-de-sac, not a road to
bigger things. Not only did he fail to crack the American
heartland, but he denied for years ever having played there.

The madness of the MainMan entourage also affected Bowie
adversely. America, Ronson said, 'changed the band for the

worse. I'm talking about feeling within the band, about money, and the position within the band. It was a bad scene – David and all those wankers.' According to this reading, Bowie had become a hostage to his manager's ambitions. By surrounding him with a retinue of sycophants, handlers and karate-suited security men, Defries had made his client untouchable, with the inevitable result that Bowie, in turn, lost touch. The man who sailed to New York in September was still – just – recognizable as David Jones; the one who returned home in September was patently a Rock Star.

There was one other, tangible result of the American tour. As the group's chartered bus droned between St Louis and Chicago (not, as Bowie later thought, Detroit), Ronson spontaneously played a pumping guitar riff in the style of Bo Diddley, or the early Rolling Stones. Bowie added a chorus, a set of lyrics dealing vaguely with urban decay, and a title. He called it 'The Jean Genie'. The song was recorded at RCA's Nashville studio and released as a single in November. It reached number two on the UK chart.

As soon as Bowie returned to Britain, he went back on the road. A Christmas Eve show at the Rainbow Theatre achieved a note of festive homecoming. Bowie came on stage to a standing ovation, went directly to the microphone and began speaking, addressing not just the packed house but an enormous radio audience. The speech, asking the fans to make a donation to Dr Barnardo's, lasted just a minute. Referring to his father, Bowie was interrupted by applause again and again, three times before he finished. On Christmas morning, a lorry-load of toys was duly delivered to children's homes all over London.

A week later, Bowie walked into RCA's boardroom in Blooms-bury immaculately groomed and made-up. To those who had not seen him in months, he looked markedly different. He wore a loose-fitting white satin suit, against which his orange hair made a stunning contrast. A polyester disc was stuck to the centre of his forehead. He had been thin before he went to America, and he had lost weight since. His face had shrunk to a gaunt caricature. In his hand was a silver-topped swagger stick. After the coughing died down, the RCA directors got to the business at hand. They had come to present Bowie with a gold record, and to photograph the event for the corporate brochure. The marketing manager made a speech before handing over the engraved disc. 'You truly have been THE main man of 1972, just as I predicted. I'll never forget the first time I heard *Hunky Dory*. I knew it was a stroke of genuis.' Bowie appeared comatose.

The executive bowed, putting his ear close enough to Defries to hear him mutter, 'You'll have to do better than that if you want a new contract.' Bowie then came forward, hastily accepted the award, and exited. Although *Ziggy Stardust* failed to win a single Grammy nomination, such ceremonies became almost routine on Bowie's return to Britain. *Melody Maker* voted him Vocalist of the Year (over Rod Stewart and Elton John) and *Ziggy* was named top album. There was a readers' poll award from *NME*. A sure sign of Bowie's ascendancy over his glam rock rivals was the emergence of what Defries called the media's tall poppy syndrome ('We grow them, we adore them, then we lop them'), a critical backlash voiced by Steve Peacock:

> When I saw David Bowie's extravaganza at the Rainbow, I couldn't quite decide whether my reaction was tears of rage, tears of hysterical laughter, or merely tears of sorrow. It was probably a mixture of all three . . . also I was angry and a bit contemptuous when I realised that most of Bowie's new-found audience didn't know anything further back than *Hunky Dory*, and were there mainly for cheap thrills, camp charisma, and a performance centred around the media creation of 'gay rock'.

Most notices, though, were all that Bowie and Defries could have hoped for. Ziggy's pyrotechnic look was widely considered both sharp-edged and radical, and introduced many a teenager to fashion. Bowie's influence extended down a line from his fans to the press, and his own peers. If, in 1972, you were in your teens or early twenties and you liked theatrical pop, your two shining examples were Bowie and Marc Bolan. No self-respecting record collection was complete without *Electric Warrior* and *Hunky Dory*; *everyone* had *Ziggy Stardust*. But Bolan's teenybop audience was fickle. After *The Groover*, many of his fans defected to David Cassidy and the Osmonds. At twenty-six, Bowie was undisputed king of a vast province: better-looking than Elton John, more wily than Slade, and allowing a personal involvement with his songs that wasn't possible with Gary Glitter. Eric Clapton remembers how 'virtually overnight, bands were trying to ride a massive hype into Ziggydom'. (Almost simultaneously with 'The Jean Genie', RCA released the Sweet's 'Blockbuster', mining the exact same blues-rock riff.) Even established stars like Mick Jagger, who now performed brandishing a rhinestone mask, showed signs of having studied Bowie. Imitation was one form of flattery. At the other extreme was the Strawbs' 'Backside', credited to Ciggy Barlust and the Whales from Venus, a satirical stab from a group that once headlined over Bowie on *Colour Me Pop*.

On its most visible level, in the high streets, the schools, the clubs and the record shops, Bowie's influence was rife, an explosion of colour and quilled hair, and almost instant. To anyone vaguely frustrated, or looking for a way to transform themselves, he was a godsend. New styles began to emerge, drawing entirely from the Ziggy character, that made their victims look like brightly painted tapeworms. Andy Peebles recalls Bowie's show that opened the Manchester Hard Rock in September 1972 – 'within a fortnight every kid in the city had orange roots'. After the first tour, a small but highly visible core of fans adopted the Ziggy cockade in American cities. In France the style – which was everywhere – was called 'le look Bowie'. The concept of wearing jeans rolled up to the shin, thick-soled boots and make-up, so startling in 1971, was near-uniform in 1973. As Michael Bracewell puts it, 'From a dubious underground incubator in which bisexuality had mingled with a host of eclectic cultural influences, a beautiful monster called Ziggy Stardust emerged. Though obviously a stranger to the dentist, he was the nearest thing to heaven on earth that a generation of pasty European and American teenagers had ever seen.' In less than a year, Bowieism became a way of life to tens of thousands. Their anthem was 'Rock 'n' Roll Suicide' and their trademark a glam confection that annoyed parents and, at its emotive extreme, made gay sex seem *fun*. These were the Bowie Boys who were a feature of London club life from *Ziggy* onwards, some of whom, like Malcolm McLaren, became a link to pop's next re-creation.

To most adults, of course, Bowie was a proverb for louche, anti-social behaviour, at best a disturbing image on a bedroom wall, and as polarizing in his way as Jagger had been. In Britain in 1973 you either loved Ziggy or you hated him. What few people did was to ignore him.

In January Bowie continued his triumphant progress through sold-out and frequently riotous provincial theatres. His fans were, above all, participants rather than passive consumers. Anybody who ventured the minimum £1 ticket price became a volunteer in the new Bowie army, thronging the halls of Glasgow, Newcastle and Preston in their Ziggy boots and caked with make-up. Like hadjis and roving nomads, crossing whole continents, lured by the holy, semi-hypnotic, thousands of believers flocked to the source. For his return to the Manchester Hard Rock, Bowie came on to a manic 'Let's Spend the Night Together'. Playing his old hits, about spacemen, and his new ones, about crack-ups and madness and America, the music was a tribal stomp of wailing guitars, screaming keyboards and bone-crushing rhythms. Humour rode the chaos with narrative raps: 'I believe in education – educate me,' Bowie cooed as he skipped across the stage, and with a thrust of the hip and a pout, segued into 'Moonage Daydream'. Here was 'Rock and Theatre', as the *Times* put it. As a performer, Bowie effortlessly worked his young audience to the brink of frenzy. Musically, his long apprenticeship showed in his all-round grasp of his roots, from lyrical ballads to factory-floor clatter, sci-fi droning to crafty pop, folk to country, heavy metal to music-hall soft-shoe.

Whether at the back of the Greyhound bus, late at night in his hotel room or on board the *Ellinis*, Bowie had been steadily writing songs since the previous autumn. Some of these, like 'Jean Genie', had been released in America. Now, along with the Spiders, a brass section and backing singers, he recorded a full album. Edgy, breathlessly dispatched, the new tracks were dark snapshots of America: race riots, drugs, guns, murder, police sirens and suicide, all set to a Rolling Stones beat. 'It's called "A Lad Insane",' Bowie announced, 'and it's crazy.'

On 17 January Bowie confirmed to a giggling Russell Harty, 'My next role will be a person called Aladdin Sane.' Whereas Ziggy's gift had been for 'flash', not nuance and tone, the new character would deal in 'innuendo and subtext – he's a situation as opposed to an individual'. Bowie told a reporter backstage in Harty's green room, 'I've always felt like a vehicle for something else, but I've never really sorted out what that was, or who Bowie is.' To the studio technicians, the answer was immediate – Bowie was a professional. Not only did he confer with Harty's director, cameramen and engineers before filming: when, towards the end of singing 'My Death', a string broke on his guitar, he incorporated the mishap, in perfect rhyme, into the final verse.

On 24 January Bowie completed his new album. The next morning he was on the *QE2* bound for New York. Defries had worked relentlessly over the Christmas holiday, first building up the MainMan empire, then negotiating with RCA – a new deal increased Bowie's advance per album from $37,500 to $60,000 in 1973 and $100,000 in 1974, with an improved royalty rate – and finally arranging a brief three-week US tour. The seven-city itinerary shunned the excesses of the previous visit. There was no MainMan entourage, although Bowie's bodyguards remained, staring out through dark glasses and threatening anyone who approached with a camera. Several did. As Bowie's fame grew, creative photographers tried bribing his chauffeur in New York, or hiring cherry-picker cranes for glimpses into the third floor of the Gramercy Park Hotel. He was mobbed when he ate in the Rainbow Room. A member of the tour party describes it as 'brilliant, how Defries brought David back after only two months. Everything we worked for on the first tour paid off. It was like *A Hard Day's Night*. From then on, David had it made.'

The tour opened on Valentine's Day at New York's Radio City Music Hall. All 6,000 seats were sold, many of them to Ziggy clones with spiked haircuts and Bowie's distinctive white disc (an idea he borrowed from Calvin Mark Lee) stuck to their foreheads. Andy Warhol was in attendance again, as were Truman Capote and Salvador Dali. The whole show, a salvo of furiously played songs from *Ziggy* and *Aladdin Sane*, was the most theatrical and elaborately choreographed even Radio City had seen: so tightly scripted that Bowie's dramatic finale, in which he fainted during 'Rock 'n' Roll Suicide', left some wondering if that, too, had been staged. (Blocked pores, due to Bowie's heavy make-up, were blamed.) The tour wound through Philadelphia, Nashville, Memphis, Detroit and Chicago to the same delirious reception.* By avoiding the low spots of the previous visit, Defries ensured capacity crowds everywhere, and a press that outdid itself to smear the prose in purple. By the time Bowie played the Hollywood Palladium in early March, he was a textbook-perfect vision, not just of a star, but of the madness that inevitably attends American celebrity.

Bowie reacted to fame with a spree of drugs and sex. That he engaged in typical rock-star conceits was no surprise: what confused and depressed Bowie's friends was to see how little happiness his success seemed to have brought him. Away from the public eye, he and Angela – thrown off the second tour, as she had been the first – could be heard in ever more frequent and furious rows. His old friends from Bromley and Beckenham noted the changes wrought by fame, and not all liked what they saw. Even Ronson thought 'David blew it' by his high-handed treatment of the Spiders. For months there had been mutterings about the group's wages. Now Bolder and Woodmansey approached their manager with a demand for a percentage of Bowie's income. Defries compromised by doubling their salaries on the condition, seemingly an afterthought, that they pay their own expenses. It was several weeks before the hapless musicians realized that this would mean earning even less money. Meanwhile, Bowie's pianist Mike Garson had begun preaching to his colleagues about Scientology – with the eventual result that Woodmansey was converted – further contributing to the group's stresses, and ultimately its break-up.

One witness was uniquely alive to the differences between the old Bowie and the new. John Hutchinson, last seen in 1969, had recently read in *Melody Maker* that his friend from the Buzz and 'Space Oddity' days was seeking a twelve-string guitarist. After a perfunctory audition, Hutchinson was flown to New York, where he found Bowie 'still friendly' and eager to see a performance by Charlie Mingus. From that high point relations soured during the

---

*One *NME* critic experienced the 'high voltage of Dave's charm' first hand at Detroit's Masonic Auditorium. 'Oh, so you're Nick Kent,' said Bowie, blowing the journalist a kiss. 'My, aren't you pretty? And I thought all English music writers looked like Richard Williams.'

rest of the tour. In Hutchinson's still-affectionate memory, 'It wasn't Dave himself who changed, as much as the whole scene around him. On his own, he was just about the same guy I'd known. With the lackeys and bodyguards, he could be a prat. I didn't care for the lifestyle, and what I saw it do to him.'

'I'm a pretty cold person. A *very* cold person,' Bowie told *Rolling Stone* in 1972. Even that frank admission fell short of Hutchinson's judgement of his friend in America. 'He was like a clenched fist,' he says, 'and he surrounded himself with people who were like clenched fists.' Bowie, certainly, could be a hard man to fathom. From his startling eyes that seemed always to look away, to his ice-cold grip, the first impression was one of reserve. 'He seemed frightened of people, and actually didn't like them to touch him,' says Helm. In London Bowie spoke, quite seriously, of his fear that a ghost was stalking him, and that 'psychic vampires' lurked under the skins of his closest friends.

Bowie could be cool to colleagues, like Bolder and Wood-mansey, and to companions, like Reed and Hunter. Even his formidable charisma was channelled to his own ends: Bowie's talent, according to Mick Rock, 'was to charm and focus people into doing exactly what he needed'. He was offhand with partners (including Angela), many of whom found their stay in Bowie's bed abruptly ended, and indifferent to family (especially Terry Burns), whose repeated wishes to see him were dashed. Until he had created his own identity, he was too self-absorbed for even his son. Bowie, in Angela's view, had been an uncaring husband, and with each passing day he showed as little concern as a father. It would be another five years, under the strain of a divorce, before he submitted to the day-to-day business of parenthood.

Bowie, therefore, identified with *Aladdin Sane*'s theme of extreme alienation. His suspicion of others, amounting in time to paranoia, began in childhood and would run throughout his life. There were those, in turn, who found Bowie repellent. For all his undoubted charisma, the combination of vermilion hair, different-coloured eyes, sunken features (his weight on tour fell to 110 pounds) and thin, lizard smile could shock as well as attract. Angela notes, too, that Bowie was in the habit of bathing only every three or four days and often appeared 'a little off, or mouldy', a feature widely remarked on by visitors to his hotel suite.

What some objected to were the very qualities of cool, passive eroticism that overwhelmed others. Bowie's glamour was only too accessible to literally hundreds of lovers. There were gay partners; but for a bisexual, at least a *poseur*, he could project rock-star masculinity. A music publisher named Brian James happened to be working in his office in Heddon Street on the night Bowie was photographed for the *Ziggy Stardust* album cover. He watched the whole process through a window: the bustling arrival of Bowie, the cameraman and two ornate-looking girls; the 'cheerful self-parody' of the actual pose, after which 'the photographer left down one end of the alley, while Bowie walked off with a hand planted squarely on each girl's arse'. Angela was later to say that she and her husband slept together for the last time in January 1973. That was only the dawn of an era that Ronson described as Bowie 'rooting himself silly' on tours of America, Japan and Britain. That February alone he bedded Todd Rundgren's girlfriend Bebe Buell, a waitress and would-be singer named Ava Cherry, the critic Lilian Roxon, Cyrinda Foxe, and numberless groupies. One member of the tour party walked into Bowie's room in Chicago to find him filming two women performing on each other with champagne bottles. 'David was absolutely sex-ridden,' says a lover, 'but of the *theory* of sex. He understood it was the ruling physical thing in life. He was fascinated by sex, all kinds, everybody's. That's different to saying he was ever satisfied by anyone.' Bowie undoubtedly enjoyed female company, especially when the woman was a dark-skinned exotic (like Bianca Jagger), or a colleague's girlfriend (who 'he screwed as a control trip over the band', according to a source who should know). There is no evidence, however, linking Bowie and a lover, in 1973, on anything but a casual basis. Ronson himself would say that 'David craved chicks' to make good a chronic lack of self-confidence.

Bowie's role-playing had, to some extent, been an antidote for his emotional numbness. 'Offstage I'm a robot,' he told Hubert Saal. 'Onstage I achieve emotion. It's probably why I prefer dressing up as Ziggy to being David.' In 1972 Bowie had been more than just dressing up. 'Call me Ziggy! Call me Ziggy Stardust!' he told the American critics who interviewed him at the Dorchester Hotel. At Defries' insistence, RCA produced posters proclaiming Bowie *was* his alter ego. 'David fell for it,' Ronson confirmed.

By 1973 the character Bowie once described as 'total anarchy' had become a straitjacket. When he changed into Ziggy it was much more than just an act, it seemed like genuine possession. His weird make-up and space-age clothes were only reflections of his own other-worldliness. The rumour went around, especially in the teen magazines, that Bowie himself thought he was from another planet. In Los Angeles, he refused to go out during the day because, he said, quite solemnly, 'I'll melt.' Bowie stopped a concert in another city to harangue the audience about a spacecraft he was certain he had seen from his hotel window. He was intrigued, he told a journalist, 'to show how a nobody can become a god, and go bonkers in the process'. He was talking about Ziggy, but it was an ominous self-sketch if ever there was one. The character, Bowie said years later, had been an elaborate front for his crippling shyness:

> Then that fucker wouldn't leave me alone for years. That was when it all started to sour . . . My whole personality was affected. It became very dangerous. I really did have doubts about my sanity.

Bowie's 'desperate need', his cousin Kristine said, was for people who would 'relate to him as David Jones'. By the early weeks of 1973 he was consciously seeking a return to, if not normality, at least some type of pre-Ziggy perspective. Bowie began to talk up his 'Bromleyness' to the press and public. An *NME* writer called him a horror-film buff, a lover of Crumb cartoons, and a frustrated painter. Bowie introduced himself to an audience in Memphis with the words 'Hello. I'm Jones.' Crossing the Sea of Japan in April 1973, he entertained his fellow boat-passengers with a cabaret, singing a medley of show tunes and Jacques Brel numbers, perched on a stool with an acoustic guitar. Bowie now went out of his way to fill up the gaps between concerts with hobbies like photography and car maintenance. According to Hutchinson, there was a deliberate plan 'to phase out Ziggy before Ziggy phased out David'.

Bowie's immediate response was to create a character called Aladdin Sane – essentially, he revealed, 'Ziggy in America'. Most of Aladdin's props came from the previous production. There were the same futuristic clothes (oriental now), and the same androgyny and perceived decadence. Bowie's transformation was achieved by way of a white circle on his forehead and, for the *Aladdin Sane* album cover, a lightning flash on his face. That red and blue stripe was revolution superbly controlled. Other than wearing a broad-brimmed hat (a homage to William Burroughs), Bowie made no further fashion metamorphoses in 1973. There was, however, a clear-cut determination that Aladdin should be his author's servant, not his master. Bowie, said Ronson, 'could always pack the character away in a box ... With Ziggy, I wasn't so sure.'

On 5 April Bowie landed at Yokohama aboard the SS *Oronsay*. The nine Japanese shows that followed were universally despised by the highbrow press and police, and hugely popular with audiences. Bowie himself began a love affair with oriental culture. He was visited at Tokyo's Imperial Hotel by the designer Kansai Yamamoto, several of whose costumes – equipped with a row of snap buttons, allowing for quick removal – were added to the stage wardrobe. Bowie also took to performing in a garment he described as a sumo thong, likened by unkind critics to a nappy. He responded with enthusiasm to aspects of Japanese society: saki, geishas, the bath-houses and kabuki, mugging gamely with the samurai warriors sent to meet him at the docks. According to Hutchinson, the lobbies of the tour hotels pulsed with kimono-clad girls, offering the bemused musicians handfuls of coins ('a role-reversal', he notes) before joining them upstairs.

Bowie was idolized in Japan as he had not initially been in America. Just before leaving Yokohama he spent two straight nights from eleven p.m. to two a.m. signing autographs at his hotel as mobs outside chanted '*Zee-gee! Zee-gee!*' He said goodbye to Yamamoto and dropped in at a bath-house on his way to the port. A member of the tour party remembers Bowie describing his experience there as 'poetic – he told them the eyes were his soul and the face was his conscience. Anything to get a hand-job.' Bowie also railed against Angela, effectively deported from Japan for throwing a chair at the final concert in Tokyo, as a 'virtual idiot', with all the finesse of a 'fucking Mack truck'. He then left Yokohama and sailed overnight to Vladivostock, surviving a scare when his boat grazed an iceberg in the Sea of Japan. From there he took the Trans-Siberian Express to Moscow ('fucking everything that moved and quite a lot that didn't', according to Bob Musel, a reporter who joined him), made stops in Berlin and Paris, and arrived in London on 4 May. Several hundred fans were on hand to see him step off the train at Charing Cross.

By then Bowie was again at the top of the charts. Released in April, while he was still in Japan, 'Drive-In Saturday' occupied the same lyrical ground as 'Life On Mars?', a parallel world where image became reality, this time set to a bracing, take-no-prisoners barrage of guitar and saxophone. The single was culled from *Aladdin Sane*, the first album Bowie made after fame struck, thought at the time to be overproduced and histrionic and now generally making for archival, rather than pleasurable, listening.

The inspiration for *Aladdin* was Mike Garson's avant-garde jazz piano and, striking a lower musical note, the Rolling Stones. As well as a revamped 'Let's Spend the Night Together' there was the *Exile*-like 'Watch That Man', where Ronson sprayed chords around like Keith Richards, and a reference to 'Jagger's eyes' in the lyrics. For the most part the album abandoned the clarity and detachment of *Ziggy* to concentrate instead on the problems and pressure of being David Bowie. As well as the familiar groove of self-pity, *Aladdin* showed that Bowie, like many a tourist before him, was simultaneously appalled and fixated by America. The best of the tracks were at once brutal and funny, especially the fame-bashing of 'Cracked Actor'. Nevertheless, some of the more 'serious' lyrics suffered from self-consciousness, and the resulting volatility of tone, swinging from the sententious to the facetious, was a mess.

Although a good portion of the songs on *Aladdin Sane* were hard rock and roll, there were some deft musical touches: the backing singers and horns; Ronson's guitar, elsewhere so muscular, on 'Lady Grinning Soul'; the salsa beat of 'Panic In Detroit'. While Bowie was already an extraordinarily gifted songwriter, it was often the Spiders' contribution that made the music soar. The reprised 'Prettiest Star' only began to sparkle after Ronson (sticking closely to the Bolan playbook) cut loose on guitar, and

'Aladdin Sane' would hardly have scaled the ladder to songhood without Garson's subversive piano. 'Time' was another virtuoso feat by the band. Garson played in a 1920s 'stride' style, with a passing nod to Kurt Weill, while the rhythm achieved moments of restraint and even subtlety. *Aladdin* wasn't just Bowie plus backing musicians, nor a laboratory for experiments between the edgy, breathless lyrics and Ronson's guitar. It was a true collaboration. 'I had so many dreams/I had so many break-throughs,' Bowie sang on 'Time'. But for much of the rest of the album, he was stuck in a lyrical rut, wallowing in his own self-doubt and grousing about everyone and everything not meeting his expectations. 'It was Ziggy's viewpoint about "Oh, God, I actually have made it and it's really crazy and I'm not sure what to make of this",' he admitted. Such was the lure of Bowie's name that over 100,000 British fans were willing to lay advance orders for the paranoid and, as the title hinted, demented posturing of *Aladdin Sane*, making it the fastest-selling album since the Beatles. It went straight to number one.

Six days after Bowie returned to London in triumph, he rang Ken Pitt's bell in Manchester Street. His ex-manager (still in the throes of suing MainMan) was 'ecstatic' at the vision in pink flared suit and yellow platform shoes at his door. Pitt remembers how, even in this glittering attire, 'David went meekly into the kitchen to make coffee'. Bowie, he confirms, was 'charming'. He spoke about having seen performances by Bette Midler, whom he loved, and Liza Minnelli, whom he 'absolutely loathed', in New York. He viewed his own career with an expected modesty, if an equally disarming certainty that it was a great one. The meeting – which Pitt puts down to 'goodwill', as well as 'evidence of how far David had come' – ended with Bowie offering to send tickets to one of his London shows.

The British tour opened at Earls Court on 12 May. First night was a fiasco. The sight-lines in the vast hall, not entirely free of the tang of a recent horse show, were appalling, and the sound was likened to a railway platform tannoy. To compound matters, members of the rowdy audience danced naked in the aisles, flung bottles and brawled with bouncers as, in the mid-distance, Bowie tearfully pleaded for calm. It was his very own mini-Altamont. As if in further analogy, Jagger himself was backstage, mumbling about his view and calling the venue 'a toilet'. 'It was a farce,' says Ken Pitt. 'Someone should have gone ahead, sat down with the promoter and *fixed* it.' 'We sucked,' was Ronson's pithy verdict on the night.

From that sorry nadir Bowie travelled by train to Aberdeen, where he was met by a Daimler and taken to a suite in the Imperial Hotel. Several hundred fans were waiting for him. Bowie not only spent an hour signing albums, he donated passes to his two (sold-out) local dates. In both he connected with his audience in a way sadly lacking at Earls Court. Although the concerts featured some serious dance music, it was not something fans were ever going to hear in their power gym classes. Bowie's songs went too deep for that, although he retained the baffling ability to swing from his public, *Aladdin Sane* image to a genial 'Bromleyness'. First he thanked the Aberdeen crowd for being 'so nice'. Then, at the stage door, he signed yet more autographs. Hutchinson agrees that Bowie's new-found affability was no doubt nurtured by his rise to superstardom in the wake of Ziggy. But just as his early disappointments in America had forced him to cancel dates and economize, so the frenzy of the British tour prompted a period of soul-searching. His Leeds show was cancelled after being picketed by angry students. A shocked *Sun* reported that a young couple had had sex in the stalls of the Glasgow Playhouse while Bowie sang 'Oh! You Pretty Things'. The *Mail* sniffed that 'self-parody [had] ruined the performance' at the New Theatre, Oxford. To the *Daily Express* 'Bowie behaved more like a Soho stripper than a top pop star.' These were isolated voices: most reviews were ecstatic, and never less than respectful, and Bowie sold out in all thirty-seven venues. There was, however, a price for the relentless schedule he imposed on himself. Early in the tour Bowie developed a deep depression that grew out of exhaustion. His health, never robust, began to fail. He lost weight. After Bowie came off stage and went to his hotel he drank and took cocaine. When he felt tired, he snorted himself awake again. In the cocktail cabinet of the Daimler he kept sample phials for emergencies on the road. A mechanic found them when the car went in for service.

Meanwhile, Defries had locked antlers with RCA's Mel Ilberman over a possible third American tour. The record label was appalled over what they described in a memo as 'chronic mismanagement' of Bowie's affairs. Thanks to massive overheads, MainMan was still operating in the red. Expenses, if not quite on their former scale, were nowhere near matched by income. Long before the first chord of Bowie's proposed tour and several weeks before tickets would have gone on sale, the company had spent something like $150,000 in advance costs. In addition to hall rentals, tens of thousands had gone on housing, feeding and paying an entourage that had again swollen to nearly fifty. RCA, stung by the Beverly Hills saga, insisted that they would underwrite only a dozen modest venues, not the eighty arenas Defries wanted. When Bowie learnt of the impasse he hit on the grand gesture of 'retiring' from the stage, allowing both MainMan and himself to regroup and, not coincidentally, wringing banner headlines. By the last week in June, Defries, Zanetta, MainMan vice-president Jaime Andrews and Ronson had all been told of the ruse. Equally affected, but completely oblivious, were Bolder, Woodmansey and the other musicians.

It was, therefore, a relatively happy group – though the old grumblings about money remained – that closed the tour at the Hammersmith Odeon. Outside, a crowd of thousands, their glitter and sequins darting like a shoal of carnivorous fish, filed under the sunlit marquee: 'WE'RE ALL WORKING TOGETHER WITH DAVID BOWIE'. The choice of slogan was ironic. Among those palpably not consulted about Bowie's ploy were the fans, whose cheers turned to groans, his band, and RCA, whose own chairman admitted on 4 July: 'We knew as much about David quitting as the audience did last night.'

Informed by MainMan that 'The massive arenas of eighty US and Canadian cities will not now, or perhaps ever again, hold within their walls the magic essence of a live Aladdin Sane', the press, not only *Melody Maker* but heavyweights like the *Times*, began to ponder the riddle of Bowie's retirement. To some it spelt the death of his career. By cancelling the planned American tour Bowie was admitting his grasp had exceeded his reach. There were critics, such as Roy Carr, to whom 'he [was] copping out before he'd proved himself'. Friends like Julie Anne Paull, who spoke to Bowie backstage, believed he was on the verge of a nervous breakdown. There were even credulous fans who felt that, by self-destructing at the peak of his power, Bowie was somehow fulfilling the prophecy of Ziggy Stardust.

A more cynical explanation was also forthcoming. A few privileged insiders had heard of the reign of terror at MainMan – rampant with firings as it was with waste – and rightly guessed that the motive behind Bowie's statement was neither his health, nor his dark vision, but his finances. Retiring was a response not only to RCA's refusal to fund an American tour; it also led to a steady increase in Bowie's stock. For the next six months, Defries watched other, failed Atlantic crossings, like Marc Bolan's, as a fakir watches a snake. He knew, rightly, that demand would build until Bowie would automatically be able to return to fill the largest arenas. A year on, and MainMan's books would go from tens of thousands of dollars in red ink to millions in the black.

Eighteen months of touring had made Bowie fanatically wary of his privacy, even as he gloried in his fame. His plan now was to go into the studio, and into films, without subjecting himself to the hysteria of his fans. Retirement was a form of inertia by which he meant to keep busy. Even when he was doing nothing, he managed to chart trends. Within a month of Bowie's swansong, Ray Davies of the Kinks announced that he, too, was quitting, while Mick Ralphs and Brian Eno left Mott the Hoople and Roxy Music respectively. (A fourth group, Slade, went on hold when their drummer was seriously injured in a car crash.) It was the start of Bowie's lifelong habit of making abrupt changes, leaving imitators in his wake. The film of his farewell concert, shot by Don Pennebaker and finally released a decade later, was itself a pioneer of rock documentary. With its collage of fast cuts, jerky camerawork, live action and disturbing close-ups of Bowie in the dressing room, *Ziggy Stardust – The Motion Picture* was a tour d'horizon of glam rock up to 3 July 1973.

The gathering that night at the Inn on the Park was a mere party. The next day's celebration in the Café Royal (known as the Last Supper) was an event. Bowie sat at a table flanked by Jagger and Lou Reed, each wearing nail polish and lipstick, and kissing for the benefit of Mick Rock's camera. To add to the already surreal mood, a long-haired guitarist from Scarborough found himself waltzing with a baroness; Woodmansey spent the night vainly trying to establish whether he had, in fact, been fired; Angela and Bianca Jagger embraced no less closely than their husbands; a woman introduced only as Laurita exposed her ample breasts in front of Barbra Streisand; Peter Cook did a revue that turned 'fuck' into the longest one-syllable drawl in history, and then went on from there to get dirty. Bowie was driven home at 5.30 in the morning.

On 5 July the Bowies attended the royal première of *Live and Let Die*. On the 6th and 7th they stayed locked in Haddon Hall. On the 8th they took the boat train to Paris. A short limousine ride, and Bowie was at the Château d'Hérouville to record his next album. Called *Pin-Ups*, it was to be an oldies collection, Bowie's homage to his favourite R&B hits from the sixties. By coincidence, Bryan Ferry had recently been recording his own nostalgic album, *These Foolish Things*. When he discovered that Bowie had had the same idea, he was enraged. 'It's a rip-off,' he grumbled. He tried to convince his label of it. Ferry, recognizing how small were his chances of outselling Bowie, asked that Island file an injunction to stop RCA from rush-releasing *Pin-Ups*. No action was taken, but he did send a telegram to the Château d'Hérouville. In the end both sides agreed to co-exist, with the result that the albums were launched on the same day, 3 November 1973. Both were hits.

Bowie would later remember the *Pin-Ups* sessions for the warm summer sunshine, the visitors to the château, where parties of twenty regularly sat down to dinner at the long refectory table, and the green Cadillac that nightly shuttled guests to the Malibu Club in Paris. Ronson, too, would speak fondly of life in Île-de-France, and of Bowie and himself alone in the limousine 'pissed, half-blinded by fag smoke' after the chauffeur abruptly quit. Also present in the studio were Mick Rock, who recalls Bowie as 'very up and relaxed' and, bizarrely, Lulu, darling of the Beat Boom, who had known Bowie as Davy Jones and who now recorded 'The Man Who Sold the World'. Absent, though, Ronson said, 'there in spirit' was Mick Woodmansey. MainMan had chosen the drummer's wedding day to fire him, quickly recruiting Aynsley Dunbar in his place. Woodmansey retaliated with a flurry of phone calls and messages to the studio. Despite these distractions, *Pin-Ups* was finished by mid-August, when the

Bowies, Ronson and Suzi Fussey (whom he later married) rented a villa in Rome. 'Sorrow', a limp retread of the Merseys' hit, was released as the album's first single, overlapping with Decca's crafty reissue of 'The Laughing Gnome'. *That* song, which Pitt recalls 'died' in 1967, now rose to number six, selling 300,000 copies and earning a gold disc in the process.

Pin-Ups itself made number one, giving Bowie a total of six albums currently in the British chart. It earned mixed reviews. *Pin-Ups* celebrated Bowie's reason for being: raw, sometimes mawkish R&B with few overdubs or edits and even fewer stylistic departures. Without straying from the songs' prototypes, the album toasted rock's sixties roots with covers of seminal hits by the Kinks, Pink Floyd and the Yardbirds. The high point was the Pretty Things' teenage anthems 'Rosalyn' and 'Don't Bring Me Down' (so faithful to the originals, says Phil May, that 'Dave even screamed in the same places I did'). The depths were plumbed by 'Here Comes the Night', ruined by Bowie's crooned vocal and croaking sax, and the Who's 'I Can't Explain', stripped of its manic beat and, in a curious decision of pacing, reduced to an aimless drone. For *Rolling Stone*, *Pin-Ups*, despite its charm, revealed an essential truth: Bowie flew higher off original work than off affectionate parody. His covers suffer by comparison both with *These Foolish Things* and the tributes on Lennon's *Rock 'n' Roll*. To *Sounds* there was a sense in which Bowie 'used R&B as a prop, not a springboard'. Another critic condemned *Pin-Ups* as 'shoddily carpentered', a work that would leave Bowie's credibility 'tottering'. It did nothing of the sort. By Christmas, *Pin-Ups* was selling 30,000 copies a week; it spent five months in the chart and succeeded perfectly as the breathing space Bowie intended.

Pin-Ups came with brief hand-scrawled liner notes, and a *Vogue* photograph of Bowie and Twiggy, earning it an entry in the list of all-time classic album covers. He was already the best-selling artist of his day. Now Bowie was adding fame as the most photogenic rock star ever. Starting with *The Man Who Sold the World*, his LP covers were almost as much part of pop mythology as their contents. Justin de Villeneuve, who designed the *Pin-Ups* sleeve, remembered Bowie's focus as like 'a bullet in flight'. Warhol added admiringly that 'David always tried out combinations that no one else would have dreamt of' and vetoed only 'dumb ideas'. A third photographer, Alan Motz, said he was 'heartbroken', because he had 'wanted to shoot Bowie met-amorphosing into an animal, but he didn't want that'. He was saving *that*.

Ziggy Stardust made his curtain call when, in October 1973, Bowie agreed to perform a television special for NBC. Shot over three days at the Marquee, the venue celebrated in *Pin-Ups*, *The 1980 Floor Show* stuck close to that album's theme of lost innocence. There was nothing naïve, however, about Bowie's last-ever double act with Ronson's guitar; about the costumes (a black leotard with a pair of rubber hands clutching at his heart for Bowie; a backless nun's habit for his guest Marianne Faithfull); or about the new, apocalyptical song '1984' with which he opened and closed the show. The special was never aired in Britain.

Late on the night of 20 October Ronson was taking off his make-up in the cold backstage area of the Marquee. Bowie, still wearing his Ziggy garb, walked in, appraising the bare concrete floor and broken window, and sat down. Even rock could have produced no odder sight than these figures in knee-breeches and fishnet leotard, the Bromley boy and the municipal gardener, slumped in the tiny dressing room of the club where they met. Nearly four years had passed since Ronson had first watched Bowie play. Their relationship had worked in close connection with their experience. And now the whole saga had come full circle. Bowie's American and British influences had been vented in, respectively, *Hunky Dory* and *Pin-Ups*. With *Ziggy Stardust* he found success with songs that soared, deceptively simple beats and a comic-book character. Then fame and all its problems, together with all Bowie's problems, had been anatomized, sum-marized and brilliantly distorted in *Aladdin Sane*. Truly it seemed that, with the *Floor Show*, the old friends were played out as a partnership. Now, as Ronson stood up, he watched Bowie gazing at himself in the filmy mirror. 'We just nodded at each other, he looked over and grunted. Then he went back to doing his face. And that was the end of me and David.'

5

THE EUROPEAN CANON

At the same time as Bowie abandoned Ronson he also left Haddon Hall. For nearly two years, ever since the success of Ziggy, the flat had become a virtual fortress against the fans. When Bowie returned home at Christmas 1972, the postman had brought six bags full of mail; the phone rang perpetually; and more than one Bowiephile tried approaching the back door by way of the Beckenham Place golf course.

On tour, Bowie was endlessly accommodating. He signed as many autographs as time and energy allowed. He posed for amateur photos, discussed his concerts, his albums, fellow stars such as Bolan, and his favourite-of-favourites Lou Reed. The lobby of his every hotel drew a large contingent of Bowie Boys, dressed as they thought he dressed, who delighted in his conversation and witty, tart remarks about pop.

During the brief periods he spent in Beckenham Bowie could barely set foot from his door. His car was mobbed, he was recognized by everyone, and his son was not neglected – a woman once tried to abduct Zowie in the street. Haddon Hall, like Ronson and the Spiders from Mars, inhabited an earlier, vanished world. When Bowie returned from his second American tour he began to complain that the flat was 'a zoo'. The pressures on him while on the road probably impaired his judgement in this case. As a public figure, Bowie was prepared to meet his fans halfway; as Ronson recalled, he went 'fucking berserk' when 'kids began to show up at home as well as the hotels'. The final straw came when, in September 1973, a teenage girl managed to climb through an open window and creep through the flat to the door of the dining room (where, as it happened, the Bowies were entertaining the Bolans). She stood on the threshold for a split second. Then the girl entered the room. She was naked.

'Joking apart,' Bolan used to say, 'it was a bad moment. The chick came over, knelt down in front of David and asked if she could kiss his foot. Instead of giving her the "I'm-not-worthy" spiel, Bowie stretched out a leg and said, "You can kiss my *boot*." Then Angie called the cops.'

The Bowies left Beckenham that October. For the next ten years Haddon Hall was a place of constant pilgrimage – and at least one visit by Bowie himself – until it was torn down and replaced by a housing estate. After briefly renting Diana Rigg's flat in north London, the couple moved to Oakley Street, on the Chelsea side of Albert Bridge. The five-bedroom house was decorated in sci-fi style, with plastic sofas, sculptures that glowed in the dark, and a gigantic Kevin Whitney painting described as 'somewhere between Salvador Dali and Norman Rockwell'. More important than even the house's decor was its proximity to Mick Jagger in Cheyne Walk. The two stars now formed a mutual appreciation society. Bowie and Jagger went drinking and gambling together; they heckled Diana Ross from backstage at the Albert Hall; they even found themselves at a heavyweight boxing fight. It was about this time that two slurs began circulating among the London rock aristocracy. One was that the Rolling Stones' single 'Angie'* referred to Angela, who was said to be Jagger's lover. The second was that the head Stone was also sleeping with her husband.

The truth was more complex. During *The 1980 Floor Show*, Bowie had reunited with Marianne Faithfull, Jagger's ex-lover, now describing herself as a poet. A floor manager remembers her reading to him from a calf-bound book backstage at the Marquee. At the end of filming, Bowie smiled shyly, literary interests quickening. The next day, having parted from Ronson, he showed up at Faithfull's flat, laden with white roses. 'Let's not talk about poetry,' Bowie said. 'I'd like to tell you something, if you won't

---

*Actually a ballad to Keith Richard's daughter, born in April 1972.

think I'm mad. The eyes are my soul and the face is my conscience . . .' The rubric had the same happy result as in Japan. Bowie and Faithfull never became what she and Jagger once were: a public item, exemplars of Swinging London. They did, however, carry on a long and undetected affair during his first winter in Chelsea.

Through Faithfull Bowie met Amanda Lear, who in turn introduced him to Fritz Lang's and Buñuel's work while sharing his bed. He dallied with the transsexual Wayne – later Jayne – County. And he renewed relations with Ava Cherry, the exotic black teenager with cropped platinum-blond hair who flew to London and, to her surprise, found herself invited to live in Oakley Street. At first the ménage à trois went well enough. Not only was Bowie Cherry's lover; he insisted that she could become a star, and spent weeks supervising sessions for her first album. Possibly it was this show of support that finally snapped Angela's patience. 'In the third quarter of 1973 [Bowie] began breaking our unspoken rules,' she writes. 'He started sleeping with a big, beautiful black woman who was *my* friend.' Suddenly, over the Christmas holiday, Angela's indifference ended. Cherry was evicted from Oakley Street and installed by Defries in a flat in King's Road. The tracks she recorded with Bowie were never released.

A meeting also took place with William Burroughs. This singular collaboration had its roots in the Arts Lab movement, where Burroughs, in *Growth*'s words, loomed 'like a male version of the Statue of Liberty'. His films *Towers Open Fire* and *Cut Ups* were constantly screened at the UFO and other London underground clubs, while *Naked Lunch* and *Nova Express* were virtually specifics for anyone interested, as Bowie was, in testing the guardrails defining the limits of normal behaviour. On 17 November 1973 Burroughs was invited to lunch at Oakley Street – a meeting he describes as 'pleasant' – where Craig Copetas of *Rolling Stone* moderated a three-way interview.

Asked about the image that people had of him, Burroughs complained, 'They try to categorize you. They want to see their picture of you and if they don't see their picture of you they're very upset.'

'You could sense David's antenna quivering,' Burroughs says today.

'I'm an awful liar,' said Bowie. 'I'm not sure whether it's me changing my mind, or whether I lie a lot. It's somewhere between the two. I don't exactly lie, I change my mind all the time. People are always throwing things at me that I've said and I say that I didn't mean anything. You can't stand still on one point for your entire life.'

Within days of finishing *Pin-Ups*, Bowie had been hankering to get back to the studio. His next post-Ziggy project was to be an adaption of Orwell's *1984* into a West End musical, with an accompanying album and film, little of which ever happened. Most nights at the Château d'Hérouville Bowie had read aloud from *The Wild Boys*, comparing Burroughs' style to the 'glitter apocalypse' of his own new songs. By the time he came to record *Diamond Dogs* early in 1974, he was eager to share his excitement over his new discovery. 'I use Burroughs' cut-up technique,' Bowie explained in the BBC documentary, *Cracked Actor*. The camera panned in to show Bowie tearing sheets of lyrics down the middle and moving the edges against each other to find new lines created in the process.

Three years later he told a reporter, 'I still incorporate a lot of Bill's ideas, and I still purposely fracture everything ... It's still a matter of taking my three or four statements and inter-relating them.'

Later in the seventies, Bowie arrived at the Bunker, Burroughs' New York apartment, carrying a four-foot-high vase of flowers which he set at his host's feet. He also had with him a Polaroid of a painting he was working on. 'It was a portrait of me,' says Burroughs. 'Nearly complete except for the face, which was blank.' Burroughs, giving only a thin smile, posed while Bowie took more photographs. 'Then David suggested that we go out to lunch for "a talk". Those are two things I don't much like – lunch and talk. He was an intelligent guy, down to earth, the antithesis of his public image – quiet, generous, smart. Inquisitive.' A friend might have thought that Bowie's probing of Burroughs' literary style was 'a fad – nothing he'd ever do again in the eighties, let alone today'. But he would have been wrong. In late 1995, the lyrics of Bowie's 'gothic hypercycle' *Outside* were subjected to a spin in his computer, industrializing the technique once limited to scissors and paste.

George Orwell's estate killed Bowie's *1984* adaption in its crib – although much of the new material he recorded in London and Hilversum tapped the same vein of urban decay. *Diamond Dogs*, the album released that spring, was a catalogue of Orwellian themes: hardly a track went by without 'Big Brother' harassing the 'wrecked-up' and 'paralysed' survivors of 'the year of the scavenger' or 'the season of the bitch'; even the love songs spoke of their heroes' 'hysterical detachment' from feeling. The first single (released, coincidentally, on Valentine's Day) was the classic, sleazy 'Rebel Rebel'. Lyrically, the song owed its rip to Bowie's lover Wayne/Jayne County, whose 'Queenage Baby' included the line 'Can't tell whether she's a boy or a girl'. Musically, it exploited Bowie's Rolling Stones connection by way of a 'Satisfaction'-like riff repeated four times. 'Rebel Rebel's distinctive two-bar hook, frequently included in the list of mighty guitar moments, has been widely credited to Bowie himself. After playing on *The 1980 Floor Show*, Ronson had succumbed to Defries' ambition to make him 'as big as David'. MainMan secured him a solo recording deal with RCA, took out advertisements (including a fifty-foot-high billboard in Times Square) and launched his first album, *Slaughter on Tenth Avenue*. Although Ronson's career was short-lived, it brought a violent reaction from Bowie. He phoned his old friend and said, loudly and repeatedly (like an 'angry MCC member', Ronson remembered), 'You're a shit, an incorrigible shit.' Ava Cherry, for one, knew what he meant. 'David felt that Mick had betrayed him [by] trying to be the star,' she told the Gillmans. 'He was very upset, very, *very* upset.' The issue, Ronson himself felt, was that 'the utterly ruthless musician' was sure to be, at least occasionally, an 'uptight' human being. Whatever the cause, the effect was that Bowie went into the studio without a guitarist.

One morning a session musician named Alan Parker, previously involved with Stevie Wonder and the Walker Brothers, took a call asking him to go to Olympic Studios in Barnes. He arrived to find 'a really friendly' Bowie perched on a stool with an acoustic guitar. 'He showed me the basic chords of "Rebel Rebel",' Parker says. 'I played it back on electric. David said, "Great" and I did it again on tape. The whole process took thirty minutes.' Parker's scorching riff helped make 'Rebel Rebel' a major hit single in both Britain and America. He was paid the standard session fee by MainMan, £20.

In March 1974 Bowie, after failing to turn Amanda Lear into a rock star, proposed instead that she should appear in an anti-Soviet romp called *Octobriana* (subtitled 'Adventures of the She-Devil'). He then conferred with John Dexter, director of the National Theatre in London and the Metropolitan Opera in New York, about his cherished *1984*. He interviewed *A Chorus Line*'s Michael Bennett, who turned down a job with MainMan on the grounds that 'David was too far out'. All of these individuals would later say exactly what Ronson said, that after years of knowing Bowie you found, suddenly, that you did not know him. He could leave relationships and pass on. He had a capacity, not just to forget, but to wipe out what no longer fitted the model of existence as he saw it. Neither *Octobriana* nor *1984*, nor the other projects he discussed with Dexter, was ever staged. Instead Bowie boarded the SS *France* to New York and his third, much-delayed American tour.

A revealing snapshot of the way Bowie and MainMan operated is given by Keith Christmas, the Beckenham guitarist last seen five years earlier. By April 1974 Christmas was at a loose end. One particular night, he recalls, he was staying with a French girlfriend in her flat in north London. No one else, to his knowledge, knew he was there. The phone rang while Christmas was in the shower and the girl announced that a man claiming to be David Bowie wanted to speak to him. 'He wouldn't even remember me,' said Christmas. He picked up the receiver. Bowie not only remembered him. He wanted Christmas to come on tour with him.

The next fortnight was C-R-A-Z-Y. First of all I had no visa. Defries fixed that, God knows how, with the American embassy. Someone gave me a ticket. Next thing I was being met in New York by a huge black guy in a limousine. He took me to the Sherry-Netherland, where David was holding court surrounded by freaks, weirdos and a guy taking hormone injections to grow tits. It was straight out of Fellini. David Cassidy was sitting on a chair outside. His career was on the skids and he wanted Bowie to write him a hit.

> David took me to a couple of gay clubs. He swung both ways – loved to tease the boys, wanted to fuck the girls. I remember him ogling this female group led by Suzi Quatro's sister. He gave *her* a seeing-to. David was doing amyl nitrate all of the time. He collapsed on the concrete stairs in one club. I grabbed him as he went down … There I was carrying a million quids' worth of rock star like a sack of spuds. A couple of nights later we were rehearsing alone in the studio. David took me into the loo, whipped out a double-sided razor and slashed into a huge chunk of coke. Sometime around then it dawned on me I wasn't going to be on the tour.

For Bowie, man's nature was to be born solitary: there was, he was fond of saying, no bond between one soul and another. Hence he had little if any understanding of friendship: his attitude toward Christmas is a gauge of his relations with fellow musicians:

> A year later, after MainMan flew me back home, I got another call from Bowie. This time I went to a studio in Hampstead. David said to me, 'Just jam for an hour.' I did. Then he said, 'Thanks, mate' and that was it. As I left he was hunched with a guitar, playing one of my riffs. He obviously liked it, because he nicked it for *Black Tie White Noise* eighteen years later.

When Bowie was told he was wrong by Defries, by the ranks of RCA and MainMan, by every concert promoter and even by his wife, there was only one conclusion to be drawn. Bowie, in staking his reputation on the largest rock tour ever, had to be right. His comeback was billed as a triumph not of musical enterprise, but of scale and revenue, the presentation more extravagant than anything he had done before, with a promotional blitz to match. Early in 1974 Defries spent $400,000 on TV advertising (billed to RCA), while in the eight weeks between 1 April and 25 May MainMan sent out seven separate mailings, each with a professionally bound book of photographs, a reproduction of the *Diamond Dogs* cover and customized gifts, to five thousand journalists across America. Now, in the space of a week, Defries announced both a new line-up (the guitarist Earl Slick took the place vacated by Christmas) and the first date – Friday 14 June – of a coast-to-coast 'theatour'. Bowie was back: official.

Diamond Dogs, released on 24 April, was Bowie's attempt to stick to the pop-rock songbook while emphasizing his literary credentials. In effect, this meant collecting influences and making something entirely fresh and new out of them, a feat not achieved by most of his highly touted contemporaries. There were nods to Orwell and to Bertolt Brecht, while 'Future Legend', the spoken piece that opened the album, 'rang several bells' for Burroughs' friend. Despite the grandeur and hype of the concept, most of the songs progressed down a raucous, R&B line, with some specific references: *Exile On Main Street*, the theme from *Shaft*, and Bowie's own 'Jean Genie' and 'Drive-In Saturday'. There were samplings of the Faces' LP *Overtures and Beginners* and Richard Rodgers' 'Bewitched, Bothered and Bewildered'. The cover art by Guy Peellaert, a Dutch surrealist much admired in Cheyne Walk, scooped the Rolling Stones by six months. (A threatened injunction by Jagger never materialized.) The album's themes of mutation, decadence and decay were brilliantly captured by the painting of Bowie metamorphosing into a dog, against a backdrop of two fat, grinning bitches. It was the very pose suggested by Alan Motz for *Pin-Ups*.

Bowie's high-flown intentions, so engaging on *Ziggy Stardust*, turned involuted and self-conscious on *Diamond Dogs*. With the exception of 'Rebel Rebel', the album was slated as a leaden nadir, the work of a tired mind that had worried itself sick. The reviews were mixed; but expectations hurt *Diamond Dogs* more than any potshots from critics. Bowie's rock star pedestal made a precarious perch. Among the album's letdowns were the production, sugar-coating some songs and making others sound as if they were recorded in a matchbox; the cynical contrivance of the whole concept, described by Lester Bangs as a 'queasily burlesque' and 'sterilely distasteful' jumble of pompous lyrics; and the unoriginality of the main theme, which was 'We Are Hungry Men' updated for the seventies.

On the credit side, much of the actual music was free, edgy and without frills. Bowie fleshed out the dozen songs with manic sound experiments: odd samplings, weird effects underneath the guitars' blur. The album was anchored by charged, garage-band riffing. There was praise, too, for Bowie's quixotic decision to tackle most of the songs without a group or even backing musicians. ('It was frightening trying to make an album with no support,' he admitted.) For the most part his playing was abrupt and real, all rough edges, spiralling guitars and sonic boom. That brutal honesty was part of *Diamond Dogs'* appeal. With or without the pretentious lyrics, the album had energy to burn.

Diamond Dogs was also the beginning of Bowie's post-modern outlook, in which a life was not a coherent story of biography, but merely a succession of moments, each unconnected to the last or the next. By 1974, not only archaic management figures like Pitt, but stalwarts like Ronson, Bolder and Woodmansey had all been erased. Bowie had already shown an impressive detachment from his friends. But he still spoke of wanting to be 'loved by the masses', rather than by his peers. At least one colleague believed Bowie was trying to use public adoration to replace what he had missed as a boy. According to Keith Christmas, 'one reason David wanted to give love [to audiences] was the desire to get it'. Here was a man crying out for it.

The result was an unprecedented fifty-date tour, elaborately rehearsed, flashily choreographed, and costing $250,000 simply to stage. The designer Jules Fisher was hired to create a set midway between *Diamond Dogs'* nightmare of urban decay and the stark, robotic world of *Metropolis*. Fisher's colleague Mark Ravitz compiled a list of props suggested by Bowie: 'tanks, turbines, smokestacks ... fluorescent lighting, alleyways, cages, watch towers, girders, beams, Albert Speer'. A young dancer named Toni Basil choreographed the whole two-hour perform-ance. Bowie himself supervised every effect. He even conquered his fear of heights to sing 'Space Oddity' while perched on a hydraulic boom that rose to a height of seventy feet above the stage and hovered over the front of the auditorium.

One of the reasons Bowie's dark vision worked was that it touched on a world that had gone wrong. In Britain millions sat, belted and shivering in unheated offices and factories, waiting out a miners' strike and the tripling of oil prices. America had been brought to a virtual civil war by Watergate and the ignominious departure of White House aides accused of perjury, deception and

obstruction of justice, culminating in the President's own resig-
nation. Bowie's themes, therefore, struck a nerve. The perverted
wreck of the *Diamond Dogs* set was, on one level, a metaphor for
the political cataclysm on both sides of the Atlantic. The tour was
also a triumph of epic production values: a brilliantly realized
package of slick ballads, hoary rock-and-roll anthems, surrealist
props and eye-bashing visuals (Bowie himself appeared in a
wardrobe of Yves St Laurent suits, tailored shirts with braces and
bright-red slippers), pregnant with a heavy, though never-
delivered message. For one reason or another, most of the other
fauna of glam rock, Marc Bolan and Slade and Gary Glitter, had
barely made the Atlantic crossing. By contrast, the *Diamond Dogs*
tour turned Bowie from a novelty act into a superstar.

Fisher and Ravitz presented the concerts as a theatrical
tapestry: it was the props and lighting and set pieces (such as
Bowie singing 'Panic In Detroit' wearing boxing gloves) that
brought the production to life. There were technical hitches. On
opening night in Montreal a motorized bridge crashed to the
stage with Bowie on it, and the sound system died; a week later
the hydraulic arm refused to work and Bowie was left suspended
in mid-air for six songs. Those were minor blemishes. A more
serious criticism was of the overkill and pretensions of the show,
in which the air of unpredictable charm once surrounding Bowie
was replaced by one of icy professionalism. To *Melody Maker*, who
sent correspondents to Montreal, it was a 'completely rehearsed
and choreographed routine where every step and nuance has
been perfected down to the last detail . . . It belongs on Broadway
or Shaftesbury Avenue rather than on the road. There isn't one
iota of spontaneity.' (A reader's letter in the same issue derided
Bowie for 'his ability to con people into buying his records – in
this respect only is he a great artist'.) Bowie brought into rock and
roll not only a native habit of introspection but also a quality that
survived and flourished in the relative isolation of English
suburbia in the 1950s: self-control. He used props to distract
attention from his extreme inhibition on stage. (Bowie, as Defries
admiringly put it, 'never sweats'.) Not only that – he demanded
equal restraint from the backing musicians (relegated to the
orchestra pit), for whom ad-libbing or deviation from the agreed
script was punished by a fine.

'I was getting all the problems every night,' Bowie remembered of the tour. 'Ten or fifteen people would be coming to see me and laying their problems on me because the management couldn't or wouldn't deal with it. It was no fun, no fun at all.' Five years earlier, Bowie had hired the bass player Herbie Flowers mainly because 'he had such an incredible name'. It was a decision he came to rue when Flowers, recruited for the *Diamond Dogs* tour, led a mutiny about money. An hour before going on at Philadelphia's Tower Theatre, Flowers and the drummer Tony Newman had a chair-throwing row with Bowie in his dressing room. Because MainMan intended recording the show for a live album, the luckless sidemen felt deserving of more than their standard fee ($190 per week, in Earl Slick's case). Flowers refuses to discuss the scene, but according to Bowie's bodyguard, 'David was hurling furniture around the room and screaming for Defries.' The musicians finally received the promise of an extra $5,000 each for their services. Two years later, they had to sue MainMan for payment.

Bowie retaliated by making melodrama of his colleagues' protest, distorting their threatened strike into grand, operatic treachery. The slightest show of disloyalty irked him; even Slick's suggestion about rearranging songs became a cause of friction. Underlying the group's frustration was the discrepancy between Bowie's accommodation at the Sherry-Netherland, the Pierre or other similarly appointed hotels, and their own lodging at whatever Holiday Inn was available – not to mention the contrast in lifestyles. In June, during an advance trip to Florida, Defries got a call from New York that shocked him. Bowie had been given $50,000 credit to last for a month, but had run through that in ten days, and needed a fresh infusion of cash. In the period from early April to late July, a member of the group believes Bowie may have spent upwards of $300,000. 'You can guess where the money came from,' he says. By the time the first half of the tour ended in New York on 20 July, Defries had borrowed beyond his debt limit at RCA and the ten backing musicians had been lured into a complicated scheme that withheld part of their wages in return for residual and other benefits that never materialized. Along with the theatrical production, this act of economic cannibalism was one of the legacies of the tour.

Among MainMan's antics were follies that made Bowie seem to possess Spartan self-discipline. By 1974 the company occupied three separate New York offices with luxurious suites for Defries, Tony Zanetta, Leee Childers, Jaime Andrews and Cherry Vanilla. A west-coast branch was opened in Hollywood, where, for Iggy Pop's drinking, eating, fighting and drugging, Defries excused him all forms of payment except one: he had to 'keep David amused' by telexing sexual gossip to New York. Expensive weekend lodges were rented in both California and Long Island. Angela, during her frequent forays on Fifth Avenue or Rodeo Drive, thought nothing of spending $5,000 of MainMan cash on clothes and shoes. Thousands more were being lavished on limousines, private planes, helicopters, and MainMan subsidiaries notable only for the sloth of their management. By mid 1974, as fast as the money came in from RCA, it was haemorrhaging out again.

On 11 August Bowie spent a week at Sigma Sound in Philadelphia to record another album. The zeal with which he took to the spiritual home of Gamble and Huff's 'Philly' sound – a crisp big-band dance beat with black flavour – showed that yet another sea change was under way. At Sigma Bowie met the guitarist Carlos Alomar, and an obscure and then vastly overweight singer named Luther Vandross. According to the bass player Willie Weeks, hired for the session, 'David was an incredibly smart guy, with a real feel for soul. He told me he'd listened to all those records when he was growing up in London.' Bowie returned to his home town for a weekend and played, uncredited, on the Rolling Stones' *It's Only Rock 'n' Roll*, as well as the glorious shambles that became Ron Wood's *I've Got My Own Album To Do*.

For the second half of the tour, starting in Los Angels on 2 September, Bowie radically revamped both his group and the set to become a kind of *Soul Train* revue. While no one doubted the sincerity of his efforts, the hard truth was that men like Alomar and Weeks, with their jazz-funk stylings, were not best placed to re-create the pure pop songs of *Hunky Dory* and *Ziggy Stardust*. Press reaction to the new production was brutal. To *Creem* it was 'David Bowie's return to the boards in Afro-Anglican drag ... a scene right out of *God's Trombones* as rendered by the Ohio Players

... a parody of a parody ... the singer/dancers all massed like the Mormon Tabernacle Choir ... as full of ersatz sincerity as Jerry Lewis ... A show that would wow them in Vegas.' In the *New York Times*' more austere view the performance was 'disappointing' and Bowie 'looked self-consciously uncomfortable without routines to act out'. Another critic claimed that the evening was 'like a huge, sumptuous birthday cake made out of cardboard with a hollow centre'. Bowie himself would reveal a year later, 'If anything, [it] helped establish that rock and roll is a pose.' By the time the tour wound up on 1 December there was a sense of physical and creative exhaustion. The last concert in Atlanta was like a case of euthanasia. At the final-night party in the Hyatt-Regency hotel, a zombie-like Bowie watched indifferently as eight armed policemen raided the room looking for drugs, finally arresting Tony Zanetta. The next morning Defries bailed his company president out of jail. Bowie returned to New York by car, and checked back into his suite at the Pierre.

The Bowie of late 1974, the corpse-pale recluse who existed on a diet of orange juice, coffee and cocaine, was brought to life by a young BBC director named Alan Yentob in his film *Cracked Actor*. Merely setting up the documentary was like a musical comedy, with dark undertones. First Yentob was vetted by Defries and Zanetta. He waited several days in his hotel in Los Angeles. One night, as Yentob was scratching notes about the 'coke psychosis' of the people surrounding Bowie, the phone rang at his bedside. 'I'll break your goddamned neck if you try to set David up – *capisce?*' a voice said. Next Yentob met Bowie himself in a restaurant. The mutual impression could not have been a better one. 'David was charming,' says a BBC staffer. 'Like the only sober person in a roomful of drunks.' A deal was struck allowing Yentob to film a concert, interview fans, and even to accompany Bowie as he sat in the back of his MainMan limousine, shrouded by his dark glasses and fedora, listlessly playing 'You Make Me Feel Like a Natural Woman' on his tape-recorder.

During his on-camera interview, Bowie dropped the mask. Far from suppressing his appetites and emotions, it seemed he wanted to chatter about them to the BBC. 'I got lost at one point,' he said, 'and couldn't decide whether I was writing the characters or whether the characters were writing me, or whether we were all one and the same.' In his view, he told Yentob, nothing was caused by people's personal failings or weaknesses, but by strange maladies. Thus Bowie's theatrical role-playing became an identity crisis. His cocaine habit was dignified as an illness. When *Cracked Actor* was first shown on 26 January 1975, it drew glowing reviews and elicited widespread sympathy for its subject. Bowie later told Yentob he had watched the film again and again, 'because it told the truth'.

In September 1974 RCA released Bowie's stage version of the Eddie Floyd–Stax pastiche, 'Knock On Wood'. A month later the *David Live* album followed. The seventeen songs fell somewhere between a radical reinvention of Bowie and the next step on a continuum from the jagged sound unveiled on *Aladdin Sane*. There were dramatic reworkings of 'All the Young Dudes', 'Moonage Daydream' and 'Jean Genie', all with a creeping transition from pop to disco. 'Sweet Thing' and 'Watch That Man' were Bowie and his group at their Philly-soul peak. With a month of studio overdubbing, *David Live* might have celebrated the essence of black culture and style while breathing new life into a career established but creatively exhausted since *Ziggy Stardust*. As it was, pressure of time meant the album was played too fast, mixed too quickly and released too soon. Tony Visconti, startled to be asked by his old – and suddenly conciliatory – friend to produce *David Live*, remembers it as 'one of the shoddiest albums I've ever done, and I'm not proud of it at all'. It was later disowned by its author. 'I've never played it,' said Bowie. 'The tension it must contain must be like vampires' teeth coming down on you. And that photo on the cover ... It looks as if I've just stepped out of the grave.' (He had, in fact, emerged from throwing a chair at his bass player.) A better title, he suggested, would have been 'David Bowie Is Alive and Well and Living Only In Theory'.

With the commercial triumph of 'The Year of the Diamond Dogs', Bowie was treated as an American celebrity, though his gravity and tensely withdrawn expression seemed to mock adulation. His silences gained weight. Rapt and reverent inter-viewers like Dick Cavett listened to the slow procession of scrupulously chosen words, rather toneless, but carrying the breath of godlike authority. In Los Angeles Bowie advised Marc Bolan to get a 'Hollywood-type image', not the 'porky pixie' look

REGISTRATION DISTRICT   Lambeth

Mb.O. BIRTH in the Sub-District of   Lambeth South   in the   Metropolitan borough of Lambeth

No.	When and where born	Name, if any	Sex	Name and surname of father	Name, surname and maiden surname of mother	Occupation of father	Signature, description and residence of informant	When registered	Signature of registrar	Name entered after registration
193	Eighth January 1947 Stansfield Road Stockwell	David Robert	Boy	Haywood Stenton Jones	Margaret Mary Jones formerly Burns	Public Relation Officer (children's homes)	M M Jones mother 4 Stansfield Grove Bromley Kent by declaration dated 9th April 1960	Fifth April 1960 To be registered 15 Grande	G.P. Curry	

CERTIFIED to be a true copy of an entry in the certified copy of a Register of Births in the District above mentioned.

Given at the GENERAL REGISTER OFFICE, under the Seal of the said Office, the ___ 3rd ___ day of ___ July ___ 19. 95

BXBZ 811318

...e birth certificate.

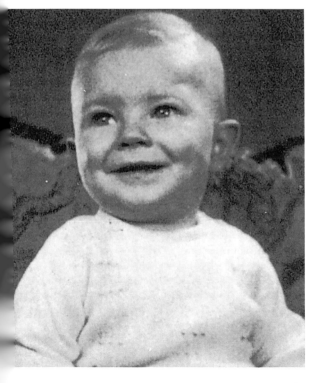

The one-year-old David Jones, whose 'knowing eyes' were much admired by his family.

Opposite page
Bowie's wedding to
Angela Barnett,
20 March 1970. His
mother Peggy *(centre)*,
though uninvited,
signed the register
and posed for
photographs
afterwards.

4 Plaistow Grove, Bromley.
Although Bowie would later
claim to be a child of the
Brixton ghetto, he spent
fourteen years living
in Kent.

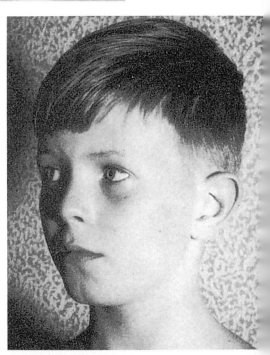

David at about
the time the
family made the
short journey to
suburbia, 1953.

Bowie's first real -
and much-maligned -
manager Ken Pitt,
seen auctioning
his ex-client's
boots for charity.

Bowie in his post-hippie,
Bob Dylan phase. Folk
music soon gave way to
guitar rock, moody
science fiction and
camp drama to
create Ziggy Stardust,
still his best-known role.

Bowie's relationship with the guitarist Mick Ronson began and ended in the same London club. In the four years in between, their stage act yielded some of the classic images of rock and roll.

Bowie would later dismiss the Ziggy look as 'a cross between Nijinsky and Woolworth's'. In fact, it was carefully designed to appeal to gays, straights and those in between.

As well as his bushy dark hair, keen nose and impeccable uniform of hip-hugging crushed velvets, unbuttoned shirt and a bare chest, Tony Defries was unblushingly frank in his own promotion. He also made Bowie a star.

After the split with Main Man-Defries, the ever-vigilant Corinne Schwab *(left)* took day-to-day control of Bowie's career. Her brief extended to aspects of his social life, including this visit to the 'lurid' Alcazar Club in Paris, raided by the drugs squad later that same night. Seated, right, is Romy Haag.

Opposite
Ziggy's farewell performan
television special for
Heavily edited in America, i
never shown in Br

Bowie, Angela and their son Zowie, also called Duncan in case,
as a grown-up, he objected to his 'kooky name'. He did.

flaunted in Britain. Iggy Pop joined the tour in the role of a wayward younger brother; Bowie allowed him to sleep on the floor of Stuey George's room in his hotel suite. There was a meeting, on level terms, with a man whose very name embodied upper-echelon rock celebrity. In September 1974 John Lennon, sitting in as a disc jockey on Radio WNEW in New York, ad-libbed a trailer for Women's Night: 'All females admitted at half price. Oh, good, Bowie can get in!' Within three months, groping his way back toward the pop scene, Lennon participated in studio sessions with the rival stars of glam rock. Elton John greeted the chance to collaborate with a childhood idol as 'stunning'. It must have been stupefying to Bowie, who was high on cocaine and vomiting before meeting Lennon in New York. A result of that tentative session was 'Fame', Bowie's first number one, and the song that made him into a household name in America.

Celebrity brought its rewards. MainMan had long been used to the nightly arrival backstage of luminaries like Bolan and Bryan Ferry. But even Bowie's head turned when, swathed in purple and flanked by six male escorts, Elizabeth Taylor appeared for his concert in Anaheim. Over the next month an unlikely friendship developed between the forty-two-year-old actress and the young rocker. At three in the afternoon, as soon as Taylor awoke, she began her day by phoning Bowie at his hotel. They talked about clothes and make-up, and transmitted the most scandalous gossip from the latest Hollywood parties. According to a woman close to Bowie, 'they sounded like sisters – it was all stuff about face cream and colonic irrigation'. Taylor's patronage extended to offering Bowie a part in her new film *Bluebird*. The two friends discussed the project one afternoon as they floated on the boating lake in the grounds of Bowie's hotel. At some stage a creative dispute seems to have occurred. According to a bellboy named Ryan Ward, 'Bowie pulled in the oars and let the dinghy drift through some lilies. I saw them coast by. David must have said something, because [Taylor] just hauled off and yelled at him: "Take me back, take me back!" Bowie reached for the oars, but missed them and fell backwards into the boat. A rope had to be sent for to rescue them.'*

---

*Bowie's other brush with Hollywood in 1974 ended equally badly. Hearing

Furious to have come so far only to have Taylor change her mind, Bowie booked himself passage to England. He spent a few days shuttling between hotels and borrowed flats before returning to Chelsea. His presence set off a ripple of excitement among rock society. One evening a party including Bolan, Ron Wood and Gary Glitter descended on 48 Cheyne Walk. Bowie, anticipating a night of heavyweight debauchery, was merely shown the Jaggers' wine cellar. When he announced plans to return to New York at Christmas, he bragged to Bolan of being 'bigger than Mick now', and told his friend Scott Richardson 'the Stones have had it'. Bowie, *Sounds* agreed, was 'king of the scene'.

In Manhattan Bowie, Angela, Zowie and Ava Cherry moved from the Pierre to a rented house on West 20th Street. The three-storey brownstone, in a tree-lined block, was furnished like a set abandoned after the feckless Soviet production that *Bluebird* became, all rumpled fabrics, heavy rugs and, in certain key places, none too hygienic. A simple wooden table stood in the attic, which Bowie used as his bedroom. Visitors to the house found it strangely depressing and claustrophobic. In the two months he visited 20th Street Defries never once saw the curtains open. Early in the new year Bowie took up residence at the Barclay Hotel in Philadelphia, commuting to Sigma Sound, where he finished his follow-up to *Diamond Dogs*, tentatively called 'Dancin'', on 12 January 1975. On the last night in the studio the group burnt the unwanted outtakes, and then invited a dozen fans into the control room to hear the album. At three in the morning Bowie substituted a new title: *Young Americans*.

A torrent of letters – unsigned, full of adjectives, superlatives and triple underlinings, and some enclosing Polaroids of their senders – had begun arriving before he got home to New York. The majority were opened by Bowie but Angela intercepted some and was aghast: long used to her husband's ways, to openly share

---

rumours of a film treatment of Frank Sinatra's life, he made it known that he would like to play the title role. Bowie and Ava Cherry then went to see Sinatra perform in Las Vegas. They waited backstage for some time. Finally a note came out of the dressing room saying Sinatra was too busy to meet Bowie, and that 'no English fag' was going to play him on screen.

him with strangers was a new experience. These were long, sometimes painfully intense love notes, hinting not just at sex but at complex emotional affairs. Bowie was seeing literally dozens of women.

There was Bette Midler, who calmly stepped into a walk-in closet with Bowie at the Plaza Hotel and emerged an hour later; a member of the Three Degrees, with whom, for a week or two, he announced he was 'really in love'; and, acting as a through-line, Ava Cherry, for whom he wrote 'Can You Hear Me' on *Young Americans*. There were hundreds of perfunctory liaisons. A year later, even after an ultimatum from Angela, Bowie thought nothing of taking Ronnie Spector and a Berlin cabaret star named Romy Haag to bed together. As Bolan put it, 'Not too many gay gods have slept with five thousand chicks.' By 1976 Bowie would describe himself as a closet heterosexual, someone whose pulse quickened when he saw a beautiful black woman. He felt off balance and promiscuously in the grip of what he later called 'Jemimas' for the next several years.

Angela would say that she and her husband had last had sex in January 1973, by which she meant as a couple. There were, of course, exotic combinations with third parties for years to come. Knowing Bowie, Angela must have had an inkling that the 'Jemimas' he met in New York and Los Angeles would satisfy certain particular needs. Nevertheless, she turned a blind eye to the steady stream of models and starlets in the attic bedroom at West 20th Street, and even brought the flesh Bowie required to him rather than allow him to prowl about like a wild animal in search of prey. So long as they shared their escapades, she was happy to act as her husband's procuress and guardian of his fantasies. She did so not bitterly but with the glee of one discovering rebellion. There were moments of genuine empathy between the couple – as when Bowie played Angela 'Golden Years', a song he dedicated to her – and, as Zanetta says, 'in the proper mood they could give stunning performances of husband and wife'. Neither tolerated criticism of the other. 'She always spoke of David's [women] in the abstract,' said Bolan, 'in a very quiet, tiny voice.' Now, Angela had a flesh-and-blood rival to contend with. She screamed in falsetto.

Corinne Schwab had started life as a secretary in MainMan's

London office, where, apart from forging Bowie's autograph, her main job was to fend off creditors. Her début public performance was in *Cracked Actor*. Schwab was seen as a plainly dressed woman with dark hair sitting with Bowie in the back of his limousine. In 1974 she was merely an assistant. Within a year her duties had expanded to include driving, cooking, nursing, procuring and in general acting as the Maginot Line between Bowie and the world. Coco, as he called her, was fiercely – some said jealously – protective of her master. Many, like Bolan, admired the calming influence she brought to Bowie's life. Slowly, she began to appropriate one after another of Defries' management duties, until even he referred to her archly as 'the governor'. The charge against Schwab is that she became over-possessive. In the matter of controlling Bowie's infrequent utterances to the press; in granting access to some and aggressively rebuffing others; in her high-handed and sometimes arrogant treatment of Bowie's ex-colleagues; above all, in her assuming of day-to-day responsibility for her employer's life, Schwab effected a relationship in which, as Ronson said, 'she lived and died for David'.

The realization that she was being replaced dawned on Angela over several months. In 1975 there was a truce, during which the two women co-existed. By 1976 the previous air of mutual goodwill had given way to one of wary mistrust. The following year war broke out. At the end of the seventies Angela portrayed Schwab as 'the gatekeeper and the assassin, [someone who] did David's dirty work for him and took all the consequences', an apt description of her own role five years earlier. By the start of the new decade, Bowie's ex-wife was almost incoherent with hatred. 'Corinne lives in constant fear that I'm going to kill her,' Angela told the Gillmans. 'It's terrifying that she's still alive. But fortunately karma always takes care and she will suffer and she will die young because of the incarnate intensity of what she has accomplished.'

Bowie's relations with MainMan made Angela's with Schwab seem positively affable. The emotional roots of the ugly and protracted wrangling of 1974–5 lay in Bowie's policy on friend-ship, which Ronson described as placing 'blind faith in someone for a year, then dumping them'. The precise cause was money. Bowie, for all his record sales (over a million copies of *Ziggy Stardust* alone), existed essentially on loose change. MainMan saw to it that he always paid the maximum in British income tax, one of the reasons he lived in America for two years and thereafter in Switzerland. He had a morbid fear of debt-collectors, and the Capricorn's eternal dread of the poorhouse. Defries felt there was something 'whipped-up and fake' about Bowie's anxieties, which he put down to 'heavy cocaine use and paranoia'. Yet if a man chose pessimism, there was evidence for it to feed on at MainMan. By summer of 1974 the company was spending thousands grooming Dana Gillespie (promoting her as a lesbian fetishist) and others, like Ava Cherry, whose albums were endlessly debated but never released. Bowie complained frequently about Defries' spending ('on everyone but me', he added), once pitifully asking Zanetta, 'How did it come to this? It shouldn't have. You know it shouldn't have. I don't understand any of it.'

MainMan's books made sorry reading. The recession, a string of bad business decisions and a year-long credit binge kept the company insolvent. In London and New York, the unpaid bills from car-hire firms, hotels, department stores, newspapers, studios and sundry bars and boutiques provided a daily and depressingly visible answer to *Billboard*'s question, Why, when the company had Bowie, were they going broke? Meanwhile, British Customs and Excise were suing for delinquent tax. The electricity and gas companies had issued multiple final warnings. Bowie's personal credit cards had been cut off. MainMan's auditors complained formally that 'Proper books of accounts were not kept' during 1974, nor had they obtained 'full verification in respect to creditors'. The company showed a 'bad debt written off' to Bowie of £222,781.90, and a total loss of £444,000 for the year. The figure would grow to £622,000 in 1975. Defries' response was to announce plans to stage *Fame*, a play loosely based on the life of Marilyn Monroe, on Broadway. It opened and closed there on 18 November 1974, adding $250,000 of red ink to MainMan's accounts at a stroke.

On 29 January 1975, Bowie, pale, trembling and dazed, went to RCA's offices in New York. He told Mel Ilberman that he was leaving Defries and asked for a cash advance against *Young Americans*. After he got it, he negotiated office space and a car. The next morning a lawyer's letter revoking 'all agreements between you and our client David Jones, AKA David Bowie' arrived at MainMan. Two months of legal haggling followed, with Defries and RCA each suing the other and jockeying for control of *Young Americans*. The dispute was the banner headline of *Music Week* and made the arts columns on both sides of the Atlantic. There were fears that the whole matter would end in court, where, as Ilberman puts it, 'it would have gone ballistic overnight'. Finally, on 1 April, lawyers representing the three sides announced a settlement after forty-eight hours of continuous negotiation in the Century Plaza Hotel in Los Angeles. As Bowie watched millions of dollars of his future earnings being surrendered to MainMan, he broke down at the conference table and began to cry. There was poignancy in his ending his relations with Defries in the same state in which he began them. According to the agreement, backdated to 1 March, MainMan was to be paid 50 per cent of all Bowie's royalties from *Hunky Dory* through *David Live*, and a further 16 per cent of his gross earnings, from all sources, until September 1982. They were uniquely generous terms for Defries. Never in the chequered history of these relationships had a manager been awarded so large a stake in his ex-client. Bowie left the room in what may have been a state of clinical shock. A day later, completing his symbolic break with the past, he instructed his lawyer to settle with Ken Pitt for £15,000. Then Bowie shut himself up in West 20th Street, where for a week his howls could be heard through the locked attic door.

Defries always spoke wistfully of Bowie, blaming cocaine for changing the shy, intelligent man into a monster of vanity and deceit, and 'severely fucking up MainMan' in the process; an ordeal for which the company was rewarded by five million dollars in the seven years following the settlement. Bowie, for his part, never tired of making the contrast between himself, working for expenses, and peripheral figures recruited to MainMan at any price they cared to name. 'I slaved and made nothing,' he remembered in 1977. A year later Bowie told *Melody Maker*, 'My anger [with Defries] was spent a good couple of years ago, and all the feelings of being used, done-out-of and whatever have more or less melted into the mist ... Without some of those initial ridiculous fusses, some of the best things never come to light. It did come to light through the efforts of him and the crazies, so I guess I'm thankful. But I'll never condone completely what went on.'

Bowie and Defries never spoke again.

Angela, who had her own views about the man she stigmatized as Tony the Nose, now offered to replace him as her husband's manager. Tony Zanetta also applied for the job, mentioning what very little work would be needed to turn Bowie into a major film star. Despite feverish lobbying, neither of their services would, in the end, be required. Instead Michael Lippman, Bowie's lawyer in the Century Plaza negotiations, acted for him for nine months, until he, too, joined the long list of ex-managers. Lippman was backed by Pat Gibbons, Bowie's tour co-ordinator in the second half of 1974, a publicist named Barbara DeWitt, and a video adviser, John Dove, all of whom RCA installed in a suite in the Algonquin Hotel. Underpinning the new team was Corinne Schwab. Even Angela was prepared to admit that, at this point, 'Coco was exactly what I thought we needed. She spoke several languages, she had an aura of being cultured ... She would have killed for David.' Not everyone succumbed to Schwab's charm. John Lennon, presciently, thought that 'she and Angie [would] fight like bitches' over Bowie. The assumption, and Schwab's brief tenure of her employer's bed, created a classic emotional triangle. Angela did, indeed, fight for Bowie, and now played the role of one of the points of the triangle – one of the few 'conventional' wifely roles she did play in the marriage, in the time-honoured tradition of philandering husbands and their loyal women – with rueful humour and, many felt, a style out of keeping with the shock tactics of earlier years.

'Young Americans' was released in February 1975, at the nadir of Bowie's feud with Defries. The British single, at more than five minutes, was a relative flop. An edited version, remixed and mining the same radio-friendly country as Hall and Oates, was Bowie's biggest American hit yet. In some views a bold, avant-garde departure, in others a shameless fling at the disco market, 'Young Americans' – if not originally styled – was lyrically challenging and musically thrilling with its gospel chorus. In keeping with demand, it also came with a new Bowie image: a short, double-breasted jacket, baggy trousers, loosely knotted tie and a look somewhere between thin and cadaverous.

The album which followed was an implausibly bold leap in a new direction. Over the years, most British rockers had tried, one way or another, to become black-by-extension. Few had succeeded as Bowie did now. Boiled down to its essence, *Young Americans* was a record of high spirits and lively, colliding ideas, like the raunchy, bass-heavy rhythm and Mike Garson's free-jazz piano. If, as charged, Bowie's 'plastic soul' pose was an act in the same way as Ziggy Stardust was a role and Aladdin Sane merely a part, it was a supremely confident performance.

The album's starting point was James Brown, feel-good merchants like the O'Jays and Sly Stone, and, closer to home, Robert Palmer, the Average White Band and Elton John's 'Philadelphia Freedom'. To the native tradition of Stax and Motown, Bowie brought a spirited mix of polemics and poetry: he was the most lyrical of rappers. Thus the wry dig of 'Win' (anticipating the media obsession with yuppies by five years); the cryptic diatribe of 'Somebody Up There Likes Me' (a 'Hitler's on his way back' warning, said Bowie); and the heartfelt plea of 'Can You Hear Me', a love song to Ava Cherry. At its worst, the music lapsed into languid, repetitive instrumentals, like the easy-listening soundtrack of a smoochy Martini commercial. There were those who thought Bowie stuck too closely to the funk-rock playbook. On *Young Americans* he took his sideline interest in black culture and turned it into a full-blown obsession. At its best, the album was both infectious and dynamic. Bowie's vocal adroitness grew with the complexity of his writing. The seeds of yet another internal revolution had borne startling fruit. *Young Americans* heralded Bowie's maturation and, finally, his arrival as a major player in America.

Elegantly packaged, as ever – the jacket photo by Eric Jacobs won another entry in the list of classic album covers – *Young Americans* made number two in the chart. Ironically, it was kept off the top position by the soul vocal group the Stylistics.

In August RCA released 'Fame', the song Bowie co-wrote with John Lennon. In fact the number evolved, via Carlos Alomar and a riff lifted from Shirley and Company, through a half-dozen makeovers and a last-minute name change from 'Footstompin''. Bowie's strategy of improvisation and promiscuous borrowing – there were nods to Bruce Springsteen and James Brown – was more interesting than the music itself. It was, Bowie admitted, 'an escapist's way out', a brazen appeal to a younger, club audience, just ahead of the Bee Gees. 'Fame' reached number 17 in Britain, number one in America.

A sure sign Bowie had arrived as a global superstar was the plundering of his sizeable back catalogue. In September 1975 RCA reissued 'Space Oddity', backed by the *Hunky Dory* outtake 'Velvet Goldmine', giving Bowie a British number one. Decca executed the neat trick of re-releasing his first, eponymous album with the sort of PR push conspicuously lacking in 1967. Meanwhile, the official greatest hits collection, *ChangesOneBowie*, recreated something of the past magic. Unfortunately, since it overlapped with the release of a new single and album, it also made it clear that Bowie could not hope to pull off the same feat in the present. While the radio played full-length early recordings of 'Changes' and 'Suffragette City', it was obvious that the new 'TVC 15' was never going to compare.

In spring of 1975 Bowie moved from New York to Los Angeles. Since his first visit five years earlier, this gifted lyricist had felt free, in his songs, to fall into the innocence of exuberant high spirits as he experienced America ('New York's a go-go'; Lorraine 'shimmered and strolled like a Chicago moll'); and so the phrases kept coming until he reached California. Already homesick for London, though home meant no more than the rented house on Oakley Street, Bowie now drifted off into a binge of addiction, diabolism and madness. How he survived the punishing, twelve-month regime of drink, heavy drugs and forty-eight-hour work jags was a mystery. Bowie himself later admitted that the whole year was a blank, bulk-erased through substance abuse. His time in Los Angeles – which he came to regard as 'the most repulsive wart on the backside of humanity' – blossomed with pre-Aids reckless sex. It was also a year of cocaine-induced mental and physical violence.

Bowie lodged with his new manager, Michael Lippman, and with a *Playboy* centrefold named Claudia Jennings before renting a house at 637 North Doheny Drive in Beverly Hills. According to Angela, the home had a rhythm typical of its time: 'David would rise sometime in the middle or late afternoon and spend the evening and night doing drugs. Occasionally he'd get involved in a little music or business, but his most compelling activity was receiving roadies of famous bands who would arrive with fat packages of best Peruvian flake in their hand-tooled leather shoulder bags and leave with fatter little rolls of his money.' Along with Bowie's drug habit and enigmatic sex life – in 1975 he started affairs with both a black actress named Winona Williams and a male friend – went self-destructive skills of a high order. His principal thought was not his new album but rather how to get through a year during which, thanks to the drugs, he scarcely ate or slept, at the cumulative cost of ruining his health. A woman who met him in Doheny Drive remembers him sitting 'pale and dazed', his long, bony fingers tracing swastikas on the cloudy windowpane. Elton John thought 'David [was] getting too fucked up and was going to die' after seeing him in Beverly Hills. At some other time, John Lennon also saw Bowie sitting and sobbing in his bedroom, holding a handkerchief to his face and wretchedly mumbling, 'Why? Why?' In this distraught state – one that even Lennon thought abject – Bowie veered between rage and despair, with long periods of introspection, broken only by Schwab and the other courtiers. Some of his misery was communicated to Mick Ronson, who told *Melody Maker* in April 1975: 'I wish that Dave would get himself sorted out. He's so very confused ... What he really needs is to have some good friends around him, somebody to say, "David, fuck off, you're fucking stupid." He needs one person who won't bow to him. He believes that everybody has to say "Yes sir" whenever he says something ... I could kick some sense into him. That's what he needs.'

Until 1975 Bowie was not a man who allowed himself to be beaten down. In the face of adversity he had always demonstrated uncommon energy. Yet in Los Angeles there were days when his family illness, repressed as though it were a shameful weakness, surreptitiously took hold of his soul. To his inner circle these fits of Bowie's – pathological in their intensity, and unnerving to watch – were either evidence of his genius or indications of a breakdown. Most never bothered to differentiate. To the public,

Bowie, who attended the Grammys ceremony in the Uris Theatre, New York, was a reed-thin figure wearing a cape and a black hat. To Aretha Franklin, who accepted her award as Best Female Soul Singer with the quip 'I'm so happy, I could even kiss David Bowie', he was an 'off-putting' and 'sinister' character whose hand she refused to shake.

Fame, cocaine, isolation – it was enough to make Bowie paranoid, and it did. Sometime during 1975 he became convinced that John Dove, his personal video adviser, was a CIA agent; Ava Cherry, 'undead – a vampire'; Michael Lippman, 'the Mafia type'. He phoned Angela in Oakley Street to tell her he was in a house somewhere – he didn't know the address – and that two witches had cast a spell over him so that he could inseminate them in a black-magic ceremony, and thus bring a son of Satan into the world. (The two women turned out to be fans Bowie had met in a bar.) He began to dabble in pagan cults. Once again calling Angela, the ex-Bromley choirboy spoke of founding a new religion dedicated to – Pain. According to one of his Los Angeles girlfriends, he developed an interest in both sadism and masochism. He discovered a form of anal-erotic pleasure he would cultivate with Winona Williams, and others.

Bowie became fascinated with the occult, specifically with the satanic rumblings of Kenneth Anger. He drew pentagrams, took to sitting cross-legged, surrounded by flickering black candles, and, on Anger's advice, stored his urine in the refrigerator so that he could drink his bodily fluids. He was fixated with Walpurgis Night, 30 April, another of the dates, he told Angela, on which he would be expected to impregnate a witch. Bowie's strange tendency to act out the plot of *Rosemary's Baby* was quite enough to convince his wife he was becoming a mental cripple. Even after he had the house on Doheny Drive professionally exorcised, the general consensus was that he was still a victim of paranoid delusions. Certain fans hold that Bowie's best work came, as a sort of therapeutic exercise, in the years after he left Los Angeles. Others, like Angela, believe he never quite recovered from going off his head in 1975.

Bowie's bizarre behaviour continued even after he moved to Europe: witness his strange use of 'signals'. Throughout 1977 and '78 his letters were filled with numbers to which he gave mysterious meanings. The minute Bowie left Berlin in 1979, the numbers abruptly stopped. The origins of this peculiar arithmetic lay in Kenneth Anger's neo-paganism. Bowie also began using variations of the word AUMGN (gleaned by Anger from the Buddhist OM) as a mantra. In the final stages of what had become an obsession, he attempted to guess the date of his death by interpreting the figures in his correspondents' letters. Everything struck Bowie as a sign of fate. His mind latched desperately onto the number of lines in a letter or the number of times a given word was repeated, or even onto the dates it was sent and delivered. Starting from 1976, he also insisted that would-be interviewers supply him with their zodiac sign and an exact time of birth. With the help of a tarot deck, Bowie would inform the journalist whether the 'numbers were right' for a meeting.

According to Angela, besides music and black magic, her husband's only other long-term relationship was with drugs. By mid 1974 Bowie had graduated from marijuana and LSD to a $200-a-day cocaine habit. 'He's using more and more of it,' Schwab complained to Tony Zanetta. 'It's the only thing that keeps him going.' Drugs may, as Schwab said, have become a daily substitute for food and sleep. They did not, however, noticeably sweeten his temper. Bowie had always flirted with self-pity, and by mid-decade, under the cocaine's stress, it became full-blown paranoia. Keith Christmas remembers 'David babbl[ing] about "enemies" the whole time we were in New York. He thought his phone was bugged and he was being tailed.' One night in Detroit Bowie spilled the contents of an ounce bag of cocaine on his hotel room floor. He said nothing, merely dropped to the ground and began snorting the rug. The next day, visiting Ava Cherry's elderly parents in Chicago, he took out a phial and began sniffing it at the dinner table. 'David was really wired,' recalled the percussionist Pablo Rosario. 'He was doing too much cocaine. He looked like a tiger in a cage going from side to side of the stage.' Paradoxically, while Bowie was 'terrified' of being arrested by drugs agents, he thought nothing of producing his double-edged razor and snorting apparatus in front of total strangers. By early 1975 he was regularly using cocaine during business meetings at MainMan, shocking even the *Pork* graduates with his glittering eyes and constantly streaming nose, and greatly exacerbating problems with Defries. Finally even Zanetta was forced to recognize the symptoms of chronic addiction.

On 20 March 1976 Bowie's hotel room in Rochester, New York, was raided by the police. He was arrested on suspicion of marijuana possession – the charge carried a possible fifteen-year jail sentence – and released on $2,000 bail. Although felony charges were filed in Rochester City Court, the case never came to trial. That same week Bowie gave an interview in which he said, 'I want to be prime minister of England.' Then he began, with the aid of his book of magic numbers, to calculate the ideal moment for him to assume power.

By then Bowie was surrounded by an intricate court and protocol system not far removed from a government. In the cabinet chaired by Michael Lippman, Schwab took the role of first minister. She assumed responsibility for literally everything that it wasn't vital for Bowie to do himself, as well as certain essential jobs such as spoon-feeding Bowie ice-cream to build up his weight. They made an odd couple. She struck one observer as 'sturdy, down-to-earth, something of a slob', strangely out of place on a rock tour, and he seemed like a wild, starving animal, tied to her solidity. Schwab's brand of personal management served to enforce Bowie's rule on friendship, in which old colleagues and relatives would be dropped, as though some inexorable and godlike judgement had annihilated them from the face of the earth. In the early days, according to Keith Christmas, everything had seemed to point to a lifelong friendship – 'the all-night booze-ups, the good times and laughs' – but a peculiar hollowness echoed through Bowie's behaviour in Los Angeles and New York which was not there in Beckenham. Some blamed Schwab for throwing up a protective wall. Others, like Bolan, thought 'David [was] a mirror', and people saw only the image they projected on to him and he reflected back to them. 'I'm a . . . very cold person,' Bowie told *Rolling Stone*. 'I can't feel strongly. I get so numb. I find I'm walking around numb. I'm a bit of an iceman.' By early 1976 it was hard to know if he was a Bromley boy burlesquing a rock star, or a rock star burlesquing Bromley. 'I liked David Jones,' he said, with his eerie habit of speaking of himself in the third person. 'I still like him, if I could only get in touch with him.' As a further symbolic break, he dropped his first name and let it be known that he would answer only to 'Bowie'. One of the reasons he adopted his stage personae was, of course, to divert attention from the inner man. He was at his best playing a role, performing to a sea of undifferentiated faces. 'I disappeared into my work so I could give my life away,' Bowie recalled in the mid nineties. 'I wanted the attention, the adoration of the masses, the audience, because I was incapable of one-to-one communication.'

Bowie backed away from emotional risk. Even his heroes encountered his vigilant self-containment in the years after *Diamond Dogs*. Lou Reed and Ian Hunter were dropped, and Ronson was reduced to raging against the man he now called a 'fucking prat' in the press. When Bowie met Bob Dylan, the two walked away from each other after only a few minutes. Dylan 'hated' *Young Americans*.

Then there was his family. Since 1971 Bowie had regularly included coded snubs in his lyrics, such as the one linking 'my mother' with 'my dog and clowns' in 'Life on Mars?'. Despite his affectionate reference to John Jones on stage in December 1972, relations with Peggy lapsed into mutual hostility. When Ava Cherry told Bowie she loved her parents, he replied he felt nothing for his mother, and couldn't remember the date of her birthday. By 1976 he spoke of his family as mere 'make-believe' which his 'tougher self' now refuted. 'I haven't spoken to any of them in years,' Bowie told a reporter. 'My father is dead. I think I talked to my mother a couple of years ago. I don't understand any of them. It's not a question of their understanding me any more. The shoe's on the other foot.' Peggy retaliated by telling *New Musical Express* her son was 'a terrible hypocrite'. She complained that Bowie had called her only once in the last five years, that his monthly standing order to her had been cancelled, and that 'he owes *me*, when one looks at everything'. Bowie was furious. ('What would you like to say about your mother?' Jean Rook asked him in May 1976. 'Nothing,' he snapped.) Restoring the standing order was an act of charity, but, on balance, the benefit was still in Bowie's favour. For years he insisted his mother never speak about him to the media again. Other family members were threatened with sanctions if they so much as mentioned him in public. No such restraint, however, was embraced by Bowie himself. His 1980 hit, 'Ashes to Ashes', contained a dig at Peggy's scoffing at his career choice. Three years later Bowie told the journalist Hilary Bonner, 'I hardly ever see my mother and I have a stepbrother [sic] I don't see any more. It was my fault we grew apart and it is painful – but somehow there's no going home.' Bowie reconciled with Peggy when she attended his second wedding, as she had his first, in 1992. But there was no way back with Terry Burns. Bowie agreed to see his half-brother after he had attempted suicide by throwing himself out of an asylum window. He brought him clothes, books and a collection of his own albums, and led Terry to expect further visits in future. Over the next three years, Bowie's office dashed such hopes with a series of noncommittal letters. The two never met again.

Bowie, therefore, was not one to make a virtue of affection. 'I believe in loving a person impersonally,' he announced in September 1967. 'All emotion can lead to sickness in the mind.' Six years later he told William Burroughs, 'I'm not at ease with the word "love".' Mick Ronson spoke of coming across Bowie in the dressing room of one of the provincial theatres on the final Ziggy Stardust tour in 1973. He was wearing gloves and a silk kimono and sitting hunched in a canvas-backed chair. Suddenly Bowie began to cry, quietly and steadily. Under other circumstances, Ronson would have reached out consolingly and touched his friend's hand. But somehow the kimono was a symbol of the difficulty of sympathizing with a man to whom life had given so much. Ronson wanted to help, but in the end did nothing. His only reaction was a quizzical shrug.

Bowie rarely, if ever, fought with people. Often his talks with Defries had touched the borders of rage, but never went further. For the most part, Bowie expressed displeasure by retreating – either literally, as when he left the stage in Detroit because someone threw a roll of toilet paper at him, or figuratively, when he broke down and wept. As for Angela, 'David was one of the most tightly controlled human beings I've met ... Unapproachable on the clear, direct level ... Sad to say, he probably didn't have an honest bone in his whole emotional body.'

*

In October 1975 Bowie, recruiting Harry Maslin, the producer of 'Fame', recorded a new album, tentatively called 'The Golden Years', at Hollywood's Cherokee Studio. 'Maybe I'm not into rock and roll. Maybe I just use it,' Bowie had said. Pale and shrivelled from drug use, subdued as ever in public, he hardly looked like a man pursuing his goal. Bowie was, however, tireless in the studio. 'I hate sleep,' he said. 'I much prefer staying up, just working all the time. It makes me so mad that we can't do anything about sleep or the common cold.' Bowie's solution was a steady diet of amphetamines and cocaine. He thought nothing of pushing his band through punishing thirty-six-hour sessions, during which, apart from the drugs, his only nourishment was a glass of milk he fortified from a flask in his pocket.

The 'Golden Years' single, another successful stab at the burgeoning disco market, was released in November. It reached number ten in America. Bowie later said that the song had been written for, and refused by, Elvis Presley. Both Angela and Ava Cherry claimed to have inspired it. Bowie's wife speaks of him 'sing[ing] it over the phone for me just the way, all those years before, he'd sung me "The Prettiest Star". It had a similar effect. I bought it.'

After nearly two years in America, Bowie's albums, singles, concerts and even his appearance at premières and openings regularly made the arts pages of the daily press. His interviews captured and held the headlines of the trade titles. His pinched, sallow features could be seen in the 'People' columns of *Time* and *Newsweek*. Only Elton John and the ex-Beatles would surpass that level. But Bowie also played to a vast TV audience beyond the reach of any other rock star. In November 1975 he mimed to 'Fame' and 'Golden Years' on *Soul Train* (one of the first whites ever to perform there); guested on CBS's *The Cher Show* (launching into an interminable bump-and-grind duet with his hostess); appeared, via satellite, on ITV's *Russell Harty Plus* (pre-empting a broadcast of General Franco's funeral mass); and sat demurely for an interview with Dinah Shore (the 1940s singing star whose chat show typically included a clientele of elderly politicians and film stars). A rock hero and rock martyr, Bowie and his legendary fickleness enacted a fable about the price of fame, the levy of fate on good fortune. To Shore he was 'a burn-out, a pasty-faced guy in drag'. To the millions who heard Bowie sing and speak about his ambitions to act, he was a generalist, a surprisingly articulate and soft-spoken Englishman who hoped he 'might have something to say' in Hollywood.

Bowie often filled out the time between studio sessions and concerts by idly composing tracks for a non-existent film. In late 1974 he played a piece for Defries, who thought it 'staggering – as good as *Diamond Dogs*'. Bowie then retreated with a portable synthesizer into the house on North Doheny Drive, with the result that, by mid 1975, he was left with a sequence of show-stopping numbers that, as yet, had no show to stop. Such scripts as arrived with Lippman or Schwab invariably called on Bowie to act the part of a space invader, frequently with green skin, a formula only varied by a plan to have him co-star with Mick Jagger in a film about Byron and Shelley. Meanwhile, an agent named Maggie Abbott, impressed by the *Cracked Actor* documentary, began to lobby Bowie about a future project by the director Nic Roeg. This, too, dealt with a marooned alien. The crucial difference lay in Roeg's track record with pioneering films like *Walkabout*, *Performance* and *Don't Look Now*, and his assurance that, as Thomas Newton, the man who fell to earth in Walter Tevis's novel of that name, Bowie would be free of ray-guns, antennae, spaceboots and other sci-fi impedimenta. Angela, too, in the throes of losing her husband, showed her best qualities of doggedness and irony – an ability to laugh at herself as a victim of the very success she strove for on Bowie's behalf – and brought Roeg to a meeting in the house on 20th Street. As Bowie recalled, 'He arrived on time and I was out. After eight hours or so, I remembered our appointment. I turned up nine hours late, thinking, of course, that he'd gone. He was sitting in the kitchen.' Despite this unpromising start, the two men got on famously. Bowie showed unexpected sensitivity to the script's subtext; he understood Newton's 'incredibly complex, Howard-Hughes-type' nature, and impressed Roeg with his lively wit and intelligence. They shook hands on a deal that night.

The Man Who Fell to Earth was filmed in the sagebrush desert around Lake Fenton, New Mexico, in July and August 1975. Bowie received a basic $50,000 fee for his role, as well as a complicated series of percentages and advances for a soundtrack.

During the six weeks of principal photography he lived in a trailer – occasionally with Angela, more often alone – and refused all offers to house him in the Albuquerque Hilton. When not in front of the cameras Bowie spent hours combing a desert trading post and an Indian pawnshop for knives, pipes, fabric, shawls, cheap pottery and native bric-à-brac. He discovered the local vampire bats, and made numerous UFO sightings in the cloudless New Mexico sky. He also impressed Roeg and his fellow cast with the patience with which he submitted to hours of make-up, and his professionalism on set.

The film opened in March 1976 to reviews that were generally positive, and never less than respectful. There was particular praise for Roeg's vivid and unconventional direction, full of in-jokes (such as the scene where Rip Torn appears in a shop wearing a Santa Claus outfit) yet achieving a kind of realism through its mix of biting satire and sci-fi. Bowie, too, was singled out for his role as the duly exotic alien whose mission to earth ends in alcoholic ruin. According to Pauline Kael in the *New Yorker*, he achieved 'true insolence in [his] lesbian-Christ leering', exuding 'self-mocking androgyny' and a 'forlorn, limp manner and chalky pallor [that were] alluringly tainted'. There were inevitable barbs that Bowie had been typecast. The line spoken to him by one character – 'You know, mister, I don't think you get enough to eat' – precisely echoed the real-life comments of Angela and Schwab. Newton was Bowie's own persona, low-key, remote and capable of surprising, bravura touches. According to his co-star Candy Clark, the part called for 'very little true acting', relying instead on improvisation and a 'star presence' that kept breaking in.

'I didn't enjoy it as a movie to watch,' Bowie admitted. 'It's very tight. Like a spring that's going to uncoil, it's got these terrific tensions ... these very inhibited feelings in it.' On a personal level, the film was clearly a form of therapy, allowing Bowie to transform from pop star to actor, to pick up a character and then drop it – not live it fully, to the hilt. (He did, however, confess to 'being Newton for six months' after playing the role.) The quality of scripts arriving at Lippman's office also improved markedly. In the next year, Bowie was offered a part in Bergman's *The Serpent's Egg* and auditioned (unsuccessfully) for *The Eagle Has Landed*.

Unlike other rock stars, his acting was not a laughing stock. His portrayal of Newton – widely interpreted as a portrayal of himself – won praise that, compared with Mick Jagger's notices, sounded like a standing ovation.

Less successful, indeed catastrophic, was the business of the soundtrack. Bowie told a friend, 'If I just acted, I'd go raving mad.' He needed the challenge of producing music as well as images. Early in July, he flew Paul Buckmaster, the arranger of 'Space Oddity', to California and wrote two separate scores – broad washes of synthesizer that became known as ambient music – but bridled when told his work would be entered in a three-way pitch. The whole project gave Bowie a taste for offbeat 'mood' music, a genre that, as he said, 'rewards attention but doesn't require it', and led directly to the austere, minimalist tones of *Low* and *'Heroes'*. It also brought a crisis with Michael Lippman, whom Bowie blamed for his failure to secure him the original commission.

Meanwhile, the album recorded in Hollywood, now called *Station to Station*, was released in January 1976. The name change was significant: 'the European canon is here' Bowie sang on the title track, over a background effect of a train gathering speed (a theme he first used ten years earlier on 'Can't Help Thinking About Me'). Bowie himself spoke of the album as 'a plea to come back to Europe for me ... One of those self-chat things one has with oneself from time to time.' On *Station to Station* he channelled his aggressive repulsion for Los Angeles in a blizzard of angst-ridden vocals and raucous, head-banging guitar. The accompaniment was violent enough, but what really made *Station* work was the lyrics' unflinching candour. Bowie may once have been accused of musical insincerity – and would be again – but no one could ever say that lines like 'In this age of grand delusion/You walked into my life out of my dreams' weren't from the heart.

For years Bowie had insisted he was an artist, an all-rounder who just happened to ply his trade most lucratively in rock. Chris Farlowe's account of his friend sitting for hours by the jukebox or waiting in the rain at the stage door of the Marquee hardly supports this claim, though Bowie certainly liked to switch tack. Relatively few fans had stuck with him since the mid 1960s, and Bowie would find a way to exasperate most of them. The chilly, techno-rock tinge of *Station to Station* was yet another departure, a first step away from a top-forty *Ziggy* sound in the direction that would produce Bowie's best work. On one level, *Station* followed down a line from *Young Americans*. On another it anticipated the stylistic revolution of *Low*. The guitar histrionics and thumping bass of a track like 'Stay' were matched by the sparse arrangement and Jacques Brel-type crooning of 'Word on a Wing'.

All the trademark features of Bowie's 'plastic soul' era were present on *Station to Station*: the Barry White choruses, choppy guitar and lavish mix. Bowie used his full repertoire of melodramatic phrasing, particularly on the ballad 'Wild is the Wind' (the theme from a 1957 Western by *High Noon* composer Dimitri Tiompkin) and the Stones-like 'Stay'. With a rhythm heavy enough to cause migraines and a barrelhouse piano played by Roy Bittan, *Station* was, however, more than a mere sequel to *Young Americans*. The album's hard, jagged beat and air of seething rage gave a tantalizing glimpse of a path Bowie would profitably explore in the future.

Station to Station was a top-ten hit in Britain and America. Its second single, 'TVC 15', a slice of singalong rock freighted with lyrics that, like 'Life on Mars?', dealt with a parallel world in which the screen became life, was released that spring. It flopped on both sides of the Atlantic.

The previous June, the nadir of his twilight year in Los Angeles, Bowie had apparently taken some hard career decisions. 'I've rocked my roll,' he said. 'It's a low form of communication and I'm through with it ... As for touring, I honestly believe that it kills my art. I will never, ever play live again.' Now, six months later, Bowie made yet another volte-face. Over Christmas, a group including Carlos Alomar, Dennis Davis (the drummer on 'Fame') and ex-Yes keyboardist Tony Kaye gathered in Jamaica to rehearse for a sixty-five-date tour Lippman promised would give 'the long view' of a glittering career. Bowie's own motivation was revealed immediately: 'It's going to make an obscenely large amount of money.' Earl Slick (like Ronson before him, banished for striking up a solo career) was replaced by Stacey Heydon, a Canadian blues guitarist. Unseen on stage, but also present on tour was Iggy Pop. After undergoing heroin addiction, a mental breakdown and confinement in the Neuropsychiatric Institute in Los Angeles, Pop had re-emerged as Bowie's travelling companion and putative star of his film production company. After two weeks of rehearsal, all that remained was for Schwab and Barbara DeWitt to coax the press into its familiar state of frenzy at Bowie's latest coming. A three-page interview in *Rolling Stone*, in which Bowie spoke of his fixation with Hitler, duly appeared in early February. The tour sold out immediately.

Opening night was in Vancouver. The evening began not with a sacrificial support act, but with Luis Buñel's film *Un Chien Andalou*, featuring a collection of surrealist images that included the slitting, in extreme close-up, of a human eyeball. As if not already shocking enough, the show proceeded with a daunting lack of props and glam-rock frippery: no lasers, no human skulls, no dancers attached to ropes pretending to be rabid dogs, and no boom to lower the star over the heads of his audience. Instead, Bowie came on bathed in stark white cross-beams of light. Given his recent right-wing effusions, the effect (influenced, said Bowie, by the early twentieth-century Brücke artists, and by Man Ray) had startling Nuremberg overtones. 'It might have been staged by Speer' was one critic's disapproving verdict. There were mixed notices, too, for Bowie's own lavish transformation. From February 1976 he now styled himself the 'thin white duke' of *Station to Station*'s title tune – a slick-haired, etiolated figure dressed in a starched white shirt, black trousers and with a blue Gitanes packet peeking from a waistcoat pocket. To a thunderous backdrop of high-tension guitars, screaming synthesizer and throbbing drums Bowie acted out a series of taut, robotic stage moves. There were those who thought his Noël Coward affectation and occasionally overwrought, Sinatra-styled crooning more properly suited a cabaret ballad singer than Ziggy Stardust. (Later in the tour Bowie would angrily claim 'I've never seen cabaret in my life', thus erasing an obsession that went back ten years.) Others believed his stiff, karate-like antics suggested the declining Elvis. Full consensus was only ever reached on the music: Howitzer-strength pop true to the high-voltage tradition of the last four albums.

Bowie, now twenty-nine, might have acquired a few wrinkles, but his nasal-edged voice remained intact, and the group's performance of virtually every well-remembered song since *Aladdin Sane* was definitive. Instant sound-bites like 'Jean Genie' and 'Rebel Rebel' mixed convivially with epic production pieces like 'Station to Station' and the reworked 'Life On Mars?' Of the 13,000 fans attending the tour's second night in Seattle, only a few bothered with platform shoes and lightning across their faces. Most had all too obviously come to listen. According to the local reviewer, 'Bowie came on like a suave French boulevardier ... Drenched in big spots and banks of fluorescent lights that caused a buzz in the sound-system ... When he wasn't singing Bowie would either walk off or dance in a sort of angular, jumpy way, with lots of squats and stiff-legged stretches. He played a little sax and I hope he meant to contrast with the band, because he did – he sounded like he was playing another tune.'

The party that night was in Bowie's hotel room. Dawn was already coming at the window when he made the acquaintance of a cocktail waitress named Cheryl Hise. There were three other women present. Bowie sat in the middle of the floor, the master of ceremonies, the director and disciplinarian of his troupe, as vigilant with those who served him sexually as those who played on his stage. 'David was a voyeur,' says Hise. 'He arranged groups, chose scenes, suggested positions and sat sketching the whole thing' – in short, established the 'protocol' of the orgy. A second woman present remembers how Bowie removed her clothes and 'very casually looked me up and down. He *posed* me – there was nothing sexual about it at all. It was more like a doctor's exam, and it was made clear that I was only one of dozens of calls on his time.' Bowie, therefore, despite or because of Angela's presence, still engaged in a variety of pursuits with fans of both sexes. Nor was any tour party with Iggy Pop in its ranks ever likely to be a stranger to drugs.

Three nights later Bowie played the 14,000-seat Winterland in San Francisco, and accepted a silver cape from Bill Graham backstage (along with a gold disc from a radio station, which Bowie left behind in his dressing room). He sold out three consecutive nights in Los Angeles, where his audience included Ringo Starr, Rod Stewart and the President's son, Steve Ford. After the final show Bowie returned to his rented home for the last time and helped load his belongings. Two U-Haul trucks took them to Los Angeles airport to be freighted to London. The tour itself proceeded in the same general direction, ending its American leg in New York on 26 March before transferring to Europe.

Although the critics were enthusiastic about Bowie's music, not all took to the conceits of his new image: the café-singer costume, the French cuffs and spats, the Gitanes, the voice so measured as to sound almost deadpan. An important part of Bowie's self-projection was that he never lose his epic *sangfroid*. To the *Melody Maker* reporter who met him backstage in Detroit he was a study in glacial reserve: Britain ('I just haven't got round to visiting'), Defries ('Is he still in the business? I honestly don't know'), Ronson ('I can't remember Mick that well nowadays. He's just like any other band member that I've had'), Dylan ('I'm not a great fan. I think he's a prick, so I'm not interested') and rock and roll ('I don't like much of it at all') were all dismissed with angry chops of Bowie's hand. There were those who, not for the first time, saw an ominous blurring between the actor and the role he played on stage. Bowie himself would call the thin white duke 'a very nasty character indeed' and admit, 'I finally did break the lines down in the mid seventies, where I couldn't perceive the difference between the stage persona and myself.'*

Bowie in the first half of 1976 was often fussy, hypochondriacal, self-obsessed and capricious. Schwab was appalled by the suddenness of his fury, and would beg him to control it for both their sakes. He would get out of her car, and slam the door. Even in this early phase of their relationship Bowie gave conflicting signals. He would propose lunch, then vanish for two weeks. He barely spoke to Angela when she joined him for the second half of the American tour. And he fired Michael Lippman.

Bowie clearly blamed his manager for the chaos of *The Man Who Fell to Earth*'s soundtrack. There was also a suggestion that Lippman had furtively raised his agreed percentage of Bowie's income, and acted improperly over funds placed in trust on his

---

*Against type, Bowie did, however, break down at the end of his first London concert in three years and leave the hall in tears.

client's behalf. The result, only a year after the Century Plaza settlement, was yet another drawn-out and acrimonious marathon of legal wrangling. Bowie opened the war with a warning shot, writing to Lippman, in tones that could only have been supplied by a lawyer, to complain about alleged breaches of contract and 'fiduciary duty'. Lippman responded by suing for 'exemplary and punitive damages' of $2 million. At the end of June the two sides met at the Hotel Trois Couronnes in Vevey, Switzerland. According to Lippman's assistant it was 'like an old-fashioned, Cold War-era summit' with Bowie, in the Khrushchev role, storming out of the room after twenty minutes. A second session, in Paris, fared little better. In Tony Visconti's words, Bowie 'went berserk' and again left the room, screaming, 'You're all fucking leeches, you all want my money.' One result was that Lippman agreed to settle for less than the hoped-for $2 million. Another was that Bowie's next album, originally planned as a celebration of his return to Europe, ended up as the stark, relentlessly pessimistic *Low*.

True to form, the lawyer who represented Bowie against Lippman in turn became his new manager. Stanley Diamond's first act was to consult an accountancy firm as to how his client could minimize his British tax bill. Their advice was to go into voluntary exile for the financial year 1976–7. That April, following in the ground-breaking mould of Somerset Maugham and, nearer to home, the Rolling Stones, the Bowies went house-hunting in France, Germany and finally Switzerland, where they settled in a seven-bedroom chalet called Clos des Mésanges, set in the foothills above Blonay on the north shore of Lake Geneva. Among their immediate neighbours were Balthazar Balthus and Charlie Chaplin. Angela describes her husband's initial reaction to his alpine idyll: 'He walked through that gorgeous house and couldn't stand it. He tried to pretend he liked it, but you could see the horror in his face. It wasn't his scene at all.'

It was Angela's misfortune to have tried to engage in a closer relationship with Bowie at this very stage. In Switzerland, Schwab more than ever became his prop, as did the cocaine and other drugs whose use he intensified. There was, however, one area where his move to Europe proved beneficial. Apart from UFO-spotting and sightseeing, Bowie's only other hobby while filming *The Man Who Fell to Earth* had been painting the scorched brown landscape and sketching his fellow actors. Later in 1975 he produced a work called *Lovers* and a portrait of William Burroughs, post-modernist images influenced, like his musical output, by a variety of sources. On several dates of the 1976 tour Bowie studiously avoided the smashing-TVs-in-hotel-rooms school of behaviour, instead drawing scenes in his notebook or snapping pictures that he would use later as references for an illustration. The back cover of *Station to Station* showed him doodling with an artist's chalk. By the time he re-crossed the Atlantic, Bowie was so absorbed by painting that he spoke of doing this rather than music for a living. He began to visit the galleries in Geneva and the Brücke Museum in West Berlin. The man who appeared in London that spring might have swapped his $200,000-per-album advance for a solo exhibition and a review in *Modern Painters*.

By 1977 Bowie was both a prolific producer and collector of contemporary art. Although his self-pitying streak found expression in his continuing quarrels over money, he was never wholeheartedly invested in them. He had a hundred things on his mind. Away from California, this rock-based pluralist seemed to live several lives at once. He devoured everything, wolfed it down. Unable to sit still, he raced about Europe in a sort of cultural rage as if trying to make up for the 'interminable wasteland' of Los Angeles. Not only did he become a well-known patron of expressionist art: locked in Clos des Mésanges he began an intensive self-improvement course in classical music and literature, and started work on an autobiography he called 'The Return of the Thin White Duke'. (One excerpt: 'My records were selling and I was being a man in demand. I thought of Vince [Taylor] and wrote "Ziggy Stardust". I thought of my brother and wrote "Five Years". Then my friend came to mind, standing the way we stood in Bewlay Bros and I wrote "Moonage Daydream".') With books and art, Switzerland and skiing, Bowie seemed to scale down if not vanquish his furies. Apart from the drugs, the only thing now separating him from his sedate, well-heeled neighbours in Blonay was his extreme – some thought demented – right-wing politics.

In his Ziggy incarnation, Bowie had represented the chaotic, liberating, free-form aspects of rock. Only three years later he was describing his ambition to be prime minister, and his reaction to Britain's economic crisis:

> I believe very strongly in Fascism. The only way we can speed up the sort of liberalism that's hanging foul in the air at the moment is to speed up the progress of a right-wing, totally dictatorial tyranny and get it over as fast as possible. People have always responded with greater efficiency under a regimental leadership.

Bowie later explained that his remarks were 'a joke', his habitual teasing of his fans, and he disowned most of his mid seventies outbursts. He had already commented, 'I think that morals should be straightened up for a start. They're disgusting.' 'The masses are silly,' he now told *Rolling Stone*. 'Just look at the cultural leaders of today. Once they were Humphrey Bogart, James Dean and Elvis Presley. Now it's Robert Redford and John Denver . . . and these are supposed to be the degenerate seventies. It doesn't look good for America. They let people like me trample all over their country.'

The fascination with supermen and the master race was a theme of all Bowie's albums since *The Man Who Sold the World*. By 1976, under the strain of cocaine addiction, he began preaching from the text of Aryan supremacy. Along with an interest in German expressionism went a growing fixation with fascism. On 10 April Bowie played in Berlin for the first time.* He immediately began an affair with the transsexual night-club star Romy Haag, a seventies equivalent of Sally Bowles, only more so. A photographer named Andy Kent shot Bowie gazing, apparently awestruck, at a bust of Hitler. Accompanied by Kent and Iggy Pop, he crossed through the Allied Checkpoint into East Berlin. After a meal of black bread and cabbage soup, which Bowie declared 'excellent', the party returned to the west and drove down Entlastungs-strasse, in the shadow of the Berlin Wall. As they passed on their

---

*In October 1969 he appeared on German television in Günther Schneider's *Musik für Junge Leute*, taped in West Berlin.

left the blown-up hill marking the site of Hitler's bunker, Bowie gave a Nazi salute for Kent's benefit. He made the photographer swear never to release the film without permission, thus showing marginally better sense than in his remarks later that month to a Swedish reporter: 'I think Britain could benefit from a fascist leader.'

By the time Bowie returned to London in May, the UK press had begun to comment disparagingly on a man who appeared to be locked in a struggle for his own soul. *Sounds* had already skewered him for the 'stormtrooper vibe' of his stage show. Now Bowie acted out a macabre piece of theatre that made headlines, and drew down rage the world over.

Early in 1976 Schwab had acquired a second-hand black Mercedes Benz (bought from the estate of an assassinated Iranian prince) in which Bowie would be conveyed around Europe. This faintly sinister machine was duly waiting on the forecourt of Victoria Station to meet the Orient Express on Sunday 2 May. Several thousand fans, as well as reporters from the daily and music press, were on hand to greet Bowie. After a delay – extended, some felt, to generate tension – the train pulled in to platform eight. Bowie, wearing a dark shirt, walked a few feet to the open-topped car, got in, stood up and thrust out his right arm. The photograph of him, standing in a black German car, apparently snapping out a Nazi salute, achieved almost mythological status in the months ahead. *NME* ran it over four columns, under the headline 'Heil and Farewell'. Bowie was excoriated in the national press, many of whose correspondents had been at Victoria to see that his gesture was neither a 'peace sign' nor a 'trick of the light' as he claimed.

Few of the reviews of Bowie's six concerts at Wembley – where he introduced himself as Winston Churchill – ignored his politics. The *Guardian* found his new image 'more Nazi than futuristic'. To *Melody Maker*, the Nuremberg associations 'raised echoes of his recent controversial comments about Fascist rule for Britain'. Nor was the backlash restricted to Bowie alone of the rock fraternity. Three months after the Victoria incident, Eric Clapton made scathing remarks about immigration from a concert stage in Birmingham. As a result the pressure group Rock Against Racism came into being, upbraiding both Clapton and Bowie – whose head they printed in profile alongside Enoch Powell's and Hitler's. For a few dizzy months in 1976–7, some of pop's leading practitioners were seen to be flirting with fascism in a dangerous way, and at a dangerous time, given the ascent of the far-right National Front. In Washington the FBI, whose file on Bowie had hitherto used words like 'kooky' and 'subversive', began stockpiling press cuttings describing him, bewilderingly, as a 'would-be demagogue' and 'apparent Nazi sympathizer'. In London it was impossible to dwell, at any length, on Bowie's albums and concerts without giving equal space to his politics. His work became part of the turbulent social history of the late seventies.

After the Wembley shows (which, seen as concerts, and not rallies, won widespread praise), the *Station to Station* tour proceeded to Brussels, Rotterdam and finally Paris. Bowie was visited backstage by the ex-Roxy Music composer Brian Eno, whose taste for avant-garde 'ambient' music he now shared, by Mick Jagger, and by Romy Haag.

The whole tour was 'done under duress', Bowie later told the journalist Angus MacKinnon. 'I was out of my mind, totally crazed. The main thing I was functioning on was mythology ... that whole thing about Hitler and Rightism ... I'd discovered King Arthur ... [the] whole racist thing.' While feature-writers chided his faulty grasp of Arthurian legend and Rock Against Racism burnt him in effigy, Bowie, travelling in Paris as 'Stenton Jones', found himself at the Alcazar Club to celebrate the end of the tour. Sometime towards dawn on 19 May a squadron of police surrounded the premises, while the head of the French anti-drugs squad appeared at the door. Each of the two hundred guests present was searched, in some cases in the body, for illegal substances. The police made four arrests, but none the Fleet Street moralists could make headlines of. A London crime reporter, coincidentally also in the club, would write of the lurid scene at the Alcazar, where 'topless girls gyrated with one another' on the dance floor and 'exotic Indian "reefers"' were passed from hand to hand, with the management's evident approval. The writer would later rue that he was denied, by perhaps twenty minutes, the defining scoop of his career – as the drugs squad were of theirs. By the time the police raided the Alcazar, Bowie was already safely back in his hotel, in bed with Romy Haag.

6
ART DECADE

The area above Blonay, a favourite residence for foreigners and particularly for the English, was one of the most pleasant in Switzerland. In contrast to Los Angeles, it was both clean and well lit. A river ran in the foothills behind Clos des Mésanges, slow and white in the sun; and throughout much of the day, and especially at night, the constant play of water could be heard by the inhabitants of the surrounding houses. From his bedroom window Bowie could look down on the village, with its steeply angled roofs, and a lush pasture grazed by cattle. Farm-workers went by the Clos and down the road and the dust they raised coated the leaves of the apple trees.

Such was Bowie's almost parodically normal life from April 1976. As well as his painting and skiing he amassed a library of 5,000 books, many of which he read. He was a popular figure in Blonay and the small neighbouring towns on Lake Geneva. Dressed modestly in slacks and short-sleeved check shirt, his blond hair swept back, Bowie was unrecognizable from the skeleton who haunted North Doheny Drive. Rock music's most famous running target paused long enough to become himself. Significantly, he even partly restored his legal name of Jones. 'Bowie was never meant to be,' he now said. 'He's like a Lego kit. I'm convinced I wouldn't like him, because he's too vacuous and undisciplined.' Apart from Romy Haag and the long-suffering Angela, his only other relationship was with Charlie Chaplin's wife (and, from December 1977, widow), the former actress Oona O'Neill. The fifty-one-year-old woman followed down a line from Elizabeth Taylor and Dinah Shore as stars of an earlier era for whom Bowie became a kind of mascot. At least one member of the Chaplin family came to believe that Bowie would propose (though she quipped it would be more like a 'merger than a marriage'). A local Vevey reporter reached a similar conclusion. Mistaking Bowie's attentions for something more, Oona apparently shared the same hope. But perhaps because he felt pressured by their expectations, he held off, and the relationship mellowed into a friendship.

Between 1972 and 1976, Bowie bred unprecedented frenzy in rock music. He was reproached from pulpits, denounced by parents and fêted by critics. Headlines made his name synonymous with decadence. Two photographs of Bowie – sucking the strings of Ronson's guitar and saluting from his black Mercedes – entered the consciousness so deeply as to become lore. His image would never be rid of this early taint. And yet without it his stratospheric success would not have been possible. From Pitt to Dai Davies to Barbara DeWitt (and above all, by Defries) Bowie had been sold in a way that made other rock stars seem woefully neglected. It was a measure of his promotional flair that even in Switzerland, while ostensibly on holiday, he was the subject of a four-page profile in *People*. Despite its faulty chronology (in which 'Space Oddity' followed Ziggy Stardust), the long feature successfully brought alive the phenomenon. Essentially, Bowie's characters were a contradiction, or a series of contradictions – 'like Houdini's underwater cages, self-set traps from which he executes miraculous escapes that work as well as the tricks they create'. The final word was from the illusionist himself: 'There is no definitive David Bowie.' As well as pieces in the *New York Times* and *Chicago Tribune*, and the still simmering debate in Britain about his politics, his first greatest-hits album now made its way to number 2 on the chart. The vast RCA PR apparatus kept Bowie in the public eye at a time when his main activities were restricted to painting, reading and sitting alone listening to the World Service.

To stay home with his family did not satisfy him for long. In June 1976 Bowie produced *The Idiot* for Iggy Pop, evolving via moves to Munich and Berlin into sessions for his own next album. Joining Visconti at the control board was Brian Eno, a composer whose *Taking Tiger Mountain* had pioneered a new musical form, in which melody was reduced to an option. Between them, these two changed Bowie's upbeat *New Music: Night and Day* into the minimal crooning and wiry backing tracks of *Low*. Eno also used one of Bowie's absences from the studio (away giving depositions against Michael Lippman) to write 'Warszawa', the first of four instrumentals on the second side of the album.

The news in September 1976 that Bowie was not only working but living in Berlin seemed to confirm the worst fears about his Weimar fixation. For years he had been held up as pop's supreme prankster, a man of legendary suppleness who treated every image as a joke, made every move a spoof. Now it seemed his Teutonic leanings were all too real. There were three specific reasons for his move. On one level, Berlin was a form of therapy, an antidote for the cocaine psychosis of California, where, as Bowie recalled, 'I blew my nose one day and half my brains came out.' The city had a perverse attraction as the dregs of a once-great society in decay. To the author of *Diamond Dogs*, a community of louche and mutant characters watched over by guard towers had much to commend it. There was even a romantic or artistic connection with the world of Christopher Isherwood, and Berlin's cultural reputation as one of the world centres for art and music. Finally, in setting up home in Germany, Bowie signified a break with his wife. The move infuriated Angela, who saw it as a deliberate snub by Schwab, exploiting her muscle as Bowie's constant companion and confidante.

Lodgings were found at the Hotel Gehrus. In early October Bowie transferred to a flat at 155 Hauptstrasse in Schöneberg, a faintly raffish quarter of West Berlin. The building itself was un-distinguished: a five-storey tenement in peeling yellow, squeezed by rising new construction. A heavy metal door gave on to an ugly, geometric-patterned linoleum floor and a flight of concrete stairs. Bowie's apartment was on the first floor. It was damp and leaky and heavy rugs as well as curtains hung at the windows. When it rained, which it did constantly that winter, water seeped through the brickwork. Apart from the three bedrooms and miniature kitchen and bath, there was a study/studio dominated by Bowie's bookcase and easel. It might have been the home of a mildly Bohemian art lecturer. Among the immediate neighbours were the Bücherhalle antiquarian bookshop, the strikingly named Amazonia Schmuck & Perlen (dealing in costume jewellery) and the Luk garage. A few doors up Haupt-strasse was the Nemesis café, a room furnished with posters of James Dean and a clientele of radical gays and lesbians with vulpine dogs. Most afternoons Bowie came in for a breakfast of coffee and Gitanes.

Some of the normality of his time in Blonay continued in Berlin. Bowie became a patron of galleries on both sides of the divided city. He frequently cycled up Hauptstrasse to the Hansa studio at 38 Kothener Strasse, shadowed by an East German watch-tower and the uncompromising bulk of the Berlin Wall. No longer were his shopping expeditions made from behind the tinted windows of a studio limousine. Now he cheerfully walked down the Kurfürstendamm, alone or with Schwab, smiling and happy to sign autographs for the few fans who recognized him. He gave an interview to the *Berliner Morgenpost*, talking up the city as an 'alternative New York' and remaking himself in the guise of 'Joe Bloggs' with 'boring habits'. As if in illustration, Bowie now kept a diary, recording slices of Berlin life, one of which ('It's two in the morning. I can't sleep for the screaming of some poor ostracized Turkish immigrant from over the street') would find its way onto *Outside* nineteen years later.

In searching for an emotional outlet, Bowie and his friends soon started to frequent the Brücke museum. Here Erich Heckel's *Roquairol*, with its stark depiction of lunacy, became the model for Iggy Pop's tortured pose on the cover of *The Idiot*, as well as for Bowie's own next-album-but-one. He also patronized nightclubs like the Roxy and the Jungle. For an early-morning meal he enjoyed the Empire bar or Joe's Beer House on the Kurfür-stendamm, where a waiter named Uwe Herz remembers him 'upchucking in the alley after a gallon of König-Pilseners'. These excursions, too, tended to be made with Iggy. Despite accom-panying an impressive number of women on the Jungle dance floor, Bowie now found himself without a steady partner. Angela remained at Clos des Mésanges. After a hopeful start, nothing came of the relationship with Oona Chaplin. Romy Haag was abruptly dropped after she leaked details of her affair with Bowie to the *Morgenpost*. So far as he had a social life, it lay with the casual pick-ups who filled out his time between recording dates, and with Schwab and Iggy. On a typical afternoon the three would take the U-Bahn into Zehlendorf, Grunewald or one of the other suburbs, where Bowie always impressed with his knowledge of local history. He continued to seek out Nazi relics, such as the former Gestapo headquarters, insisting that he had the right to be an 'ordinary tourist'. But to his colleagues at Hansa, this tendency to see himself as both Bowie the star and Bowie the common man wasn't entirely a virtue or necessarily an admirable thing. As one musician puts it, 'Dave forgot that the rest of us didn't make the distinction.' When he was criticized for an over-enthusiastic reaction to Goering's Air Ministry, Bowie flew into a rage, prodding his fingers towards Schwab's face, and shouting, 'Fuck you! I changed the world! Kiss my arse.' Then he burst into tears and stalked off.

Drugs, though not on their previous scale, continued. Bowie was a promiscuous user of cocaine and began most days by locking himself in his bathroom, from which Schwab and Iggy could hear the unmistakable sounds of retching. With a characteristically perverse gift for self-mortification, he still attributed his condition to 'over-eating', and tantalized himself all summer by refraining from the ice-cream he loved. Apart from drugs and sightseeing, Bowie's main hobbies in Berlin were coffee-housing, smoking and listening to the local techno-rock group Kraftwerk. He cropped his hair to *Virgin Soldiers* length, and affected a wardrobe of baggy trousers and dowdy shirts, topped off by a peasant's cloth cap. Reserved and serious, he was, in one German friend's words, 'a slight figure, of medium height' with a 'pallid complexion', a 'dull, toneless voice', and no sense of humour. Nor did he participate much in the convivial social life in the bars and restaurants around Hansa. 'His job was work, and his joy was in discussing it – if a mumbled "yep" or "nope" could be elevated to the level of discussion.' Furthermore, he had a peculiar habit of looking down and away from people with whom he was talking and of doodling with a pencil while listening. Not the traits that legends are made of.

Bowie, despite Iggy's and Schwab's constant presence, grumbled frequently at Angela's preference for Switzerland and London. The arrangement had, admittedly, its drawbacks. He enjoyed being looked after in the obvious sense – of having the toothpaste squeezed onto the brush for him, or having his clothes cleaned and a new shirt laid out whenever he wanted it – and the business of actually fending for himself was so tedious and time-consuming that he never made much more than a few brief stabs at it. He was a dab hand at brewing coffee, but that was his one and only accomplishment in the kitchen. Without either Angela or Schwab, therefore, there was a tendency for unwashed dishes to pile up in the sink and for discarded drawings and clothes to be strewn across the floor. Left to his own devices, in short, without mistress, maid or wife, Bowie was unable to cope. Visconti was so appalled, on one occasion, at the chaos he found at Hauptstrasse that he insisted on taking Bowie home there and then and looking after him until Schwab returned. On the other hand, however, the life of a wealthy bachelor – on a part-time basis, at any rate – did have its privileges, and Bowie was rarely without an attractive overnight guest. His closest friend at the time was a chronic womanizer and alcoholic, and the temptation to follow in Iggy's footsteps was almost impossible to resist.

Bowie had been a binge drinker for years. Two or three times a month, according to a friend, he 'sank' a bottle of whisky, then indulged in a show of morning-after remorse and mumbled pledges to cut down in future. Now, however, egged on by Iggy (whose own drinking recognized no limit but unconsciousness), Bowie's intake reached a new high. Thus, while keen to develop his artistic and political interests in Berlin, he also gave rein to the side of him his friend calls the 'aggressive introvert'. His frequent visits to Joe's Beer House followed a familiar routine. Bowie would sit at a corner table in the plush, panelled bar; his voice rose in volume with every König-Pilsener ordered; the noise brought a steady stream of fans and autograph-hounds; their attention drove Bowie to more drink. Uwe Herz remembers the near-nightly ritual of holding Bowie up by his belt as he vomited in the dark alley next to the beer garden. A friend in Schöneberg saw 'Dave staggering up Hauptstrasse with his head down and that hooded "don't fuck with me" expression of his, really mean.' When Bowie appeared for breakfast hours later at the Nemesis he shouted at the waitress for the tactless remark, 'Hello, David. How are you?' and invited a young fan who approached him to 'Go dick yourself.'

By November 1976 Angela, at least, was determined to settle the deadlock in the Bowies' marriage. She flew to Berlin and presented her husband with an ultimatum. He was to fire Schwab – whom Angela saw as the real crisis in their relationship – or face the prospect of a public and ugly divorce. Bowie counter-proposed that she should 'stay at home and be the wealthy wife and breed more offspring'. When Angela rejected that, Bowie began to stammer and hyperventilate. Afraid that he was overdosing, Angela rushed him to the British Military Hospital, where a doctor later denied there was anything 'organically wrong' with Bowie, who had 'overdone things and was suffering from too much drink'. Bowie's wife then took a taxi to Haupt-strasse, dumped all Schwab's clothes on the floor, doused them with brandy and lit a match. She took the next flight out of Berlin to London.

Bowie turned thirty on 8 January 1977. Iggy and Romy Haag were at his table at the Roxy. Bowie always provided good copy for journalists, and later became very nearly a fully fledged journalist in his own right. His articles were published overseas, especially in America, and he distributed his favours among *Modern Painters, Q* and the Internet with almost equal generosity. He was still, however, quick to take offence if a reporter or photographer pestered him. A man took a picture of Bowie and Haag at the Roxy, resulting in a shoving match and the smashing of the camera against a brick wall. Bowie then turned his rage on Haag, whom he believed had 'fucked up' his birthday for her own ends. Their affair cooled from that day on. In the first weeks of 1977 he complained almost daily about his ex-lover, and her apparent desire to exploit the relationship. After one long harangue at Joe's Beer House, Bowie began sobbing when he described, to a comparative stranger, how 'leeches' were bleeding him – the same word he once used to Visconti. Thus Uwe Herz detected what only intimates of Bowie discerned: beneath the arctic exterior was a fragile ego.

Low was released the week after Bowie's thirtieth birthday. It was, by that simple yardstick, the work of a mature man. There were few enough laughs in the music, and the adult theme was a key to the appeal. The album did, however, feature one blatant pun: a silhouette of Bowie from *The Man Who Fell to Earth* below the prominent title, making the obvious link – 'low profile'.

The album was a failure; at least a failed experiment in ambient music. Bowie's original plan was to record one side of raw rock and roll, not the odd clatter that resulted, and a second that revolved around the synthesizer. The idea was to release this hybrid with no editing or overdubbing, no polishing, and no production. Bowie himself told *Melody Maker* he felt he was 'very predictable, and that was starting to bore me . . . I was getting too successful in the wrong way.' It was *Low*'s impressive ambition to mix chilly electronics, new wave and the kind of languid, lovelorn pop that gives self-pity a good name. Although the concept fractured into an uneasy truce between Bowie and RCA's quality-control department, it was still so complex in its failure that it worked better as an album than either *Aladdin Sane* or *Diamond Dogs*. Virtually overnight, Bowie had invented a new kind of rock song: a half-verse, if that, flung in the general direction of the melody. The chugging, industrial beat would launch a thousand failed imitators. Few would ever match the weird blend of primal, wordless chanting, quirky, naïve tunes delivered via computers and digital keyboards, relentless solemnity and comic under-tones. To a sordidly commercial ear, *Low* was hardly worth releasing, but, because of its influence, it did more than any other album to establish Bowie as the *éminence grise* of art rock.

Low's starting point was Eno's *Taking Tiger Mountain*, like much of John Cage's work as important for its example as for what it actually did. Eno's real contribution was to steer Bowie away from narration. *Low* mechanized the system, begun on *Diamond Dogs*, of pasting the occasional verse on to the repetitive music – what Bowie called 'the idea of processing, the abstract of communication'; in short, surrealism. As Eric Tamm puts it, 'Eno was able to nudge [*Low*] beyond the limits of rock.' His musical personality was all over the album's second, mostly instrumental side. There were mutterings that, apart from his co-credit for 'Warszawa', Eno's name might have appeared on the cover alongside Bowie's. In some quarters, *Low* was seen as practically a joint album. But the production credit fell to Bowie and Visconti alone. As Eno himself explained, where several people contributed ideas, it came down to 'who was paying for the studio time'. Thus 'Art Decade', nominally Bowie's, was largely improvised during his absence in Paris; 'Weeping Wall' and 'Subterraneans' both grew out of the aborted *Man Who Fell to Earth* sessions with Paul Buckmaster. The single 'Sound and Vision' and the album's yards of recycled guitar riffs raised a smile from Mick Ronson.

At its best, *Low* was Bowie's mental state turned into novel and rousing music. 'Breaking Glass', a characteristic warning-off of an encroaching lover, was quirky, singalong rock. 'Sound and Vision' was a classic anti-social pop song – as Bowie put it about leaving America and sitting in a 'little cold room with omnipotent blue on the walls and blinds on the windows'. Yet both this and the mawkish plea of 'By My Wife', complete with faux-cockney vocals, somehow made the leap to hit singles. By welding pop choruses to piston-hissing noises filched from the factory floor, Bowie managed the rare feat of being accessible and avant-garde in roughly equal parts, with consistently winning results. Even at its nadir, *Low* crackled with something that sounded like grunge's elder brother, all enviably simple tunes, jagged edges and a firm grasp of the first rule of modern rock writing: exploit your pain. The album both justified the past and anticipated the future. While Bowie delivered the chorus of 'Sound and Vision' ('Blue/That's the colour of my room') with a conviction that suggested much of the music came from his own depression, the freshness and spark he put into *Low* was the stuff of new beginnings.

Among those horrified by the album's seemingly impenetrable mix of mood music and random salvos of punk guitar were RCA, agitating for 'another *Young Americans*', who even offered to buy Bowie a house in Philadelphia. (One executive recalls listening to *Low*'s second side and taking the instant decision to pull it from the label's Christmas list. There was 'no way', he says, people were going to give it as a gift.) Tony Defries, still with a 16 per cent interest in *Low*, tried desperately to stop RCA from even releasing it. The critics were generally hostile and never less than sceptical. Charles Shaar Murray, a known admirer of Bowie, was almost demented in *NME*. *Low*, he wrote, was 'so negative it doesn't even contain emptiness or the void ... a totally passive psychosis, a scenario and soundtrack for total withdrawal ... Futility and death-wish glorified, an elaborate embalming job for a suicide's grave . . . Stinks of artfully counterfeited spiritual defeat and emptiness.' The press had to be educated up to *Low*, which many of them later touted as a classic, paving the way for the likes of Joy Division, Human League and, ultimately, U2. Only the public, it seemed, could hold in its head simultaneously the ideas that Bowie was an inveterate tunesmith who, for reasons of his own, needed to regroup (just as he had with *Pin-Ups*) and to explore new musical ideas. *Low* reached number two on the chart.

Visconti explained much of the album as taking its mood from Bowie himself. Recording in Paris was 'absolutely the worst', he said. The bonhomie of the *Pin-Ups* sessions dissolved in a series of tense, ugly scenes involving 'useless' staff at the Château d'Hérouville, uneatable meals and the 'reading of the riot act' by Schwab concerning leaks to the press. Then there was the stand-off with Michael Lippman. It was a miracle, says Iggy, that, under the circumstances, a record was made at all – let alone 'one as balls-out as *Low*'. For ten years, Bowie had been threatening to release an album that increased the whole specific mass of rock. *Hunky Dory*, *Ziggy Stardust* and the rest had all had their fans, but the possibility of his ever making an artistic breakthrough, despite the confident prediction of Bowiephiles, had come to seem increasingly remote. It was, after all, almost incredible that a man famous for singing pop songs about an alien, with an all-too-fickle musical persona, should record a work successfully covered by Philip Glass and still widely respected twenty years later. To go from *Diamond Dogs* to *Young Americans* to *Station to Station* was an achievement in itself, particularly in just eighteen months, but to move from there to *Low* was something that virtually beggared belief. It was astonishing enough that Glass – one of the pioneers of minimalist music in the sixties, when Bowie was still writing 'The Laughing Gnome' – should now be speaking of him as an equal: it was even more astonishing that Glass hailed *Low* as 'a work of genius', complex music masquerading as simple.

It was typical of Bowie that, at the crowning moment of his solo career, he was already seeking a purely anonymous berth in a group. On 29 January 1977, *Melody Maker* reported that he had cast himself as the keyboard player in Iggy's touring band. RCA announced extensive dates in Britain and America throughout

March and April. Ostensibly meant to promote *The Idiot*, which did, briefly, graze the UK charts, it was also an opportunity for Bowie to flex his punk muscle at a time when other well-heeled rock stars were being stigmatized as 'dinosaurs', 'old farts' and worse. The five-piece group, in a break with Iggy's past, rehearsed for several weeks in the new year. Apart from that, Bowie's chief activities were drinking, painting and trawling the Kumbaba boutique in Hauptstrasse for the latest fashions. He distinguished himself by being the first rock star to make the critical transition from flared to straight trousers, and displayed a renewed interest in black bomber jackets. Bowie also spent an hour most afternoons sitting in Schöneberg library where, shoulder to shoulder with thugs and the homeless, he queued for the single copy of the *Morgenpost*.

The tour began on 1 March at the Friars Club, Aylesbury, the very scene of Defries' epic press junket in 1972. Iggy's six British shows were a triumph. Playing stripped to the waist, flailing the stage and frequently the audience, the singer had half the crowd spellbound and the other half running for the car park. There was praise, too, for the stripped-down, vicious rasp of the band – though the question remained, said *Sounds*, whether Iggy was using Bowie, or Bowie was using Iggy. Certain critics made it a point of honour to cast doubt on the real motivation behind the tour. Unlike most of his contemporaries – his old sparring partner Elton John springs immediately to mind – Bowie had ploughed anything but a straight musical furrow since becoming famous five years before. Singing adaptions of Jacques Brel one minute and collaborating with Lulu the next marked him out as a reviewer's worst nightmare: the restless, creative artist. The sixty journalists at Iggy's first, sold-out show at the Rainbow were left to ponder the chain-smoking sideman stage left, who sat quietly at his piano, plunking notes that seldom scaled the musical ladder to tunefulness, and not acknowledging the manic roar of the crowd. Onstage, Bowie rarely did more than listlessly prod his keyboard. Offstage, he was meticulous about not taking any of Iggy's press. According to *Sounds*, 'If you wanted David, you also got the band ... a collective.' It was an early example of Bowie's periodic bids to retreat into one-of-the-gang anonymity, fulfilled by Tin Machine* a dozen years later. While some detected a kind of snobbery in the pose – he was 'slumming it' according to Don Gunn – others applauded his modesty. In 1977, Bowie shunned ostentation. While he loved to engineer publicity, he shrank from overtly *personal* publicity. He was averse to having his picture taken, at least for public use. At the Rainbow he would not pose for a backstage photograph without the other musicians. He dismissed his Mercedes and travelled in the hired tour bus.

Whilst in Britain, Bowie spent a weekend with Marc Bolan. Time had not been kind to the 'porky pixie' encountered in Los Angeles two years before. His single 'New York City' (with its lines 'Have you ever seen a woman coming out of New York/With a frog in her hand?') was his last top-twenty hit. He revamped his band with his girlfriend Gloria Jones (and Bowie's old nemesis Herbie Flowers on bass) and launched a TV series called *Marc*. Bowie was astonished, he admitted to a friend, at the wretched man's refusal to lie down after being pronounced dead by the critics. A member of Iggy's group heard him mutter, after leaving Bolan at his hotel, 'Such talent, such a waste.' With only six days before the tour resumed in North America, Bowie then gave in and agreed to fly again after more than five years. Even this logistical footnote made a feature story in *NME*. 'I think the aeroplane's a wonderful invention,' Bowie told Lisa Robinson on landing in New York, before taking the train to Montreal.

The month that followed, a zigzag excursion ending in San Diego, was a lesson in raw guitar and punk-style blurting – suitably dramatized by Iggy howling 'China Girl' while holding a yellow torch under his chin – in which Bowie, recalling Defries' earlier phrase, never sweated. At the Paramount, Seattle, the band performed a medley of '1969' and the Stooges' 'No Fun' and '96 Tears'. An hour later Bowie walked unrecognized out of the stage door, strolled down Pike Street to the waterfront and sat before a plate of 'olde English fish and chips' while a single

---

*The drummer and bassist on Iggy's tour, Hunt Sales and his brother Tony, later became Tin Machine's rhythm section.

teenager came and gazed doubtfully into his face.

'You're *someone* aren't you?' she asked him.

'No, I'm not,' Bowie said.

A week later, in San Francisco, Bowie strayed out of character and sang 'Fame'. In Los Angeles he and Iggy appeared on *The Dinah Shore Show*. Bowie's old flame was gushingly effusive to have 'Sister Midnight' and 'Funtime' – successful on stage but somehow crude and dull in the studio – blared a few feet from her face. As a metaphor for social assimilation (the ex-mental patient and the Nazi apologist playing to a huge daytime TV audience), the scene was memorable. The governing image was, again, one of change. Bowie was praised in the media for having 'grown', 'mellowed' and 'straddled the shifting public taste'. His appeal was not, however, merely that of the matured rock star. He also took the time to renew relations with Mick Jagger. Now separated from their wives, the two spent a long evening heckling a black cabaret singer with whom, inevitably, Bowie spent the night. The next morning the woman dressed, drove home and returned with her sister. Jagger then reappeared, according to one of the women, 'casually sucking a candy bar' (though not a Mars Bar), and allegedly joined them between the sheets. A disappointingly short time later, the four met Iggy and his companion for lunch in Bowie's favourite club. Both sisters remember the comic disparity between Iggy ('a complete lunatic', who ordered everything on the menu), Jagger (sitting with 'folded arms and pursed lips' – and in the end, an even tighter wallet) and Bowie, who surveyed the whole scene with the impersonal pleasure of 'someone watching the view'. There was no view.

Opinions vary as to whether Bowie 'made' Iggy or vice-versa, but the tour served both their purposes. Bowie's presence enhanced interest and ensured sell-outs at all twenty-one venues. Iggy's support in turn helped Bowie escape the wrath of punk rock. While men like Jagger were berated for having grown soft, Malcolm McLaren, the Sex Pistols' guru, made his switch from designer to music fashion 'largely because of the [Ziggy] factor'. McLaren, like most other London style pundits, was fascinated by Bowie's lavish transformations. His influence reached down to the musicians themselves: Johnny Rotten, whose hairdo and dazed stare exactly mimicked the front cover of *Space Oddity*, five years earlier; and Sid Vicious, who in Rotten's words 'arse-licked David'. In defining just how he proposed to be a godfather of punk, Bowie was suitably unspecific. In early 1978 he helped Eno produce the seminal *Q: Are We Not Men? A: We are Devo!* A decade later, Tin Machine mined the same seam of aggressive, breakneck riffs and approximate melodies as the Pixies, Dinosaur and, ultimately, Nirvana (who repaid the compliment by covering 'The Man Who Sold the World' on *Unplugged*). In late 1995, Bowie appeared on stage with both Nine Inch Nails and the prince of misery, Morrissey. But his patronage of even those, like Iggy, whom he genuinely admired rarely went beyond a desultory project and mutual exchanges of goodwill. If Bowie was truly punk's *auteur*, it was because of the same restless spirit and dread of the pigeonhole that vexed RCA's marketing department. Put simply, he never stayed still long enough to become a target.

The Iggy tour ended on 16 April 1977. Bowie returned to Berlin. Meanwhile, his nominal tax exile in Switzerland was renewed for twelve months, as it would be every spring for twenty years.

In rapid succession, Bowie next helped to write, arrange and produce Iggy's follow-up to *The Idiot*, significantly titled *Lust For Life*. Astonishingly, this prototype of the wasted punk now became a health addict. He and Bowie regularly cycled or walked from Hauptstrasse to the Hansa studio and Iggy took up weight-lifting. The results not only showed in *Lust*'s grinning, full-face cover photograph, but inevitably fuelled the music. Full of lithe, upbeat songs and lyrics that celebrated sex, the album was a top-thirty hit in Britain and America.

At the same brisk speed, Bowie began work on his own sequel to *Low*. Orthodox ways of recording, with their interminable retakes and endless delays, never appealed to him. He detested having to overdub his vocals, disliked technicalities and was annoyed at being bothered with details, though his ability to master a complex piece was as brilliant as ever when time demanded. He took a mischievous delight in improvising varia-tions – 'uncannily', according to his co-producer – over Eno's painstaking arrangements. After virtually ad-libbing a song as he went along, Bowie was apt to jump up, put on a *Goon Show* accent and clown his way around the room. A friend speaks of such

outbursts as 'physical necessities, compensation for a quick mind
. . . the results, as well as the reflection, of pure genius'.

While Bowie rarely joined the other musicians at the end of the
day's work, he took to walking alone up Kothener Strasse
between creative frenzies. A woman named Gitta Fuchs remembers meeting him twice in the Aufnahme bar at the foot of the
studio stairs. On the first night Bowie was 'laughing and pulling
faces like a schoolboy'. Twenty-four hours later Fuchs saw him
with his head in a plate, sobbing, '*Why?*' 'I thought it was moving
he could still suffer for his art,' she says.

Bowie's all-things-to-all-people appeal had led him to some
strange associations, not least with women like Cher and Dinah
Shore. Shore herself felt 'David hated being painted into a corner
that wasn't his natural scene.' Judging from Bowie's outtakes at
Hansa, it was as if he had one style to please himself, and another
for the crowd: as well as the art-noise experiments with Eno there
were dozens of blissful, nostalgia-strewn songs. Bowie's voice,
fuelled by his forty-a-day cigarette habit, was frayed around the
edges but its warmth and character were still intact. Hearing its
owner reassess his life from the other side of fame made for
compulsive listening. In the memories of his Berlin years, as so
often in the past, there seemed to be two Bowies, the one
prominent and familiar, the other almost opaque or unseen.
Scores of fans knew him as the now imposing, now shrinking
singer, songwriter, producer, style plate, androgyne, the brisk,
intelligent man hurrying from role to role. To those who met him
at Hansa or the Nemesis, Bowie in 1977 was a sober-suited
figure, concave from drugs, whose knife-point slacks, open shirt
and crucifix gave him the look of a Cuban tourist. Others saw him
as strained and tightly strung, physically as well as in personality.
'David was a very tense person, always hurried,' Shore said,
remembering his striding across the cavernous sound stage. 'He
walked tense, and when he walked he could really cut out. I
mean, he didn't have a leisurely, graceful gait.' A musician also
recalls him pumping his arms 'like he was going for gold' in a
race. To the journalists who Bowie met that summer, he seemed
to care more about winning approval. 'I believe in the last two
albums more than anything I've done before,' he told one writer.
'I look back on my earlier work and there's not a great deal that

I actually like.' For the privileged few who met him after hours at Joe's Bar or Hauptstrasse, he frequently complained, as he had to Shore, about being typecast. 'I admired Ziggy,' he told one woman privately. 'I didn't *like* him. Singing folk songs was too slow a road, and [I] went for broke. I became a rock star. It's what I do. It's not my whole life.'

Bowie's next project, which could easily be taken for instability, actually concealed deep sentiment, an eclecticism which constantly took critics by surprise, a love of show business, and a quirkiness which took no more account of the cost in album sales than *Low*. He duetted with Bing Crosby.

This bizarre collaboration took place in London, where Crosby's twenty-first (and, as it turned out, final) Christmas special was filmed that September. The two men, separated by forty-five years but both short-haired and wearing identical Yuletide blazers, looked distressingly alike. Not only that: Bowie's mannered phrasing and husky, nicotine voice joined with the Groaner's, still full-bodied and with all its natural insouciance, in an eerie match of laid-back vocal styles. Crosby, who paid Bowie the compliment of asking his home phone number, died less than a month later. The special was shown on schedule. A single of 'Peace on Earth' backed by 'Little Drummer Boy' released by RCA in November 1982 (by which time Bowie had left the label) was a Christmas hit five years after the event.

From *Hunky Dory* onwards, Bowie had written songs in which he obliquely charted family life and the breakup of his marriage. By the time of *Low* he was drawing more than just the significant title from reality. The familiar theme of marital tension of 'Be My Wife' was not pure invention. After her incendiary display at Hauptstrasse the previous November, Angela had returned to London and ultimately to starring in a lunch-hour lesbian knockabout called *Krisis Kabaret*. By mid-1977 the Bowies had agreed to rotationally occupy Clos des Mésanges, with Hauptstrasse and the house on Oakley Street as their own respective pieds-à-terre. Bowie himself was living in Switzerland that September. Early in the month he took a call from Bolan, asking if he would appear on the final episode of the *Marc* TV show. By a miracle of timing, Bowie had just told Schwab and Barbara DeWitt to 'stick me on a conveyor

belt' to promote his new, unreleased album, to be called
'Heroes'. He agreed to perform. It was the first time the two
rival icons had worked together since 'The Prettiest Star' session
more than seven years before.

Right away, in Bowie's Manchester hotel, there was evidence
of tension. It centred on Bolan. He looked haggard; about forty;
already moving in that nebulous age where talk of retirement
was a sort of occupation in itself. More specifically, as host of the
show, Bolan resented what he called the 'Prince Charles' overkill
of Bowie's entourage – Schwab, DeWitt, a driver and two
bodyguards. Bowie in turn was appalled to find a press pack,
corralled by Bolan's publicist Keith Altham, barking out questions about Ziggy Stardust. Not even pop could have produced a
more poignant scene than this: the founding father of glam
reduced to exploiting his one-time disciple, who sat silently
smoking a cigarette and scowling out of the Post House window.
After Bolan and the press left the suite, Bowie extemporaneously
wrote a song called 'Madman' which he played to his ecstatic
retinue.

Tempers flared the next evening, 9 September, at the Granada
TV studio. The continued presence of the media brought an angry
reaction from DeWitt. Voices got louder. Then Bowie learnt that
Bolan's bass player, and thus a member of his own backing group
for the night, was Herbie Flowers, shop steward for the dis-
gruntled *Diamond Dogs* musicians in 1974. On that unpromising
note, and harassed by Granada's own floor crew refusing to work
overtime, the band played the first bars of a song hurriedly
rehearsed for the occasion, 'Sleeping Next to You'. Bowie stepped
forward to sing and was knocked sideways by an electric shock.
Next, as if in sympathy, though excessive green-room hospitality
was blamed, Bolan fell off stage. The production crew, with their
union deadline looming, then pulled the plug, leaving Bowie and
Bolan respectively enraged and in tears. (An acceptable minute or
two of music was later patched together on videotape.) At the
Post House, Bowie completed work on 'Madman', hastily proposed to Bolan they 'do lunch' ('Bowie-ese for "Get lost",'
according to one friend) and exited. He took the train home to
Blonay.

Eight days later Bolan was killed when his car, driven by Gloria

Jones, swerved off the road into a tree. Bowie was at the funeral at the Chapel, Golders Green, on 20 September. He sat next to Visconti and immediately in front of Dana Gillespie, who was moved by his weeping. Following the service, Bowie announced that he was setting up a trust fund for Bolan's son. He quietly donated a substantial sum of his own money. Beyond the sorrow and self-reproach of the moment, the death of a friend his own age sparked feelings in Bowie about his own mortality. After leaving Golders Green, he ordered his chauffeur to drive slowly down Stansfield Road. As the Mercedes pulled up outside number 40, Bowie got out and stood for a minute gazing up at the lace curtains of the room where he was born. He did not go inside. The car then continued down the A204 to Beckenham. At Haddon Hall, still then with its original Gothic façade, Bowie again got out, staring at the house where, six years earlier, he had reached out and fashioned something more than a new 'look', a process that bordered on reincarnation. According to a fellow passenger in the car, Bowie's mood was 'wistful – he was talking about Ronson'. He was moved by some premonitory sense to remind himself of his roots. As Bowie contemplated the decaying Edwardian stucco and weed-covered towers there was a noise from the basement and his ex-landlord, Mr Hoy, emerged to hand him a bill for unpaid rent. It had been a trying day for Bowie, but even he must have been struck by how it ended: fumbling in the pockets of his funeral suit for a few pounds to finally settle up with his past.

After a month in Switzerland, Bowie was in London again in October to promote his new album. He spent two days at the Dorchester Hotel, where he informed the press that *Low* and *'Heroes'* were angry anthems to his own survival. '*Station to Station* and *Young Americans* was a terribly traumatic time ... I was in a terrible state. I was absolutely infuriated that I was still in rock and roll.' Professing himself 'pessimistic', Bowie told *Melody Maker*, 'There is, I hope, some relief in compassion – not a word usually flung at my work – and *"Heroes"* is, I think, compassionate.' He talked about his son. The next morning, Bowie and Joe (as he now became) flew to Nairobi, where they stayed at Treetops, the safari home of the royal family, and visited among the Masai tribesman.

One of the results of Bowie's Kenyan trip was 'African Night Flight', included on his 1979 album *Lodger*, and the first statement disowning his mid-seventies tirades. The song dealt with the plight of the large contingent of ex-Luftwaffe pilots, 'permanently plastered and always talking about when they are going to leave', exiled in Mombassa. There was similar revisionism to be heard on 'Fantastic Voyage' and 'Repetition'. At the end of the decade came the event that had been implicit in the critical attack and Bowie's own personality from the start – his conversion to rock-star liberalism. By the time Tin Machine formed in the late 1980s he was a staple at show-business charity events, a patron of the Brixton Community Centre, and a writer of antifascist diatribes like 'Under the God'.

It was not always so. Bowie would later speak about his fixation with 'the magical side of the whole Nazi campaign, and the mythology involved'; the myth of national regeneration and of the 'new man', encapsulated in the search for a New Order to transcend the futile drift of modern politics. Bowie saw fascism as a direct result of Europe's pre-1914 crisis, when Darwin's biology, Nietzsche's fatalism and Freud's psychology destroyed at a stroke the moral certainties of the age. He saw the core of the movement as the appeal to personal growth through the leadership of an all-wise guru, who like Nietzsche's 'superman' dared to stand apart.

Bowie, therefore, justified fascism with that familiar mix of the personal and the semi-occult. But the musician with a restless, original mind was but a salute away from the neo-Nazi who made music. Bowie later denied that his flirtation with German expressionism had extended to the Third Reich. Yet, apart from the incident at Victoria and Andy Kent's furtive shots in Berlin (and the seizing of Bowie's Nazi 'research materials' by authorities on the Soviet border) there was ample evidence that he saw in Hitler a messianic, Ziggy-like mastery of his audience. 'He was one of the first rock stars,' Bowie said. 'Look at some of the films and see how he moved. I think he was quite as good as Jagger . . . Hitler used politics and theatrics and created this thing that governed and controlled the show for those twelve years. The world will never see his like again. He staged a country.' That Bowie saw megalomaniac traits in himself was confirmed by his

quote to *Rolling Stone* in February 1976: 'I think I might have
been a bloody good Hitler. I'd be an excellent dictator. Very
eccentric and quite mad.' Then there were his lyrics to 'China
Girl', written for Iggy's *The Idiot*:

> I stumble into town just like a sacred cow
> Visions of swastikas in my head
> Plans for everyone . . .

Bowie came to Berlin with more than a passing interest in Nazi
history. While some of his effusions can be looked at as simple
curiosity, they can also be seen as an attempt to express the core
myth of man's godlike potential, a theme of all his work since
1970. When Bowie met real Nazi fanatics living all around him
in Schöneberg – an orthodontist in his own building kept
reproduction skulls of each one of Hitler's cabinet members,
which he used in order to demonstrate the dental merits of
'Nordic blood' – he quickly reversed himself. He was appalled,
not only by the backlash against him in the British press, but
by the steady procession of rabid nationalists, racists and moral
deadbeats at his door. Late one night at Hauptstrasse, a down-
and-out art dealer attempted to sell Bowie a half-life-size bust
by Hitler's favourite sculptor, Arno Breker, and had to be
physically evicted by Iggy. There was a second incident when
Bowie, strolling alone near Hansa, was shocked to see his name
daubed on the west side of the Berlin Wall, with the last two
letters twisted into a swastika. As early as 1972, Ronson had
warned his friend against 'coming on like Genghis Khan' when
talking politics. For five years there seemed no hope of such an
outbreak of sanity. All that changed in Berlin. By the time of
'Heroes', Bowie's romantic attachment with Germanism had
given way to a belief in the consolation of human feeling. The
process accelerated on *Lodger*. With 1980's 'It's No Game',
Bowie's reinvention of himself as a sane social and political
thinker was complete. 'To be insulted by these fascists – it's so
degrading,' he sang. It was always a measure of Bowie's
complexity and strength that while privately enmeshed in an
identity crisis he could still think rationally, and in retrospect
his political makeovers, like his style metamorphoses, seem
strangely logical. But in choosing to include Hitler among his

role models, and putting in a good word for the unspeakable, Bowie came close to derailing his whole career.

Sex, the throughline of Bowie's life, was identified with the same concept of perpetual change and turnover. In June 1977 he escorted the actress Sydne Rome to the French première of *The Man Who Fell to Earth*. Later that summer his name was linked, yet again, to Bianca Jagger's. The two had dinner in Paris and, in one version, spent a romantic weekend together in a Spanish villa. By 1978, Bowie's policy of safety in numbers was fulfilled by Schwab, Viv Lynn and Monique Van Vooren.

All his life, Bowie seemed to divide women between the good girls and the good-time girls. He was attracted to big-boned negresses and would marry or make long-term mistresses of at least three of them. But friends who knew the women in his life described their roles as ornamental as much as sexual. According to one ex-lover, 'The second David decided to move on, the woman went too. We were all accessories. When we broke up he told me I had a "loving soul", almost as if he were describing my tennis stroke or something else irrelevant to the relationship.'

Among those discarded were Romy Haag, who continued to fulminate in the press, and MainMan's ex-protégée Cherry Vanilla, whose 1977 'Little Red Rooster' was an open letter to the man for whom she 'screwed disc jockeys across America'. Angela, meanwhile, still commuted between London and Switzerland, prudently timing her visits to avoid her husband. When the two did meet, in December 1977, the result was a final marital crisis, headlines in the *Sunday Mirror*, and ultimately divorce.

In addition to the lovers who joined him at Hauptstrasse or Blonay, Bowie had for some months been building up a private entourage, composed for the most part of single young women, who acted as his interface with the world. Supervised by Schwab, these 'back-room girls' would arrange travel and hotels, book dinner tables on their master's whim and, at the higher level, correspond with the record label and publishers. Where a serious strategic decision arose, the matter would be referred to an *ad hoc* committee of Schwab, RCA's Mel Ilberman and a representative of Bowie's accountants. If this committee came up with any solution which did not suit Bowie, he would sabotage it and tell

Schwab to try again, this time with Pat Gibbons' help. 'Every-thing depends on organization,' he used to say. And so, even from his austere flat in Berlin, Bowie controlled a staff that was one of the best managed in rock. Most members of the entourage cheerfully accepted the burden of serving a pleasant but essen-tially unknowable boss: someone, an ex-secretary says, who 'loved people as statistics, but didn't want to deal with them one at a time'. The recording of every album, and the running of every tour, came to depend on the advance work of the relevant section of the 'boiler room' and its endorsement by 'the guv'nr'. Over the years more than a dozen women were employed there.

At the street level, Bowie increasingly came to rely on a bodyguard-driver named Tony Mascia. This ex-bank-robber emerges as partly attractive, partly the reverse, and even Bowie's friends emphasize his paradoxical character. If Bolan's version was that 'David always had a weakness for tough guys', other colleagues' memories are less flattering. As one musician recalls, 'A kick in the nuts from Tony – that counted as a friendly hello by his standards.' Mascia continued down a line from Stuey George and Tony Frost in keeping unwanted photographers and fans from Bowie's door, often by brute force. He was apt to use plain language and he gave the impression of being formally uneducated. However, despite these drawbacks Mascia had a quick tongue, a wry Brooklyn humour, and put himself wholly at Bowie's service. He was also an excellent driver. That Bowie himself lacked the last skill was shown when he wrote off the black Mercedes whilst drunkenly steering through an under-ground garage. From then on, Mascia always took the wheel.

'Heroes', the album recorded that summer at Hansa, was released in October. The sarcastic punctuation of the title was deliberate. Bowie included the quotes not only to convey a sense of irony about the whole notion of heroism, but as part of his lifelong policy of keeping his songs, and by extension himself, emotionally distant. All his best albums share this sense of gently deflating expectations. That is not to say his fans were incapable of any strong opinions about him. Some of Bowie's new album made for thrilling listening, its lyrics characterized by the familiar neuroses, and its music by a guitar-packed wallop. Other parts served as a grim reminder of what can happen when technology and a musician's vanity run riot. *'Heroes'* was not a record that seemed to inspire any lukewarm feelings.

Like *Low*, the album roughly divided into two parts: a first side of left-of-the-dial rock songs, and a second of largely instrumental pieces, where Eno's influence was paramount. The opening cut, 'Beauty and the Beast', was a motley jumble of pop ideas wedged into a dance track with a title that referred to the Burns' madness. The music itself, hopscotching through rock history, was oddly schizophrenic. 'Joe the Lion' was even stranger, inspired by an American performance artist who nailed himself to his car, and allowing Bowie to explore his fascination with dreams in the curious refrain 'YOU GET UP AND SLEEP'. 'V-2 Schneider' was a warbled mix of electronic noodling and the bazooka blast of Carlos Alomar's guitar. It also featured a deliberate back-to-front intro, in which Bowie played a frighteningly effective sax on the offbeat instead of the onbeat. 'Sense of Doubt', 'Moss Garden' and 'Neuköln' fleshed out basic tunes with eccentric, hypnotic bursts of white-noise, guitar treatments and a Japanese koto strummed by Bowie. 'The Secret Life of Arabia' returned, yet again, to the parallel world of 'Life On Mars?' This blurring of the art-life divide, where Bowie suggested that a film scene was just as good as a real one, was a theme that came increasingly to reflect his own career.

All this paled beside the title track, a rock anthem fuelled by Robert Fripp's guitar, whose wit, depth and polish the song embodies, a clanging, metallic rhythm (produced in part by Visconti hitting a studio ashtray), and Bowie, whose quavery, melodramatic lyric achieved, as he insisted, real emotion. 'Heroes' was a brilliant collage of Kraftwerk's atonal synthesizer explorations, Phil Spector's technical finesse and Freddie Mercury's excitable choirboy vocals. Accompanied by a video of Bowie (dressed in skimpy black leather and dramatically backlit by a single spot), promoted on *Top of the Pops*, 'Heroes' reached number 24. A second single from the album, 'Beauty and the Beast', made a top-forty hit in January 1978.

'Heroes', the LP, spent eighteen weeks on the chart, longer than either *Young Americans* or *Station to Station*. Not only was it a commercial hit, it reaffirmed Bowie's talent for bending critics to maximum effect. In October 1977 he again submitted to

interviews in London and New York, spent an evening on a live radio phone-in, and took the unprecedented step of releasing 'Heroes' in both German and French. The results were all that Bowie could have hoped for: warm reviews, profiles in Berlin and Paris, heavy rotation of the video, strong word of mouth and impressive sales. *Melody Maker* chose 'Heroes' as its record of the year. Even the album's design wrung praise from the media. The black-and-white cover photograph, like *The Idiot*'s, took its source from the Brücke Museum. It, too, won Bowie a critics' award. The only discordant note could be found in the fine print dividing copyright of the songs between Bowie's own Bewlay Bros and Fleur Music, the company formed by Defries to bank his 16 per cent of the action.

Bowie's songwriting frequently worked in connection with his private life. *Low* had dealt, in part, with his feelings of betrayal by Michael Lippman. 'Heroes' was packed with layered meaning and coded references to Bowie's marriage, as when he bawled on 'Blackout', 'I've been told someone's/back in town/the chips are down'. Now, just before Christmas 1977, he met Angela for a rare week together in Switzerland. It was a disaster. Bowie announced that he was spending the holiday itself in Berlin, with Schwab and Joe. Angela fled on the first plane out of Geneva to New York, returning in January to an empty Clos des Mésanges. Desperate for money, she decided to sell her side of the story to the papers. When Tony Robinson of the *Sunday Mirror* arrived in Switzerland he found his hostess nearly senseless with drugs, a state later dramatized as a suicide bid. Pausing only to launch divorce proceedings, Angela again flew to New York and a second incident in which she was pulled from her bathtub, comatose from an overdose of Equanil. The paramedics then dropped their patient on the way downstairs to the ambulance, breaking her nose.

For much of the winter, Bowie was at home in Hauptstrasse with Joe, the boy's nanny, and sometimes with Schwab. Now and then he showed the intuitive awkwardness of a single man relating to his son. Uwe Herz recalls a day when 'David and Joe sat outside in the beer garden, both gazing up into the sky' and unable, apparently, to find common conversational ground. An increasing percentage of the time, however, Bowie was spending the whole day taking Joe to the zoo or a museum, reading together, or cycling on a tandem around Berlin's parks. The new arrangement seemed to suit him.

Inevitably, Joe became an issue in the Bowies' divorce. Here Angela would fall prey, not so much to a legal barrage, as to the leaking to her husband of a single photograph. In the Polaroid, later produced in closed court, Angela was seen posed in an exotic combination with a girlfriend. According to an official who saw it, 'It was *Hustler* stuff. That bad. As soon as the judge sat down, it was obvious which way the hearing would go.' In the eventual settlement two years later, Bowie was given custody of his son, who was to be available to Angela twice a year. Later in the 1980s Joe decided to disown his mother.

During his brief stay in Switzerland in December 1977, Bowie was visited by David Hemmings, the star of Antonioni's *Blow-Up* and a host of lesser, happy-go-lucky pop skits. Hemmings persuaded him to appear in *Just a Gigolo*, a film celebrating Weimar Berlin, also starring Sydne Rome. As an extra induce-ment, Marlene Dietrich was given a supporting part – her first screen appearance in seventeen years – although, in the event, she and Bowie never met. Principal photography began in Berlin in January 1978.

For his role as a 1920s gigolo, of mixed parentage, Bowie was supposed to be a symbol of inter-bellum Germany. The concept was good for a laugh, but not for his serious-acting aspirations. Heavy with a never-delivered message, *Just a Gigolo* was, as he put it, Bowie's 'thirty-two Elvis Presley movies rolled up into one': an unadulterated flop that saw him deliver a series of inane one-liners in an oafish script making light of street violence, marching Brownshirts and the rise of Hitler. Not only was the direction flat and the plot abysmal; due to distribution problems, twenty minutes were cut from the first half of the film (largely of Bowie), with the result that there was little scene-setting. What emerged was a threnody to decadence. Bowie played a Prussian army officer, Paul, who through a series of mishaps becomes an accidental hero. Returning to Berlin, he makes a living dredging the bars and sex clubs on the Ku'dam. At the climax of the picture, Bowie's character is killed in the crossfire of a street-fight between rival militias.

A profile of Bowie at work on *Just a Gigolo* was written for
Melody Maker by Michael Watts, author of the legendary 'I'm gay'
interview six years before. He described a scene filmed in the Café
Wien, with Bowie 'as hippy and angular as ever' and looking
uncannily like the stage performer of *Station to Station*, gliding
across the dance floor with the fifties sex siren Kim Novak. 'Look,
Maw,' Bowie announced gleefully to the few people standing
around. 'I kin tango at last! Kin ah go into town and git me a gal
now?' He had always been a glutton for accents. Perhaps sensing
the enormity of the film's defects, he increasingly filled out his
time between takes by re-enacting *Monty Python* and *Goon Show*
scripts, goosestepping around the set, and using a tin helmet for
sound effects. 'There were no quarrels, he was very friendly,'
Hemmings' assistant told the Gillmans.

Others remember a quality of the solitary, of apartness in his
social life. Though Bowie never joined the nightly parties most of
the cast frequented at the Berlin Hilton, he broke off from his
impersonations from time to time to play the piano, his music
sometimes drawing a small crowd of listeners before he shyly left
without lingering to talk or make friends. A revealing portrait of
Bowie at play is given by Stuart Mackenzie, then a young
paratrooper attached to a British regiment in Berlin:

> One night in January I came across David with Iggy Pop and
> Coco Schwab in Joe's Beer House. Bowie was being mobbed.
> There were kids literally ripping at his clothes and begging
> for an autograph. I steamed in and sorted them out. David
> was so grateful, I found myself invited to move in with him
> at the Hilton. Two other paras showed up and we formed a
> Close Protection Squad. We were Bowie's Boys for a week.

According to Mackenzie, Bowie's bedroom contained a flower-
vase of cocaine with which Iggy, in particular, would refresh
himself. 'David's own thing was drink. It was booze, booze, booze
all night,' after which Bowie would 'get maudlin' and 'talk about
Angie – he loved her but couldn't live with her'. Mackenzie saw
Bowie in tears after ringing Clos des Mésanges and thought him
'shot full of guilt. Iggy and the others might run Angela down.
David never would.' In the Hilton or at Joe's Bar Mackenzie
watched him drink and act aggressively in an obvious effort to

overcome his innate shyness and to win the very approval his intensity sometimes prevented. 'Maybe it was a kind of power thing,' another soldier says of Bowie. 'I don't think he had much self-confidence.' To still others, though, the effort was too convincing. 'He had an almost ruthless side to him,' says Uwe Herz, 'which was the reason some regulars avoided him.'

'David didn't have any close friends,' concludes Mackenzie, who remembers, on being introduced to Schwab, asking if her nickname was 'like the clown's'. At this Bowie nodded to the table where Iggy was even then adding to an already mountainous bar-bill and muttered, 'No. *There's* the clown.'

'He's so changeable,' Gitta Fuchs reflects. 'He had a tendency to downgrade himself.' Like some of the film crew who saw him on set, she felt an underlying unease and awkwardness, a deeper unfulfilled need. 'He seemed so lonely in the Aufnahme,' she thought, watching him laughing and often surrounded by people, yet somehow isolated. 'He didn't know how to mix. He was smart and sort of set apart. I think he was unsure of himself, deep down.'

Just a Gigolo opened at the Gloria-Palast in West Berlin on 16 November 1978. It was not a triumph. In talking up the film to the media, Hemmings had described it as 'highly ironic, tongue-in-cheek, about the period . . . The character [Bowie] plays makes things happen by default. His presence is always there in the action, but he never gets it right, he always slightly misses'; over ninety minutes, not quite enough. The intended note of light comedy fell flat with the critics. *Just a Gigolo* was shown at the Cannes Festival to resounding boos and was turned down by several major British distributors. Bowie, who advised his friends not to see the film, later scrapped plans to air concert footage of himself shot by Hemmings, and spurned efforts by the same director to have him appear in a biopic about Buster Keaton. The two men did not speak again for several years.

Bowie and his film agents followed up the experience aggressively. In 1977 he was turned down for a part in *The Eagle Has Landed* (where his audition was uncharitably dubbed The Ego Has Landed); he also met Rainer Fassbinder to discuss a remake of *The Threepenny Opera*. This, too, failed to occur, although Bowie released a version of Brecht and Weill's 'Alabama Song' as a single in 1980. Meanwhile, in summer 1978, plans were made to film *Wally*, a life of the expressionist painter Egon Schiele. Clive Donner, responsible for *The Caretaker*, was hired to direct, and Charlotte Rampling was touted as Bowie's co-star. In the end, due to stage commitments and the usual problems about money, he pulled out. Bowie's next wide-screen appearances would be in 1983, when he starred in *The Hunger* ('one of the most incoherent and foolish pictures in years', said the *Observer*) and *Merry Christmas, Mr Lawrence*, the most accomplished film performance of his life.

Over the next few years, Bowie became a missionary for rock video. As early as 1973, with men like Mick Rock and John Dove, he had shown a gift for recruiting the genre's brightest stars. In 1979 he met the director David Mallet, with whom he made three ground-breaking films to push his album *Lodger*. 'D.J.' and 'Look Back in Anger' were both clever vignettes, taking the songs' lyrics as their text. On 'Boys Keep Swinging', fashion, transvestism and gender were explored by some neatly drawn stereotypes. On one level, the picture was a straightforward romp and an ironic jab at sexual mores. On another, it was a brilliant throwback to the days of Ziggy and *The Man Who Sold the World* cover – Bowie appeared in three different types of drag – and a parody of the Village People. In New York, RCA rapidly decided that *Lodger*'s accompanying videos were more interesting than the actual music. An edited, four-minute collage of Mallet's work was sold in to record stores and theatres across America.

In 1980 Bowie and Mallet came up with the haunting images that accompanied 'Ashes to Ashes', the follow-up to 'Space Oddity'. *That* video would be recognized as Bowie's supreme creation, 'as touching and poignant as anything any of our best young artists have ever done', according to the *Guardian*. From then on things deteriorated. Bowie was always given to sweeping pronouncements about challenging his audience, and the grander the statement, the shorter the time before he would somehow contradict it. Thus by 1983 he was reduced to parodying the Burt Lancaster role in *From Here to Eternity*. For at least a year or two, though, Bowie's videos, surreal and yet always entertaining, were among the most intriguing contemporary films anywhere.

Within days of finishing *Gigolo*, Bowie was at Treetops for another Kenyan safari. From there he flew to Dallas, where rehearsals began for a year-long tour. Alongside the *Station to Station* group, Bowie added two new keyboard players, the violinist Simon House, and Adrian Belew on lead guitar. Belew had been playing in a bar in Nashville when Frank Zappa happened to walk in one night. The result was a place on Zappa's 1977 world tour. While playing a club date in Berlin Belew met Bowie, and soon found himself virtually retracing his steps around the US, Canada and Europe. 'I had exactly a week between gigs,' Belew told a reporter. 'During it, Bowie taught me thirty or forty of his songs. He works fast.'

Opening night was on 29 March 1978 in San Diego. Visually, the set was again out of the Speer school of drama: hundreds of white neon tubes lit the stage, and Bowie came on in a range of eye-bruising costumes, with baggy slacks and short-sleeved shirts, frequently adorned by a sailor's hat. The outfits were designed by Bowie's old lover Natasha Kornilof, who, meeting him for the first time in five years, found him 'healthy, physically and mentally, with some really epic ideas'; his surprises were almost never mere twists. Musically, the concerts stayed close to the *Low* and *'Heroes'* playlist, with ample helpings from *Station to Station* and nostalgic renderings of *Ziggy Stardust*. Eccentrically, Bowie went through the Jacques Brel and Brecht–Weill song-books, as well as his own. After a fist-pumping medley of 'Beauty and the Beast' and 'Fame', the group shifted down into 'Five Years'. The week-long rehearsal had left Belew and the others apparently only on nodding terms with Bowie's most famous songs. A ragged 'Soul Love' and a brooding 'Rock 'n' Roll Suicide' that engaged the mind, if not the ear, gave way to an interminable 'Art Decade'. The signs of Bowie's dissatisfaction with the moody joys of ambient music were readily apparent as he abruptly segued into 'Rebel Rebel'. A leisurely journey through 'Alabama Song' and 'Sound and Vision' followed: reflections on solitude and isolation, set to typically bizarre, whimsical arrangements packed with unexpected melodic twists, and sung in a low, crooning, occasionally disturbingly approximate rasp. As the house lights came up in San Diego, one woman turned to her companion. 'That was so cool,' she said. 'What will he do for an encore?' The woman would never know. In true superstar tradition, Bowie had already left the building.

Two shows in Philadelphia in late April were recorded for the double album *Stage*, released in September. As with *David Live*, the 1974 souvenir from the same theatre, it was a curiously sterile affair. The best-known tracks, like 'Soul Love' and 'Fame', were slowed down and saddled with a whistle-like synthesizer chorus. Newer cuts like 'Warszawa' were a parody of the watertight studio versions. To add to the confusion, Bowie and Visconti – in a variation of the cut-ups technique – all but capsized the running order of the original live set. *Stage*'s seventeen songs appeared in the sequence Bowie first recorded them, not as they came in Philadelphia. Visconti scrubbed Bowie's harmonizer playing from all but the *Low* and *'Heroes'* cuts, and similarly wiped audience applause. The result, rush-released to stop bootleggers and pacify RCA (where an argument arose as to whether *Stage* comprised one or two albums towards fulfilling Bowie's contract), deflated the label's hopes of a Christmas hit. The residual loyalty of Bowie's fans took the record to number five in Britain, and most local reviews were forgiving. The rest of the world never adopted this attitude. *Stage* flopped in America.

When the group played in Germany in mid-May, Bowie plunged into the usually thankless, perfunctory job of promoting the tour with conspicuous zeal, overseeing ticket sales and arrangements for the media, and donating a charcoal self-portrait to publicize *'Heroes'*. At one point in the Berlin concert, Bowie broke off from 'Stay' to ask a bouncer, in fluent German, to stop manhandling a fan. The morning's press outdid themselves in their praise of the man dubbed simply The Star. For Bowie's return to Earls Court six weeks later, the critics drew on his disastrous appearance there in 1973. Seven albums on, Aladdin Sane had become a more relaxed, if not uninhibited character. The audience, who charted Bowie's career via an array of red hair and Ziggy suits, were treated to a night of enjoyable nostalgia. Bowie frequently referred back to the earlier concert, and playfully introduced 'Art Decade', as 'Half Decade'. What's more, 'Five Years' was in the repertoire.

When the first leg of the tour ended on 1 July, Bowie continued to shuttle between his homes in Berlin and Switzerland. He spent three weeks at Mountain studios in Montreux, recording new tracks with Visconti and Eno. In August, Bowie again showed the wily, show business trouper inside the radical rock star. He played on German ZDF TV's *Musikladen* and (wearing a half-grown beard) submitted to an Italian *Vogue* photo-shoot. The group then re-assembled for further dates in Australia and Japan. By the time of the last show in Tokyo, Bowie had played seventy concerts, in a dozen countries, to nearly a million people. Critics swiftly and discreetly interred the tour, but it was Bowie's watchword and comfort that he had 'finally made it' as an entertainer.

Visitors backstage at Earls Court had witnessed a touching scene. Before going on, Bowie had left his dressing room, in full make-up and a pair of Jacobean pantaloons, to walk to the royal box. There Peggy Jones was arranging her seat and scanning the tour programme when her companion gasped, 'David's coming upstairs!' They had scarcely turned to look when Bowie was there, 'grinning all over', a friend remembers. 'You didn't have to come up here to see me,' Peggy said. And Bowie replied, 'You're my mum.' Nineteen seventy-eight was the year the two finally achieved some sort of rapprochement, if only a cursory one. Though never again close, they worked steadily towards improving relations from their low point of 1976. Two years later, Bowie would arrange for Peggy to fly to watch him star in *The Elephant Man* on Broadway. He introduced her to every member of the cast and crew and took her to dinner with her grandson. In 1992, Peggy, seventy-eight and in poor health, was guest of honour at Bowie's wedding party in Florence. By then he was not only the grand old man of art rock, but had also earned himself a fair amount of money. This latter aspect of his fame even caused Peggy to acknowledge, in private, that her son had finally done something right.

Bowie not only took financial responsibility for his mother and tried to give her a decent life: the same policy soon extended to other members of the family. When Bowie's cousin Kristine contracted cancer, he gave generously towards her treatment. There was a donation, made anonymously, to one of Peggy's elderly sisters. More importantly, Bowie took increased responsibility for raising his son. There was a practical and highly visible symbol of this closer relationship in May 1978. The previous autumn (after Peter Ustinov and Alec Guinness turned down the job), Bowie had recorded Prokofiev's *Peter and the Wolf* for RCA. He dedicated it as a gift for Joe. By spring, the album was up for a 'Best Children's Recording' Grammy alongside *The Muppet Show* and *Sesame Street Fever*. That Bowie's narration failed to hold off the challenge of Kermit the Frog was widely smiled at behind his back; but no one, including Angela, doubted that he was characteristically thorough, and now surprisingly tender, in dealing with Joe.

Over the years, Bowie developed steadily warmer feelings towards both sides of his family. They exchanged letters frequently, full of mutual concern about health, wealth and happiness. Distance, of course, helped to make the relationships better, as they could not interfere in Bowie's life. When an aunt did so – complaining in the *Sun* that he was 'callous and uncaring' and adding that it was 'time his fans knew the other side of David' – he reacted with a show of indifference. He still 'choked' he said, when reflecting on the past, but he also could realize that the survival instinct he learnt in childhood had become part of his adult character. He told a Berlin friend he felt he had 'grown up at last' in 1978.

Bowie had always relished the chance to travel. Now, with the time and money to indulge himself, he became a virtual nomad. From December 1978 to May 1979, he flew between London and New York a half-dozen times, went to Australia, and continued to migrate between Blonay and Berlin. A measure of the distance he had travelled personally came on 14 February when, before attending the British première of *Just a Gigolo*, he told Jean Rook, 'Now I look at other people. I even go into shops and, if somebody talks to me, I chat back. Three years ago I could have no more done that than fly – literally. They couldn't drag me on an aeroplane screaming, at one time. Now, every day, I get up more nerve and try to be more normal and less insulated against real people.' Stirring other memories of the Ziggy era, he gave interviews at the Café Royal. Valerie Singleton asked Bowie if he was concerned about the media tendency to see rock stars as being 'a bit thick'. 'No, I'm not concerned,' he said, smiling broadly. 'I'm *very* thick.'

After sitting through the black-tie première (for which he wore clogs and a blue kimono), Bowie returned to New York. Five years earlier he had written of the city as 'full of kooks, droogs and Light People, but also full of flies and shit. It is very beautiful and quite obscene.' Now Bowie saw only the kooks and droogs. He accompanied Joey Ramone to see the Clash and watched Talking Heads and Nico. Although no longer friendly with Reed, he met John Cale and recorded two songs with him, 'Velvet Couch' and 'Pian-Ola', that made even *Low* sound rootsy by comparison. Later that spring, Bowie would leave the Hauptstrasse apartment and exchange it for a loft on the fringe of Chelsea and Greenwich Village.

Early in May, an internal memo circulated through RCA in an effort to generate interest for the new album recorded in Montreux, *Lodger*. 'It would be fair to call it Bowie's *Sergeant Pepper*,' Ilberman contended; 'a concept album that portrays the Lodger as a homeless wanderer, shunned and victimized by life's pressures and technology.' The record dashed such high hopes with dubious choices, and production that spelt the end – for fifteen years – of Bowie's partnership with Eno. Lyrically, *Lodger* was a review of the seventies, the decade that records like *Ziggy Stardust* and *Low* had helped define. In particular, 'Look Back in Anger' may have been too cleverly titled for its own good. Almost every track was a gloomy, vengeful retrospective. Still obsessed with psychological breakdown, Bowie widened his scope to project alienation on a global level ('African Night Flight'), as well as through droll vignettes ('D.J.', 'Boys Keep Swinging'). Sonically, *Lodger* followed down the same moody path. Bowie's new album appeared as a piece of self-plagiarism, with nods to all the usual suspects. Like *Young Americans* and *Station to Station*, *Lodger* borrowed sounds from a variety of sources and liberated them from their original context.

Thus 'Fantastic Voyage' pirated the chorus from 'Word On a Wing'; 'African Night Flight' was the basic tune of 'Suzie Q' played backwards; 'Move On' achieved the same trick with 'All the Young Dudes'; 'Boys Keep Swinging' echoed the Beach Boys' 'You're So Good to Me'; 'Red Money' lifted *The Idiot*'s 'Sister Midnight' riff wholesale. Laden with over-familiar arrangements, a lavish mix and conventional, narrative lyrics, *Lodger* was a slick, calculatedly disposable record that didn't have the pretension of being anything more than a homage to Bowie's standard sources

– even though, unlike *Pin-Ups*, the tributes were oblique ones. The songs were only connected conceptually through the broad theme of being part of a fixation, Pinteresque at its edges, with failed, dysfunctional relationships.

The album's three singles were twangy, foot-tapping tunes, with solid rock-and-roll momentum provided by galloping drums, fast and furious guitar solos and Simon House's violin. 'Boys Keep Swinging' was an immediate British hit; its follow-ups, 'D.J.' and, in the US, 'Look Back in Anger', fared less well. *Lodger* itself reached number four on the chart. The popularity of the album was no doubt helped by David Mallet's state-of-the-art videos. One magazine heralded these under the title 'Sights of the Seventies', printing a half-page, foppish photo of Bowie in his Bromley Tech regalia of 'Boys Keep Swinging'.

After the innovative, raw-edged excursions of *Low* and *'Heroes'*, *Lodger* showed Bowie creeping to safer, pre-Berlin musical ground. Recorded in Switzerland, it was tainted with some of that country's famed blandness. As the album progressed, Bowie and Eno had 'argued quite a lot about what was going to happen' on certain tracks, and much of *Lodger* emerged as a compromise between the two styles. Bowie himself signified that an artistic crisis had been reached. 'I've learned some of Brian's methods quite thoroughly, and I'm fairly competent with them, so I can utilize them on my own,' he told one reporter. Almost the last line on 'Red Money', the Eno-less song that closed the album, was the repeated chorus: 'Project cancelled'.

Lodger's title was significant. By the time the album was released in May, Bowie had moved from Berlin. He now divided his time between Switzerland, his New York loft and a rented flat in London. In the three years since leaving Los Angeles, Bowie had become a more rational human being. Phil May, who knew him in both the sixties and the eighties, believes it was a 'cathartic and even life-saving' interlude. Ronson, too, thought 'David aged about twenty years' in Berlin. Although Bowie was friendlier, paradoxically he became even harder to know on an intimate level. 'I wear shades and no one even asks for my autograph,' he reported happily of New York. It was not just the fans, though, who Bowie was shunning; his disguise, ostensibly worn in order to be left alone on the street, was also symbolic. It was the same pattern he had used all his life. As a child and adolescent he had retreated to his room to make the household reality disappear. Now, at thirty-two, he employed the same tactic, still firmly believing that involvement was a curse to be avoided. The Bowie who returned from Berlin was sane, lucid and, on the surface, friendly. He was also businesslike, cryptic and self-contained. He left in his wake in New York the same shifting mixture of admiration, hostility and confusion that was to be the response to his career and personality, the chemistry of his public image, to the end.

Bowie's three studio albums starting with *Low* were among the most significant of the seventies. Although, in the last resort, he thought they belonged 'among the electric lights, brilliant and dazzling, but no heat', even John Lennon acknowledged the 'strange pull of David's work', as well as his life. *Low* and *'Heroes'*, in particular, influenced everyone from Gary Numan to Talking Heads to Culture Club. In October 1992 Philip Glass débuted a symphonic piece at the Brooklyn Academy of Music consisting of a cycle of Bowie's Berlin trilogy. These were the songs, as much as the quirky concepts of *Ziggy* or *Diamond Dogs*, that allowed him to collaborate on equal terms with Simple Minds, to socialize with the Ramones, and casually record with John Cale. Bowie's self-imposed exile had produced thrilling work, and played a large part in creating a climate for long-term credibility. He had gone to Berlin as a rock star. He left it as the consummate artist: actor, painter, folklorist, performer, and, now, father figure to a musical generation coming up behind, fast.

His influence was both global, touching Europe and America, and deep. Bowie's *Low* period helped usher in the New Romantics and the synthesizer bands spearheaded by London nightclubbers clutching their copies of *The Face* and *i-D*. His concern with guilt, anxiety and the split personality set the agenda for a new era of songwriting. His pessimistic view of humanity and fascination with style appealed to bands as diverse as Spandau Ballet and U2. Lennon would admit that his own return to the studio with *Double Fantasy* was partly in order to 'do something as good as *"Heroes"'*. *Rolling Stone* was right to declare that Bowie – more than any other performer of the decade – had foreshadowed the music of the future and would become a major figure in rock culture.

Bowie's sales, while not astronomic, were at least holding steady. Two years after release, *Low* had sold 230,000 copies in the US and the same number in Europe, roughly the same total as *'Heroes'*. *Lodger* reached a sorry 140,000. Bowie had to his credit only one platinum album (*ChangesOne*) and one gold single ('Fame'). Thanks to his RCA advances and tour revenues he was a rich man; he needed to be, and never felt himself wholly secure, but by the standards of most thirty-two-year-olds, even those in his own business, Bowie had little to complain of. In 1979 alone he collaborated in the release of the *Just a Gigolo* soundtrack; a reissue of *David Live*; an Australian compilation called *Chameleon*; and *1980 All Clear*, a nostalgic prank charting his career since 1969. Bowie was a major beneficiary of the modern fad of the record industry to endlessly recycle itself. Now, and over the next two decades, it was to be a strategy worth hundreds of thousands of pounds to his own and RCA's coffers.

Bowie was also deeply disturbed by the knowledge that whole fortunes were being made illicitly bootlegging his live performances. (One 1976 set, *Thin White Duke*, was said to have outsold even *Station to Station*.) It was partly in response to the widespread misuse of his name that Bowie enlisted the Copyright Protection Society to prevent the sale of illegal recordings in Europe. Towards the end of the seventies, he filed a second suit with the British Phonographic Institute. Bowie was shrewd, uncompromising, and never failed to use Schwab or Pat Gibbons to recover what was rightly his. When, early in the nineties, Vanilla Ice 'sampled' Bowie's and Queen's 'Under Pressure', the rapper in turn came under a barrage of writs and demands for compensation.

After *Lodger*'s release, Bowie briefly reunited with Iggy to write a song called 'Play It Safe'; had lunch with David Byrne; and squabbled furiously with Lou Reed over dinner, bringing the intervention of Mascia and Reed's own bodyguard.* He returned for a third time to Kenya. So industrious was Bowie's promotion

---

*The journalist Allan Jones, present at the same table, believed the crisis arose because 'David demanded Lou clean up his act before he, David, would work with him again.'

of *Lodger*, so well aimed and publicized his forays on all issues of music and art, that the press outdid itself to flatter him for the rest of the year. They did so because Bowie sounded interesting, which was to say, newsworthy. Beyond his obvious desire to boost sales of his records, he led no rock crusade, spoke as readily of his paintings and woodcuts as of his albums, and cheerfully admitted to his ambition to be a director. He might have been, judging by his press cuttings – a self-reinforcing record from which profiles of him were usually drawn – a Renaissance Man with a consuming interest in books. It was a measure of Bowie's intuitive knack for publicity that, a few years later, when his career hit a standstill, his name and at least an impression of his work would be remembered by millions, while many of them had forgotten Marc Bolan. Yet hidden in the public image was an equal diligence towards the promotion of his albums, and attention to his own interests, especially to retrieving 'David Jones', that was much more than perfunctory.

That diligence began and ended, as always, with the media. While Barbara DeWitt churned out releases and syndicated radio tapes, Schwab and Gibbons maintained the old contacts, in constant touch with their sizeable journalistic claque to buff their client's image. By now, Bowie generated almost anthropological interest. *Rolling Stone* studied him during a 'typical day' towards the end of his stay in Berlin. The impression was of an affable if unexciting man who painted and stuck photographs in an album while listening to *The Four Seasons*. The reporter watched Bowie, dressed in a conservative wool suit, sit down at a table in the Café Wien. 'I know what I'd like,' he said cheerfully in broken German. 'Steak and eggs and chips and a glass of milk.' Throughout the meal, Bowie laughed 'boyishly'. He had a 'genial, perplexed' air. For much of the afternoon he sat working at an expressionist painting. After a simple dinner, Bowie put on bicycle clips and rode home to Hauptstrasse. 'I'll be going back to my room to watch one hour of telly – got to catch the news, you know – and go to sleep.' Smiling, he showed his eyeteeth. 'I've got into the habit lately.'

When in 1980, he began refusing to co-operate with any biography, the motive may have been to shield the real Jones behind the fictive Bowie. It was a curious paradox that the more journalists wrote about him, the less visible he became. Bowie's interviews, though entertaining, were invariably self-serving, tongue-in-cheek sorties in projecting whatever mask was currently worn. He routinely achieved his ends by a winning mix of boffo British humour, erudition, rock-star hauteur, and an added dash of surrealism. In one writer's vivid phrase, 'Meeting him was like going ten rounds with a flyweight trained by Dali and managed by Harold Pinter.' Bowie's own diary, parts of which he later published, scattered chronology to the winds; excavation of the text in search of a factually coherent account of the author's life was as productive as listening to his records backwards for coded messages about black magic. (A cult of Los Angeles fans did this, with the rapid conclusion that Bowie was a warlock.)

Bowie saw out the decade by appearing on TV simultaneously on three continents. On New Year's Eve, Dick Clark's *Salute to the Seventies* showed taped footage of 'Space Oddity'. On the Australian show, *Countdown*, Bowie was interviewed about his career. In Britain, Kenny Everett's programme aired a new video, the extraordinary, brilliantly compact capsule of Bowie's past, 'Ashes to Ashes'. It was a triumphant note on which to end the decade that, as *Sounds* put it, 'would have been pretty boring without him'. The applause began even before the final frame of 'Ashes' faded from the screen. 'I want to thank—' Everett began. But only the first words could be heard over the roar of the studio audience, and he had to start again. It was as if Bowie were a young pop neophyte, basking in the glory of overnight fame, not the veteran of sixteen years and over twenty albums.

He next appeared on *Saturday Night Live*. Over the years, *SNL* has had the enviable knack of showcasing major stars in a necessarily intimate setting, with some often stunning results. Nothing in the programme's history even approached Bowie's performance there on 5 January 1980. He first appeared on camera in a diver's body-suit which allowed only his head to move. Somehow, in this demented garb, he got through 'The Man Who Sold the World'. Next Bowie changed into a Chinese airline hostess's uniform to croon 'TVC 15'. The song ended to wild applause. For the third number, a studio technician superimposed a marionette body over Bowie's torso. From behind this bizarre effect, he belted 'Boys Keep Swinging'. His limbs seeming to

gyrate like the song's subjects, frequently achieving a full 360°
rotation, he kept America spellbound for three and a quarter
minutes. When the broadcast cut to a commercial, the studio that
had seemed silent and funereal an hour before was now
thronging with fans. Overwhelming his bodyguard, they
'mobbed' Bowie, as he happily put it, grabbing his hands and
pleading for autographs until a floor manager intervened. For the
second time in a week, TV brought him unstinting critical
acclaim.

While in New York, Bowie recorded a new album. Then, at the
same brisk clip, he negotiated the sale of the outtake, 'Fuje Moto
San', re-edited and used to advertise saki in Japan. He later gave
three reasons for returning to the medium abandoned after the
LUV commercial in 1969. 'The first one being that no one has
ever asked me to do it before. And the money is a useful thing.
And the third, I think it's very effective that my music is on
television twenty times a day. I think my music isn't for radio.'

Throughout the autumn, Bowie and Angela had submitted to
final divorce proceedings in Switzerland. The war lasted for
months, shattering the privacy of all the participants. No two
stories were alike. Some hinted at Angela's promiscuous lesbian
affairs and negligence of Joe. Other versions had Bowie physically
attacking his wife. The eventual settlement, announced on 8
February 1980, gave Angela alimony of $750,000 spread over
ten years, and nothing else. A gagging order prevented her from
writing about her marriage for the same period. Despite the
restriction, Angela published a ghosted autobiography, *Free
Spirit*, in 1981 and a sequel in 1993. In 1986, she made a
typically brave and ill-advised bid for independence with a series
of articles in the *Daily Mirror*. The real target of these broadsides
was Schwab. It was obvious now that Angela had taken against
this 'cold, insensitive, rude woman' in a way which few had ever
suspected. Years later, she was still seething at Schwab in the
press and threatening 'ultra-violence' should their paths cross.

Some public figures actually take a perverse delight in scandal.
Bowie was not among them. In later years he privately portrayed
Angela as the rock wife from hell, a sex-fuelled opportunist who
married him for neither love nor money, but his British passport.
Publicly, he responded with grim forbearance. Bowie's friends

took up the war on his behalf. One anonymous source told the *Sun* that Angela had been a 'virtual zombie' for seven years. Another spoke of her shortcomings as a wife and mother. That the vengeful view of Angela was something of a simplification the preceding pages have, perhaps, shown; and in the nineties a reaction set in which portrayed Bowie's wife as the real genius behind Ziggy Stardust. This, too, was a mistaken picture of the woman.

Bowie and Angela had married just eleven weeks into the 1970s. They divorced in the second month of the eighties. Like Bowie's best music, they are powerfully identified with one decade. It would be straining belief to say that, on that simple basis, there was something inevitable about their breakup. One of the most interesting comments on the marriage is the fact that Bowie had turned to Angela not only without duress but enthusiastically, and when she suggested a new image in 1971, responded with Ziggy. The fabric of compromise between husband and wife was their shared lust for fame. As Bowie later said, 'Angie bit me and I went mad.'

7
LET'S DANCE

At the time he divorced Angela, Bowie wasn't sure whether he was a British, American or Swiss resident. He played at being all three, regarded them as virtually interchangeable for his purposes, and was prepared to live in whichever country suited his tax needs. As ever, he counted on Schwab to arrange details of his travel and housing. By spring of 1980 Bowie eked out his time between a new home in Lausanne, his London flat and the loft in New York – the last, like Hauptstrasse, furnished by a large bookcase, an easel and a fold-down bed. As usual there was a new car, again a Mercedes. After (he admitted) escaping lightly from the divorce, Bowie lived a comfortable, upper-middle-class existence, free to spend the margins of his RCA advances as well as his publishing royalties, money that, without a Swiss tax shelter, would have been almost certainly eaten away by his agents', accountants' and lawyers' fees, not to mention Defries.

While Schwab looked after his three homes, Bowie continued his simultaneous, whimsical and ultimately doomed relationships with different women. Like D.H. Lawrence – whose life he admired – he seemed desperate to remarry as soon as possible. Bowie liked to worship women from afar, in letters and in song. When he drew dangerously close to them, he became overwrought and insecure, and deliberately – if unconsciously – ruined his chances. There was a strong contrast between Bowie's highly disciplined songwriting and the emotional eruptions of his love letters. In his volatile confrontations with women, he invariably lapsed into the romantic clichés and operatic gestures he shunned with Angela: falling to his knees, offering flowers, weeping. Stuart Mackenzie, to whom Bowie spoke in Berlin about his love life, believes that Angela's refusal to 'stay home and breed more offspring', whatever the other stresses in the marriage, had deeply hurt her husband. 'David was someone who needed a mate', and he constantly recycled the feelings, if not the actual words of his love letters to woman after woman. 'Be My Wife' had a more literal application than some thought.

There was Bowie's close friendship with Oona Chaplin. Untypical in that it seemed (at least to Oona's daughter-in-law) that they were 'completely open' with each other, the relationship progressed by way of long walks around Lake Geneva, dinner in Chaplin's home and, ultimately, a rendezvous in New York. In September 1980 Oona was on hand to watch Bowie's Broadway stage début. 'I'm crazy about David,' she informed the *Sunday People*. 'But it's a purely platonic thing.' She recalled being introduced to Bowie by her son Eugene (the assistant engineer on *Lodger*). 'This very charming, very intelligent, very sensitive fellow, who came from the same part of London as Charlie, walked in and wanted to talk. It was as simple as that.' Among the other similarities, of course, were the two men's brilliant hijacking of the Pierrot-Harlequin mime routine and a genius for confronting audiences in the subversive guise of a not-wholly-comic character. A year later, Bowie would assure a mutual neighbour that he and Oona were 'just good friends'. He sympathized with her loneliness and drinking, minimized their age difference and spoke fondly of exchanging gifts under the Chaplins' Christmas tree (a change of venue made necessary when the lights on Bowie's own tree exploded and caught fire). Oona reacted to the cooling-off in relations by regressing to infantile dependence, telling Bowie that she couldn't survive without his support. He immediately renewed his offer of friendship. Thereafter they saw each other once a year for the remainder of Chaplin's life.

When, five years before, Bowie had recorded 'Fame' with John Lennon, he met Lennon's assistant and lover May Pang. Now, as he prepared for his Broadway début, he was visited by Pang in Greenwich Village. When the loft proved inadequate for their needs, a friend obligingly put his penthouse at Bowie's disposal. Pang also accompanied him to rehearsals at the Booth Theatre. Like Oona Chaplin, she sat in the front row on opening night.

Six months later, Bowie accepted the nomination for Best Male Singer at the *Daily Mirror* Rock and Pop Awards in London. The presenter was Lulu. Friends remarked how they enjoyed the conventions of dating – eating out, going to events about town, sitting up talking while Mascia waited outside in the car – though deeper involvement was not thought to be on the agenda. It seemed to others that Bowie valued Lulu's company both as a link with his past (the two met in 1965) and as evidence of how far he had come. The relationship was apparently not sexually charged.

In spring of 1982 Bowie co-starred in an ill-conceived piece of sub-vampiric dross, with lesbian undertones, called *The Hunger*. While on set he met the actress Susan Sarandon. Bowie enjoyed a number of intimate dinners with the woman he described as 'pure dynamite'. His commitment, however, fell short of endorsing Sarandon's radical feminist agenda. Bowie's eyes glazed over at the talk of Equal Rights Amendments and increased welfare payments to single mothers. Seemingly his sole point of interest was Sarandon's work with the Imagination Workshop, a therapy unit for schizophrenics. Bowie enthusiastically supported the project. Archly, he told Sarandon that the Burns family had always denied their history of mental illness and 'refused every offer to help them'. (Terry Burns was in fact confined in Cane Hill at that moment.) A year later, Bowie met an actress named Jee Ling, with whom he re-enacted the notorious love scene in *From Here to Eternity* for the 'China Girl' video. Life promptly imitated art. After keeping company for most of 1983, the two broke up in a clash about marriage. Still reeling from Ling's rejection and with Joe now at boarding school in Scotland, Bowie, in his late thirties, retreated altogether from socializing and fell back for support, once again, on Schwab.

Bowie's volatile love life, in which his hopes for a second marriage were dashed in a series of disastrous affairs, concealed equally bleak feelings about his music. By 1980 groups like Bauhaus and Ultravox had embezzled some of the studio techniques of *Low* and *'Heroes'*. Boy George was about to launch his particular line of post-Ziggy transvestism. Bowie himself recognized the dangers of stooping to imitate his imitators. 'I felt I was becoming static,' he said. 'I wanted to break away from that. Every few years I have to redefine what I'm writing. I had to do it when I went to Berlin and [now] I had to do it again.' After drifting apart from Eno and Iggy, and falling out with Reed, Bowie lacked an obvious career strategy. Some, like Oona Chaplin, thought that he would turn to full-time acting. Others believed he would take the opportunity to write the novel that had threatened to emerge from his songs anyway. During a spring visit to London, Bowie was seen in a number of bookshops, and leaving a publisher's office in Covent Garden. He visited the ballet, the Tate Gallery and, curiously, made a lengthy trip to the London Hospital in Whitechapel. About his new album he would say only that it was 'painless' and the single, released in August, was 'long overdue – the end of something'.

It proved to be. 'Ashes to Ashes' was a bid to update and thus resolve the saga of Major Tom in 'Space Oddity'. It was also one of Bowie's most poignant lyrics. After eleven years in orbit, the major had become 'a junky/strung out in heaven's high', looking down on a glowing planet. In its references to love, drugs and depression – and its glancing blow at Peggy – 'Ashes' was a rare exercise in writing autobiographically. Bowie rued his own self-containment in the lines:

I've never done good things
I've never done bad things
I never did anything out of the blue

over a jittery, beautifully crafted beat. True to form, the song was that unique mix of the routine and the novel, a tribute to Bowie's talent for forging new material which seemed to have been around for years. No one hearing 'Ashes to Ashes' could fail to recall it. Upstaging the Police and Abba, the single gave Bowie his first British number one since 1975.

The video, too, was a spacily-shot mixture of traditional and modern. At its simplest, the film was a look at a post-nuclear apocalypse, full of continually shifting scenes introduced by Bowie holding a miniature TV set. On another level, it was a surrealist parade of fashion changes. In its eerie fade-out Bowie was seen as a morose clown, trekking along a jet-black sea, being harangued by his mother. Not only did the images brilliantly evoke the music, they were the very forerunner of the rock video revolution.

Inevitably, RCA linked 'Ashes to Ashes' to 'Space Oddity' as an obvious way to gain attention. In one US promotion, the two songs were released as a medley. Press advertisements hammered the same theme of continuity. As testament to Bowie's now panoramic career, the label declared that 'Ashes' was the latest single from an 'enduring icon' already in his third decade in the business. Bowie was on his way to becoming famous for merely being, rather than for anything he said or did. He suffered the fate of a legend.

Scary Monsters, 'Ashes'' parent album, cast Bowie's career in a new light. Like other rock stars, he had a basically limited range, but he played one character to absolute perfection: the wry, vain but self-lacerating observer of twisted humanity, himself included. He found this character early, in *The Man Who Sold the World*, and refined it in *Hunky Dory* and *Ziggy Stardust*. But, not content with this gift, Bowie tried to branch out in most of his later albums – dabbling in disco (*Young Americans*), Euro-rock (*Station to Station*) and avant-garde (*Low*) – and earned himself five years of grief for his trouble. With *Scary Monsters* he found his voice again. The need to reinvent himself, apparently endless with Bowie, stopped dead. The album was a mid-term career self-assessment; it reviewed Bowie's progress through the decade since 'Space Oddity'. *Scary Monsters* was a moving, melodic affirmation of themes like madness, alienation and the redeeming power of love that had obsessed Bowie for years – only now he was allowing the listener in instead of freezing him out. Added to dementedly chirpy choruses, tearaway rhythms and Robert Fripp's madcap guitar, it was easy to see why *Scary Monsters* was a hit (if not quite the global smash RCA wanted), Bowie's first British number one since *Diamond Dogs*.

Scary Monsters caught Bowie between the extremes of senti-mentality and cynicism. Musically, it breathed new life into a small-scale but eclectic pop sound hijacked by the likes of Talking Heads. The first number, sung in strident, warbling Japanese by Michi Hirota, and apparently accompanied by a vacuum-cleaner, gave due warning that the album was something other than all-round family entertainment. The same song both opened and closed *Scary Monsters* in a frame, but, in between, the dense music veered between quicksilver bursts of Roy Bittan's piano, short, hot blasts of Fripp's Gibson and the sort of cocktail-bar crooning on which Bowie thrived. Aside from 'Ashes', the highlight was 'Fashion', a number in the same footstamping groove as 'Fame'. Originally titled 'Jamaica', the song evolved through a guitar make-over and a significant name change into a satire on knee-jerk style victims, a theme extended in 'Teenage Wildlife'. 'Scary Monsters', the song, set up a nightmare vision of Bowie 'running scared' from a stalking lover over a beat that evoked a homicidal pursuit. 'Scream Like a Baby' was a similarly paranoid vision of being victimized for being different. Pete Townshend guested on 'Because You're Young' (dedicated to Joe), in which Bowie offered lessons from his own varied love life. Never had his singing sounded more real or his songwriting more heartfelt. But the album was a comic wallow, too: Bowie's drill-sergeant singsong in 'Up the Hill Backwards', the samurai vocals, the puckish key changes. The result was cutting-edge avant-rock. Bowie's songs soared with manic glee and routinely achieved a bluesy languor when introspection called. Nearly every track recalled the best of his early work. There were touches of 'Space Oddity' and Ziggy, but relatively few excursions into *Lodger*-like techno-pop. Stripped of the gadgets, *Scary Monsters* drew its charge from within.

The album spent thirty-two weeks in the UK chart. It was heavily plugged by the label. Even the British campaign was minor compared to the onslaught in America. RCA spent a half-million dollars on radio and TV and sent out two pre-recorded radio tapes, with Bowie answering questions supplied on a printed list. He was presented to the public as virtually back from the dead. 'I don't see any sense existing when you could *live*,' he said. In keeping with this almost mythic sense of survival and rebirth, Bowie appeared on the *Tonight* show and polished anew some of the tall tales about his past. He collaborated with David Mallet on two new videos. Of *Scary Monsters'* ten tracks, no fewer than seven were released as singles or B-sides over the next year. (Only 'Fashion', reaching number five, was a hit.) RCA even made headway with the album's title. It was of a piece, they claimed (and Bowie denied) with his next, ground-breaking project.

The previous Christmas, Bowie had met Jack Hofsiss, then recasting his production of Bernard Pomerance's play *The*

Elephant Man. Within days, the director had offered him the chance to take over in the title role. Bowie, pressed for an overnight decision, accepted. 'I was familiar with his music,' said Hofsiss. 'But the piece of work he did that was most helpful in making the decision was *The Man Who Fell to Earth*, in which I thought he was wonderful, and where the character he played had an isolation similar to the Elephant Man's. His perceptions about the part and his interest were all so good that we decided to investigate the possibility of doing it.'

Bowie next met with the play's producers, Elizabeth McCann and Nelle Nugent, who insisted on a month of rehearsals in San Francisco and a six-week road tour before reopening in New York. Bowie agreed, accepting a $3,000-a-week fee and even submitting to an interview with American Equity (who waived their ban on alien actors), before returning to London. While there, Bowie and Schwab visited the hospital where John Merrick, the Victorian hunchback of the play's title, had gone into care. They made a pilgrimage to the hospital museum. Bowie saw Merrick's skeleton and death mask, his clothes and the model church he fashioned from cardboard. He grilled the archivist about how Merrick moved and spoke. A doctor called in to furnish medical detail claims he saw tears in Bowie's eyes. 'David told me it reawakened one of his strongest boyhood feelings, of being alone.' For his final motivation, Bowie went back to the same source that fuelled both *'Heroes'* and Iggy's *The Idiot* – Erich Heckel's *Roquairol*, whose graphic portrayal of madness also made him weep.

Through most of the summer, Bowie was bound to a familiar regime of hard work and rehearsal. He took voice and mime lessons, and offered ad-lib variations on the script – all to the mounting admiration of Hofsiss and the cast, to whom he apologized individually on the one occasion he was late. *The Elephant Man* opened in Denver on 29 July. The curtain rose to show the star, clad in little more than a nappy, acting out the role of a man – so bent he was barely recognizable as such – with restrained, agonized gestures. Somehow Bowie projected himself in the 750-seat hall in a way he never did in a 20,000-seat arena. The morning's press were fulsome with praise. One reviewer called it 'the most haunting performance in the theatre's [twenty-eight-year] history'. To *Variety*, 'Bowie now [had] the chance to achieve legitimate stardom'. Overnight, *The Elephant Man* became the most talked-about stage production in America.

If personally awkward at small talk and jokes, Bowie understood almost reflexively the needs and expectations of the media, and handled them as a matter of business no less deftly than his role. By autumn of 1980, there were two publicity machines working flat out on his behalf. The play's producers wooed the 'straight' or arts correspondents, while RCA could be relied on to raise interest among rock critics in *Scary Monsters*. When *The Elephant Man* transferred to Chicago, Bowie found himself talking, in quick succession, to *Stage*, *Sight and Sound*, *Theater* and *Rolling Stone*. To the last, he 'exude[d] an air of contented family-man composure', dressed in faded blue slacks and a simple knit shirt, and escorting Joe to the local museum. 'Over the last three and a half years, I've been getting happier and happier,' Bowie said. 'I feel I can travel about in some kind of anonymity and circulate within cities I've always dreamed of going to see. More and more, I'm prepared to relinquish sales, as far as records go, by sticking to my guns about the kind of music I really wish to make. And I'm trying to stretch out ... to get involved in all the other avenues.' Elsewhere, the cumulative press interest in his work amounted to a frenzy. In retail terms Bowie now joined the junk food of celebrity, vying with cancer cures and UFO sightings in the supermarket tabloids. 'How does it feel to be a homosexual and a father?' he was asked on ABC's *20/20*. The two worlds of theatrical and rock media met on *The Tonight Show* when, after singing 'Ashes to Ashes', Bowie took a seat and spoke movingly about Merrick's incurable plague of bone and skin tumours.

The Elephant Man began a three-month Broadway run on 23 September 1980. Among the first-night crowd were Elizabeth Taylor, Oona Chaplin, May Pang, Diana Vreeland, Andy Warhol, David Hockney and Christopher Isherwood. Ken Pitt flew in from London. 'David was stunningly good,' he says. 'It was particularly gratifying for me, because so much of it seemed to flow from his mime training around the time of *Love You Till Tuesday*.' (Bowie confirmed this thesis backstage.) William Burroughs also attended. 'I admired David for doing it straight,' he says today. 'It took guts to use only his body, instead of yards of make-up.' For Oona

Chaplin, 'he was breathtakingly good at expressing physical agony', yet never hamboning. The reviewers followed in kind. Bowie was 'preternaturally wise' (*New York Times*), 'piercing and haunted' (*Daily News*) and 'simply electrifying' (the *Post*.) The third group of critics, the Ziggy clones and Bowie Boys, were also represented. At least once every performance, a cry of 'Starman!' or 'Rebel Rebel!' would surge up from the stalls.

Accustomed to seeing his name in print, to weekly mentions in *Melody Maker* and *NME*, Bowie was still not fully prepared for how effectively Barbara DeWitt exploited him to the heavyweight titles, and for what now began to unfold. The *Sunday Times* sent Gordon Burn to interview him in New York. French and German theatre critics jockeyed for position backstage in the theatre. Tim Rice (who remembers Bowie as alternately 'very charming and charismatic' and 'utterly focused') arrived for the BBC. Two ITV crews followed. On the afternoon of 7 December the disc jockey Andy Peebles met Bowie in the RCA Building on 6th Avenue. To Peebles and the others he was a revelation, a Broadway star, a Renaissance man, an interviewee who made the interview enjoyable and, not least, a rock fan. 'I was in town to meet both him and Lennon. David was spellbound by that,' says Peebles. 'All he talked about was the Beatles.'

The next night Lennon was murdered. Bowie had just come off stage. While much was made of the physical vicinity of the two men – the more imaginative versions had Bowie hearing the shots from thirty blocks away – the truth was shocking enough. Mark Chapman, Lennon's killer, had attended a performance of *The Elephant Man*. At the stage door, he got off a shot of Bowie with his camera. Chapman later bragged to a girlfriend that he could have slain either man. His plan was to lie in wait for Lennon and, should that not work, walk back to the theatre. Among the items found at Chapman's hotel room was a programme for *The Elephant Man*, with the star's name ringed in black.

Bowie went on as usual the next night. He turned down the producers' suggestion of extra security. A few days later, after visiting Yoko Ono and May Pang, he also declined Hofsiss's offer of a renewed contract. Bowie gave his 157th and final perform-ance as John Merrick on 4 January 1981. Reflected in the critical

and popular acclaim was a fundamental truth of his achievement. Bowie was quite simply more intelligent, more resourceful,
by any odds harder working than most of his rock music peers.
What he lacked in raw talent he made up for in improvisation and
a genius for realizing other people's ideas. His three months on
Broadway planted a self-confidence and changed his reputation
forever, lifting him to true celebrity and erasing the Ziggy image
at last.

The Elephant Man employed Bowie and legitimized him. He
became an actor–composer, rather than a musician who did
impersonations. But it did not, at least at first, ensure him a
future. It was more than a year before another play of his reached
the public, and two years before he next appeared on screen.
Bowie's sole appearance in front of the cameras in 1981 was
Christiane F., a graphic tale of teenage dereliction and drug
addiction in Berlin. His cameo as himself at a German concert
was in fact a composite, largely shot in New York. The accompanying album, released in April 1981, was made up entirely of
songs taken from *Low*, *'Heroes'*, *Stage* and *Lodger*, thus making a
soundtrack out of an anthology. For all the glowing reviews of
The Elephant Man, Bowie found himself in the quandary of nearly
every actor other than the biggest stars. He did get offers, but
mostly from producers who lacked financing for their dubious
scripts (still chiefly concerned with guitar-playing aliens) and
who were counting on Bowie's fame to get their projects made.
He had to take what roles were offered and play them because
they were available to him, or opt for semi-retirement. He chose
seclusion.

Bowie spent much of the year as a virtual hermit in Switzerland. He still saw May Pang and Oona Chaplin. He accepted his
Best Male Singer award from Lulu. But he refused either to tour
or to capitalize on his Broadway hit by turning his interesting
enough life into a science-fiction farce. For a year, his name
almost disappeared from the gossip columns and the entertainment trade news. When Schwab and others visited Lausanne
they found a scrupulously polite, taciturn Englishman, dressed in
a ski sweater, more anxious to discuss snow levels than music.
His sole albums were re-releases, scraped together by RCA, full of
spurious rarities, and inevitably celebrating Bowie's past rather

than his present. Nowhere was this more true than with *ChangesTwoBowie*. Nobody close to him, not even Schwab, claims he took the slightest pride in this cynical project. The album's crude reworking of old hits was dangerous, if not impossible material to wed to Bowie's self-image as a man on the move. *ChangesTwo* was not only shamelessly nostalgic; it also followed the same well-beaten path as the previous year's *The Best of David Bowie*. Despite objections from Pat Gibbons, RCA never let up on its attempts to recycle its two star products, widely referred to by insiders as the 'king' and 'queen' of rock. Elvis Presley made three posthumous top-forty appearances in 1981. Bowie now walked the same self-caricature tightrope, and induced the same law of diminishing returns. One result of *ChangesTwo* was a listless video promoting 'Wild is the Wind'. Another was a growing rift between Bowie and Schwab on one side and RCA on the other. The record company took a dim view of the Berlin trilogy, and angered Bowie with their overheated promotion of *Scary Monsters*. By summer of 1981 he was comparing the relationship to a 'bust marriage', and suggesting a familiar legal solution. 'I've had enough,' he said. 'I want a divorce, like my divorce from Angie.'

He had reached this conclusion after comparing notes with Freddie Mercury and the other members of Queen. Bowie met the group in July 1981 at his local studio in Montreux, where they were recording their album *Hot Space*. After the inevitable jam session, they pooled resources on 'Under Pressure'. The single, in some views a simple duet, in others an all-out war between Bowie's and Mercury's caterwaulings, was recorded and mixed in less than a day. Both camps later tended to disown the hastily improvised lyrics. Although 'Under Pressure' featured some seriously inept lines, it also possessed Queen's winning formula of balladry, hard rock and heavy metal; something for everybody made it a number-one hit in Britain.

From Mercury, Bowie heard of the positive feedback and healthy royalty flow Queen enjoyed from EMI. According to an engineer at the Montreux session, 'you could see his one good eye gleam when Freddie used the words artistic control. After that, David was all over him for details. Were the advances prompt? Who paid what? Stuff like that. Bowie had reached the end of his rope with his label.' A year later, Ronson also said that money was 'a pitched battle between David and RCA', but added that the real cause of his defection was his fear of becoming 'an old fart', pigeonholed as an AOR stalwart and 'a kind of joke' to the caricaturists. Bowie had already been lampooned by the Strawbs. Now a comedy team called the HeeBeeGeeBees parodied *Scary Monsters* on a song called 'I'm Quite Ahead of My Time'. Bowie was featured as David Bowwow and A-Lad-In-Sainsbury's, a freak posing as, among other things, an elephant. Although Bowie's response was never recorded, Ronson believed 'it was one more nail in the coffin'. In the course of a discussion with Mel Ilberman, Bowie made it clear 'he wasn't happy with RCA ... he wanted to go'. A second executive had the same sense that 'David was losing direction' and needed to reboot his career. RCA's action in allowing what Bowie considered to be the exploitation of himself and his work gave a fillip to the uneasy feeling that some form of reinvention was necessary, if not vital. He asked Mercury for a contact at EMI.

By 1982, the depth of his dissatisfaction and, more important, the shifting mindset of his mid thirties remained largely hidden from his fans. By *Scary Monsters* there was already emerging the patterned duality of Bowie's politics – the right-wing bigot still smeared in the press and the man and liberal campaigner rarely openly seen. He remained an unwilling icon of the National Front. *Bulldog*, the party's youth newsletter, said in an article on 'White European Dance Music' in November 1981: 'Perhaps the anti-Communist backlash and the aspirations towards heroism by the Futurist movement has much to do with the imagery employed by the Big Daddy of Futurism, David Bowie. After all, it was Bowie who horrified the music establishment in the mid seventies with his favourable comments about the NF [sic] ... Bowie who, on the album *Hunky Dory*, started the anti-Communist musical tradition which we now see flourishing amidst the new wave of Futurist bands.' Sixteen months later, Bowie's vision of 'swastikas in my head' in 'China Girl' was seized on as proof of a continuing fixation with Nazism. Yet that song, like the Victoria Station salute, dated from 1976. By the time of *Scary Monsters* he was showing a vague but decisive swing to the left. Fatherhood, too, brought new variations into his thinking.

As Bowie grew closer to his son, so he made an effort, however clumsy, to blunt the sharp edges of his isolationism. It pleased his new friends and surprised his old ones to see how he cared for the boy. More often than not he would drive Joe to school and visited on parents' day. On holiday in Kenya, Bowie bought him a camera and a book about native culture. Any sign of intolerance on Joe's part roused Bowie's disapproval, for example when he playfully referred to 'darkies'. By the mid eighties the two presented a close mutual relationship to the world. Bowie openly credited Joe for giving him a more relaxed view of life. He also spoke movingly of his new-found ability to see 'the long-term – issues like health care and ecology' because of his concern for Joe's future. In July 1985, introducing 'Heroes' from the stage at Live Aid, Bowie made the dedication: 'To my son, to all our children, and to the children of the world.'

After the one-off success of 'Under Pressure', Bowie's musical career languished for a year. The RCA sales department kept his name in the public eye. As well as the *ChangesTwo* and *Best of David Bowie* compilations, there was a glut of reissues, doodlings and studio outtakes, some dating back to an era of pre-'Space Oddity' innocence. This professional cannibalism further contributed to his feeling that he was 'nothing but a product' to RCA; a brand name which they shamelessly peddled at the obvious risk of swamping the market. Fortunately for Bowie, he had several things on his side that combined to carry his career. First, *The Elephant Man* had been such an enormous hit that other producers desperately wanted to profit from his name. In summer 1981, Bowie accepted an offer to star in a BBC dramatization of Bertolt Brecht's *Baal*. For the title role of the shiftless, homicidal poet, he appeared unwashed and hiding behind a flimsy beard. The part was not especially big, nor particularly sympathetic. Rehearsals occupied Bowie for weeks. He was paid the standard fee by the BBC, £1,000.

David Bowie in Baal was broadcast on 2 February 1982. It earned mixed reviews. Rock critics, some unfamiliar with the script, saw little to praise in Bowie's half-awake performance. To *Melody Maker* there was 'none of the dramatic dominance which made *The Elephant Man* so memorable'. Moreover, by scheduling

Baal against Laurence Olivier in *Voyage Round My Father* on the rival channel, the BBC invited viewers to choose between Bowie and one of the world's most watchable actors. He was the heavy loser in the ratings war. There was praise from those, like Ken Pitt, for whom 'David scored a personal hit in a weak production'. But the general consensus was that Bowie was a mumbling cartoon of a German poet, just as he had been of a Berlin gigolo. The part seemed beyond his reach. He did, however, release a soundtrack EP of five of *Baal*'s songs (proving, if nothing else, that Bowie and Brecht were strangers to each other's tempos), achieving a modest success.

As 1982 progressed, so Bowie retaliated against RCA with a series of stage and film projects. He refused to deliver a follow-up to *Scary Monsters*. The simmering clash of wills now boiled to a crisis. Not only was there a standoff over, as an RCA memo put it, 'what type of artist David really is'; there was the matter of his obligation to Defries through September 1982. Bowie was in no great rush to release records that served in large part to enrich his enemies. He said as much to *Rolling Stone*. That he intended to pursue his other ends was shown by *Baal*; by his choosing to attend several nights at Sadler's Wells (where Mascia snored in counterpoint to the performance); his dabbling with taking the role of Satan in *Brimstone and Treacle*; and his contribution to the soundtrack of Paul Schrader's *Cat People*. The last yielded a number 26 hit in April 1982. While RCA went to ever more cynical lengths to squeeze as much product as they could out of Bowie, he obliged with a string of bizarre collaborations, duets and soundtracks like *Baal*. His fiftieth and latest single followed in this perverse tradition. With Bowie's trademark bombastic vocals and a score by Eurodicso producer Giorgio Moroder, 'Cat People (Putting Out Fire)' was a darker, more edgy treatment than the cover which appeared in 1983. Bowie, above all, knew that a suggestive, fragmentary lyric could cast a telling shadow over a song: 'Those who feel me near/pull the blinds ...' he murmured, and the sense of menace loomed when he completed the line: '... and change their minds'. Again, there were long faces at RCA. One executive evidently thought Bowie's partnership with Moroder would lead him back in the user-friendly direction of *Young Americans*. 'If it isn't too much trouble,' he minuted a colleague, 'it would be nice if DB went into the studio and recorded a *real* album.'

He did not. Bowie followed *Baal* by co-starring in Tony Scott's *The Hunger*, described by MGM as a 'female vampire' movie, but existing mainly as a long series of soft-focus poses with a lesbian subplot. For the part of Blaylock, Bowie was called on to age 250 years in a day. Much the same geriatric fate befell the script, which came on moody and atmospheric and ended up struggling vainly to be decadent. 'Incoherent and foolish' was the *Observer*'s verdict.

Despite sharing top billing, Bowie was on screen for less than thirty minutes. It was ample. Critics were quick to skewer his deadpan cool as no more than wooden acting. 'Bowie and Catherine Deneuve,' wrote one, 'make Bill and Ben look like Olivier and Gielgud.' In this view, the high promise of *The Man Who Fell to Earth* had been dashed in a series of vacuous roles, with only their alleged eroticism in common. Bowie's looks and cue cards carried him through *The Hunger*, which he later disowned (while praising the quality of the camera work). The film also introduced him to Susan Sarandon.

Meanwhile, a radical Japanese director named Nagisa Oshima (whose *In the Realm of the Senses* had resulted in a lurid obscenity trial) began casting for his version of Laurens van der Post's *The Seed and the Sower*. The story was an unflinching treatment of life in a wartime prison camp. Oshima's plan was to have Robert Redford appear in the starring role. In the end, for budgetary reasons, that proved impossible. By a fluke of timing, Oshima, who had met Bowie during the New York run of *The Elephant Man*, then saw his saki commercial on television. He placed a call to Lausanne. 'I'd just wrapped *The Hunger*, and the last thing I wanted to do was make another movie,' Bowie admitted. But he admired *In the Realm of the Senses*, and would automatically be favourably disposed to anyone who was, like Oshima, struck off by his own directors' guild. He agreed to take part in the film, renamed *Merry Christmas, Mr Lawrence*, without reading the script. Within a fortnight of finishing *The Hunger*, Bowie was on location in the Cook Islands.

The screenplay for the project was written by Paul Mayersberg, who had worked on *The Man Who Fell to Earth*. Some felt that he too freely adapted van der Post's story to suit Bowie's character. There was the enigmatic opening line ('Why shouldn't it be?'), the snub made by Bowie to his captors ('My past is *my* business') and a lengthy flashback to life as a bullied schoolboy. However arrived at, the result was an actor more than usually attuned to his role. In most critics' judgement, *Merry Christmas, Mr Lawrence* was the finest film Bowie ever participated in and featured his finest work. His character, Jack Celliers, was another in Bowie's gallery of life's misfits, but this version had several subtleties. Celliers was meant to be 'the devil' to his captors. a neurotic, twitchy figure yet with a vulnerability that was to be revealed only slowly, so that Bowie could not hope to enlist the audience's sympathy until the film was nearly over. Then, in front of the entire camp, and shown in slow-motion, Celliers stopped the execution of a fellow POW by marching forward to kiss the Japanese commandant on his cheeks. For that he was beaten, and buried up to his neck to suffocate under the blazing sun, while the rest of the prisoners were spared.

Merry Christmas, Mr Lawrence premièred at Cannes and brought Bowie unstinting critical raves. The *New York Times*, which had panned *The Hunger*, called him 'mercurial and arresting'. In a long piece in *Vogue* entitled 'The End of Gender', Anne Rice praised the androgynous quality of his acting: 'Bowie, through the alchemy of his subtle strength and yielding beauty, emerges as [a] new and thoroughly contemporary star.' The film was still widely circulating four months later, when Bowie won the ultimate media accolade, a *Time* cover story. By then, freed from the irksome deal with RCA, he was again travelling around the world, enjoying a hit album and generally being a global rock star.

In the summer of 1982, prompted by feelings that his back catalogue, and thus his name, was being used, Bowie fell into a familiar pattern of behaviour. When he had no regular group and no songs, he was glad to accept a salary for doing film work. But after he had been on location for six months, his resentment built up again. He got tired with working hard for little pay, increasingly wanted to get back to music, but was equally weary of RCA and Defries. Bowie faced a demoralizing crisis. He was a victim of the very versatility he had striven for as an artist. In the nearly two years since *Scary Monsters*, he had appeared on the Broadway stage, acted on TV, and co-starred in three films, one of them a major critical hit. Yet he never gave up on plans to return to the studio. By the time he finished *Merry Christmas, Mr Lawrence*, there were the old deep ambiguities in his thinking: was he a movie star who made music, a composer who acted, or, rather, a Swiss tax-exile who wanted to ski and paint? Even Bowie had no clear answer to RCA's question about 'what type of artist' he really was. Record-label pressure for a hit, condescending attitude and criticism of *Scary Monsters*, combined with Bowie's paranoia about Defries and embittered moods, led to a summer of constant ferment. Bowie sent RCA an angry letter attacking plans for yet another cynical anthology. He brusquely vetoed plans for a charity concert in London, and called instead for an audit of his royalties. His grumbles were wide-ranging, even contradictory. Bowie wanted to keep his name in front of the public. He refused to tour. He spoke about not needing a hit single. He carped when RCA failed to release 'Boys Keep Swinging' in America. Bowie's frustration and anger were fuelled by loyal friends, like Mercury, who made good on his promise to arrange a meeting at EMI. Preliminary discussions took place that September. When Bowie was told of the sums on offer elsewhere, he promptly wrote RCA another letter (eventually crossing Ilberman's desk), rambling and strewn with expletives, expressing all the frustration he felt about his career. Not long afterwards, Ilberman left the company.

Bowie sat tight. To wait out the end of his contract suited his purposes. There was also a sense of artistic exhaustion, that, at thirty-five, most of his really epic songs were behind him. 'Under Pressure' and 'Cat People', for all their success, did little to suggest Bowie was doing anything other than tread water on a larger budget. In Britain, meanwhile, a younger crowd started to pick up on him for what he represented. The advent of the New Romantics did wonders, as one critic said, for 'the oldest romantic in rock'. Bowie's flame was kept alive by a clique of dedicated journalists, by the fan magazine *Starzone*, and by the hardcore movement who took *Low* and *'Heroes'* as their manifesto. The 'gender-bender' cult, pioneered by Boy George, served him well, too: Bowie was frequently cited as a reference point.

Between bouts of depression and self-lacerating wit, Bowie played up to the myth. He became a self-admitted elder statesman – 'the Ronald Reagan of rock'. One journalist who visited Lausanne suspected him of having a weakness for titles, as in his preference for being called 'Mr Bowie' in public. The rumour that he had tried to buy the rights to a baronetcy was obviously a slur, but nevertheless expressed a quality that people saw in him. It made him more attractive that he preferred harmless vanity to megalomania, but it still left Bowie's judgement open to doubt. Visitors to Switzerland in the latter half of 1982 were treated to long screeds about RCA and the conviction, eerily reminiscent of 1975, that 'agents' were out to get him. The sharp inward division between the clarity of Bowie's rational mind and the overpowering strength of his irrational rages was reflected not only in his speech and letters but also in his suspect professional choices. Buying the novel *Miracle Jack* to work into a film was one thing; appearing as 'the Shark', with a rubber fin stuck to his back, in the pirate pastiche *Yellowbeard* was an act of almost surreal inanity.

Over the years, Bowie had quarrelled with nearly everyone he ever met and alienated more than one person capable of helping him. By 1982 his own life – as opposed to that of his fictional characters – was no longer tainted by this unhappy knack. With his neighbours and friends he won, in both Lausanne and New York, a warm, ungrudging popularity. Immaculately groomed, with a soft voice his visitors remembered as a trademark, Bowie could be the picture of English civility. In Switzerland he threw open-air parties in which, says a friend, 'he worked the crowd like Princess Di'. Sometimes two or three hundred people would gather in a marquee to hear him sing. 'He was the consummate host,' says another guest. 'Just a word from him was enough. If you ever saw Robert Redford in *The Great Gatsby*, you have a good idea of what David was like.' Many of his fellow-musicians never forgot him. 'He was without doubt the nicest, most professional, *intelligent* rock star I ever met,' says Willie Weeks. 'Bowie seduced you,' another man says. 'He used to tell you what he thought you wanted to hear, then ask your opinion. It's very flattering.'

With security came self-confidence. Bowie could be genuinely affable, self-mocking and a considerate friend and father. Phil

May believes that Berlin had been a kind of closure for 'the old David – the bugger who got what he wanted'. Others felt uneasily that Bowie's surface charm stopped short of real warmth. Loyal colleagues like Terry Cox and John Hutchinson, told to 'keep in touch', found their letters unanswered. While some blamed Schwab for shielding Bowie from his past, Cox argues that 'she could never have done it without David's say-so'. The policy extended even to Ronson, who by October 1982, touring America with T-Bone Burnett, referred to his old friend as 'a twat', and still in need of 'real friends – he doesn't have any'.* Even this was mild compared to Angela's outburst in the *Daily Mirror*. The headline, MY BITTERNESS, said enough.

Since the low point of 1976, Bowie had worked hard to achieve some sort of rapport with his mother, if only a casual one. While most of his letters generally contained news bulletins, with little or no emotional input, they did nonetheless show some of the concern he felt for his family. In June 1982 Bowie's half-brother Terry Burns threw himself out of a window at Cane Hill in an apparent suicide bid. He fractured his arm and leg and was taken to Mayday Hospital in Croydon. Later that month, a nurse (whom, Terry noticed, had hurriedly put on make-up) informed him that 'Mr Bowie' was in the visitors' room. The two men spoke alone for an hour. Over the course of the next year, at Mayday and Cane Hill, Terry gave the nurses to believe that Bowie would be back to rescue him. When she realized that that promise was not going to be kept, Peggy's sister Pat called in the press. In her version, Bowie was afraid of losing his sanity and 'terrified' to visit Terry. This brought an angry response from Peggy, though no comment from her son. As the true emotional bonds between Bowie and his half-brother had been broken so many years before and never repaired, he may not have experienced any great shock

---

*There was a reconciliation a year later, when Ronson was invited to Bowie's concert in Toronto. The two joined together on 'The Jean Genie' – Ronson borrowing Earl Slick's guitar – and were seen deep in conversation in the dressing room. Proof that there was a way back into Bowie's favour finally came in 1992, when Ronson guested on *Black Tie White Noise*. He died the following year.

at Terry's desperate plight. Then again, as an expert at hiding emotion, even from himself, it is also quite possible that he was not at the time truly sure of how he felt. It was another ten years before Bowie wrote about his brother in a song.

Some friends would remember Bowie for a need to dominate, and a petulance when prevented. The fallings-out with both Defries and Lippman had thrown him into fits of tears, a show of self-pity that had marked similar experiences of setback or trial in the past. Their other result was to persuade him to 'take control ... to make my own decisions'. The Bowie emerging in the early eighties would stress that virtue among all others: control. Though he took advice from Stan Diamond, Pat Gibbons and the rest, by the time of *Scary Monsters* he was self-managed. Bowie had learnt that he could just as easily use MainMan's tactics to make a deal without using Mainman. Don Gunn calls him 'an incredibly quick study ... He has a great head on his shoulders and he catches on fast.' Even in an industry teeming with lawyers, accountants and sinister 'market-penetration' men, Bowie was famously awake at the wheel. On 9 September 1981 he applied for, and obtained, a Tax Exempt Certificate, number FD617010220, establishing him as a Swiss resident. He took an interest in no fewer than six companies administering his songs, and struck a deal with United Artists enabling him to develop his own film projects. It was enough to make Bowie confident of his position, and it did. He told RCA he would be leaving the company 'the split second' his other commitments allowed.

On 15 March 1982, in the High Court of Justice, a winding-up order was made against MainMan. Six months later, Bowie's support of Fleur Music also ended. From then on, Defries would take only 50 per cent of his ex-client's royalties from *Hunky Dory* through *David Live*.

When his contract with RCA then lapsed, Bowie received bids from CBS, Geffen and EMI. Money, to these three conglomerates, was apparently no object. The offers that poured in were significant not only to Bowie's immediate plans but also to his future. An example of the lavish attention he always enjoyed in boardrooms, the interviews each touched on his long-term security. A last-minute doubling of advance, the result of muscular pressure from Gibbons, and Mercury's endorsement won the auction for EMI. By charm, opportunism and a strong arm, by using and being used with equal skill, Bowie had pulled off a major negotiating coup and extended his career into the next century.

According to the terms of the deal, effective from 27 January 1983, EMI paid a $20 million advance against five albums. Even at the peak of the industry's generosity, when the Rolling Stones could earn twice as much or more, new groups had only to move to be signed, and a company like EMI actively relished a loss-leader, it was a notable feat. Bowie, after years of being rich, entered the realms of Elton John and the ex-Beatles.

The new label's A&R men soon found how Bowie functioned. The suave and soft-spoken star was Mr Outside, attending the meetings, signing the papers, but otherwise invisible. Gibbons was Mr Inside, riding herd on the staff, organizing details and, with Schwab, taking responsibility for literally everything it wasn't vital for Bowie to do himself. In the boardroom, one executive recalls, it was 'Coco who was the Great Satan'. 'She had the two absolutely priceless traits of the PA,' a friend says. 'She could pick horses *and* jockeys. She could spot a good idea, and she could tell if the people running with it were any good.' Others credited Schwab with greater insight than Bowie into the needs of his career. Over Christmas, plans had already been made for a new world tour, his first in five years. Now EMI booked Bowie studio time at the Power Plant in New York. With Barbara DeWitt dancing attendance, the press and publicity machine once more became a giant needle stuck in one groove. The three words stamped on a million souvenir badges read simply: 'BOWIE IS BACK'.

If 1973 was remembered as the year a mass market discovered Bowie, then 1983 would go down as the year Bowie discovered mass marketing. As well as EMI's badge campaign, there were to be home videos, a TV special, reissues of Bowie's material, logoed souvenirs and accessories, all coupled with a strategic year-long media blitz that would lead to stories in *Time* and *Newsweek*. Such publicity could not have been bought, particularly for an album that had yet to be recorded.

Tony Visconti had been under the impression that he would be producing the project. He put off a number of other plans accordingly. Shortly before he was due to start work, Visconti rang Schwab to confirm the arrangements. 'She phoned back,' he told the Gillmans, 'and couldn't even tell me. She phoned my secretary and said, "Well, he's met someone else".' Visconti's replacement was Nile Rodgers, the New York guitarist and songwriter responsible for hoary disco hits like 'Le Freak' and 'Good Times' and, more recently, producer for Diana Ross and Debbie Harry. He met Bowie in the bar of the Hotel Carlisle in Manhattan. The occasion was only slightly marred by a gaffe when Rodgers, 'expecting Ziggy Stardust and not this average-looking guy', failed to recognize his new employer. From that low point things improved. After a perfunctory jam, the two men hit on a sound that blended *Ziggy*'s irresistible tunes with funky dance beats influenced equally by James Brown and *Saturday Night Fever*. Rodgers located the perfect musicians. By mid-January, the group was already recording 'Vampires and Human Flesh', a working title quickly shelved in favour of the simple-but-self-explanatory *Let's Dance*.

'It's very easy,' Lennon had told his collaborator on 'Fame'. 'Say what you mean, make it rhyme and put a backbeat to it.' Some of this raw appeal carried over into Bowie's new album. *Let's Dance* was recorded in three weeks. Bowie then flew to Switzerland, where he was joined by David Mallet to work up storyboards for the record's first two videos. The reference text for the films was to be racial prejudice. In what some praised as a new-found altruism and others thought reeked of play-acting, Bowie persuaded EMI to finance a shoot in Australia, where he proposed to take up the cause of Aboriginal rights. (In private he also discussed plans to play the role of Lincoln in *The Civil War*, an avant-garde opera by Robert Wilson portraying the president as a genocidal racist, and to take part in an unnamed play slating Enoch Powell, neither of which took place.) Bowie and an entourage of five, including his son, then took off for Sydney.

Visitors to the Sebel Town House Hotel found Bowie at his most engaging. Since his previous visit in 1978 he seemed to have softened and to have begun, perhaps unconsciously, to come to terms with himself. He was no less anxious to be liked than he had been, but he was now old enough and experienced enough to seek favour on his own terms. The unfocused character with the live-wire hair had become a genial, relaxed man wearing shorts, bush boots and a felt hat. For the 'Let's Dance' video he drove to the sheep-country outpost of Carinda, walking into the one-room pub of the local hotel and charming the locals by talking cricket. A day later, returning to Sydney, Bowie was exotically employed with his new girlfriend Jee Ling on the 'China Girl' shoot. 'As much as I love this country,' he told Kurt Loder, 'it's probably one of the most racially intolerant in the world, well in line with South Africa.' Fourteen years on, Bowie appeared to be groping his way back to the hippie idealism of *Growth* and the Beckenham Arts Lab: 'It occurred to me that one doesn't have much *time* on the planet, you know? And that I could do something more useful . . . I feel that I'm thirty-six years old . . . I've got a certain position . . . I want to start utilizing that position to the benefit of my . . . brotherhood and sisterhood.' He winced but continued. 'There's a lot of injustice. So let's, you know, *say* something about it.'

Bowie returned home with Jee Ling. Mark Ravitz, co-producer of the *Diamond Dogs* tour, then found himself picked up and flown at a moment's notice (the method Bowie typically used to summon colleagues) for a design conference in Lausanne. He arrived to find his host smiling and tanned, fresh off the ski slopes. Bowie stipulated that the new tour had to have a 'topflight production' and he insisted that topflight people be in charge. Shy and affable he may have been, but there was nothing self-effacing about the way he dredged money from EMI. These funds in turn gave Bowie the means to retain his grip on his tour crew, many of them seconded from the Rolling Stones. One executive left with the impression of a split personality: the unassuming family man who drove a modest Volvo, and the self-styled 'control nut' whose obsession with order and compulsion to classify was reflected in computerized print-outs and a card index with details of his every stage performance over ten years.

Part of Bowie's own ego was a naïve but unshakable faith that whoever represented him was the best at what he did, whether he was a lawyer, stagehand, musician or producer. Following a reference from Mick Jagger, he had insisted on Stevie Ray Vaughan, the virtuoso blues guitarist, to play on *Let's Dance*. He hand-picked Nile Rodgers. A combination of these two, said

Bowie, gave the album a 'dynamic, enthusiastic quality', making it his 'commercial début' and, he gloomily predicted, unleashing 'the media attack-dogs' in the process.

But there was no attack. Certain critics were more polite than moved. *Rolling Stone* called it a 'functional' album that came alive only through Rodgers' touch-of-funk production. The *Commonweal* reviewer dismissed it as a 'disturbing failure'. But such grumbles were either too few or too late to stop Bowie's success. Not only was it his commercial début: it revived his whole career. In 1978, Bowie had told *Melody Maker* he had 'decided to adopt the doctrine that a man reaches his most creative strength at around age 35'. *Let's Dance* now bore out the claim. It was a rock album in the classic mould. In Bowie's case, that meant collecting influences and seamlessly mixing styles: his own gravelly vocals, the trademark R&B horns, thickened bass and drum parts and the blues tour-de-force of Stevie Ray Vaughan. Bowie, if nothing else, had a clear idea of how a rhythm-based album should sound. The result could be heard in the bass-heavy swing of 'Modern Love' and, most spectacularly, in the title track. Elsewhere, *Let's Dance* flaunted its disco beat without yielding an inch of rock muscle or punch.

The album featured some of Bowie's most tuneful songwriting. But it was often the producer's touch that made the music work. Under Rodgers' baton, the playing emerged as digitally sharp, and instantly amenable to the huge mainstream audience deserted after *Young Americans*. Bowie would later come to rue this rare surrender of artistic control. 'I only kind of touched the edge of what I really want to do,' he recalled. Years later he would admit, 'It was more Nile's album than mine.'

Like the best of Bowie's records in the seventies, the music had a spirit and exuberance that chimed oddly with the words. 'There's no sign of life/It's just the power to charm' he sang in 'Modern Love', over the metronomic beat of the drums. In so far as the album had a theme, it was that familiar one of love gone awry, touched on variously in 'China Girl', 'Without You' and 'Shake it'. 'Ricochet', a song with no noticeable tune, followed in the leaden, Orwellian style of *Diamond Dogs*. 'Criminal World', the sole cover, had been recorded in 1977 by the glam rock duo Metro, a case of Bowie parroting his mimics. Like 'China Girl',

'Cat People' was a reprise: stripped of the moody arrangement it, too, became a dance-floor staple.

Released in April 1983, *Let's Dance* topped both the British and American charts by early May. Thereafter word-of-mouth, the accompanying tour and hyper self-promotion buoyed the album for a year. It yielded three hit singles and sold six million copies. EMI would describe it as their fastest-selling release since *Sergeant Pepper*. Bowie was no longer the relative cult figure who lived decently, but not lavishly, chiefly on his guarantees from RCA. He was reborn, a man of substance and fame, one of the best-known entertainers in the world.

Nineteen eighty-three was his year, and a new, or almost new Bowie greeted it. His 'commercial début' soon extended beyond the mere accountancy of album sales. The multimedia bonanza also featured Mallet's two videos, a third film shot on stage, two in-concert specials and a slew of new and re-released singles, all coupled with a PR offensive that dwarfed even the Rolling Stones' best efforts of 1982. A sign that Bowie had ceased to be a moral crusade and become a marketing opportunity was RCA's reissue of twenty singles, from 'Space Oddity' to 'D.J.', in new picture-sleeves. 'Let's Dance' itself was a number-one hit. As a song, it possessed all the virtues of the host album, including Vaughan's neatly fluid guitar solo. As a video, it mixed elements of corporate satire (via an American Express card), political comment on the plight of Aborigines and straightforward tourist footage of Sydney. At least one critic worked the five-minute film into an entire article, writing of the 'messages and structures' somehow glimpsed in the heroine's pair of red shoes. Elsewhere the journalist Mick Farren asked if 'the native Australians are objects of compassion, social comment or just Pacific chic?' Everything he had set out to do with 'Let's Dance' Bowie succeeded in doing. On a superficial level, it was a pop song of riveting style and wit. Deeper down, it touched on issues like racism and genocide, and relaunched Bowie as a very different character to the Nazi romantic of 1976, ideologically of no fixed abode. The controversy about the film's themes quickly became a talking-point, and the letter pages bristled with comment. 'Let's Dance' was put into heavy rotation on MTV.

Six years earlier, 'China Girl' had provided Iggy with a modest hit, boosted his album sales and rekindled interest in a career thought, creatively speaking, to be on the way down rather than the way up. The song repeated the same happy trick for Bowie, though on a higher scale. It, too, came with a David Mallet video. It, too, was salvaged by a brilliant blues guitar hook. By autumn, 'Modern Love', accompanied by live concert footage shot in Montreal, became *Let's Dance*'s third consecutive hit. For six months, from March to September, Bowie was a fixture in both the album and single charts. Sales, however, were only one measure of his success. Although other records of 1983, including Michael Jackson's *Thriller*, outsold *Let's Dance* several times over, no other was so much discussed, or enjoyed such reviews. His reputation soared off the promotional work of EMI and Barbara DeWitt, and the year-long tour of Europe, North America and the Far East brought headlines and features wherever he went. People who had never been to a rock concert suddenly knew the name and, above all, the face of David Bowie.

On 17 March, the day after returning from Sydney, Bowie held a press conference at London's Claridges. He was the soul of charm and dandified civility. Whatever their reasons for being there, the media showed in force. In thirty minutes, Bowie was asked more than a hundred questions, from 'Whose suits do you wear?' to 'Are you queer?' He answered them all. He could not complain, as he had in 1972 and even 1978, that the mainstream press ignored him. At Claridges there was a frenzy of voices, a buzz of gossip, reporters from the *Times*, the *Telegraph* and the *Guardian*, a battery of photographers. 'You're only here to relive your youth,' Bowie quipped. It was funny, and had the added value of being true.

Unmentioned in the talk about album sales and dates was Bowie's divorce. It was specifically vetoed by Schwab. That same week, Bowie had his solicitors send Angela a letter warning her away from his tour. For the past three years, a sure sign of a crisis in his ex-wife's finances had been the appearance of a ghosted article in the tabloids. The publication of *Free Spirit* had proved the last straw. Instead of an invitation being sent to her New York home, Angela received a court order. Her exclusion was the talk of the tour headquarters.

That was mild compared to the clash that disrupted rehearsals, and nearly derailed the tour, just ninety-six hours before opening night. Throughout the spring a group, largely recruited by Rodgers, had practised under Carlos Alomar's eye, first in Dallas, and then in Paris and Brussels. Bowie himself appeared in early May. He gave the musicians a long leash. But all the leashes ultimately were held in his hand – logistics, staging, lighting, costumes, publicity, money. That his colleagues looked on him with respect and trepidation, rather than warmth, was shown by the drummer Tony Thompson's comment ('David had a good sense of humour, provided the joke was in the right context'), and the group's nickname for him behind his back ('His Ladyship'). The pairing of Bowie and Stevie Vaughan was particularly volatile. The Texan guitarist, a blues fanatic in a line from Buddy Guy and Albert Collins, had already turned down a berth in the Rolling Stones on the grounds of their being 'not ballsy enough'. The same cutting line was now used to Bowie. As Vaughan recalled, 'I told him to his face he was full of bull, playing us dirt and telling us to dress up on stage like fairies.' As well as a familiar dispute about money, there was a suggestion that Bowie was heavy-handed in ordering his musicians to neither drink nor take drugs, a restraint not necessarily shared by himself. Then there was Vaughan's proposal that his own group, Double Trouble, appear as the tour's opening act. When *that* was vetoed, the result was a scene that spun heads the length of the rehearsal room. Vaughan was a folksy, down-home character with fundamental ideas about right and wrong. He was, as one friend puts it, 'no rocket scientist', but he possessed a certain earthy frankness. He was also capable, gruff, and kissed up to no one, including Bowie. His friend remembered coming into the middle of a Vaughan rampage: 'Stevie was shouting at David, "What the fuck do you mean, no dope? What the fuck are *you* on?"' Bowie, the friend recalled, looked at Vaughan with the faint contempt of a prefect dressing down a new boy: 'Look, I've bloody well got to put on a show. If you don't like it, perhaps you should leave.' Vaughan did. He was replaced by Bowie's old accomplice Earl Slick, who, summoned overnight, learnt the entire twenty-eight-song set in three days.

Slick found, beneath the hard-driving, chilly exterior, an unexpected sympathy. 'There was communication,' he told the

Gillmans; 'a lot of joking and fooling around. In the old days I'd show up at the theatre and literally not see [Bowie] except for the stage part. Now it's back to normal. Business as usual.' After dispensing with Angela and Vaughan, and a single dress rehearsal, Bowie's tour – named 'Serious Moonlight' after a phrase in 'Let's Dance' – opened in Brussels on 18 May. The reviews could not have been more sanguine. There were mutterings when Bowie cancelled a show in Nantes in order to play at the US Festival in California, for which he received a million dollars; and when he returned to Hammersmith Odeon, ten years to the week after his final Ziggy show, for a concert which raised not only funds for a Brixton charity but also mixed reviews. In Paris, Kevin Rowland, mouth of the support act Dexy's Midnight Runners, informed the crowd that Bowie was 'full of shit'. But these were lapses. For the most part the tour advanced like a well-drilled army, and the unprecedented voltage of EMI's PR crusade ensured sell-outs everywhere. Not everyone claimed to like the new Bowie, but everyone began to talk about him.

The set was a wholly-owned subsidiary of the minimalist design of 1976. Ravitz produced a row of shimmering, *Star Trek*-like light columns, warmer than the stark white shafts of *Station to Station*, bathing the stage in bright red for the fast numbers, blue when moodiness called, and sickly green for 'Scary Monsters'. Props were kept to a minimum. The group themselves were dressed as if a 1950s Singapore bar band – the conceit that so enraged Vaughan. Thus a saxophonist played in a pith helmet, the bassist wore a sailor's cap and the two backing singers dressed in flannels and striped blazers, like extras from *The Prisoner*. Alomar's garb transformed him into a guitar-wielding Nehru. The costumes, like the stage's open lines, were a deliberate strategy. As with all Bowie's concerts, the performance was endlessly drilled. Even the moments of seeming spontaneity were worked out beforehand. When Alomar strode backwards in time to the drum outro of 'Life On Mars?', he wasn't reacting to the transcendent music so much as following a script. 'Fashion', 'China Girl', and 'Cracked Actor' all emerged as slices of theatrical rock. The synchronized riffing on 'White Light, White Heat' would have done justice to Status Quo. As one reviewer pointed out, the tour's basic premise, once stripped of the vicarious thrill of Bowie's name, was 'utterly conventional arena rock . . . a slick one-man show, rehearsed and blocked' in which spontaneity by the sidemen, or deviation from the routine, was scrupulously avoided. As a musician recalls, 'Most nights David was the easiest guy in the world to work for, always or usually friendly, disciplined, in control of himself, but if anyone expected him to boost their egos, they made a big mistake.'

Bowie himself came on, bleach-haired, in a series of rakish suits, the jackets cut to his waist, with braces and a bow-tie. He was one of the few rock stars to wear a watch on stage. Much as it was an achievement in itself to create such an air of steely efficiency, Bowie's exceptional control over his fans brought only a feeling of mutual respect, not the true sense of abandon. There was enthusiasm and affection, but very little in the way of audience participation. (When Bowie draped his jacket over one girl who had rushed on stage and fainted, she calmly walked off with it.) Thus the title of his new album was ironic, particularly as Bowie himself couldn't really dance. Rather, he illustrated each song by a gentle rocking motion, bow-legged and swaying on the balls of his feet. For 'Rebel Rebel' he unveiled a silly walk out of John Cleese's repertoire. The Lower Third's Graham Rivens, who saw a British concert in July 1983, would say that Bowie borrowed traits from the old days for much of his act. He could have been singing 'You've Got a Habit of Leaving', for instance, instead of 'Golden Years'. John Hutchinson is another who thinks 'David's changes have been exaggerated. There was a consistency in the songs and the stage show from the sixties to the eighties.' There was also a feeling that, by the time of *Let's Dance*, Bowie was acting himself, not another exotic artifact. The businesslike atmosphere and anaesthetized calm of many of the 1983 concerts flowed from a man who (as he frequently reminded crowds) was called Jones. 'For the first time in his thirteen-year career, Bowie played Bowie straight,' wrote the *Express*. 'I'm smart enough to know my best bet in life is myself,' he confirmed.

As Bowie recalled, he did the tour 'for the money, and to remind people how great the songs are'.* He also, of course,

---

*He referred to the tour in private as 'my pension plan'.

wanted to be taken seriously as a cultural idol (just as so many
cultural idols wanted to be rock stars). Thus he remade himself in
the role of all-round entertainer, the 'great average' first seen in
1978 and now extended into a paragon of sober values and self-
restraint. Bowie not only cut back on drink, drugs and his faithful
Gitanes; he travelled with a portable library, his art materials and
his ever-present diary. The habits of self-discipline begun in Berlin
now ruled him, became virtually reflexive. He rationed his time as
though a stopwatch ticked in his head. Minutes waiting for an
appointment, minutes in a hotel lobby, minutes between interviews added up to hours – productive hours if he used them,
hours forever lost if he wasted them. He did not waste them. The
cocaine addict of 1975 was now saying: 'I can't see spending a
whole day out of my head.' Journalists led into Bowie's dressing
room by DeWitt or Schwab found a brisk, down-to-business
character more eager to sell the tour than dwell on the past.
What little he said of the seventies followed the same middle line
as his music. Bowie was too sensible a man to make extravagant
claims for what he did. He knew better than anyone that the
so-called revolution attributed to him was on the surface only.
The counter-revolutionary enemy was waiting, ready to mobilize
whole armies of heavy metal, vacuous pop and life-threatening
industrial rock, in order to ensure that Bowie's best work would
remain the exception, rather than the rule. As he disarmingly
admitted, his own tour was in keeping with his detractors'
conservative musical values. By such a mix of self-effacement and
self-confidence, Bowie charmed the public and press. He was
written of favourably in *Vogue*, and without reproach in the *New
York Times*. *Newsweek* declared him 'a study in blankness ... the
supreme pop chameleon, a true modernist ... our Pulcinella of
the id'. *Time*'s cover announced the return of a 'mercurial
superstar'.

On 8 December Bowie's tour ended at the Hong Kong
Coliseum, where he sang 'Imagine' as a tribute to John Lennon.
The ninety-eight concerts, spread over seven months, were seen
by two and a half million fans on four continents. Box office sales
were impressive enough, but Bowie profited even more from the
marketing blitz fuelled by his new management company, Isolar,
in New York. The approaches to every arena were awash with

designer merchandising and exclusive souvenirs. Sales of *Let's Dance* and RCA's hastily compiled *Golden Years* both flourished in response to dogged hype and the tour's ecstatic reviews. Plans for a double live album were eventually dropped. There was, however, a tour documentary and a TV special, both later released on video. 'The real Bowie' was promised in the production company's blurb. What emerged was an endlessly polished entertainer whose performance veered between irony and sarcasm.

The material success of the album and tour was matched by an equal failure of Bowie's critical nerve. His efforts to follow up the commercial triumph of *Let's Dance* led to one of his poorest albums. The spectre of yuppies singing along to his best songs was, said one critic, 'absolutely the wrong world' for Bowie to work in. Rarely had an artist repudiated his fame as potently as he did in the mid eighties. Despite, or because of his show-stopping performance at Live Aid, he began to question his whole reason for being in rock. In 1975, Bowie's golden years were still ahead of him. A decade later they were behind him, and he realized that he was paying a price for trying to please a vast audience. One of his most precious assets – relevance – died in 1983.

Let's Dance gave Bowie no respite from the endless recycling and looting of his archive. In January 1983 RCA had released *Rare*, an eleven-track anthology of rejects, B-sides and the Italian version of 'Space Oddity'. Both Pat Gibbons and Tony Defries wrote protesting to the label. RCA responded with a frenzy of dubious outtakes, padded by uninteresting souvenirs and faulty biographical data, climaxing in the reissue of *The Man Who Sold the World*, *Hunky Dory*, *Ziggy Stardust*, *Aladdin Sane*, *Pin-Ups*, *Diamond Dogs*, *Low*, *'Heroes'*, and *Lodger*. The result was that thirteen of Bowie's albums spent a total of 198 weeks on the British chart in 1983. He eclipsed even his record of ten years before. While he ranted at RCA for their exploitation – butchery, he called it – of his catalogue, Bowie was glad of the income it generated. The loss of what had been his unique quality began slowly to undermine his popularity later in the eighties. As each successive new release did worse, so he reaped a royalty from his past. That he was never an innocent at selling his wares was shown by the merchandising salvo of *Let's Dance*, and strange offerings like the cover art of *Scary Monsters* made into a Bowie calendar.

Another branch of the Bowie industry worked exclusively on film projects. The various promotional and live videos were followed, in October 1983, by Don Pennebaker's documentary of the final Ziggy concert, a decade earlier. Bowie himself remixed the soundtrack ('I don't know what I was on when I did it the first time,' he revealed). According to Bowie, his reasons for bringing Ziggy back were neither financial nor nostalgic, but comic. 'That's something I couldn't look at for years,' he said of his alter ego. 'I was so fed up with him ... But I dragged it out last year and had a look, and I thought: This is a *funny film*! This boy used to dress like that for a living? My *God*, this is funny! Incredible! Wait till my *son* sees this!'

Ken Pitt, meanwhile, chose 1983 to revive *Love You Till Tuesday*, the film project shot but never released in 1969. As Pitt says today, 'the movie was completed, but the planned spoken narrative that was to link the sequences was scrapped [when Bowie signed with Defries] and the film was shelved. With the coming of the video market I spoke to PolyGram about it ... They were emphatic that the production should be left as it was, otherwise, they said, "it might lose its charm".' It was released in May 1984. Although the cinema was by no means a new fad, film work now came to occupy a larger space in Bowie's life than ever before. His relationship with David Mallet (who shot the Serious Moonlight videos) was obviously a prime factor in this area. In 1984 he would join forces with Julien Temple, director of *The Great Rock 'n' Roll Swindle*, before working with John Landis, Martin Scorsese and Julian Schnabel. It was rather to Bowie's credit that, amid such company, he privately admitted to 'loving' the lost innocence and primitive production values of Pitt's film, and eagerly advised his friends to see it.

Bowie spent much of 1984 reaping the fruits of 1983. As well as the pillaging of his back catalogue and the EMI marketing mania, there were dozens of nominations and awards. The new year had hardly begun when he was named Best British Male Artist in a ceremony at London's Grosvenor House. *Let's Dance* was up for a Grammy, which it lost to *Thriller*. 'China Girl' won

Best Male Video at the first-ever MTV Awards in New York. The media competed to heap honours on him. Bowie was *Playboy*'s Man of the Year. He made the covers of *Rolling Stone*, *Paris Match*, the *Face* and the *Observer* magazine. Meanwhile, with the approximately seven million dollars he earnt in 1983 – the first real money he ever had – Bowie expanded his life in Lausanne and New York. He renovated the Greenwich Village apartment, which he painted fireapple red. He traded in his Volvo for two new Mercedes and bought a car for Schwab. With the help of Oona Chaplin, who had decorated for some of his friends, Bowie ransacked London art galleries to furnish his Swiss home. He spent a good part of the year on a wandering trail mapped out for him by EMI and Isolar, collecting awards and antiques, and being courted by Hollywood moguls. He was reported to be writing the score for an adaption of Raymond Briggs' *When the Wind Blows*. He auditioned alongside Mel Gibson for *Burke and Speke*, while Cubby Broccoli hinted that Bowie might be in line for a role in the latest Bond film: 'David would make the perfect villain. We plan to exploit his unique physical oddity – his different-coloured and different-sized eyes.' Although the part went elsewhere, the panegyrics for Bowie rolled on and on. His face loomed out from the covers of music and movie titles, *Let's Dance* spent fifty-six weeks on the chart, and continuous reviews and profiles held the public's attention for a year. The deluge would have been even greater if Bowie had not refused many interviews, including those with any would-be biographers.

Late in 1983 Bowie and Schwab had been joined by Iggy and a girlfriend for a post-tour holiday in Bali. Jee Ling, the young Chinese woman from New Zealand with whom Bowie romped on Bondi Beach, joined the Rolodex of ex-lovers. 'I don't have any great attachments to anybody,' he announced. 'I've got a number of girlfriends that I see around the world – I'm a bit sailorlike, I suppose . . . I think I just find it hard to live with anybody. I'm a very solitary person, actually, kind of selfish that way. I like my own company.' While unnamed 'industry insiders' continued to hint that Bowie and Schwab would marry, others were sceptical that two such mismatched souls could come together: day and night, cat and dog, David and Coco. The differences between them could have filled a slim book. Schwab was blunt, displaying what she was; Bowie was disguised, veiled, going through social motions. He wanted to charm the world; she seemed to delight in goading. These were the very qualities that made Schwab so formidable in the boardroom. Her temper was more than a kink in her personality. It was the wall that protected Bowie. In every way she could, she screened and shielded, organized and arranged, and became a human link between her employer and the world. This was the mutually dependent relationship that some mistook for love.

Besides himself and his work, Bowie's only other long-term attachment was to his son. At thirteen Joe had matured into a genial adolescent, bright and alert, though, his father rued, 'over-fond of playing the drums'. Bowie adopted the role of a protective big brother. He included Joe in his lunches with rock business friends at the Plaza Hotel. On one occasion, with Mick Jagger and Keith Richards around the table, Bowie launched into a proud recital of Joe's feats in the school cricket team. He also proved to be gifted at art. Early in 1984 Bowie took Joe with him to Montreal, where he began work on a new album, almost devoid of original songs but completed at the same wild speed as *Let's Dance*. Father and son then spent the summer in Switzerland. In September Joe entered Gordonstoun School in Scotland. The spartan, all-male establishment with its stress on discipline and physical fitness was as far as one could get from the louche world of rock and roll. Angela, meanwhile, settled in New York with her four-year-old daughter and the girl's father, a rock musician named Drew Blood. There was an embarrassing scene when Joe refused to see her. Angela's letters came back from Gordonstoun unopened.

For years the friendship between Bowie and Mick Jagger had been matched by the lively interchange between their organizations. The Serious Moonlight tour had borrowed a number of key personnel from the Rolling Stones. In 1985 Jagger hired Nile Rodgers to work on his own first solo album, *She's the Boss*, in the hope that the producer would somehow repeat the success of *Let's Dance*. Bowie, meanwhile, was introduced to Julien Temple, *enfant terrible* of the National Film School and director of the Stones' 1983 hit 'Undercover'. The result was 'Jazzin' for Blue Jean', an extraordinary twenty-two minute video promoting the first single from the Montreal session. Bowie played both victor and victim, a prancing rocker dressed like Valentino's *The Sheik*, and a wide-eyed fan ogling from the floor. It touched skilfully on the Bowie–Jones personae, something Bowie had done years before by taking two incompatible drafts of a fan-club autobiography and saying to Ralph Horton, 'Mix them together'. The film was widely aired as a trailer. Edited to three minutes, 'Blue Jean', occupying the same rabble-rousing ground as 'Rebel Rebel', was a top-ten hit on both sides of the Atlantic.

Montreal yielded two other singles. 'Tonight', released in November 1984, was a lacklustre reggae duet with Tina Turner.* 'Loving the Alien', in which Bowie brought off a passable impersonation of Bryan Ferry, was at least a stab at the old writing technique: the words dealt with torture and crucifixion, but the cloyingly romantic arrangement made a potentially ugly rendering as starkly beautiful as an Ecce Homo. The single, remixed from the album, came with a video in which Bowie acted out various scenes from religious history. Like 'Tonight', it flopped.

In 1971 'Changes' had plotted the course of an erratic but unstoppable career; until 1983, at least, Bowie's endless innovations were never boring. Now, however, when Lionel Ritchie nestled comfortably at the top of the chart alongside Billy Joel and Paul Young, Bowie released an album that wasn't so much bad as completely redundant. Chapter two in the EMI saga brought no new characters or major twists in the plot: *Tonight* touched each of the familiar bases – the hard-rock drums, wheezing saxes and overwrought vocals were all present. 'Blue Jean', whose chorus grabbed instantly, was a worthy follow-up to 'Let's Dance'. 'Loving the Alien' was one of Bowie's best lyrics. Elsewhere, however, the album was filled with blatant castoffs – flabby retreads of old hits and swiped tracks from Iggy's *Lust for Life*. *Tonight* was Bowie's first serious studio misfire since the days of 'The Laughing Gnome'.

---

*Bowie had been backstage at the Ritz, New York, in December 1982 for Turner's comeback. He was a loyal supporter and collaborator in the years ahead.

With only two new songs of his own, Bowie substituted pointless remakes of Lieber and Stoller's 'I Keep Forgettin'' and the Beach Boys' 'God Only Knows', which sounded 'adult' in all the wrong ways. 'Tonight' itself lost the spoken introduction – and thus the plot – of Iggy's original. 'Tumble and Twirl' sank under the effects of Latinized riffs, mock-operatic vocals and rushing wind. The arrangements by Alomar and the album's co-producer Derek Bramble were beyond reproach. More revealingly, they were also completely beside the point. Too many of the tracks were poor fare pretentiously wrapped. *Tonight* closed with an outright disaster, 'Dancing with the Big Boys', overexcited and saddled with lazy clichés. 'This can be embarrassing,' Bowie muttered before the final fade-out.

A decade earlier, Bowie had written his post-Orwellian vision *Diamond Dogs*. It was ironic that, after all his years of anticipating 1984, when it came it caught him flat-footed. According to the guitarist Reeves Gabrels, who heard the demos for *Tonight*, the music sounded 'great', but 'all the life got squeezed out of it in the studio somehow'. Other critics were less forgiving. As Bowie's friend Kurt Loder wrote, 'the album is a throwaway, and David knows it'. *Tonight* was a calculated effort to wring another hit from the smash *Let's Dance* formula. Buoyed by residual goodwill and another far-flung sales campaign, the album did, briefly, touch number one. There its similarity to its predecessor ended. Whereas *Let's Dance* enjoyed more than a year on the chart, *Tonight* vanished after three months. It made Bowie fewer friends than enemies. Only a tiny band of dedicated fans praised the album, and its maker soon aligned himself with the consensus. 'A bomb', was Bowie's pithy, private comment.

The truth was that, for the next several years, Bowie virtually gave up on music. He needed months to prepare for a new record, and even then things would go wrong. His next major tour, in 1987, tried to revive the theatricality of the Year of the Diamond Dogs on Serious Moonlight's scale, and failed. 'I seriously thought of pulling back ... just being a visual artist,' he remembered. In 1988, for the first time in seventeen years, Bowie was in neither the album nor the singles charts. As failure swiftly followed success, the plot became a series of footnotes – bizarre, one-off projects, pretentious interviews and regular features in *Hello!*.

Bowie's comeback, tentative in the late eighties and accelerating in the nineties, gave him a fresh start – literally a fresh face before the world. Within the space of a few months, he would grow a goatee, dye his hair and have major work done on his teeth. He also released two critically acclaimed albums and played to packed houses in Europe and America. Just when rock needed a jolt in a new direction, Bowie's latest reincarnation somehow managed to be the right idea at the right time.

'David Bowie Ponders His Newfound Popularity' ran the *New York Times*' perceptive headline in November 1984. The article saw him as a victim of success. According to this reading, *Tonight* was an ambivalent album, full of self-doubt and anxiety about satisfying the market. 'He ruminates on whether, or how much, he's compromised; he also vows to please his audience, suggests that sweetness and light are not on the agenda and wonders how long his new fans will stick around.' Bowie was a bundle of contrasts: a man often accused of élitism, yet one whose album, shot off in three weeks, had sold millions; an androgynous queen who now presented himself as 'sailorlike' in his relations with women; an avant-gardist who taxed his audience, yet a pragmatic who could knock out a hit single to order.

Above all, Bowie was the man of deeply held irony. On 25 November 1984, after being moved to tears by a harrowing news report from Ethiopia, Bob Geldof organized the cream of British rock into an *ad hoc* group he called Band Aid. Their single, 'Do They Know It's Christmas?' became the fastest-selling release in chart history. Bowie was unable to make the recording date. He did, however, send a taped message that Geldof mixed into the B-side. 'It's Christmas and there are more starving folk on this planet than ever before. Please give a thought for them this season and do whatever you can, however small, to help them live. Have a peaceful new year. David Bowie.'

8
JARETH, KING OF THE GOBLINS

On 31 December 1984, a black Mercedes carried Bowie, Joe, Schwab and the newly-wed Iggy and Suchi Pop into the Swiss resort of Gstaad. The entourage arrived in their hotel and dispersed into three suites; a fourth was set up as a rehearsal space and artist's studio. The party that night was in Bowie's room. On New Year's morning he was on the ski slopes with his son, playfully fencing with their poles, each trying to topple the other and become 'king of the hill'. It amazed the loyal Iggy to see how much pleasure fatherhood seemed to have brought Bowie. Away from the paparazzi, he and Joe could be heard in long, animated discussions, behaving, as a friend says, 'in the childlike way that David relaxed'. It went beyond that; an almost mystical aura seemed to come out of their relationship, the portrait of a man so sparing of himself elsewhere, who treated Joe like a brother.

In mid-January the Pops returned to their loft in New York, Joe to the rugby fields of Gordonstoun and Bowie and Schwab to Lausanne. On the morning of the 16th Peggy Jones rang from her flat in Beckenham. There had been an accident. Bowie's half-brother, Terry Burns, had been struck by a train and killed. Word had already leaked to the London *Standard*, who had sent a reporter to the scene. The story was making the rounds of the TV news editors. Before lunchtime two rival film crews were jostling on Peggy's doorstep, each shouting endlessly varied questions on the single topic: 'What happened?'

The truth came out by degrees. Over the Christmas holiday,

while the Bowies relaxed in Switzerland, Terry had scaled a wall at Cane Hill and walked to the nearby Coulsdon South station. He lay down with his neck on the rail. As the London express bore down, shedding sparks over the icy track, Terry jerked his head away at the last second and rolled on to the frozen embankment. Then he began scooping up handfuls of sleeping pills and crushing them between his teeth. He was jumped by two railway workers, who up-ended him on the ground and held his feet high while a third man gripped his throat. Terry had already lost consciousness. An ambulance returned him to Mayday Hospital, where emetics and a stomach pump were applied. At some time during the undignified struggle over the next fifteen minutes, Terry regained his senses, demanding to be driven to Peggy's home, where 'David would be waiting' for him. Instead, social workers arrived to consult with the doctors. The next morning, Terry was taken back to Cane Hill and left to his own desires.

History repeated itself three weeks later. By then southern England was swept by unremitting gale-force wind, lashed by alternating rain and snow, and, for all practical purposes, at a virtual standstill. Several of the staff at Cane Hill were stranded at home. Terry left the hospital grounds unchallenged, passed over the empty road and through the station booking hall. The trains that morning were running late. The few other passengers ignored the heavy-set man who walked casually to the end of the platform. It was a bright, cold day, the ground covered with a sleet that had frozen so that it seemed that the wooden station, the platforms and all the embankment and the bare rail had been varnished with ice. Terry waited until the express appeared from the south. Then he lay down with his head on the track, looking away. The driver tried to brake but was too late. All ten carriages struck the body, the cry giving way to the more urgent tempo of a woman's scream.

Terry Burns was forty-seven. There were eleven mourners at the funeral at Elmers End cemetery in Beckenham. His mother and aunt, ignoring each other throughout, represented the family. Bowie did not attend but sent a wreath of roses and a card: 'You've seen more things than we could imagine but all these moments will be lost, like tears washed away by the rain. God bless you – David.' Terry's illness had shocked Bowie from the start, tempting pop psychologists to conclude that his every lyric had been shaped by a fear of insanity. Whatever the similarities may have been, and however enticing the comparisons, the younger brother had shown a nerve that converted his own problems into effective means of achieving his goals and sustaining his career. In the months after Terry's death, his aunt Pat portrayed both Bowie and his mother as callous, unfeeling schemers who had known of his plight and ignored it. Such a charge was consistent with the icier extremes of Bowie's public image. Yet, after 1976, he enjoyed long family friendships, and a warm rapport with Joe. He made flying visits to his mother and invited her to stay in Lausanne. Indeed, Peggy, her son and grandson often travelled together and, in a friend's words, 'did every kind of mundane thing'. There may have been less neglect in Bowie's relations with Terry than some thought. The two had grown apart; by the late sixties the fabric of childhood had been torn up, and there was no way to stitch it together again. Bowie stood accused on the basis of tabloid stories and charges that were often flagrant lies. He also stood accused by a woman who had long been cast as the family black sheep. As things were, he was wise to ignore his aunt and scoff at those who trivialized his career as a mere deterrent against madness.

Bowie emerged from Switzerland early in February. He joined Tina Turner on stage in Birmingham for a medley of 'Let's Dance' and Chris Montez's hit of the same title. He also entered into discussions with Julien Temple about appearing in a film version of Colin MacInnes' novel *Absolute Beginners*, a slice of 1950s London street life. In the end Bowie's role was pared to a cameo. He did, however, contribute three songs to the soundtrack: the title number, 'That's Motivation', and an overhaul of the 1958 hit 'Volare'. The album's shifting moods of nostalgia and state-of-the-art pop would, briefly, earn it a place in the Top Twenty.

In between writing, auditioning for Temple and a handful of interviews puffing *Tonight*, Bowie got down to his long-deferred plan of writing a script of his own. He hoped to produce and direct a film in 1986. In all, Bowie spent nine weeks at work on the first draft. It was read by a friend who urged him to make 'drastic' cuts. Doing his own screenplay turned out to be an exhausting process. Bowie carried the MS all over New York to conduct interviews with Tony Scott and John Landis; he saw old friends in the city, including Bruce Springsteen and Luther Vandross; went out to the country, on Long Island, for a weekend with his cousin Kristine; and back to Manhattan again, to hear a lecture on screenwriting, before flying to London for an *Absolute Beginners* costume fitting. He caught a cold from the English spring and flew home to Geneva with sinusitis and a buzzing in the ears. That did not stop him from rewriting his script, or dropping in on Oona Chaplin, or from hosting Joe for the Easter holiday. Bowie showed his son the rough second draft. It was less a plot than a montage of scenes designed to show that Bowie had inscribed his various phobias into a text shot through with sub-Joycean monologues. Joe was taken aback by it, and complimented his father on his style. He made him promise to finish the work one day.

What Bowie was doing, patently, was assessing his role as a rock star. By the time *Tonight* hit the market stalls early in 1985 he was again speaking of a life in art or films. Bowie's post-mortem account of his career crisis showed a detachment that can variously be described as offering shrewd, well-informed insights into his predicament; or, to critics, monumental self-indulgence in deserting the fans who made him famous in the first place. Bowie the man was in conflict with Bowie the pop icon. Reluctant and ambivalent, he had gone along with EMI's plea for 'another *Let's Dance*'. With that comparative flop, he entered a transitional phase when his commercial ambition had run out of steam, but there was no clear-cut replacement. Bowie busied himself with interim projects like writing the theme for John Schlesinger's *The Falcon and the Snowman* and taking a cameo alongside Jeff Goldblum and Michelle Pfeiffer in *Into the Night*. Those were bit jobs. During the months that followed Terry's death, he seemed eager to do nearly anything rather than lock himself away and face the problems inherent in making a new David Bowie album. As Visconti put it: 'He is a very hard worker and he knows what he wants. Proof of that is the fact he's into films these days. He couldn't care less about music at this stage.'

As the year went on, Bowie seemed to retreat further into the solitude of his Swiss exile. Certain EMI directors complained out loud about his inaccessibility. Mick Ronson, who found his own relationship one of growing warmth, noted how 'David did nothing by halves. When he dropped out, he vanished.' Accounts of Bowie as a recluse became commonplace.

And they were true. Bowie received strangers with courtesy, even kindness, but with anxiety that came from self-consciousness, or wondering what the other person really wanted. This self-consciousness or insecurity explains why he could be comfortable sitting in a room with Schwab for hours without responding – or even thinking about responding – to any demands. After *Scary Monsters*, overwhelmed with the reality of the frustrations of multimillion-selling success, Bowie more and more followed his natural tendency to brood: about how well he was being served by his label or understood by the world beyond EMI; how much, if at all, he enjoyed being a matinée-idol rock star; and whether, as with Ziggy, he should change his public image and kill off his new character. Aladdin Sane was not dead; he was alive and living in Lausanne, and with a lot to be mad about.

The critics were a good example. Reviews for *Tonight*, which came off as a botched plot between Bowie and his record company, quickly erased the happy smiles that followed *Let's Dance*. A backlash began. Because he took a lucid view of his fame, Bowie himself could participate in the debate. For instance, there was his confession that his 'worst time was 1986 . . . I really did look at the prospect of just working as an artist until something else generated my interest in music, or unless it never came back and I would be expressing myself in some other form.' Even in the spring of 1985, Bowie would tell a colleague on *Absolute Beginners* he was going through that stigma of the creative conscience, an 'artistic crisis'. To another friend, 'David was riding the crest of a wave and of ten years of superstardom. It had an awful effect. Stubbornness and a manic desire not to be tied down . . . were still his values. Success only proved to him that he hadn't aimed high enough.'

Bowie was angry with himself for blatantly pop-mongering on his last two albums. He was also in a frenzy with the critics. In April 1985 the *Sunday Times* published excerpts from Peter and Leni Gillman's *Alias David Bowie*, with its central theme that Bowie's career depended on his troubled, chaotic life and, specifically, a fear of insanity. EMI promptly responded with a demand that all copies of the book be pulped. Bowie himself snapped at an American interviewer, in tones that echoed Jack Celliers: 'The past is *my* business.' Later in the year he complained of his Aunt Pat and the other 'long-lost relatives with their unbelievable, blatant lies' constantly recycled in the press. He had a lawyer's letter sent to a second biographer.

Bowie's increasingly bad mood was barely distinguishable from self-hatred. He told his friend that he was a 'guilt-ridden sod', that what kept him awake at night was the 'cop-out' of his recent work. 'I was better off before [*Let's Dance*]. At least I kept up the fight. I had fantastic luck. Now what?' Bowie's ability to be simultaneously angry, self-accusing, sincere and self-aware found expression in his private conversation, and in a public show of contempt for the critics. Hostile reviewers found themselves struck off the VIP list for Bowie's next tour, their credentials revoked. Even a venerable Radio One star was denied access on the grounds of having the 'wrong badge'. Anyone making the transition from writing about Bowie's music to discussing the man himself knew that they crossed the Rubicon dividing passive resistance from all-out war. Besides the EMI legal department, there was Isolar and an entertainment lawyer named John Eastman (Paul McCartney's brother-in-law) combining in fierce protection of their client's interests. In his own off-the-record estimate, Bowie was a has-been, a now middle-aged winner of an early prize, a writer who had failed to live up to his promise. He was alone as a rock star. Bowie belonged to no school, and though he still had fans in the business (most of the New Romantics, for example) he had fewer standard-bearers in the media. While he commanded respect, his last album had failed to excite the audience. He had no new songs, and no new ideas about how to 'put across' his old ones. Unfortunately, at this point – in mid 1985 – neither did his record companies.

The year after *Tonight* brought a fit of singles and albums. Even the most hardened collector would have been satisfied by the remnants, anthologies, barrel-scrapings and repackaged collections of past glories that kept Bowie's name before the public. It seemed a churlish technicality to suggest that some of this activity might be linked to writing new material; or that, between them, EMI, Isolar and the rest were engaging in a cynical cash-in. Thus, in May 1985, Bowie released 'Loving the Alien' after reading a review of *Tonight* which thought that the song might make a hit single. (It didn't.) Following the same backward-looking policy, RCA then issued *Fame and Fashion*, culled from Bowie's mid-seventies archive, while a second collection in the same month featured a cross-sample from the Pye and Decca catalogues. Meanwhile, a Scandinavian company named Krazy Kat hit on the idea of releasing three songs from Bowie's pre-Ziggy laboratory, Arnold Corns. EMI chipped in with 'I Pity the Fool' and 'You've Got a Habit of Leaving', the long-forgotten 1965 flops. Bowie himself would choose to cover the old Martha and the Vandellas hit 'Dancing in the Street' as a duet with Mick Jagger. His next three singles were taken from film soundtracks. The number of re-releases does not detract from Bowie's place in history – it may even add to his stature. But it remains a fact that, by 1985, he was surviving almost entirely on residual goodwill at the cost of a fresh creative stance. For the first time in nearly twenty years, Bowie was boring.

The charismatic attraction that he possessed – the fame of being Bowie – still made itself felt. Early that summer a group of musicians at work in Abbey Road studios under Thomas Dolby each received a letter from EMI saying they had been hired for a session with 'Mister X'. (The drummer Neil Conti was given a partial clue as to his employer's identity by the murmured aside from an EMI staffer: 'He has a glass eye.') This cryptic utterance was followed, in time, by the arrival of Schwab, Tony Mascia and Bowie. The guitarist Kevin Armstrong recalls the last as 'charming', though uncertain of his new group's ability. 'David came in with the song "Absolute Beginners" half written. The whole band helped out, whether it was a missing chord or a rhyme for the last verse. Over an afternoon it evolved into the backing track, which we recorded. *That's* how Bowie operated – from the germ of an idea, which the group polished up into the master. Once he saw what we could do, he relaxed. We fitted.' As Matthew Seligman, the bassist, recalls, 'David liked to work at top speed. He said he loved the Abbey Road session, which reminded him of *"Heroes"*.'

Seligman, Armstrong and the others were old Bowie fans; Thomas Dolby's own mix of minimalist tunes with synth-pop

The 1974 comeback tour, a brilliantly realized package of slick ballads, hoary rock and roll anthems, surrealist props and eye-bashing visuals, cost Bowie $250,000 to stage. In America, it turned him from a novelty act into a superstar.

Bowie spent three years living at 155 Hauptstrasse in the then West Berlin. His apartment was on the first floor, over the costume jewellery shop and the garage.

The 'thin white duke' on tour in 1976 - a slick-haired, unsmiling figure Bowie himself would later call 'a very nasty character indeed'.

Bowie's haunting portrayal of isolation in *The Elephant Man* received widespread critical acclaim. Despite *Variety*'s suggestion that he 'now had the chance to achieve legitimate stardom', however, his career as a serious stage actor remained in limbo.

Eight Changes ...
Above, Bowie at the time of his first single (1964) and his first album (1967).

The punishing regime of drink, heavy drugs and diabolism that filled out his year in Los Angeles gave way to a more relaxed style around the time of *Let's Dance*.

The Man Who Fell to Earth and the *Scary Monsters* look.

Nearly twenty years later, Bowie still knew exactly how to seduce the camera, when to scowl and when to smile, effortlessly drawing the spotlight.

13 July 1985. Bowie's Live Aid set was among the night's show-stopping moments. 'We should make it an annual gig,' he said, bringing a sarcastic quip from Bob Geldof.

The Glass Spider tour of 1987. While some praised the shows' flamboyance, to others the much-vaunted props were the product of narcissism and vanity, and strangely reminiscent of *Spinal Tap*.

Although Tin Machine made obligatory gestures towards band democracy, the eye still fixed stubbornly on the famous lead singer.

DB first met Andy Warhol in September 1971, an event that fascinated Bowie because 'nothing happened'. Twenty-five years later, in a fright wig and black leather, he played Warhol in the film *Basquiat, Build a Fort, Set it on Fire*.

After exchanging platinum rings and mutually suffering the tattooist's needle, Bowie and Iman were married in Switzerland in April 1992. The church service in Florence a month later brought the city to a standstill. Their life together soon changed him: he was more effusive, less wary and even enjoyed a social life.

rhythms owed much to the mechanized tones of *Low*. Now the wheel had come full circle. 'Absolute Beginners' was the result of Bowie's and his group's mutual influence on one another. A second session became a variation of the kind of free-form interplay of the first. The band provided a framework for Bowie that was open and flexible, accommodating his improvisational flair. A solid rhythm section set his style into a mainstream pop groove. And although Bowie – whose bodyguard never left his side – was clearly the star, he was an artist who tapped into his musicians on a personal as well as professional level. One day he meekly enquired about how to use a new guitar pedal. The next Bowie arrived in the studio carrying a painting which he hung on the wall; he then took several random photographs around the room, pointing the camera blindly over his shoulder, and spent five minutes filming an empty glass he set on the studio console. As Conti says, 'He was bright, witty and above all ready to experiment, and he never told anyone what to play. It was always something like: 'Think green' or 'Think Brazilian', and not a technical hassle. He used the natural strengths of his musicians. Bowie also worked at the speed of light. He wanted to record a moment, not an idea.'

'Absolute Beginners' was released as a single in March 1986. Although it scraped the lower reaches of the chart, it failed commercially. At five and a half minutes, the song (of which Bowie's reference to being 'absolutely sane' was the sole point of note) was a long though underweight tune, accompanied by a video in which the star, in classic 1958 regalia – trilby, mock camel-hair coat and the look of the Strand cigarette commercial – cavorted with a woman painted bafflingly like a zebra. An extended version, effectively a preview for the full-length feature, was shown in 300 cinemas across Britain.

When, a year earlier, Julien Temple had approached Bowie to appear in *Absolute Beginners*, he touted the work as a 'small-budget genre flic', a triumph of economy and quality, yet with mainstream appeal. Since then the budget had grown to £9 million and the genre become a hybrid of nostalgic-documentary styles, with *West Side Story* undertones. As Bowie, Temple and the cast laboured at Shepperton studios, there were rumours that *Absolute Beginners* had become a monster, a musical folly fuelled

by narcissism and vanity, whose desperate excesses threatened to
bankrupt the producers. Julie Burchill in *Time Out* gave ten good
reasons why nobody would ever watch the film, among them that
'everyone will be too old by the time it finally hits the screens'.
Absolute Beginners made such virtue of its being British – British
financed, produced and directed – that there was only one thing
for it: it was a commercial flop. The film nearly ruined its backers,
Goldcrest, and made sense only as a morality tale of epic
spending, where costs rose in inverse proportion to quality and
shooting proceeded months behind schedule. Compounding the
problem was the near-constant rain that summer. Back-lot and
outdoor location scenes were delayed, then shelved, then abandoned and reshot on an interior studio replica of Soho. A sound
stage caught fire when flood water slopped into an electrical
junction box. Two cast members came down with pneumonia.
Bowie himself spent much of the summer sneezing and morbid
with flu.

  Absolute Beginners caught London at the precise moment
before the plague of pop music. The film bristled with references,
visual and verbal, to the teenage demi-monde of the day: Vespas,
mock-crocs, rumbles, Italian suits, frothy coffees and jukeboxes.
Poignantly, this was the world of Terry Burns. As Bowie played
the part of Vendice Partners, an amoral (though tap-dancing)
ad-man, images of his half-brother could scarcely have failed to
surface. A musician who worked on the soundtrack says, 'Just
walking up Great Windmill Street, dressed up like Elvis, brought
back the memories ... He didn't hide his feelings.' Bowie's other
reference point, of course, was his own apprenticeship. 'I worked
in advertising when I first left school,' he told Paul Gambaccini.
'And I loathed it.' Bowie went on to explain that his boss at the
time had affected a mid-Atlantic twang, a conceit he in turn
brought to *Absolute Beginners*. 'There was this continual fluctu-
ation between English and American, which I thought was a
good way to play Vendice. And I enjoyed playing him. He's such
a bastard.'

  According to his fellow actors and musicians, the reverse
applied to Bowie on set. Conti, Seligman and Armstrong all have
fond memories of the *Absolute Beginners* soundtrack. His co-star
Patsy Kensit would speak of his extreme briskness – he hated to

be kept waiting – his efficiency and his courtesy to everyone in the cast. In Alan Freeman's memory, 'David was the epitome of warmth and charm.' From the cradle, if less so from *Let's Dance*, Bowie's behaviour had been frequently disruptive, always para-doxical. The desire for greater fame, one actor recalls, 'was the whole reason he got into movies'. By summer of 1985, the incongruities that marked his career were almost as well known as his song titles. The so-called loner and bookworm was a man about town who struck Conti as 'in the thick of life'. The timid son of pious and self-effacing John Jones had dabbled in exotic combinations of sex, drugs and rock and roll, embraced politics from fascism to near-anarchy, taken up acting, and could comment wryly on the slump in his own career. A continuing pattern of Bowie's life became one of assertion and counter-assertion, contradictions that defied explanation and encouraged controversy. He was an inspired choice to play the schizophrenic Partners. Bowie's performance earned lavish reviews. His slick set-piece, 'That's Motivation', reminded some of Chaplin's *The Great Dictator* with its inventive use of a world globe. To others Bowie was still on permanent audition for the role of Frank Sinatra, swaggering through the city streets with his hat and a mac tossed over his shoulder. His impressive grasp of pop culture brought much-needed depth to the film. Bowie, wrote Philip Norman, 'surprised everyone with his straightforward profession-alism, his intuitive comic gift ... his eye for detail'. 'David had a very good memory for that kind of thing,' says Temple. 'Like knowing the jackets he wore shouldn't be padded. And E-type Jaguars were an important part of the period for him.' Bowie himself would remember hearing of the 1958 Notting Hill race riots, the climax of the film, on the Plaistow Grove wireless.

Despite extensive pre-release hype, including the dread phrase 'the future of British cinema', *Absolute Beginners* died at the box office. After the première in April 1986, crowds dwindled to a hardcore of Bowie fans and those who came out of morbid curiosity to see whether it was as bad as the critics said. London Weekend TV paid the film the backhanded compliment of parodying it on *Spitting Image*. In North America, it made a respectable $96,000 in its first weekend of exclusive engage-ments in New York, Los Angeles, San Francisco and Toronto. But after a seven-week run, *Absolute Beginners* had grossed a total of only $300,000. *Variety* cited the film's distinctly English flavour as one reason why it had not done 'as well as expected'. Others found the plot's sentimentality (out of the *Love You Till Tuesday* school of drama) hard to take, panning it as a 107-minute inflated pop video.

On 4 July 1985 Bowie was backstage at a Bruce Springsteen show at Wembley. He struck a passing journalist, Roy Wendt, as an 'odd' character. 'There was an episode when he snarled at some kids to leave him alone ... Their sin was to walk by him and say hello. He sort of crouched down at the side of the stage and didn't say anything, didn't do any dancing. I never saw him move.' Bowie told another reporter that he was not there to enjoy himself, but as a 'working professional'.

Shortly after wrapping the *Absolute Beginners* soundtrack, Bowie had appeared at Abbey Road and told his group, 'I've got this little gig – can you do it?' After affirmative grunts, arrangements were made with the producer Clive Langer. The next evening Armstrong, Seligman, Conti and sundry percussionists and singers were sitting in a semi-circle learning the chords to 'Dancing in the Street'. Bowie told them that he had decided to record the song after a night on the town with 'Coco and Mick'. As if on cue, a limousine swept into the studio courtyard. Neil Conti remembers Jagger as 'being "on" the whole time ... strutting around and trying to upstage David. It was a *huge* ego trip for him.' After a technical hitch, the basic track was cut the next morning. Bowie was happy with the first take. Jagger wanted the bass and other parts redone. 'David,' says Conti, 'just sat there, Sphinx-like, smiling and chatting with the band, while Jagger snarled at the engineer. We suggested some more lyrics. Mick fumed some more.' A video of Bowie and Jagger was then shot by David Mallet in London's Docklands. After filming, there was a moment's delay before the stars' limousines arrived at the door. Bowie hugged his musicians and talked to their family and girlfriends. Jagger, furious, flew with the master tape to New York, where the song was embellished by a horn section and Earl Slick's guitar.

By mid August, the single was number one in Britain and number seven in America. Meanwhile, the video (rush-released when plans for a transatlantic duet between Bowie and Jagger broke down) was also a bestseller. It was shown – twice – in front of a TV audience of a billion, in 143 countries, before being aired in 5,000 theatres across America. For the millions who watched or taped the three-minute clip, the two antiques, with a combined age of eighty, gave a thrilling illustration of the song. Unkinder critics saw Bowie and Jagger 'tottering like music-hall artistes', 'mincing' and 'jigging about' to their risible version of the Motown hit. With much of his enigma peeled away, Bowie, in particular, was seen as toppling from several of the thrones he once occupied and cheapening himself in the process – although 'Dancing in the Street' raised millions for charity and paid a handsome dividend to Marvin Gaye's estate.

The 'little gig' he referred to was, of course, Live Aid. In the frenetic weeks leading to 13 July, when Bob Geldof's office began to resemble 'something between a travel agency and an executive nanny service', he placed several calls to Isolar in New York. Like virtually everyone else who had heard of it, Bowie was moved and appalled by the famine in Ethiopia. He told Schwab that 'something must be done'. That, for the next several months, was the limit of Bowie's commitment. He found himself sympathizing with the relief effort, but at the same time trapped by a principal article of his faith – his reluctance to take a stand on issues. The collision with reality came later in the spring. Geldof remembers that Bowie 'dithered' about appearing at either the London or Philadelphia events: he would express interest in the evening, yet ring back the next morning with more misgivings. The slate was constantly wiped clean. When Bowie did agree to perform, he had a list of conditions about the production and stage-management of his segment. A secretary told him that he would have to go on at Wembley without a sound-check. Bowie looked ill at the prospect. He did, however, keep his word to Geldof, and allowed his name to be used to promote the event and attract other stars, including Jagger.

Rehearsals took place on three consecutive Sundays at Bray studios and on a sound stage at Elstree. On the morning of the first, Schwab's assistant appeared with a computer print-out of all Bowie's songs – there were over 200 – for him to browse. The band rehearsed seven, of which four made the final cut. Bowie

was keen to do 'Fascination' from *Young Americans*, but at the last
minute substituted 'Modern Love' as a sop to EMI. The sessions
were recorded and each group member was sent a tape. Bowie's
last words at Elstree were 'Be lucky' and 'Wear blue.' He then
enlisted the engineer Mike Robinson to produce his slice of the
show, forcing a last-minute disruption of arrangements. He
micro-managed every detail of his performance, including how
he was announced on stage. Andy Peebles, who introduced
Bowie at Wembley, remembers fondly how 'his army took over'
from the house staff as if by a silent coup. A sound engineer,
working backstage at midnight on 12 July, found Bowie and
Schwab poring over a blueprint of the stadium and discussing
'dead spots' and volume settings, while also consulting a copy of
the next day's weather forecast. His preparation for Live Aid, even
more than the organization of his world tour, impressive as that
was, showed the rock-hard core at the heart of Bowie's planning.

The master tactician seen at Wembley should give pause for
thought to anyone who thinks Bowie was concerned only with
broad strategy. He insisted on taking personal control; judging
from the letters, telexes, calls, memos and enquiries that flowed
from Isolar, his addiction to detail was obsessive. A friend recalled
that the long hours Bowie spent at his office, many of them
duplicating Schwab, horrified his staff. When the friend tried to
remonstrate on health grounds, Bowie replied, 'The kids aren't
fussed how well I sleep. They're worried how well I sing.' In
striving for his ideal world, he had an image of perfection which
he had to measure up to himself. Here he was quite different from
Jagger, who, though vigilant, had long since learnt to say 'Fuck
it' to menial tasks that were done better by others.

Bowie returned to Wembley by helicopter, landing on a nearby
sports ground. By coincidence, a couple were inside the cricket
pavilion, holding their wedding reception. They were Bowie fans.
At the groom's signal, he wheeled away from Schwab, Mascia
and the others and posed for photographs with the newlyweds.
Backstage, he found himself in a Portakabin teeming with his
eight-piece band, sundry friends, technicians and event staff.
Bowie's star status found expression in a cracked mirror, a folding
table and a child's make-up box. He changed into a light *Diamond
Dogs*-era suit, the jacket cut tight, the loose trousers almost

covering his white socks and the heels of his black shoes. Thus attired, he spent an hour in the royal box, exchanging quips with the heir to the throne. Then he walked backstage. He gave his well-practised wave to fans who called his name, and muttered the word 'vibes' several times. There was a generous minimum 'vibe' quota at Wembley, but, even so, Bowie seemed to be aiming for a world record, inserting it into the most banal sentences to the point where, for the first time, the word seemed to have reached the end of its usefulness: 'How you vibin'?' he asked Elton John's horn player, to the man's patent bemusement. Bowie then came on Geldof himself, lying face down on a flight case and moaning in pain from a sprained back. The two men had never been close. Geldof, like so many evangelical new wavers, had admired Bowie as a teenager. He had heard the stories about his time in the dead zone of Los Angeles and listened to the weird Berlin albums full of shrewd yet icy self-doubt. The very qualities that were the essence of Bowie carried with them a potential for coolness. The negotiations with Isolar had seemed to confirm that here was a man of more than usual self-restraint. Geldof, in short, expected nothing from Bowie, and certainly not in his undignified prone position. He was surprised, therefore, at the warmth of the greeting. Not only that: Bowie rolled up the sleeves of his jacket and began rubbing Geldof's back. He kept up the procedure for a full fifteen minutes. Bowie had come a long way from North Doheny Drive, but even he must have been struck, as others were, by the scene outside Dressing Room A: a demure figure in a shirt and tie, his face registering nothing but concern, massaging a stranger's spine. In short order, Bowie and another suited figure then began frolicking among the potted palms. The two men struck poses for a gaggle of photographers with schoolboy glee, mimicking their shouts of 'Back to back!' and stooping for a round of mock fisticuffs. Mugging with Paul McCartney was not exactly a novelty by the standards of most rock stars, but for the press, the backstage scenes would distract from and in some ways trivialize the main event. On the basis of this particular incident an American journalist, apparently on sabbatical for the last dozen years, would write that Bowie had 'really arrived' in the top flight.

At 7.15 on the now balmy summer evening, Peebles made his

announcement. Bowie ducked through a flap in the canvas backdrop, grinned, waved, and, on the first bar of 'TVC 15', dropped into his patent bow-legged dance. The number segued into 'Rebel Rebel', the song that staked out a claim bordered by the Rolling Stones and Iggy's manic despair. The guitar and saxophone deftly traded lines; the percussionist grew increasingly frantic, and Bowie, *pace* Defries, sweated profusely. 'Modern Love' followed. The tune was so strong that it could sustain even quirks such as a mid-paced tempo and retooled lyrics. By now Armstrong, Dolby and the rest had blended into a band. This type of destructive reinvention had been much noted at rehearsal. Bowie, according to one of his musicians, 'always said there was more than one way to start a fire'. 'Modern Love' was slow to ignite. Bowie first unbuttoned his jacket, then loosened his tie, strutting onto the runway beneath the stage and finally rousing the crowd into fist-pumping frenzy. His fourth and final number was 'Heroes'. As the band vamped a repetitive tune, and heard themselves publicly thanked, Bowie came forward with the dedication 'To my son . . . and to the children of the world.' This, along with Queen and a barely audible McCartney, were the night's show-stopping moments. Bowie's vocal, and the obvious moral of the song, cut to the heart of Live Aid's reason for being. This was not just rock music on an epic scale. Bowie's parting words and the film of Ethiopia he introduced in place of a fifth song led to more money being pledged than throughout the entire event.

Bowie returned for the finale, miming his way through the Band Aid single. Backstage again, wearing a 'Feed the World' T-shirt, he was asked his opinion of the day. 'We should make it an annual gig,' he grinned, prompting a sarcastic quip from Geldof. Then he thanked his band (all of whom, except Armstrong, had followed his advice to wear blue), draped his arm around Schwab and walked out into the night. As he was crossing the road to his car, a fan approached and asked if he would pose for a photograph. This time, Bowie refused.

It remains arguable whether Live Aid did any lasting good for the suffering in Africa. But it undeniably rocked the world of pop music. Album sales soared. Careers were revived. Those who suspected cynical self-interest in most rock stars believed they found it at Wembley. Bowie himself did not suffer by his appearance. His was not, however, one of those names rescued from semi-death by the CD boom that followed Live Aid. *Tonight* stubbornly failed to reappear in the chart, and there was minimal interest in his back catalogue. In fact he gained nothing but a renewed sense of self-confidence, and some reviewers said as much, dismissing his recent work even while praising his turn at Wembley. It was not a glorious future he was pointing to, wrote Albert Goldman, but a glorious past, namely the flamboyant, knockabout world of vaudeville and the music-hall. Bowie was surely one of the shining stars of Live Aid, a physically charismatic singer who drilled the crowd like a vast workout, yet moved them with his few, well-chosen words about Ethiopia. It was a consummate performance. But whereas other artists used Live Aid as a springboard, immediately taking to the road amid a flurry of self-seeking projects, Bowie flouted all the unwritten rules of rock careerism. He gave no interviews and barely set foot inside a studio. There was only one public performance in the next two years. Asked by a disc jockey what he had to say to his fans, Bowie replied: 'Nothing.'

At the very time that EMI were organizing with Isolar and John Eastman to discuss plans for a new tour, Bowie was drawing up his own wish-list for the year. This included another film, the building of an island home, monitoring the US–Soviet summit at Fleur d'Eau on Lake Geneva, and, acting as a throughline, his art and books. Other than a casual collaboration with Iggy there was, however, very little by way of music. Bowie, for all practical purposes, was semi-retired. He had no new songs, no producer and, above all, no group. After effusively thanking his band at Wembley, Bowie had told each musician he hoped to work with them again. Yet nothing happened. Matthew Seligman would receive a sole Christmas card from Isolar. Conti heard nothing more from Bowie until 1994, when, like Keith Christmas before him, he was summoned overnight to the studio. Dolby, complaining that Kevin Armstrong, not he, had been credited as Bowie's musical director, drifted off into film work with Ken Russell. Armstrong himself kept in touch via Isolar and, like Conti, re-emerged years later.

Bowie returned to the sound stage that autumn. By then he

had already vetoed plans for a new album. On one of his frequent drop-ins on EMI, he steered the conversation around to *Let's Dance* and rendered his succinct verdict: 'Disco sucks.' On another visit, he was bolder. 'I don't give a shit about a hit record.'

Bowie did, however, give a shit about his son. In 1977, he had recorded *Peter and the Wolf* as a gift for Joe. Eight years later, he dedicated his new film project to him. The picture was *Labyrinth*, a $20 million extravaganza, directed by Jim Henson, creator of the Muppets, and written by Monty Python's Terry Jones. As befits that collaboration, the plot was a fantasy, with a cast mainly of puppets, some of whom disturbingly resembled the live actors. Bowie, Henson and the producer George Lucas invited the press and TV cameras in to watch them work. Fourteen journalists recorded Bowie's first day of shooting and his gushing comment: 'These guys organize thousands of crew and eight-hundred-mile-per-hour equipment with less trouble than I have buying a pack of cigarettes.' This was what he had been reduced to – TV cameras eagerly recording him speaking to his own camera so the scene could then be reproduced on *Entertainment Tonight*. It was a hall of mirrors, a self-referential McLuhan universe where all that ultimately mattered were the images – not the disruptive genius Bowie once struggled to tame.

Jones's script was that histrionic blend of sorcery, surrealism and boffo Python humour. Bowie played Jareth, King of the Goblins. Clad in a jerkin and an alarming Tina Turner wig, he hammed his way through the negligible plot: teenage girl goes in search of missing baby brother, whom Bowie has kidnapped and goblinized. The girl, played by Jennifer Connelly, undergoes initiation into Jareth's lair, seduction, imprisonment and other rituals before emerging triumphant. *Labyrinth* was accompanied by pre-release hype on a scale that Lucas had pioneered with *Star Wars*. *Rolling Stone* gave the film lavish advance publicity. A preview cut was shown in cinemas across America. Print and TV advertising, along with a national poster campaign, broke in spring of 1986. Much was made of the relationship – what the publicists called the 'chemistry' – between the two human leads. The media gave its deep sigh, halfway between joy and disgust, whenever contemplating Bowie's sex life. 'Where have we failed that this papery old queen is a hero to our kids?' barked the *Star*.

Jareth himself admitted to being drawn to his fifteen-year-old co-star. 'Jennifer's extremely pretty ... She looks rather like the young Elizabeth Taylor as she was in *National Velvet*.' Bowie spoke of his own mid-life *modus vivendi*: 'I still splash paint onto a canvas once in a while, and I collect twentieth-century woodblock prints and first editions of twentieth-century writers. I don't do gardening.'

Released in June 1986, the *Labyrinth* soundtrack spent a week in the British Top 40 without troubling the *Billboard* chart. Bowie supplied seven songs, including the single 'Underground'. The inevitable video saw him cavorting in a subterranean maze of caverns and tunnels and standing his image on its ear by singing the chorus amongst Henson's puppets. For many critics, the bizarre evolution of his backing group marked the only discernible virtue in the performance. Those who cast their minds back to *The Man Who Fell to Earth* understood why Bowie looked so wretched in *Labyrinth*: put the two roles side by side and one could hear the old Yankee advice to lost tourists, 'You can't get there from here.' It was a cruel spring for Bowie. In April he was basking in good notices for his cameo in *Absolute Beginners*; two months later the critics panned him for *Labyrinth*. The accident of scheduling meant that within the course of a few weeks Bowie had gone from respected actor to abject ham. 'Eye of newt and tongue of mole, David Bowie has become a troll,' wrote *Melody Maker*'s Ted Mico. *NME* chose to parody both the film and the *Jackie* school of pop journalism: 'Most of us are familiar with David Bowie from his role as Vendice Partners in the sparkling musical comedy *Absolute Beginners*, but how many I wonder know that David is also a talented all-round entertainer and singer?'* Another video, 'As the World Falls Down', showed Bowie reflecting on former glories while semi-yodelling the slight, wistful tune. Elsewhere, the soundtrack shunned altitude in favour of the kind of sleepy-time ballads and family favourites best left to Elton John.

---

*Few of the reviewers mentioned Bowie's long-time penchant for writing children's songs, a subplot of his career since 'The Laughing Gnome', which *Labyrinth*'s second single, 'Magic Dance', neatly mined.

Lucas accorded *Labyrinth* the full panoply of Hollywood publicity, the marketing machine cranked up, and the film was a hit. It topped the British box office over Christmas 1986. Children loved the mix of fire-fights, castles, mazes and gospel-singing goblins. For adults, the big surprise was not that Bowie was a bad actor, but that the charisma was gone. The performance radiated blandness. In a Phil Collins film like *Buster*, that would have been fine. From the star of *The Elephant Man* and *Merry Christmas, Mr Lawrence*, it was a disaster. Even for someone who had tried on nearly as many personae as he had written songs, *Labyrinth* was a weird career choice. Bowie returned to Switzerland a million dollars richer, but an actor whose reputation outweighed anything so paltry as his recent roles.

Iggy Pop had spent summer of 1985 recording an album with Steve Jones, the former Sex Pistols guitarist, in Los Angeles. He offered to perform at Live Aid, but his services as a fundraiser were not required. Instead, it was Iggy himself who then travelled, as he says, 'in reduced circumstances', to New York. There he met Bowie, fresh from shooting *Labyrinth*. After a quantity of cocaine snorted, bottles of wine drunk and an assortment of other substances smoked, the old friends were ready to review Iggy's work. Bowie, of course, had long carried a torch for the man suddenly canonized at thirty-nine as the godfather of punk. Now his praise soared to baroque heights. Iggy had had no intention of asking Bowie to produce the album. He was simply proud of how much he had achieved on a tight budget. It was that same mutual admiration, and striving for the other man's approval, that friends had noted since 1971. Bowie was so moved by what he heard that he volunteered to help write four extra songs and co-produce the final product. Iggy then announced he wanted a commercial record. 'I can make this as commercial as hell,' Bowie told him.

In November the two, alongside Steve Winwood and Ron Wood, performed as an *ad hoc* group at New York's China Club. Iggy and his wife then joined Bowie and Schwab for a pre-Christmas cruise in the Caribbean. It was an odd place to be writing post-punk rock songs. Odder still was that Bowie spent most afternoons lying on the sun deck with Iggy, both strumming their Martin guitars, while other passengers milled around, took pictures and asked for their autographs. At Christmas the Pops joined Bowie in Switzerland. There they got in their annual skiing trip and wrote more songs.

Bowie booked studio time at Mountain (where he enjoyed a cut rate) that May. By then Iggy's purse strings had loosened. A year and a half since release, some of *Tonight*'s songwriting royalties had finally filtered from ASCAP to the Pops' apartment. Iggy opened a bank account and learnt to balance a chequebook. He decided the time had come to get organized. Visitors to Montreux found a resurrected, apparently healthy man whose only self-laceration was a shaving scar. As always in the studio, Bowie worked at dizzy speed. Basic tracks were cut at the rate of one a day, and the entire album was completed within a month. On the last night of recording, he and Iggy sat at the control board and smoked cigars. A source recalls Bowie also 'read *The Times* a lot'.

The result was *Blah Blah Blah*, released in October 1986. It revived a career once seemingly bound for the 'Where are they now?' rock trivia pages. Not only was Iggy back on the chart, he performed for the first time ever on *Top of the Pops*. By this yardstick alone, his life and career took a few recognizably normal, if not banal twists. The achievement was Iggy's, but he was quick to credit his patron. As a friend, Bowie could be generous of his time, his ideas, his connections, and, by all accounts, his money. He was good company to boot. Thus, if you sparked his interest, you had it all – the lively companion, the benefactor and the artistic soul-mate. Bowie did not, as was rumoured, join in Iggy's subsequent tour. He did, though, frequently do favours for friends in no position to return them. Here was a departure from the angst-ridden 'numb iceman' character of the seventies. If schizoid tendencies can be gleaned from Bowie's family – and if they seem to be supported by his early career – it was because he was indeed tortured by inner frustration, anger and guilt, and persecuted by a mix of ego and insecurity which had caused his sado-masochistic dreams and fantasies, feelings he was tempted constantly to project onto the world. That cruelty and compassion are closely linked was well known to Bowie. While a Buddhist, he had made a study of them. Alongside the 'thin white duke' persona, there were numerous clues from Bowie's past indicating compassion – his behaviour to his son was one example. He cried constantly. Bowie's senti-mentality, therefore, was very real. By his late thirties he had converted lachrymose outpourings of goodwill into something approaching true friendship. His support of Iggy was striking because it showed a part of Bowie that fits poorly with the iceman stereotype. Kevin Armstrong, who played on the *Blah Blah Blah* session, remembers 'David [as] just *supremely* nice' and making time to socialize with the band. Whatever the problems of his own career, Bowie went out of his way to help others, whether lending them money, producing their albums or, as Armstrong puts it, 'being aware of their particular needs' in the studio. That he was cognizant on a deeper level was shown by 'Shades', a ballad he co-wrote for *Blah Blah Blah*, based on his observation of Iggy's relationship with his wife.

A bacterial infection from contaminated water felled Bowie shortly after he returned to Lausanne for the summer. It was only after he recovered from his illness that he could settle into his new lifestyle. He spent most of that year alone in Switzerland. As much a creature of habit as ever, Bowie followed a routine that included morning walks around Lake Geneva, work on his sculptures and paintings, an afternoon siesta and dinner with the many individuals who constantly grappled for his ear. Weekends he relaxed with Schwab or Oona Chaplin. Occasion-ally he worked on his screenplay. Despite extensive edits, a final draft remained frustratingly elusive. Bowie's own contradictory comments about it confirmed that he had lost his way. He could not make up his mind whether he was writing an existentialist tract or a caper. Each year he gave a wildly different plot synopsis: a Gothic tragedy, a fantasy, a farce; later still, a surrealist tale that charted the rise and fall of a Ziggy-like character. Bowie had given up on producing the film, but he was too proud to admit it, even to himself. One day he informed *Rolling Stone* he was working on the project 'eternally'. The next he ripped up the entire first draft of the manuscript and told a friend he had thought of a wonderful new storyline. 'I could probably do something serious, but I wanted to make it into a rock folly, a satire of what happened to me.' Those were his plans, and he talked as though the projected characters were embedded so deeply in his head that putting them on paper was only a minor matter, like joining the dots on a child's puzzle.

By his own account, Bowie spent much of the year in Lausanne, reading 'eighteen books a week' – a guest remembers him weeping at Oscar Wilde's stories – and listening to news on the World Service. Bowie dressed simply, preferring slacks, sport shirts and discreet chunks of costume jewellery. His main meal of the day usually consisted of an English-style fry-up. He often prepared his own food. His personal computer, recently installed in his study, was an endless source of diversion. As was the case in Berlin, Bowie's routine exuded a frugality that did not square with published accounts of his exotic bents. One visitor to Lausanne came across Bowie sitting cross-legged on his bedroom floor polishing a pair of black lace-up shoes. Several garments he recalls as 'sane, bankers' suits' were on hooks nearby. Bowie then showed his guest his latest work-in-progress, which he planned to hang in a London gallery in order to prove 'I'm more than a metal-headed moron'. The exhibit drew respectful, curious crowds but did not change many minds.

Despite extensive discussions between EMI, Isolar and John Eastman, Bowie refused to tour in 1986. Instead he gave a single charity performance, duetting with Jagger at a Prince's Trust gala at Wembley. Nearly fifteen years earlier, once he had made the decision to concoct Ziggy, Bowie had confided to Ronson, 'Every day is the *last – make it count.*' The guitarist was shrewd enough to note at the time that 'he said it as much to gee himself up as the band'. It showed a shaky commitment to rock and roll that Bowie so often needed to flaunt it with slogans. Anyone who had been paying attention would have known that music, to him, wasn't necessarily the solution. Once he achieved his starting ambitions – to be noticed and make money – Bowie was hard-pressed to motivate himself. He spent nearly two years out of view and enjoyed the mystique of a Garbo.

Later in 1986, in August, Bowie began a brief affair with a young actress. The experience itself was paltry, but its significance was enormous. He had already overcome his fear of sloth, his fear of flying and even his fear of madness. It was time to celebrate the birth of the real David Bowie, the man who could make light of his own foibles. This exultant trumpet-blast echoed in almost all his dealings with his new lover. She recalled how, at the critical moment in bed, Bowie had cried 'The iceman cometh!', reducing both parties to tears of laughter. His writings on sex took every imaginable form, from masturbation to buggery, mutilation, cunnilingus and bestial copulations in fancy dress. Yet he leavened his own erotic activities, hidden beneath a veil of propriety, with humour the woman found 'sexier than the act'.

As he neared forty Bowie must have known that his days as a front-line rock star were, if not over, then perilously close to being so. Many of his old friends from the early seventies had already vanished from the scene. Rod Stewart and Elton John were still in the saddle, but T Rex, Roxy Music, Slade, Sweet, Mud and Gary Glitter had all either folded or taken well-earned semi-retirement. Eno was now making a living producing massive AOR hits for U2. Bowie himself was physically still capable of projecting a character ten years younger. But it was a character that audiences were finding harder and harder to credit. Bowie lost thousands of his old fans each time he released a new single. His charity performances were more than adequate, but they tended to celebrate the past – his Prince's Trust act was praised for its 'sly sentimentalism' – rather than dare skirt the cutting-edge. As Bowie had negotiated huge guarantees from EMI, it was relatively easy for him to keep the fact of his eroding popularity largely to himself. Seeing him in his public role as the smiling millionaire rock superstar, few would have suspected that he was enduring agonies of doubt about quitting. While his output had now ground down to one new album every two or three years (he had made one every six months in the early seventies), stories about Bowie continued to appear regularly in the fan magazines. He was still seen at all the fashionable openings in London and New York. So far as the general public was concerned, as well as a good part of the business, Bowie was one of the very few glam-rock stars who had managed to survive.

The secret was not as easily kept from the financial powers at EMI. After paying Bowie $20 million for five albums, the label was well aware of the downward sales trajectory from *Let's Dance* to *Labyrinth*. There was growing concern, as a corporate insider put it in October, about the 'declining prospects of a viable product' from their star turn. Bowie himself stayed away from

New York, its liaisons and power rows, its lunches and lifestyle –
'I hate that thing where the company becomes your life. I just like
to make an album, you know, and go home.' He hated most of all
the label's belief that an artist was best served by a steady diet of
hit singles and tours that ploughed down a straight line, one after
another, with little scope for stylistic departures and none for a
wholesale change of public image.

While Bowie lived as a virtual hermit in Switzerland, his
reputation went into a tailspin. EMI had wanted him to release a
new album in 1986 before it headed too far south. But Bowie
raised an objection about dates, promising only that 1987 would
be 'a year of great endeavours'. In the meantime, *Tonight* was
reduced to slumming in the bargain bins, the *Labyrinth* soundtrack flopped and 'Magic Dance' barely nudged the chart – all at
a loss of millions for EMI. Bowie's refusal to deliver a son-of-*Let's
Dance* had cost the label a huge potential profit. And now they
were carrying him only so he could collaborate casually with Iggy
Pop for a rival firm. Finally, in a frenzy of inter-office memos,
EMI's detachment ended. No more delays in recording, they said.
And no more years off – never again.

The result was an intense month of writing and recording at
Mountain Studios. Bowie assembled a band again quarterbacked
by Carlos Alomar and including a classically trained Turkish
multi-instrumentalist, Erdal Kizilcay, also involved on *Blah Blah
Blah*. The cosmopolitan flavour was enhanced by the bassist
Carmine Rojas and Philippe Saisse on piano. More exotic still was
Bowie's choice of lead guitarist. Live Aid's Kevin Armstrong was
replaced by the man dubbed 'The Face of '68' by teen magazine
Rave, who went on – briefly – to become a mainstream golden
boy, and re-emerged in 1986 with an ill-advised synth-pop
hybrid called, with unconscious irony, *Premonition*.

Nearly thirty years had passed since Davy Jones had come
under the benign aegis of Owen Frampton, the man he credited
with prodding him into art. Now Bowie repaid the debt by
rescuing his son's career. Even for one who downplayed consistency, it was a curious decision. Despite releasing the best-
selling grandfather of the live-double-album era, Peter Frampton
had rarely been more than a journeyman guitarist; there were
literally hundreds of more talented session men. Bowie's choice

made little sense done in the name of technical genius. It may
have made more sense in the name of nostalgia. Introducing the
album six months later, Bowie peppered the press with his
approximation of a south London accent and matching slang,
both suggesting that, at forty, another sea-change, illustrated by
his appearing in scuffed jeans and a sweater, was under way.
Frampton, too, was more than usually receptive to Bowie's
compulsive ad-libbing and speed-of-light work in the studio. Neil
Conti remembers: 'He gave you complete freedom with your part,
but he didn't give you the encouragement you needed to really
develop it. You accepted that as part of David. And he's fast. I've
never worked faster in my life, you just do it – stand-and-jump
music.'

The Montreux session, co-produced by Bowie and David
Richards, spawned twelve songs and dozens of noodling, fusion-
style vamps, some of which circulated freely on bootlegs. Elation
wreathed the faces in the EMI boardroom. They were on their
way to releasing a new, upbeat album, but more importantly, one
that marked the first time in three years that Bowie had agreed
to tour. He had steadfastly endured the rigours of self-imposed
exile and the pressures heaped on him to follow up the Serious
Moonlight extravaganza. But the one arrow that had pierced him
most deeply was the observation that, in Kim Gordon's terms, he
was an 'old fart'. Bowie's comeback would not have been
complete without the expunction of the stain on his record for
risk-taking and abrupt switches. With varying success, but a
shrewd instinct for the market, Bowie now engaged in a
calculated display of his punk credentials. He went to the right
clubs in Los Angeles and New York, ending up backstage with
Iggy. He allowed himself to be photographed wearing a torn
T-shirt. Though his superstar rank and privileges had been
restored, proper rehabilitation called for the wearing of the right
uniform. That Bowie chose to dress alternately like a Bromley
actuary and a refugee from the Ramones told more about his self-
image than many of his fans, especially EMI, wanted to know.

From Miami he took the small commuter jet to Mustique, an
otherwise bleak outpost of the Grenadines developed in the sixties
by Colin Tennant and his friend Princess Margaret, and now a
virtual colony of rock stars. Late in 1982, Mick Jagger and Jerry

Hall had begun the process by building a beach cottage, surrounded by a series of adjoining Japanese pavilions and guest houses, connected by polished hardwood walkways and bamboo railings, they fondly named Stargroves. On Christmas Eve 1986 Bowie and Schwab joined them on the estate. The 'international set', as one villager dubbed them, turned the island into their playground. If Bowie's goals as a rock star had been merely to make money and win the adoration of the masses he could probably have brought them off; indeed, more than most, had done so. But he also sought social success, which meant acceptance by the élite, and benign tolerance had never been a virtue of his tax-exile neighbours. With the exception of Balthus and the Chaplins they refused to recognize the ex-Brixton boy of dubious origins, despite his niche on the celebrity A-list. In 1973, Bowie had ranted to his wife that 'Mick has all this bread – I'm skint', setting in hand the events that led to Defries' ouster, and ultimately her own. Thirteen years later, Jagger still acted as a contrast-gainer. Bowie quizzed him for hours about Mustique property prices and zoning laws, exchanging notes on furnishings, antiques, international paperwork, customs clearances and touching on knotty problems like that posed by desalinization and the sewage pump. Later that evening the two men attended the carol service in Mustique's Anglican church. A London public relations executive, Nick Miles, remembers them 'mugging, not singing' their way through a hymn, letting their arms drape across the back of the pew onto each other's shoulders. Here was a different Bowie to the New Wave avatar glimpsed in New York. His commitment to shock tactics was fully matched, as ever, by his conservative personal code; they were two sides of the same psychic drive. For every crowd-pleasing display of punk muscle, there were still the rites, manners and insecurities of the suburban Englishman keeping up with (reverting to, in Bowie's case) the Joneses.

Early in the new year, Bowie bought a plot of land up the hill from Jagger and Hall. He commissioned the architect Arne Hasselqvist and New York designer Robert Litwiller to oversee the building of a series of oriental pavilions, eventually filled with fourteen cargo containers' worth of antiques shipped in from Indonesia, Italy, France, London and New York. Bowie would no longer spend his Christmas in Gstaad. From 1986 he began an expansion policy worthy of a small conglomerate. There would be houses in Switzerland, Ireland, New York, Los Angeles and a boat in the Mediterranean. Bowie, his war chest bulging with EMI money, pressed forward with developing his Mustique estate and made frequent inspection tours. The home, like Jagger's, became a magnet for visiting celebrities. Although Bowie complained of being treated like a tourist attraction, holding court in his Balinese-style dining room was an essential part of his day, and he loved it. The opportunity to talk to rich businessmen especially amused him, and he mesmerized vacationing record chiefs and lawyers, for whom he was a living legend. These sessions almost always turned into rambling reminiscences, often characterized by outrageous distortions or misstatements of fact.

Bowie turned forty on 8 January 1987. A decade earlier he had stood on the brink of great things: an uninterrupted row of thrilling albums – the brave new music of Berlin; an escape from what he called the 'blinkered' lifestyle of most rock stars; stage and film work; the commercial accolade of the EMI deal. Bowie's golden years had been ushered in by a crisis, his twelve-month-long binge in Los Angeles. By 1985–6 his mid-career pomp had dwindled to a few *ad hoc* projects, soundtracks and increasingly desultory albums. His fans liked to put him in a class with other long-running stars like Jagger, Dylan and Clapton, and tended to make the simplistic assumption that if these old-wavers could rock, so could he. The giant forces that now returned him to the stage were dealing not with a young *flâneur*, but an old pro. A cynic might note that – as with Clapton and the rest – Bowie was doing no more than reshuffling stale formulae. The glibness of his recent songs, the recurrence of commercial ploys and the laughable self-caricature of his duets with Jagger and Tina Turner all suggested a man, creatively speaking, on the point of menopause. It had been a good decade for Bowie. It would be increasingly difficult to build on the momentum in the years ahead. The problems he had to confront would have severely tested him in his prime. As it was, the tour needed careful, sustained attention, and each new strategy session, brainstorm and audition kindled his devotion to the grail of self-management. The hands-on style Bowie preferred included an extreme reluctance to delegate or say no. Jealous of her place next to the throne, Schwab stood ready to prevent others from intruding.

Late in 1986 Bowie had gone on a safari of the New York clubs and told one aspiring band that his new album was 'punker than you'll ever be'. A week later he was crooning carols with Mick Jagger. The pendulum swung again in the course of a birthday interview with *Rolling Stone*. Bowie praised the film *Sid and Nancy*. 'How did Vicious strike you as a person?' he was asked. 'Just a mindless twerp. I didn't find anything at all romantic about him, or even interesting.' Did he still feel, as he had in *Diamond Dogs* days, that the end was near? 'No, I don't feel that at all. I *can't* feel that. I always *have* to look for some kind of light at the end of the tunnel. Having a son does that. You change a lot.' Bowie ended by insisting he was 'more like I was in 1967, say, than I was in 1977 . . . I feel as bright and cheerful and optimistic as I was then – as opposed to feeling as depressed and nihilistic as I was in the seventies. I feel like I've come full circle in that particular way.'

For any analysis of Bowie's character, 1987 was the testing year. The album and world tour were planned for the spring. EMI and Isolar were coaxing the press and whole assembly-lines were turning out T-shirts, posters, and other relics, elaborately inscribed with the gaudy hieroglyphics of the tour logo. The stage managers, the carpenters, the caterers, the truckers, the accountants and the group were all put on standby. John Eastman sold the TV and video rights and struck a sponsorship deal with Pepsi. Yet again, Bowie was back. The only question was: which one?

The first clue came in March 1987, with the release of 'Day In Day Out'. Bowie's sixtieth single opted for the 'plastic soul' sound of *Young Americans*, all riffing bass, jungle drums and lyrics that tried to be meaningful. The song was about the creeping paranoia of urban America, a tourist snap of the moronic inferno. Musically, it blazed no new trails. At a time when his imitators were experimenting with a harsh style of hammering, assembly-line music and dabbling with the primal tones that became grunge, Bowie elected to retreat to disco. 'Day In Day Out', released in a riot of formats, including a limited edition box in blue vinyl, was a minor hit on both sides of the Atlantic. It came with a Julien Temple video which saw Bowie, looking disturbingly like Daryl Hall (and his drummer got up like William Burroughs) following the heroine's progress in Los Angeles. By using complicated arrangements to swamp rather than build on the slight, disposable melody, David Richards achieved a truly awful, Bee Gees-era mix. 'Day In Day Out' sounded so faithful to the mid seventies, one could almost see Bowie, arm extended, wiggling under a mirror-ball as he sang it.

'Time Will Crawl' followed, a simple pop tune packed with twisted, unresolved feelings of romance, loss, obsession and self-doubt, and a British top-forty hit. The album's third single, 'Never Let Me Down', also stuck close to the *Young Americans* playbook – or that part of the album where Lennon breathed life into the lyrics. The romantic undertones and hand-me-down social comment were matched by a chorus that fell short of the giddy expectation generated by the title. 'Never Let Me Down' tossed rock in favour of a four-minute ditty which had Bowie whistling in the outro. It, too, came with a video: a pastiche of *They Shoot Horses, Don't They?*, and Bowie and a young girl sauntering down a corridor, the former all suave elegance and exuding the jaded aesthete look of Bryan Ferry.

Never Let Me Down was a British number six. It gave innocent pleasure to over a million people. Fans pointed admiringly to Bowie's ability to reinvent pop music, invigorating tired riffs and rhythms with off-the-wall but danceable tunes. Others felt the album was a depressing return to 'Little Drummer Boy' form, a throwback to the days of Bing Crosby duets and *The Dinah Shore Show*. This was a record of popular themes – the power of love, love as power, sexual tyranny and emotional dependency – weighed down by Bowie's mannered vocals and the consistently weak production. There was little that was flat-out awful, but too many of the album's eleven cuts flowed on clichéd guitar hooks and Steely Dan-like grooves instead of any house style. The result was a shoddily constructed work, with the occasional disruptive twist to bring the message that this was a David Bowie LP. Its author soon joined the negative consensus. 'What, for me, was a bitter disappointment was the way it turned out. It wasn't played with any conviction ... It was studio-fied to such an extent that, halfway through the sessions, I was going out to lunch and just leaving everyone to it.'

The upside was that Bowie was generous with his musicians, giving them room to breathe, and occasionally to salvage the unfinished, featherweight songs. Thus 'Beat of Your Drum' worked an ingeniously melodic, sweatily incarnated blitzkrieg of bass, keyboards and drums (all played by Erdal Kizilcay) into a palatable, dance-hall riff. 'Zeroes' used some of Prince's *Purple Rain* as a launch-pad to Ziggydom. 'Glass Spider' built from a spoken intro, via a steady upbeat progression, into a meaty, full-band arrangement. Those were the exceptions. 'Too Dizzy' was at least two steps removed from its primary source – 'Young Americans' by way of 'Day In Day Out'. 'New York's In Love' devolved into messy jamming, and a pasted-on guitar solo. Real indignity befell Bowie's version of Iggy's 'Bang Bang'.

As a critic said, had anyone else released *Tonight* and followed it with the dreary *Never Let Me Down*, they would have been ignored. Yet the response Bowie had to face was more akin to scorn. People were angry. Bowie was trading on the loyalty and dwindling affection his fans still had for him. Since 1983, while commanding respect, he had failed to excite new audiences. Even Live Aid was no more than a milestone down the road to looming obscurity. His decline seemed unstoppable. Residual goodwill from his tour kept *Never Let Me Down* in the chart for sixteen weeks; after that Bowie's name vanished for the first time since *Ziggy Stardust*. His most conspicuous appearance was as a waxwork dummy in Madame Tussaud's.

That kind of fame was far from what Bowie wanted. Humiliation and embarrassment haunted him, inevitably contributing to both anger and determination. In 1987 he was forced almost literally to crawl back on stage in the 'Glass Spider' guise foisted on him by others. During the tour itself, Bowie was alternately displayed before the public with confidence and uncertainty. The theatrical vision of 1974 came across as silly and contrived in 1987. Bowie himself admitted he was close to giving up. He suffered pangs of doubt about performing live. After a histrionic scene in Lausanne, he found himself taking motivational courses in order to become 'David Bowie' for six months. From a practical point of view the result was an extraordinary blunder as well as an extraordinary tour.

On 17 March, Bowie held a press conference at the Diamond

Club, in Toronto, to announce dates and a multi-million-dollar sponsorship deal with Pepsi for the North American shows. In the next two weeks he held seven further events in the US and Europe, turning the process into a tour of its own. By ripping through tracks from *Never Let Me Down* to three hundred journalists at a time, Bowie was ensuring the attention that he had hoped for, but he also took critical heat. 'Day In Day Out' and the rest were not so much seized on as accepted. He was forced to defend the album as 'a progression from *Scary Monsters* rather than my last two records'. Asked if he was 'past it', Bowie pursed his lips, promising to be 'totally candid' in his answer, which turned out to be no. He denied that he had arthritis and bristled when one critic suggested that the tour be dubbed not Glass Spider, but the Antique Roadshow.

Such cynicism, well-founded as it was, was almost certainly not shared by Bowie's fans. The reason why EMI and Pepsi were willing to ante up millions before the first chord of the first show, and several months even before most venues went on sale, was the growing worldwide demand for reunion and nostalgia acts. In America, in particular, nothing sold concert tickets like a comeback tour. More pertinently, comeback on an epic scale. Glass Spider saw Bowie attempt to revive the Broadway conceit of the Year of the Diamond Dogs for his new arena audience. Opening night, at Feyenoord stadium in Rotterdam, had all the trappings of a musical première. For his entrance, Bowie was lowered to the stage from inside a translucent spider's belly; a troupe of dancers abseiled down from the scaffolding, leading one cynic to wonder if he was witnessing a rock concert or an SAS-type storming of an embassy; films were shown; each song was choreographed. In a final gimmick, Bowie emerged atop a radio tower sporting wings and them shimmied down for the encore. While some praised the show's flamboyance, for others it was a travesty of the 1974 blueprint, a *folie de grandeur* with no unifying concept except the star's ego. It was Bowie at his most self-indulgent. There were mutterings, too, about the originality of the central theme. Those with long memories made the link to the Who's 'Boris' and other arachnoid names in rock history, including, of course, the Spiders from Mars.

The show drew inspiration from the usual sources: *Metropolis*,

1984, Albert Speer, Pink Floyd and Lindsay Kemp's epicene mime routine. So far as there was a focal point it was the sixty-foot-high spider that hung forlornly from the scaffolding above the stage, and the spotlit and over-amplified musicians, whose power chords rapidly descended into headbanging. Frampton, whatever his merits as a touchstone to Bowie's past, proved sadly inept as a lead guitarist. His playing lacked dynamics. Instead of rising and dipping in volume and intensity, the fast numbers lashed out in a blitz and maintained their exhaustive pace throughout. The ballads seemed in danger of stalling. Even a closing salvo from *Let's Dance* elicited only a lukewarm response. An MC appeared after the final encore at Rotterdam to urge everyone to leave peacefully, but there was no problem – most of the subdued audience had already fallen silent.

After a stop in Belgium, the tour reached Berlin on 6 June. A mark of Bowie's respect for his former home was his insistence on a morning-long rehearsal at Hansa followed by a press conference in the very room (now a recital hall) where he recorded *'Heroes'*. He spoke fondly of his experience in the studio. It made him sad, he said, to look out of the window, as he had a decade ago, at the Berlin Wall. The wall became an important theme in Bowie's next few hours. He took an ordinary city taxi up Entlastungstrasse, past the Brandenburg Gate, and down the east–west axis, skirting some of the most potent visual symbols of the Cold War. He paused for photographs outside 155 Hauptstrasse (though, as in his previous visit to Stansfield Road, Bowie declined to go inside). He returned to his hotel by way of Kochstrasse and Checkpoint Charlie. When the car finally reached the Kempinski, Bowie groaned, in German, from the back sea, 'I cannot leave you. I am paralysed.' After that it became usual for him to travel with Tony Mascia in the Mercedes.

That night Bowie headlined a three-day festival taking place on the Reichstag lawn, within earshot of East Berlin, as part of the municipal 750th birthday celebrations. The scene threw poignant light on the divided city. As Bowie performed on the Platz der Republik, several thousand East German rock fans massed on the opposite side of the wall, rousing the border guards to disperse the impromptu concert with clubs, dogs and finally tear gas. The pictures of bloodied teenagers being chased down the street by armed police achieved global circulation in the days ahead. *Bild* described the scene as 'a defining moment' in coalescing grass-roots agitation into a national crusade to unify the two Germanys. According to this reading, Bowie was as responsible as anyone else for a huge upswing in anti-Communist sentiment, and ultimately for the fall of the Berlin Wall.

A fortnight later Bowie was in his home town for two sold-out shows at Wembley Stadium. That London, like Berlin, held special merit for him was shown by his agreeing to perform live on *Top of the Pops* (where, in an apparent protest against sexual exploitation, he wore a jacket adorned with Page 3-type photos across each shoulder), his granting of multiple interviews at the Hilton, and his insistence on three separate rehearsals at Wembley, the last held in driving rain. ('When you're born in a place,' Bowie informed a press conference, 'that becomes the big one.') 'He always liked to be working,' says Alan Rea, a London staffer. There was never a question of waiting for the muse to descend. 'David was a very obsessive type of musician, not inspired,' he says. 'Everything was blocked out: how many beats, what would happen on each beat.' An assistant would chart this data on three-by-five cards, and as the rehearsal progressed, Bowie would shuffle the cards if he needed to alter the structure.

After a lengthy guitar solo from Alomar, during which voodoo-clad dancers swung on ropes and, apelike, prattled at the Wembley crowd, a single spot picked out Bowie, descending in a steel office chair and cradling an antique phone. In this arresting pose he got through 'Glass Spider' and 'Day In Day Out'. After an attempted audience singalong and an hour dense with cuts from *Scary Monsters*, vague memories were stirred by the early chords of 1971's 'All the Madmen'. In "87 and Cry' Bowie was tied up by a goon squad; in 'Heroes' he broke loose again. When 'Let's Dance' materialized, following a noodle of Frampton's guitar, fans roared; clearly the Serious Moonlight sound was what they had come to hear. Bowie and the dancers managed a bit of business in 'Fame' and left the stage after 'Modern Love'. There was no second encore. Due to gale-force winds, Bowie declined to fly on a wire for 'Time', as he had in Holland and Germany.

Bowie had introduced his son, sixteen years old that day, to the crowd at Rotterdam. The sound of 60,000 voices duly crooning

'Happy Birthday' proved the tour's most human moment. Elsewhere Bowie's comments between numbers, once seized on almost as eagerly as the songs themselves, veered between endless variations on 'How ya doin'?' and the ominous 'Here's a new one.' At Wembley he offered the pat 'It's good to be back', but otherwise brought the noise with lordly control and no great warmth. Bowie's sinewy body language was his communication with his audience.

The tour's outward features were the routine ones of arena rock: scuffles at airports, brawls about tickets, oafish stewards, injuries, deaths (a lighting engineer was killed when he fell from a scaffold in Florence) and carefully staged photo opportunities with pop luminaries and minor royals. Bowie himself grew increasingly morose as the year progressed. So full of hope in late May, he was a punctured balloon by early July, incapable of reflation. Since 1983 Bowie had become known as a predictable performer and now the inquests after his tours also ran on familiar lines. They followed down one of two tracks. On the one hand, the tabloids and certain reviewers praised the shows' scale and enterprise (quoting bizarre statistics like the number of kebab meals served backstage). The alternative view was taken by those who measured Bowie by his own high standards. They judged him alongside names like Prince and Madonna and found him wanting. To them, the much-hyped props were the product of narcissism and vanity, the playthings of a spoilt child transported into middle age. At the very least, the combination of Bowie, a giant spider, the band and a chaotic running commentary was thought risibly inane, as though *Spinal Tap* had never happened. As one reviewer said, 'Bowie has simply smashed his blonde head into the wall of the pretentious end of a cul-de-sac. If this is the way rock music is going to get back its meaning, the answer is no.'

Under the theatrical mechanics the inner workings of the tour also went awry. By his early forties Bowie had become obsessed with the idea of absolute, relentless perfection in everything, and in so doing he naturally increased his already large corps of professional foes. One of his own group was found backstage at Wembley, coiled in the foetal position and sobbing after an apparently scathing remark. There were the inevitable scenes about money. A member of Big Country, Bowie's support act, recalls a 'volcanic' reaction when the wrong brand of lacquer was produced for the star's hair. In the past it had been impossible to predict when his hidden combustibility – often fuelled by drugs – would erupt into public outrage. Now Bowie merely seethed when a roommate from Beckenham arrived, uninvited, in the hospitality suite. He had Mascia throw the man out. A few moments later, Bowie and a second ex-colleague (this one wearing a VIP badge) passed each other on the stairs, and each turned his head away from the other. The first man then reappeared through a side door. This time, Bowie exploded.

Life for Bowie was insipid without the interest given by some morale-boosting partner. Now, for the first tour in twenty years, he was alone. A friendship with Marie Helvin failed to ignite; another companion abruptly left him after taking money from his wallet; the connection with Schwab drifted along, obscurely and indeterminately, but without resolution. When Bowie mingled with his attractive female fans he walked the sexual-harassment tightrope. On 9 October 1987 a woman named Wanda Lee Nichols alleged he had assaulted her 'in a Dracula-like fashion' in his Dallas hotel room after a concert. Two years of litigation followed, during which Bowie denied the charge, though admitted sleeping with Nichols. The case was dismissed in February 1990.

Personal difficulties were mirrored by professional setbacks on the US tour. Bowie, competing with the likes of Dylan and the Grateful Dead, took his lumps at the box office. Despite sellout crowds for opening night in Philadelphia, an effort to improve total grosses by adding dates in key markets backfired; in southern California, for example, extensive TV advertising was needed to boost sales for Bowie's Anaheim show. The critics groaned the same chorus as their British counterparts. Bowie, who 'thought [he] knew how terrible writers could be' to him, was shocked by the violence of the negative reviews. According to *Rolling Stone*, the performance at Giants Stadium was, like the glass spider itself, 'large and meaningless ... When Bowie cast off the frills and ripped through "Rebel Rebel" and "China Girl", he displayed all the authority for which his shows are renowned ... Unfortunately, they only served to make the excesses more apparent – and the experience of suffering through them more frustrating.'

The tour was a self-contained cocoon of Bowie's imagination, a testament to his obsessions. Probably no other rock star demonstrated his personal compulsions so consistently in his work; stubborness was Bowie's great strength as well as his weakness. Despite variable ticket sales, more than three million fans saw the shows in ten countries. The set, widely slated as a child's prank (and derided by Bowie as 'too messy'), was later recycled wholesale by artists like Prince and Paula Abdul, who had her group abseil down to the front of the stage at the Grammys. Madonna would also salvage much of the discarded material. Bowie's fate always to be the prototype, rarely the production-line rocker, thus continued. He symbolically burnt the unfortunate spider in a field after the tour's final night. Then he returned to Switzerland, thoroughly depressed.

The mixture of alcohol, tranquillizers, fatigue and post-tour *ennui* easily matched the limit of his reserves. Bowie was in a bad way. After dinner one night in Lausanne he could walk only if others supported him; unable to lift his legs, he shuffled between them. Schwab had booked dates at Mountain Studios during the autumn. On the first day of recording, it was clear to all that Bowie would be unable to attend, but the difficulty was in persuading him to stay home. Surprisingly, he acquiesced, saying Mascia should start the album in his place. Bowie did, however, come to his senses one morning in November, when he listened to a tape given to him by one of the tour's PR women, Sarah Gabrels. It brought Bowie back into contact with rock and set up his next self-avowed pose – the unlikely one of singer in a garage-band filled out by Gabrels' husband and the comedian Soupy Sales' two sons.

Bowie's other immediate role was a cameo in Martin Scorsese's *The Last Temptation of Christ*. The film was released to wildly mixed notices in 1988. For years Bowie had been so anxious to protect himself against the lure of Hollywood ambition that he wore integrity as a kind of chastity belt. His dread of selling out had led him into some curiously ill-conceived and feckless projects. *The Last Temptation* was not one of these pictures. Scorsese's work drew down howls of rage from America's Christian right, and warm critical acclaim elsewhere. Bowie dramatized his part as Pontius Pilate in a quiet, unadorned style that carried a lethal chill.

He also tapped into his life-long fixation with mysticism, astronomy and the supernatural by enthusing about the (supposedly chaotic and apocalyptical) Aquarian Age and the coming of Halley's Comet. Bowie's mother had taught him to be passionate about memory, and he shared with her the ability to experience various fragmentary moments of mental telepathy. He entertained a visitor to Lausanne by describing a long mind-reading conversation he had just had with Joe in Scotland. Seeing the man smile, Bowie challenged him to concentrate on any five-figure number, which he would in turn call out. At that he went into an apparent coma. After ten minutes, just when his friend suspected an anarchic hoax, Bowie opened his eyes and spoke in a high, reedy voice. Four of the sequence of five were correct.

By mid 1988 it seemed that the sexual outlaw and the man who played stoicism with irony and style, had been replaced by the mellowing entertainer. There was truth to one critic's claim that he was 'punked out'. But it was also true that Bowie was still capable of stirring his public with his intelligence, his emotional lurches, his restlessness, his prophetic insights into pop culture. Within days of listening to Sarah Gabrels' tape, Bowie was on the phone to her husband. The result was Tin Machine, a group of four middle-aged men whose uniform was a dismal costume of goatee beards, and suits or T-shirts and ripped jeans, who drew a bead on the dark sounds of Seattle. Reeves Gabrels, a guitarist whose classical pedigree met a liking for loud, electric rock and roll, was joined by Hunt Sales and his brother Tony, respectively Iggy's drummer and bassist on his 1977 tour of Britain and America. Bowie told his cohorts he 'wanted to be a working musician' again, and Tin Machine preached collectivism over star appeal. As Hunt Sales put it: 'The thing that makes us different from other bands is that the lead singer's a millionaire. But that's where it stops.'

Except, of course, it wasn't. Had Bowie thought about it deeply, he would have realized that his income and celebrity would always guarantee him a special place in the limelight. In practice, therefore, his decision to seek an anonymous berth in a group led him into situations where his superiority would be effortless and unrivalled. Bowie's apparent effort to disown his pop audience was by no means a bid to evade this special status: on the contrary, he relished it. He knew full well that in rock music, like other performing arts, success tends to be a function of mystique, not technical ability. It is even possible that the fickle, perverse side of Bowie – his living affront to the mores of conventional celebrity – was the basis of his appeal.

Bowie's formidable ego allowed him to continually recover from failure by creating radically new styles for his next work. Just as critics began to observe a staleness in his songs, even a slump into self-parody, he returned with another volte-face. First he placed a call to Gabrels. Next the guitarist found himself being flown to Switzerland, where Bowie startled him by choosing 'Ziggy Stardust' as a first rehearsal number. Gabrels remembers that 'David sounded exactly like he did all those years ago on the original' and that 'he had all these different voices' in his bottomless internal wardrobe. From Lausanne the two flew to London, where they staged a short piece for an ICA benefit. Recruiting the Sales brothers, they then returned to Switzerland and the studio.

Over the years the exchanges between Bowie and EMI usually began with an enthusiasm of the label's. The high hopes of the $20 million deal were followed by wild acclaim for *Let's Dance* and grudging acceptance of its successors. It was fair to say that, with Tin Machine, all the company's warm feelings were converted into their opposites. Although the group's début album wasn't rejected (except in a few markets), there was much unpleasantness and stress involved in its release. An EMI memo referred to 'repetitive tunes ... lyrics that preach ... minimalist or no production' and a general lack of potential hit singles. Bowie himself spoke of 'a massive falling-out' between himself and the label. At a stroke the contented family man had regressed into a punk misfit and corporate liability. Tin Machine had done nothing but casually rehearse and record a few numbers; they were – in the derogatory term by which they became best known – 'only Bowie's band'. Their primary identity came through their relationship to him, and because of it they were tainted by association. It was a mixed blessing.

9
SOUND + VISION

The fourteen tracks that went to make up *Tin Machine* were almost all recorded, at breakneck speed, live in the studio. The reckless attack of the music sounded like the bizarre result of a clinical trial involving both stimulants and sedatives. Beatlesque melodies were coated in the super-distorted guitar noise of a Sonic Youth or Nirvana. The lyrics dealt with neo-Nazis, drugs, despair and death – and the songs achieved a startling personal wallop as a result.

The album's premise was that Tin Machine was a democratic band, not Bowie with his latest sidemen, and that *Tin Machine* was its mutual effort. The truth was that the group ran as a virtual dictatorship. Of *Tin Machine*'s tracks, thirteen were written or co-written by Bowie; the exception was Lennon's 'Working Class Hero'. The band's manifesto aggressively repudiated subtlety and finesse in favour of stripped-down tunes and explicit lyrics. Yet the man emerging from his Swiss exile in 1989 was no mere team member. He was player-manager of Tin Machine, whose rough edge and left-of-the-dial artistic punch was a form of recovery after the Glass Spider débâcle. This was Bowie pleasing himself as much as the audience. His achievement was to make the album seem both liberating and enlightening. Framing the eighties, *Tin Machine* and *Scary Monsters* were polar opposite examples of Bowie's talent for writing intelligent and influential rock songs. One was smooth, one was blunt, but the two had this in common: both were superior to anything else that Bowie did in the decade, so full of ironic twists, so rich in manic energy that they might almost have been written by a different person. In a sense, they had been.

The Bowie of May 1989 was an older and richer version of the doom-monger who wrote *Diamond Dogs*. In an interview that summer he foresaw a bleak future for his own son: 'It's very hard for him to understand the structure because, in fact, I think the structure is decaying rapidly.' *Tin Machine* was dipped in a slough of such gloomy predictions. 'Crack City' (whose riff mined the Troggs' 'Wild Thing') was a series of crude observations on America's drug problem. 'I Can't Read' was about TV's erosion of literacy, while 'Video Crime' snarled at the same medium: 'Late-night cannibal – cripples decay/Just can't tear my eyes away'. The album's title track took violent exception to, among other things, 'Humping tories/Spittle on their chins/Carving up my children's future'. 'Under the God' was a political tirade, what Bowie called a 'simplistic, naïve, radical, laying-it-down about the emergence of neo-Nazis'. His writing had never been less oblique. Nor had it ever been more ironical: Bowie had made a quantum leap, from hoary topics like DJs and China girls into a stylistic and narrative world of his own. It took nerve to denounce drugs, fascism and TV – three of Bowie's staples in the seventies – in terms that reached the literary level of a comic book. It was hard to miss the songs' point; the vocals were too loud in the mix. Tin Machine, the band and the album, was a type of therapy, a way for Bowie to purge his past while making his usual deft assault on the market. The lyrics were one thing, but the music consistently demonstrated a preference for the centre ground (and a willingness to loot old riffs) when it served his purpose.

FM radio, in 1989, veered between seventies headbangers and the pre-grunge bands Tin Machine most resembled. Their first single, 'Under the God' – a cannibalization of 'Break On Through' – enjoyed heavy airplay. For the rest of the summer it was impossible to avoid the welter of cover stories and features about the group, to ignore the critical debate, or to switch on MTV without seeing the video. *Tin Machine* sold a million copies worldwide. It reached number three on the British chart. Money was a serious consideration for Bowie at the time, since he had spent wildly on his last tour and depended on the EMI deal for living expenses. *Tin Machine*, like *Low* before it, recouped the sort of income needed by a man with eight people on his payroll, yet within an 'alternative' format. It polarized Bowie's critics at a stroke. John Peel, a fan for twenty years, thinks the band was 'awful – lousy . . . all noise and thrashing about'. There were those who thought of Bowie in a group as a contradiction in terms, his whole persona existing as a solo performer. Gus Dudgeon, the producer of 'Space Oddity', called the Tin Machine project 'dreadful, and the crazy thing is he spends his whole time saying he just wants to be the singer in the band. As if he *could* be. He *is* David Bowie, for God's sake.' EMI, despite the respectable sales figure, hated the group's album. Isolar began to hawk Bowie's contract to other labels, but it was turned down. One company said 'a band like Tin Machine could bankrupt the whole enterprise'. While Bowie's management was making these difficult forays into the record industry, his new group made their first worldwide tour.

'We're not really ready,' Bowie told *Melody Maker*. 'We just wanted to get our feet wet and make sure that we really like working together as a band and, as it happens, it's a real buzz.' On a commercial level, the tour certainly achieved its modest ambitions. At the 1,500-seat Paradiso Club in Amsterdam, a crowd of 25,000 brawled and fought with police in the forecourt. British audiences were responsive and never less than curious about Bowie's latest transformation. Gone was the lavish melodrama of Glass Spider, replaced by simple sets, utilitarian lighting and a bearded singer who alternately appeared in jeans or a dark suit, shirt and tie. Some of the band's low-key approach extended offstage. Tin Machine travelled everywhere by bus. The spartan tour arrangements chimed perfectly with Bowie's own new persona. He enjoyed games of cards while on the motorway. He liked its food, too. Bowie's culinary taste was not elevated; nor did he demand a high standard of presentation. As in his youthful visits to London, he liked to take his meals at a cheap high street restaurant where he could eat steak and chips and nobody bothered with a wine list.

John Cambridge, Bowie's drummer before being replaced by Mick Woodmansey, recalls driving to a Tin Machine show in Bradford. Apparently there was a matter of £5 still owing from 1970, and in the days before the concert the debt was aired light-heartedly on the radio. On the evening in question, Cambridge appeared at the stage door of St George's Hall. He told the obtrusive guard there that he was a friend of Bowie's and that he would like a word. 'I'm not waiting,' Cambridge added. After a short delay, Bowie duly appeared. He was 'very friendly and all over me . . . It was constantly "Do you remember so-and-so?" and a lot of jokes about the old days. I'll say this for David: he had fantastic charm and a knack for making people melt.' Cambridge left the hall impressed by his friend's new-found poise. Bowie remarked on this himself; in consequence he thought he had better give up his solo career. 'I've lost my ego,' he told a friend. 'It's a young guy's thing, being a rock star – you get less cocky as you get older.'

As usual, opinion varied as to whether his current incarnation was the 'real Bowie' or merely another front. With Tin Machine, he seemed determined to slough off his past. His name was not billed separately; he said little, if anything, between numbers; he performed none of his old hits. Bowie's failure of ego does not seem to have worried him. Advancing years made him more considerate and less inclined to Delphic utterances about his art. There was a part of Bowie that was genuinely affable, and that part spoke in his dealings with Cambridge and others. Kevin Armstrong, who played a number of dates with Tin Machine, calls Bowie 'a case of someone who got less assuming and more human as the years went on'. A second man involved with the group insists that 'it really was a band ethic. Tin Machine worked because everyone checked their egos at the door. It was like a killer cocktail: everyone added something to the mix.'

All of that was true. But it was equally true that Bowie was the straw that stirred the drink. Even in the corporate identity of Tin Machine, there were times when he wore his fame badly. Bowie saw himself as living on Olympus and yet had a grating awareness that not all the world agreed. While *Tin Machine* was being recorded, he entered into new negotiations with EMI in which he was to be paid handsomely to return with a solo album and tour; in the end he left the label and arranged for a major reissue set called *David Bowie: Sound + Vision* with an independent Massachusetts-based company called Rykodisc. The same firm would release a double CD of thirty-nine of his singles. In 1990, meanwhile, Bowie would again take to the road for a lucrative outing of the old hits. These were not the actions of a 'half-bright bloke', as he described himself in Bradford, 'called Jones'.

In mid June Tin Machine played their first American dates. Jon Pareles' piece in the *New York Times* was a spot-on analysis of the group's inherent contradictions. 'Mr Bowie couldn't completely give up theatricality any more than Johnny Cash could give up wearing black ... The lighting, while not too fancy, provided more variation than the average club setup – white-and-shadow effects designed to emphasize how stark the setting was. And Mr Bowie has retained his easy grace onstage; he swivelled his pelvis, dropped to his knees (and then jumped around as he knelt) and moved in streamlined angles.' Amid wild sheets of power-chord guitar, Tin Machine made obligatory gestures towards band democracy – as when the drummer sang one of his own songs – but the eye fixed stubbornly on the chain-smoking frontman with the arresting stage act. Away from the spotlight, Bowie's band were still subjected to his relentless self-absorption, an exhausting barrage that had struck friends like Cambridge in the old days. The freedom of Tin Machine was exhilarating: it allowed him to rationalize his past, and worked brilliantly as the stopgap Bowie needed. That he could be charming to men like Cambridge and Armstrong was undeniable. But it was also the case that the old Bowie was alive and well, and planning a comeback.

After the initial honeymoon, the critics' love affair with Tin Machine dwindled to a few footnotes and the occasional photo in *Rolling Stone*. Bowie entered one of his frequent troughs. He continued, as always, to write songs. (It was, he told a friend, 'a kind of addiction'.) Bowie kept working for a number of reasons, one of which was that he had 'grown used to living inside a writer's skin' and to sitting down daily and producing a certain number of lyrics. He worked also because there did not seem to be any point to accepting retirement, or near-death in Las Vegas. But perhaps the most important reason of all for Bowie's prolific output was one he hinted at in his best work: his world, centred for so long on the idea of himself as a rock idol, was falling apart. For long periods in 1989–90 his name was kept alive largely through the patronage of Steve Sutherland in *Melody Maker*. Tin Machine's singles flopped and they never graduated from the college and town-hall circuit. Bowie himself grew weary of his one-of-the-guys affectation. As the group's tour progressed, so some of the conceits of *Let's Dance*-era celebrity resumed. Bowie abandoned the bus in favour of Mascia's Mercedes. He squabbled furiously with EMI, then left the label altogether. His conversation was laced, in its droll way, with barbs at his enemies in the press ('I can't get anything right. I can't go big. I can't go small. Whichever way I go is wrong'). He began to agitate for a return to the mainstream. Bowie complained to one friend that 'nobody was talking' about him. It was all too much.

By mid 1989, most of Bowie's vast back catalogue was hard to find. Although RCA and the rest had done their best, many of the early albums were out of stock. Even *Let's Dance* and *Tonight* were making furtive appearances in the second-hand and speciality shops. Bowie's response was to contact Jeff Rougvie, the Rykodisc manager responsible for the definitive Hendrix and Frank Zappa anthologies. *Sound + Vision* followed in October. Bowie helped unearth rare tracks for the set, including the original Clareville Grove demo of 'Space Oddity'. The compilation was a tidy hit on both sides of the Atlantic. Along with the critical plaudits, there was praise for Bowie's foresight and business acumen in recovering his masters from Defries. 'It's rare when an artist gets his own catalogue – it was a pretty shrewd deal he made,' says Rougvie.

Bowie now assumed a new mask. The last form he had taken had been a singer in a garage band. Now, after an interval of two years, he returned to consolidate his status as a rock god. The old guise was clearly inappropriate, and it was no good embarking on an arena tour with a repertoire of neo-grunge tunes. Bowie meant to profit from his reputation and recoup all the privileges and rewards his long career brought. He made his reappearance on the world stage as an ancient *revenant*, a sort of hip Rip Van Winkle, blinking sleepily at the upturned faces, or turning away to ponder his old memories. His pro-Tin Machine effusions and Tin Machine's occasional pro-Bowie displays of unity were matched by a hankering to reinvent himself as the global icon of *Let's Dance*.

Bowie first flew to Mustique. Work continued to import the European and Asian antiques that would fill out his tropical hideaway. The house itself was ready, however, except for finishing touches, by Christmas 1989. To ring in the new decade Bowie threw a party with a 1970s theme. Several of his guests

came dressed as Ziggy. A few pursued the theme still further and
spent the evening snorting copious amounts of cocaine. Bowie
himself chose to recall his own *anni mirabili* by dressing in a
simple suit, with a scarf and high heels, and a glass of champagne
in one hand. Towards dawn he ascended a makeshift podium
overlooking Britannia Bay and gave a speech so effusive, in one
guest's words, 'he might have been someone from the tourist
board'.

Bowie and Tin Machine then departed for Sydney, where they
spent three weeks recording tracks for their second album. Of the
twenty-five numbers hummed, ad-libbed and jammed in the
studio, a dozen would make the final cut. By late January he was
back in London. At a press conference in the foyer of the Rainbow
Theatre in Finsbury Park, Bowie announced dates for his Sound
+ Vision tour. The choice of venue (scene of Bowie's homecoming
triumph in 1972) and the hall's décor (a facsimile of the *Ziggy
Stardust* cover) were significant: as recently as 1987 mere
mention of Ziggy was high on the list of Bowie's pet hates. Later
in the morning he strummed a few verses of 'Panic in Detroit' and
'Amsterdam', mugged his way through 'The Laughing Gnome'
('I still love the chorus,' he said) and ended with 'Space Oddity'.
It took all of Bowie's formidable self-confidence to pose next to a
plaster effigy of himself as Ziggy. He meant it ironically; but Bowie
ran the risk that others might not see the joke. A number of the
tabloids duly billed Sound + Vision as a shameless nostalgia *fest*.
This was, at best, a partial understanding of the tour.

During the press conference Bowie revealed a bias for indoor
stages because he felt his act 'got lost in stadiums' – a lesson
gleaned at Wembley and the other Glass Spider venues. He talked
up Tin Machine. They were 'on hold' until Sound + Vision was
out of his system. He claimed, and repeated, that once the tour
was over he would no longer perform his old songs in concert.
The staging would be somewhere between the lurid extravaganza
of 1987 and the back-to-the-roots minimalism of 1989. Bowie, in
short, was attempting the difficult trick of playing on his past in
order to fend off his own obsolescence.

In the next six weeks Bowie worked hard to consolidate the
euphoric advance publicity. He granted follow-up interviews with
a few, highly privileged reporters. He summoned and rehearsed a

group, including the guitarist Adrian Belew (music director of the 1978 tour), Belew's drummer and pianist, and Glass Spider's Erdal Kizilcay on bass. He brought his usual microscopic attention to the choreography and lighting. Bowie adored endlessly ironing out wrinkles in his songs. If they did not exist he sometimes felt obliged to create them. One musician recalls rehearsing a number, four bars at a time 'over and over, until it was *exactly* right. And then David did it again.' Even in an era when rock tours were organized by the likes of Michael Jackson with Ziegfeld precision, Bowie showed an exceptional grasp of detail. Another man might have delegated: Bowie scrutinized bills, micromanaged budgets and personally chose the food and drink for the crew party.

He also, to his credit, found time for outside projects. He supervised several remixes of his 1975 breakthrough hit, released by EMI as 'Fame 90'. A video of the song, showing Bowie reflecting on his former selves, was shot by Gus Van Sant. He hammed a part in *Twin Peaks: Fire Walk With Me*. He continued to paint and riffle promiscuously through other art forms. After admiring the design for Zeffirelli's *Aida*, Bowie collaborated with Edouard Lock, leader of the Montreal-based dance troupe La La La Human Steps, to create a set that adapted flamboyant operatic tradition to rock and roll. Its most successful and innovative feature was a transparent scrim on which video footage of Bowie was projected around and above him: for much of the concert he would sing live to images of himself miming, recalling the parallel worlds of 'Life on Mars?' and 'Drive-In Saturday'.

'I know I'll miss them desperately,' Bowie said of retiring his golden greats. 'They're very fine songs to work with and I love singing most of them, but I don't want to feel that I can always fall back on them. I want it to be forthrightly known that that should not be expected anymore.' Bowie's pomposity was leavened by an engaging streak of self-doubt. 'I approached [the tour] with trepidation,' he said. His gloom lifted in the days following the Rainbow event. Two concerts at the 12,000-seat London Arena sold out immediately. A third went in eight minutes. The 70,000 applications which arrived soon afterwards forced him to add extra dates. By August Bowie had played to 250,000 British fans, more than turned out for the Rolling

Stones, and five times as many as originally planned.

Bowie presented himself as a relaxed, genial figure who had nothing to prove. It was an important part of his self-image that, as with Tin Machine, he was one of the band. After years of struggle, Bowie's life had achieved a much-needed balance. He was a jobbing musician, a singer-songwriter and (in his own words) 'someone who belong[ed] in rock and roll'.

Bowie did not obey all his own axioms. He may have taken shelter in rock, but singing twenty-year-old hits was not his natural habitat. He was too intelligent for that. Even as he announced the Sound + Vision tour, he was writing yet more material for Tin Machine, redrafting his screenplay and arranging through Isolar to star in his first feature since *The Last Temptation of Christ*. For the role of Monte, the gnomic bartender in *The Linguini Incident*, Bowie was called on to emulate or parody aspects of his iceman persona. A deadpan 'Hello. I love you' was among his first lines in the film. The negligible plot saw him proposing to an American woman in order to acquire a Green Card. There was an escapology theme that uncoiled slowly over two hours, and a striking combination involving Rosanna Arquette, a rope and a pineapple. *The Linguini Incident*, shot in late 1990, was released by Rank Films the following year. Critics consigned the modest caper to a niche somewhere between *The Hunger* and *Just a Gigolo* and it hit the video shelves overnight.

The Sound + Vision tour opened barely a month after being announced. Despite the promising response in London, doubts lingered about the speed of ticket sales elsewhere. Was Bowie, who had not had a major hit for years, a strong enough draw? In a market dominated by quick-change artists like Prince and Madonna, would audiences respond to a leisurely stroll through nearly a quarter-century of a fashion *flâneur*'s career? Outside the NEC, Birmingham, both box offices were open minutes before Bowie's appearance. As the *Independent* said, 'It was not a night for the entrepreneurial fringe, which was failing to unload fistfuls of tickets on to groups of unimpressed couples.' In 1972 a concert by Bowie was an event. Eighteen years later it was a pleasant night out. A sense of mild expectation, not Ziggy-like abandon, greeted the slender, suited figure who strolled to the front of the stage strumming his guitar. His frail voice surprised people. Half-hidden behind a bank of microphones, Bowie looked small, tired and old, like an ageing actor battling through a part he hated. There was perplexity in the audience as he crooned a solo 'Space Oddity'. Only on the last 'Here am I/Floating round my tin can' did Belew and the band, lurking in the wings, render the song vertebrate.

The tour's staging, at least, was meticulous. In 1990, unlike 1987, the sight-lines were exemplary and nobody needed binoculars. Bowie solved the visibility problem by use of the giant backdrop and a pair of circular close-circuit screens flanking the stage. One of his gifts was his ability to attract people who helped him innovate – in this case, Edouard Lock. There were some startling moments when Bowie's video image echoed the live one, a matter of unerring timing and gadgetry. His deadpan delivery, though strained, was a kind of benchmark of cool. And Bowie's stage moves were more intentionally guarded than since the early seventies. His new persona was not about drop-dead entrances and three-hour maquillage; Bowie sauntered on, smiled a lot, and kept up a stream of banter between numbers. 'You're very quiet,' he told the audience at Birmingham, instantly raising an ironic cheer. 'You sound about my age, but I guess you probably are.' Bowie laughed self-effacingly, then launched into 'Changes'. As the final notes of 'Ashes to Ashes' dissolved in an audience singalong, Bowie suddenly became a music teacher chiding his huge class. 'No, no, no. It changes there. It's a three-part melody over a four-line sequence. How very interesting,' he chortled, then cued in the power chords of 'Fashion'.

Bowie's performance was also impeccable, asides in exquisite taste, buoyed by an open, apparently happy demeanour. Unfortunately, his troubled character had also been the primary source of his inspiration. As one reviewer said, 'Bowie's "hello, I'm normal" bonhomie has stripped a lot of tension out of the music ... "Station to Station" was no longer recognizable as the work of a man clawing at the bars of his own sanity, and "Young Americans" sounded sadly routine.' Heard in this context, some of the material from *Ziggy Stardust* and *Aladdin Sane* came across as evanescent, bubblegum pop. The tunes were pleasant enough, but it was hard not to cringe at the suicide-note lyrics when Bowie sang them with a grin. Nor were his efforts to 'illustrate' the songs entirely successful. The back-projection was the tour's most ingenious prop, but the dance routines revealed a basic truth: it was only when he tried to be young that Bowie seemed old.

Many rock critics had grown up with Bowie. For them his strange and much-admired mix of ego and irony – not to mention his link to the past – was an article of faith. They made a nostalgic connection between Bowie's songs and the vanished world of their youth. Those for whom he created an image of childhood and home were prepared to suspend judgement. Others were less forgiving. For Adam Sweeting in the *Guardian*, Bowie 'seem[ed] like a good-looking bloke who can act a bit and write a few songs, and is making the best of what he's got while the going is good'. There was widespread criticism of Bowie's band. *Melody Maker* pegged their performance at Birmingham as 'pitiful . . . The turgid tub-thumpers are thankfully hidden behind columns, but the terminally pratty Adrian Belew, with his ghastly tie and ponytail, bounces about nauseatingly and labours under the delusion that weird guitar noises are automatically art.' A general consensus was that the group were more comfortable with Bowie's newer canon than with the *Ziggy* era.

Aside from Below and the common-man affectations of the show, the other doubts were about Bowie's voice. There was a moment at Birmingham, halfway through 'Queen Bitch', when his baritone cracked into a gruff near-rasp. (Bowie recovered by a quick bit of mime.) Less than a month into the tour, the set was cut back in order to give the star instrument a rest. Production numbers like 'John, I'm Only Dancing' and 'Rock 'n' Roll Suicide' were dropped and others were retooled. The band flaunted itself as a result, bulldozing through parts that should have been subtle and each taking interminable solos. A grating, heavy-metal beat made itself heard in every nuance of Bowie's lyrics.

But so, too, was every song shot through with surprising, bravura touches. 'Life On Mars?' was a case in point: slabs of Rick Fox's synthesizer topping off the brick wall solidity of the bass and drums. There were improvisational swings of key and tempo in 'Changes'. Nor did Bowie's enigmatic statement on the medium, 'TVC 15', seem to have involved too many stints in the rehearsal mill. For every critic, like the BBC's Jeff Griffin, who thought the band 'ill-suited and anaemic', there were others, like the *Guardian*, for whom 'there [could] be no complaints under the Trades Description Act ... Bowie's Sound + Vision tour is exactly what it's billed as – the best-known songs from his back catalogue, played more or less perfectly straight.'

By allowing the band unprecedented leeway with his best tunes, Bowie proved himself to be artistically shrewd as well as commercially astute. The result, in his own view, was a successful tour. He told a group member that they were his most enjoyable dates since the days of Ziggy and Aladdin Sane, but added that his pleasure was qualified by the fact that he still found the characters almost painfully real; some of Bowie's old complaint that 'that fucker [Ziggy] wouldn't leave me alone ... My whole personality was affected' returned with the persona he killed off in 1973. 'Suffragette City' and 'Jean Genie', the *Ziggy* title tune and an encore of 'White Light, White Heat' – all these passed in a blur, brought to life with a manic intensity that made Bowie's other hits seem half-awake, or merely lazy by comparison. When he *sang* them, as opposed to stooping to parody, they still bore his characteristic blend of the threatening and the comic.

The tour weaved a meander through the US, opening in Miami on 27 April, before reaching Giants Stadium in New Jersey in August. By then there was near-universal praise for the inventive work of the band, the concept of the screen and Bowie's own dramatic embellishments of songs like 'Fame'. To the critic Amy Duncan, it was 'just about the perfect retrospect' with the full range of theatrical Ziggy-era stunts: in 'Young Americans', Bowie collapsed to the floor when he reached the line 'Ain't there one damn song that can make me/Break down and cry?'. According to Duncan, 'he stayed down so long that people began to wonder – is he really all right? Then, suddenly, he leaped to his feet and charged into an aggressive, rocking "Suffragette City" and finally "Heroes".'

A few days earlier, during his Cleveland stop, Bowie was joined onstage by Bono for a version of 'Gloria'. His fellow professionals became grist for the desire to remake himself, yet again, as an approachable, loyal friend. Some found their very cachet enhanced by his patronage. A listless record-release party for Iggy's new album *Brick By Brick* suddenly became a media event when Bowie strolled in. Reporters strained to catch the exchange between the two self-styled 'graduates of Defries University'. Iggy confessed he had had trouble reaching Bowie at his hotel – 'I don't have the secret name you use,' he complained. Bowie, in turn, called Iggy 'Jim'. Later in the evening he heaped fulsome praise on Madonna and Prince, seen by some as the logical successors of the overblown production and sexual gibing of his previous tour.

Bowie ended 1990 in greatly better fettle than he began it. With Sound + Vision he retrieved his ambition of achieving respect over adulation. In an era of pop nonentities like Bros and Milli Vanilli, Bowie constituted a figure of substance, of continuity and even, it seemed, of permanence. Also humour. As the tour progressed, his comic sense manifested itself more subtly, not leaden and dull like the faux-cockney patter of Glass Spider, but wry, mischievous and, in a curious way, affectionate. Warmer, too; Bowie managed some jokes at his own expense. For this, and the unbeatable quality of the songs, he now reclaimed his place in the rock pantheon. Bowie passed from a musical has-been, his achievements lying in the past, into the realm of a Living Legend.

When Bowie had said that 'something good' had come from the Glass Spider fiasco, he may have been referring to his determination never to repeat the experience; to his introduction to Gabrels, and thus to Tin Machine; or to the boost it gave his flagging love life.

At various moments during the tour, most notably during Iggy's 'Bang Bang', Bowie had been joined onstage by a woman in the crowd, apparently an ordinary fan, but, in fact, a professional dancer named Melissa Hurley. Hurley was a dark-haired, statuesque New Yorker, young, with striking Latin looks, a soft, expressive voice and a manner that alluringly mingled familiarity and an old-fashioned deferential politeness. Bowie was smitten. It was hard to say at what point the friendship evolved into dating, sex and a full-blown affair. The speculation for most of the summer of 1987 was that Bowie was involved with Marie Helvin, or a second woman with whom he was seen smiling and carousing backstage at Wembley. There were rumours that he regularly entertained a well-known actress at home in Lausanne. Yet by early 1988 Bowie and Hurley were an item. He kept the relationship private and tried to ensure that she was never photographed. Bowie was an expert at doing this. When the two went to dinner, a Mercedes with a blacked-out window deposited Hurley at the restaurant. The car then snaked around the block and returned to discharge Bowie. The same arrangements were in place in Lausanne. Tony Mascia, promoted from factotum to Bowie's full-time driver, came to play a key role in eluding the press and paparazzi, or, failing that, in getting out fast.

The couple were together, intermittently, for the rest of the eighties. Hurley joined Bowie when he was recording, and later on tour, with Tin Machine. She learnt a variation on the same evasive technique, hurrying out the stage doors of provincial clubs and cinemas and making her way to safety in the Mercedes. She appeared backstage at the last Sound + Vision dates in 1990. When the tour ended, Hurley joined Bowie in Mustique.

Bowie always went back to the island as soon as he could, and each time with relief. His life there did not provide him with new interests; rather, he read, painted and worked on his perennial screenplay. With the exception of Mick Jagger, he was careful to avoid such expatriates as lived nearby. Bowie's home boasted a formal European living room with nineteenth-century furnishings and an antique crystal chandelier, a Javanese dining pavilion and two koi-filled ornamental ponds that overlooked a swimming pool and the mountainous outline of Britannia Bay. It was, as he said, somewhere he had 'absolutely no motivation to do a thing'. In six weeks Bowie had only two visitors, Schwab and his new publicist, Alan Edwards, another Rolling Stones fugitive. At some point in this tropical idyll he ended the affair with Hurley. It was a clean break: both parties agreed to remain 'good friends', and, for once, this hackneyed phrase conveyed the truth of a relationship. His aunt would later speak of the age gap as one reason for Bowie's decision.

By the early nineties Bowie had abandoned most of the habits of his youth. Like Pete Townshend and Keith Richards he was paraded in support of a new, drug-free lifestyle, exemplars of the 'just say no' crusade launched in America. He was also weaning

himself from the deadliest drug of them all: celebrity. Watching
him browse in London bookshops or queuing for his lunch in a
New York automat, it was clear another reincarnation was under
way. By the time he arrived in Los Angeles in October 1990 to
reconvene Tin Machine, Bowie was almost a paragon of normality. His way of thinking – what he called his 'loving the alien' –
underwent a major change in the months after the Sound +
Vision tour. Until then, Bowie was constantly dredging up every
old grievance, break-up and feud, reconsidering what he might
have done, or what could have been. His emotional writhings
over women, nearly all brought to grief by his legendary coolness,
continued into his forties. If 1990 had been good for anything, it
was because he had learned to stop living in the past, to admit
that once something was done, finished or gone, it was truly over.
His behaviour in Los Angeles was that of a contented bachelor,
easy in his own skin, someone who, as he said, 'had just come out
of one relationship and was completely uninterested in forming a
new one'. Almost inevitably, he fell in love.

The woman was Iman Abdul Majid, a thirty-four-year-old
Somalian actress and model. After a glittering career on the
catwalk and a failed marriage, Iman had moved to Los Angeles
to carve out a life for herself in films. In her first year in Hollywood
she landed parts in a *Star Trek* sequel and *House Party 2*, and a
television movie called *Lies of the Twins*. Although not an
overnight sensation, it was a respectable enough transition. Iman
found herself occupying the same niche as Grace Jones as an
exotic, physically arresting type, whose lack of conventional
acting skill was offset by an intimacy that came through on
screen. Some of this presence was equally at work socially, and
her night life became an extension of her perpetual auditions and
rehearsals. Hostesses thought of her as 'fun' – a striking contrast
to other struggling actresses. On 14 October, a mutual friend
invited both Iman and Bowie to dinner.

Later that autumn the two enjoyed an interlude in Switzerland. Although the gossip columnists deemed it insignificant,
members of Bowie's court were persuaded that he had already
chosen his next wife. Their first public appearance together was
on the set of *The Linguini Incident*. Iman was seen in a cameo in
Richard Shepard's film in which Bowie's character completed a

triangle with the actresses Rosanna Arquette and Eszter Balint. By early 1991 he was openly speaking of the affair to friends, and an enterprising gossip columnist picked up the story. A photographer shot Bowie and Iman leaving a New York restaurant – described as 'a place couples go to see and be seen' – in the early hours of the morning. By spring the secret was known by too many people to be denied. Bowie took Iman to England to meet his mother and son. He also introduced her to Schwab.

That summer the couple took a six-week boat trip up and down the Italian coast, ending in Florence. They strolled in front of the jewellers' shops on the Ponte Vecchio and patronized the Via Calzaiuoli. Their burst of luxury spending on clothes and shoes was impressive enough. But what really struck observers was their subsequent mutual suffering of the tattooist's needle. Iman, logically enough, chose a design in the form of a bowie knife. Her lover was more oblique. Sometime over the summer, Bowie had read a book called *Grave for a Dolphin*: the European hero's wanderings in Somalia squared with his own self-image as a refugee at last finding home. His tattoo was of a dolphin, a phrase of Japanese and a female bottom, all etched into the back of his right calf.

In conversation with a friend in September 1991, Bowie remarked almost parenthetically that it was time for him to marry and settle down. Few were surprised that the woman he would choose was Iman. Over the years there had been a coterie of black lovers, of whom Ava Cherry was only the longest-suffering. More importantly, Iman's personality was supremely suited to the man who unapologetically emerged in 1990 as a 'closet heterosexual'. The relationship undoubtedly had its basis in physical attraction, as well as in shared values. Bowie would later tell a reporter that he was 'well surprised' to meet a model who was 'devastatingly wonderful and not the usual sort of bubblehead that I'd known in the past ... I make no bones about it: I was naming the children the night we met. I knew that she was for me, it was absolutely immediate. I just fell under her spell.'

Bowie's courtship was conducted in surprisingly formal – what he called 'gentlemanly' – fashion. His memory of 'lots of being led to doorways and polite kisses on the cheek ... flowers and chocolates and the whole thing' quite accurately conveys an affair that, at first, was discreet to the point of invisibility. It was only after weeks of cruising the Adriatic, and the first appearance of their names in the scandal sheets, that Bowie began to comment freely on the relationship. After briefing his family and colleagues, he took to dropping hints in his rock-music interviews about the pleasures of monogamy. 'It excites me,' he told the journalist David Sinclair. 'I've gone from the extreme promiscuity of the 1970s to a changing set of attitudes in the 1980s, and hopefully to some sense of harmony in the nineties.'

   When Bowie was in France with Tin Machine that autumn, he looked better than he had in years. He had put on weight since coming off tour, so much so, he noted elatedly, that his *Diamond Dogs*-era suits no longer fitted. He recognized certain personal danger signals (such as too many and too frequent excessive crying jags), so, to keep in shape for the gruelling daily task of recording and going back on the road, he did something totally uncharacteristic: he stopped drinking and started to take long jogs around the streets of Paris. (Bowie still chain-smoked his way through two to three packets of cigarettes a day.) He resumed a course of psychotherapy. A happy consequence was that he began to regain some of his lost memory. When Bowie once admitted that whole years of his life had been bulk-erased through drug abuse, now, like Peggy, he fastened on dates and anniversaries with compulsive detail: everything had to be related to everything else in the right order, and at the proper interval. A side of Bowie measured time with obsessive relish, and that side spoke when, on a bâteau-mouche cruising down the Seine, he proposed to Iman on 14 October, the first anniversary of their meeting. The couple had already exchanged rings in Florence. While passing through Japan, they then obtained their mutual tattoos. Next, as a final engagement ritual, Bowie agreed to an Aids test and finally swore off all drugs. Thus, by late 1991, he was probably in the best physical shape of his adult life, and since he normally looked younger than his age, the nine-year gap between them was not as great as the literal figure might seem.

   News of the engagement broke on 2 November. Alan Edwards made the announcement in a curiously terse press release; no place or date was given for the wedding. There were notably muted expressions of goodwill from the Burns family. One woman referred archly to Iman's colour and the prospect of mixed-race children. Another aunt read the news in the local paper.

At the same time as Bowie went public with Iman, his first wife emerged in New York to gleefully tell *The Joan Rivers Show* of her ex-husband's sexual exploits, and, in particular, his liking for Mick Jagger. The audience was enthralled by Angela's tales. She was wildly applauded. When she left the TV studio the crowd which had gathered outside chanted her name for several minutes and queued for autographs. Her central allegation about Bowie and Jagger would recur in the years ahead, forcing both men, with varying degrees of tact, to deny the slur. Elsewhere, opinion about Angela varied. Even after ten years, she was one of the most polarizing figures in Bowie's past. To the journalist Mick Brown she became 'the rock missus from hell', capable only of lurid reiteration of all that had contributed to her displacement as the key figure in Bowie's life: namely, Schwab. Angela replayed what she should or could have done to prevent it from happening with everyone who cared to listen, from interviewers to the numerous women to whom she became an avenging angel, a feminist icon and, at worst, an object of curiosity and pity. There were those who still swore that Angela had been the real power behind the throne. The Bowies' friend Jayne County insists that, without his wife's vision, 'David would have been just another singer with floppy hair'. Others point to Angela's pivotal role in organizing Bowie's life at Haddon Hall, and her willingly accepting jobs he chose not to do himself, including dealing with Terry Burns. Her exuberance had made good his inwardness. Reaction to Angela was nearly always based on the individual's emotional response to the couple's sex life, but to look beyond that was to see a curiously empty marriage. Bowie himself would say that 'It was very short . . . By '74 we rarely saw each other. After that she would drop in or drop out for a weekend, but we were virtually living our own separate lives. There was no real togetherness.'

Meanwhile, *Tin Machine II* was released in Britain by Victory. Between their first and second albums, the group moved from riff-rock to blues-based pop. They managed a miracle: welding the same thunderous beat to a set of virtues – ringing slabs of guitar, a range from metal to folk and songwriting of classic pedigree – that emphasized tunefulness and an ear for the hook. The single, 'You Belong in Rock 'n' Roll', mixed intelligent, enigmatic lyrics with fuzz tones, a neat tempo change and punk commitment and passion. *Tin Machine II* exulted in the band's basic premise: no frills, raw R&B. It vaulted several barriers. The very fact that the album wasn't a 'long-awaited follow-up' allowed for telling departures from the formula: the guitar on 'One Shot', the wry lyric of 'Shopping For Girls'. *Tin Machine II* contained enough choruses to grab the most demanding Bowiephile, while the playing revelled in feedback, distortion and pumped-up bass. This was strange and oddly elevating rock and roll.

Bowie himself would speak of the album (along with *Diamond Dogs*, *Scary Monsters*, the *Low* era and half of *Let's Dance*) as among his all-time favourites. Responding to his enthusiasm, Alan Edwards predicted 'the public [would] make this David's biggest smash in years'. They didn't. True to his principles, Bowie had challenged his audience on the first Tin Machine record; he paid the penalty with the second. The album confirmed and established his post-*Let's Dance* slump. Sales were disappointing enough, but Bowie was incensed even more, if possible, by a row of rare ferocity and entertainment value with his record company. The group had wanted a front cover depicting themselves as classical, nude statues. Bowie considered this 'in exquisite taste'. The label responded by taking action to stop 'a show of wrong, obscene images' that had already caused two national retailers to refuse to carry the album. In the end Bowie compromised. Out of deference to public sensibilities, the four figures were airbrushed to appear sexless, while a variety of strategically placed stickers were added for the American market. The whole farce, widely aired in the tabloids, enabled Bowie to get off at least one pun about 'geeks censoring the Greeks'. It also allowed him to blow off steam while his career continued its free-fall.

In early August, after his boat trip along the Italian coast, Bowie assembled Tin Machine in a converted factory in Dublin to rehearse their second tour. His pique at the record company was mixed with high spirits: he had just fallen – heavily – in love. *Melody Maker* found him 'customarily lean, newly tanned and unusually relaxed ... this year's Bowie is a very different proposition from the neurotically nervy character who shuffled a trifle uneasily through his farewell-then-greatest-hits tour'. Bowie continued to insist on the collective ethic of Tin Machine, meaning that all four men had to be interviewed together. (He still did most of the talking.) But democracy was no substitute for a group identity. The band had still not shaken off the taint of being Bowie and three lackeys. Standing 6″ 1′ in his Italian heels, with a Riviera tan and a Somalian lover waiting in the Mercedes, he was not someone who fitted easily in a corporate format.

When Tin Machine toured Britain in 1989, Bowie had struck old friends like John Cambridge and Kevin Armstrong as a changed man. No longer the spiky, petulant character who tortured himself by inventing conversations in which he imagined his fans sneered at him, Bowie now declared himself 'whole'. In a variation of his penchant for self-flagellation, he told a reporter he was 'blissed out'. That was more than a year before meeting Iman. Yet it would be a mistake to confuse a supposedly affable, relaxed outlook with any dereliction of his superstar duty. In 1989 Cambridge talked his way in through the stage door. Two years later, Bowie's old friend Phil May (the man he called 'God') found himself sharing a bill with Tin Machine. Not only did the two men not meet; when May asked to do so he was told to go through 'management', that nebulous bureaucracy that controlled all access. A second friend thinks this 'typical ... as always in a situation where he felt uncomfortable, Dave retreated, internalized everything as his own social failure, and then relied on Isolar to bail him out'.

In October Bowie proposed to Iman. He also continued the round of interviews and club dates with Tin Machine. He denied he was playing another character role – that of a singer in an obscure rock band – and talked up Gabrels as 'an extraordinary musician ... absolutely extraordinary. Probably the nearest in [technical] terms to Fripp.' His new fiancée and his new guitarist had, at a stroke, swept away all the anger, the pain, the bile and frustration Bowie felt in the months and years after Live Aid. They had a corrosive power on him that he found intoxicating. One reporter came away 'dizzy' after a twenty-minute panegyric on Gabrels, whom Bowie compared to not only Fripp, but Hendrix,

Robert Johnson and, bizarrely, all four of the Monkees. The guitarist repaid the favour. 'Bowie doesn't have the bias of technique to hold him back,' he said. 'He comes up with these great parts that I would never have thought of.' Another colleague would call Bowie 'the Neil Young of the saxophone', an intuitive, if flawed talent. ('He plays like Bill Clinton' was a less charitable view.) Bowie would stress the improvisational nature of his music: 'It's OK for me to break rules on instruments because I have no embarrassment – I don't know if I've done anything wrong.'

By late November Tin Machine were again trawling the eastern seaboard of America. Bowie seemed to have lived far more than two years since the last tour. He came onstage at the New York Academy dressed in yellow-and-black-striped breeches and a bright jacket, shirt and T-shirt that he successively removed. Virtuoso technique took the place of structure as furiously dispatched songs followed one another in a salvo. By 'Heaven's In Here', late in the set, Bowie was bare-chested, howling and flailing the stage, and reminding older fans of Iggy. Then, in another nod to the past, he fell to his knees and appeared to chew at the strings of Gabrels' guitar. Whereas in 1972 the gesture had been heavy with 'meaning', now Bowie paused to wink archly at the crowd, thus sheathing the act in a giant parody, a huge protective Durex signifying the irony of the whole scene. He left to a standing ovation.

Over the next two years there was a live Tin Machine album, *Oy Vey, Baby*, also released on video, and a half-hearted effort to regroup in America. By 1994 the Sales brothers had learnt what literally dozens of musicians had found out before them: a collaboration with Bowie was no lifetime guarantee. The recollections of those concerned with the split vary slightly; even today, an Isolar staffer insists that the group are 'viable'. A decisive factor in the break was Bowie's desire to resume a solo career, first as a pop-inflected rock star, then as the 'outsider' who revived some of the macabre fixations of his Berlin exile. The least defensible part of the rift was what happened to the luckless musicians. In July 1995 a fan named Dale Freeman asked Bowie, by way of the Prodigy computer bulletin, if he had plans to reunite Tin Machine on tour. The nine-word answer read:

'Reeves will be with me. The Sales brothers, no.'

Warmed-over punk rock was only a detour along the road to Bowie's next transformation. By 1993 he was again touting his credentials as a generalist, and not without success. His friend the art dealer Bernard Jacobson introduced him to Karen Wright, the editor of *Modern Painters*; in turn, she invited Bowie to join the board. He religiously attended the quarterly meetings, and the informal dinners at the Gay Hussar (where the owner, Bela Molnar, remembers him as having 'a courtesy that seemed to come naturally'). Bowie spoke eagerly of his plans to collaborate with Eduardo Paolozzi and his new friend Damien Hirst. He interviewed Balthus and wrote a piece on the Johannesburg Biennale. Above all, Bowie stressed the distance he went both forwards and back. Dressed in his black polo-neck and wraparound shades, he made an aesthetic connection to the Beat Generation of the fifties. He admired the world of Ginsberg and Kerouac, while he enjoyed a panoramic view of modern literature. That spring Bowie composed the score for an adaption of Hanif Kureishi's *The Buddha of Suburbia*. The now-proficient writer returned to his own work-in-progress with renewed self-confidence. Bowie admitted to getting up at 5.30 in the morning to work on his screenplay.

A part of Bowie, not surprisingly, was perversely nostalgic for the early seventies, even for the laughable extremes of his own saga. 'The Swiss Larry Grayson' he once called himself to a colleague in the Gay Hussar, and, in terms of high camp, Bowie's act had certainly been alpine. During all his years as a would-be critic and author, and as a father, husband and small corporation, Bowie rarely passed up the chance to send an obscure signal about his roots. When not passing himself off as a poet-hipster, even his dress code was a delightfully reliable giveaway, dominated as it was by boots, blouses and scarves flaunting a conflict of styles such as might have been favoured by Gary Glitter in his 'Do You Wanna Touch?' era. Whatever Bowie might say about being a Renaissance Man of contemporary art, there was still no mistaking the world he came from.

As proved by his pre-grunge excursion with Tin Machine, he moved with the times. Bowie loved American hardcore bands like the Pixies and Dinosaur Jr, and expressed interest in working with the Jesus and Mary Chain. His own influence as a guru-figure extended to groups as diverse as Suede, Blur, the Auteurs and Smashing Pumpkins. In November 1993 Nirvana covered 'The Man Who Sold the World' on their MTV *Unplugged* set. Trent Reznor of Nine Inch Nails would admit to listening to *Low* on a daily basis while recording *The Downward Spiral*.

Such kudos gave a vital boost to Bowie's reputation. He needed it, and never reconciled to the idea of retiring from rock gracefully. When he was irritated (at the flop of *Tin Machine II*, for instance) Bowie would burst out in exasperated rage at the fans. He told a friend 'he didn't know *what* the fuck they wanted'. Seized with remorse, Bowie then admitted to *Rolling Stone*, 'Frankly, I've made a lot of money over the years. If I want to make music outside the mainstream, I can't expect massive sales, so there's no self-pitying to go on.' His friend remained indignant; and puzzled too. Such fits of violent and contradictory emotions were not to his taste. Gradually he came to the conclusion that 'David never made up his mind about being a pop star.' After a year on the outside, he was 'panting to get back in again. He wanted his old life.'

What kind of life? As an ambiguously clever chameleon, a rock dinosaur or a man who still had big things to say, and who needed a more prominent platform than his occasional albums from which to say them? Bowie's view of himself in *Who's Who* aimed for altitude. He was an 'International recording artist and performer: film and stage actor; video and film producer; and graphic designer.' In this take, Bowie's extracurricular activities were almost as important as his records. It may be unfair to single out his entry in the reference books, but there was something about the lines 'Artiste from age of 16' and 'Recipient of international music and entertainment awards' that was almost satirically quaint; as though Bing Crosby had offered his services as Bowie's CV writer.

Bowie's fixed centre was, as ever, difficult to place. On one level he was clearly in revolt against the cliché of the 'moronic pop star'. Although he lived in the rarefied world of celebrity, he still knew how to breathe real air. He had patently not stopped thinking. In his Prodigy bulletin alone, Bowie spoke of Balthus,

Warhol, Bosnia, Aids, the *Sunday Telegraph* and Kurt Cobain. He was particularly interested in the European Union and his proper political role for the twenty-first century. Bowie claimed to have read 'literally thousands of books' in an effort to tutor himself. Apparently successfully; several of Bowie's arguments were extremely influential among even the highbrows he met at the Gay Hussar. His views on the relationship between the 'abyss of life' and its consolatory artistic release attracted attention, not all derisory. He now believed that art should become a therapeutic tool used, for example, 'to establish how a coma patient responds to beauty'. More and more, the idea of painting became para-mount in Bowie's thinking. He interpreted art in conceptual terms of the individual's response to it and belief about it. In some respects, Bowie's half-baked theories were ludicrous; but not his claim to have found personal happiness. By 1992 he had come to admit that his 'iceman' persona was conducive neither to solid achievement, nor even to the most ephemeral pleasure. Thanks to Iman, he was a more garrulous, human version of the man who said 'I can't feel strongly' and 'I get so numb', a considerate employer to Schwab, Mascia and the rest, and a practising heterosexual who now insisted, 'I was never gay ... I was physical about it, but frankly it wasn't enjoyable. It was almost like I was testing myself. It wasn't something I was comfortable with at all. But it had to be done.'

Bowie had mellowed. Where once there were drugs, now there was skiing. Where once Angela, now Iman. For all his recent forays into the real world, Bowie remained an essentially private character. The dynamic energy he possessed in abundance was warped early on into a defence mechanism that divided others into a minority of loyal supporters and a mass of enemies, out to get him. Bowie acquired a self-vigilance he never lost. Whether hiding behind different accents and disguises, or mimicking the – deeply resented – cries for Ziggy at Tin Machine shows, he was still driven by his own demons, the isolation he felt, and the fear of madness. Bowie was aware of his public alter ego – an untouchable, superstar image that hid the shy boy from Bromley. The hard-edged businessman who negotiated his own deals and threatened to sue Vanilla Ice for copyright infringement was not a new persona, but another dimension of Bowie's increasingly complicated personality. With a few exceptions, he dealt in concrete facts rather than abstracts, and, as Ronson said, had the gift of 'steering for the bottom line'. It was an effective system.

On 27 February 1992 Bowie and Iman were at Elizabeth Taylor's sixtieth birthday party. After interludes in Lausanne and New York, they flew to London on 18 April. Over the next forty-eight hours, Bowie rehearsed for his appearance at the largest blue-chip rock event since Live Aid – the Concert for Life, otherwise known as the Freddie Mercury Tribute. The BBC's Jeff Griffin remembers 'David doing his usual meticulous job', not only in drilling his musicians, but in having Schwab tick off a check-list to do with catering, lighting, security and other facilities. Bowie's mere presence at a sound check often produced among the technicians and other staff a reaction verging on panic, which was intensified by the speed and variety of his demands. Among his orders at Wembley was a curt 'Fuck off' addressed to the various bystanders watching him from the wings.

The concert on 20 April left many in the 70,000 crowd dry-throated. After the surviving members of Queen played their own segment they became the house band for a parade of vocalists: Joe Elliott was followed in turn by Seal, who gave way to Paul Young. At dusk Bowie walked on in a violent green suit. A woman in a ballgown and implausible make-up, later revealed as Annie Lennox, joined him for a capable duet on 'Under Pressure'. Bowie then turned time back with surprising success in 'All the Young Dudes'. Added poignancy came in the choice of guitarists: Ian Hunter and Ronson himself, grey-skinned and suffering from cancer, but laying down the trebly pop-guitar hook to perfection. As at Live Aid, Bowie then sang the anthemic 'Heroes'.

He might have left it there. It had been an emotional night, the first public outing with Ronson in a decade, and proof that Bowie's old songs shared the fire of the moment. Instead he gave in to his flair for drama. The last time Bowie had dropped to his knees in Ronson's presence, it had been to simulate oral sex on his guitar. Now, to puzzled glances from the crowd, he knelt and recited the Lord's Prayer. Bowie's quixotic gesture might have made him, as he later said, 'the most surprised man in Wembley', but after a minute of listening to him wheeze through the prayer, his fans could have made a strong bid for second place. There was palpable embarrassment among Bowie's ex-colleagues as he reached the line 'And forgive us our trespasses'. It was, as David Buckley wrote, 'just about the most controversial thing he could have done'. And the oddest, particularly as Bowie was not really religious. Rather, he had a 'thrusting, rampant' spiritual need that he described as 'an unshakeable belief in God ... I look to Him a lot and He is the cornerstone of my existence – even more as I get older. But it is a one-to-one relationship with God ... I've never bought in to any organized religion ... I tend to judge a man or a woman by their actions – the way they are with me and the way they are with their friends.' Bowie later revealed that one of his own friends, a playwright named Craig, had slipped into an Aids-related coma the day before the concert. The prayer was his public response.

Whatever his previous doubts about Elizabeth Taylor and Liza Minnelli, both women were at the party that night in Bowie's hotel suite. On 22 April he flew to Lausanne with Iman. The couple were married there on the 24th. A magistrate named Michel Perret performed the brief and private city-hall ceremony. Pictures of the event tended to make both parties resemble a photographic negative. The bride, in sunglasses, wore a plain white trouser suit with a black jacket and carried a bouquet of white flowers. Bowie opted for a black suit and tie with a white rose in his lapel. Besides an exchange of platinum rings, the newlyweds also paid £2 million for a 640-acre estate in the County Wicklow hills above Dublin. They then flew to California to honeymoon and house-hunt. In his daily life, as in his songs, Bowie's picaresque wanderings for their own sake had become increasingly rarer. For long periods in the eighties, he hardly left Switzerland. Now, as well as the Lausanne mansion, he had addresses in Ireland and Mustique, and a plan to buy a 'work apartment' in Los Angeles.

The couple arrived there on 29 April. It was the very day that the acquittal of four policemen in the Rodney King case triggered America's worst outbreak of civil disorder in three decades. That night the Bowies were forced to cancel plans for a celebration dinner after the extension of a curfew to cover the entire city. From the window of their hotel they could see the glow of smouldering rubble. 'This was one of those things waiting to happen,' said John Mack, president of the Los Angeles Urban League, expressing a widely held view of the riot. 'Out of frustration and anger you have people resorting to this kind of behaviour, and then it feeds on itself.' Despite the disruption of his own plans, Bowie joined the consensus. 'The whole thing felt like nothing less than a prison break by people who had been caged up for too long with no reason,' he told *Rolling Stone*'s David Wild. One result was the song 'Black Tie White Noise', a soul-tinged duet with Al B. Sure! inspired by the week-long violence. Another was that the Bowies quietly dropped plans to look for a property in downtown Los Angeles and began searching in neighbourhoods synonymous with good race relations.

'Black Tie White Noise' was only the first of dozens of songs Bowie composed that spring. There was an instrumental, complete with church bells, he wrote for his wedding; a new draft of a Tin Machine reject called 'You've Been Around'; a fragment of a ballad to Iman. But at this ostensibly optimistic time in Bowie's life, the romantic element was strangely muted. His wife was certainly mentioned: she appeared as his 'angel for life' in 'The Wedding Song' and maintained a shadowy presence elsewhere. But for the most part his material was that stock mix of dark, dramatic lyrics, bombastic vocals and poignant rationalizations of the past. Among the new titles was one dealing with the suicide of Terry Burns.

Bowie was in Mustique in late May to celebrate his son's twenty-first birthday. Having survived Haddon Hall and five years at Gordonstoun, Joe (clean-cut and bearing a passing resemblance to the rugby player Rob Andrew) was studying philosophy at university. He, too, like his father, wanted to be a writer.

A week later Bowie formalized his marriage in true celebrity style, in a small ceremony with Joe, sixty-eight guests and the effervescent *Hello!* magazine. The service took place at St James Episcopal Church in Florence. Throughout the day, local fans and paparazzi whipped up an atmosphere of Colosseum-type frenzy, with reporters setting the scene from the Bowies' luxurious Villa Massa hotel. There was something approaching hysteria by mid-afternoon, when a news helicopter circled overhead and the bride and groom arrived at the church, escorted by police cars and motorcycles speeding through red lights and causing traffic jams in the Via Nazionale. The fifty-minute ceremony was conducted by the Reverend Mario Marziale; as at the registry wedding, Bowie and Iman dressed in black and white (the groom with his Caribbean tan showing in his face, and a silver stud in his earlobe). Among the guests were Yoko Ono, Eric Idle, Thierry Mugler (who designed Bowie's suit), Schwab and the publicist Alan Edwards. Peggy Jones also attended. At seventy-eight, Bowie's mother had matured into a stout, matronly woman in a polka-dot dress who appeared in photographs, even at relaxed moments, as tense and contained. In response to *Hello!*'s question, Peggy announced that her favourite singers were Nat King Cole and Bono of U2. The magazine's twenty-one-page spread quoted her as hurriedly adding, 'And David, of course.'

Also present in the church was Bowie's Berlin accomplice Brian Eno. The meeting was mutually fruitful for both men. Eno later spoke of the wedding in a public lecture on the theme of 'how we deal with pretence and ritual, style and privacy, and how the best thing we can do in life is to make a drama of ourselves'. While in Florence, the two friends listened to a tape of Bowie's Los Angeles material. The songs burst on them with the recognition that they should work together again. By the end of the day they had agreed to a further meeting, and, ultimately, to the sessions that produced *Outside*.

It was a time of real choice for Bowie, because this was the moment his solo career resumed after five years. By midsummer he was in Montreux, recording the soundtrack for *The Buddha of Suburbia*. From there Bowie moved, via London and Mustique, to New York's Hit Factory studios, home of *Let's Dance*. Some of that album's winning touch-of-funk formula now returned, though with startling avant-garde flourishes from Lester Bowie's trumpet. Songs that started out sounding like Isaac Hayes suddenly swerved into multiple key changes and free-jazz stylings. The new material was striking for its collection of gospel, soul, rap, disco and pop influences, earning praise from some quarters for its willingness to experiment, and jeers from others for whom the final album had direction but no destination. The sessions were also notable for a number of reunions. Nile Rodgers returned as producer; after seventeen years Mike Garson reclaimed the pianist's stool; and Ronson, though now terminally ill, played on the hoary Cream hit 'I Feel Free'. Bowie was a self-confessed tyrant when it came to dominating his rhythm section. Even with old friends, and a jazz master like his namesake, he was the emperor and the musicians the defeated gladiators, anxiously awaiting the thumb to twist upwards or down. Bowie would later say that the new songs were the most 'evolutionary' of his career. His comment was intended to fend off criticism about the album, but he found that it applied equally to himself. With marriage, Bowie became a reformed character who, having lived a life of dissipation and excess, not only relinquished those activities in middle age but tried to urge others of any age at all to give them up as well. 'I have someone who loves me for me,' he happily told a journalist visiting the Hit Factory. For Bowie, that was better than any drug.

10
OUTSIDE

As he explored his life in mutual analysis with Iman, Bowie was also deeply involved in the practicalities of his career. Although he was well aware of Victory's loss from the second and third Tin Machine albums, he constantly belaboured the label with new projects. He entered into an agreement with BMG-distributed Savage Records to release his solo album. And he finished work in Montreux on *The Buddha of Suburbia*. Bowie's renewed experiments with sound texture would foreshadow his next collaboration with Eno. His television score was a dense, calculatedly stark treatment that died commercially. It also contained some of Bowie's best work since *Scary Monsters*. No one else in the theme-music business had attempted an album of such depth, let alone scope; as always, Bowie danced to the beat of a different drum machine. *Buddha*'s soundtrack played avant-garde with wit, feeling and style. It was also of a piece with Kureishi's novel – the plot was the perfect setting for the songs.

The year saw two major Bowie retrospectives. Rykodisc released *The Singles 1969–1993*, transporting the listener back to the world of the alienated, strung-out astronaut by way of some of the finest rock of the seventies. *Bowie: The Video Collection* achieved much the same trick, although here it was the later work that jumped off the screen. Each of the twenty-five clips took risks that paid off artistically, the more so when Bowie (as in 'Blue Jean') commented wryly on his own neuroses. He did his most vivid and unconventional work in the videos that charted his best-known incarnations. The performances were as quick-changing as the artist. Bowie was especially adept at locating the madness that attends celebrity. Time and again, the films proved the inevitability of any intelligent rock star finding at least part of his audience ridiculous. They also confirmed that Bowie could laugh at himself. Mallet's scripts, in particular, provided the perfect vehicle for his near-panoramic sense of irony. Bowie was the ultimate pop satirist, and the *Video Collection* was a treasury of his best jokes.

Both the video and singles anthologies were unashamedly nostalgic, a frequent and usually disparaging description of Bowie's role in the early nineties. In one sense, his barrenness was very real. After completing *Buddha* and the New York sessions, Bowie did little creative writing. He marked time by occupying himself with other things – painting, travelling and giving interviews that were frankly sentimental. In March 1993 he led David Sinclair on a voyage round his old Ziggy haunts. There was one striking scene in Wardour Street:

> In a dingy alleyway in Soho, London's notorious red-light district, David Bowie stops in front of a doorway. Uncertain of whom or what he will find on the other side, he pushes a buzzer.
>
> 'Yes,' says a voice on the intercom.
>
> 'Hi,' says Bowie. 'Did this used to be Trident Studios once upon a time?'
>
> 'Indeed so, a long time ago,' comes the voice from inside.
>
> 'This is David Bowie. I used to record here. Do you think I could come in for a second?'

After similar detours to the Thomas À Becket pub, Heddon Street and the Marquee, Bowie found himself on the deserted stage of the Hammersmith Odeon (now the Apollo) repeating his fateful 'retirement' announcement of July 1973. He explained the Ziggy phenomenon in full to Sinclair. After a lifetime of elegant evasion, Bowie was now the most directly open and revealing of pop stars, the closest to the memory of what he once was. And simultaneously he was the most social, historical and moral artist in the best and highest (nonconforming) sense of morality. This factor explains his willingness to talk about his own past and the past in general – rather than any self-indulgent cash-in. It was also why Bowie in his twenties, his thirties, his mid forties, became one of the most perceptive critics of a changing pop scene, a student of the revolution he helped bring about.

The celebration of the past continued in titles from *The Times* to *Der Spiegel* to *Q*. In a chest-baring interview with *Esquire*, Bowie spoke of having been drug-free for two years, of the mental illness in his family background, and of his own fears of madness. Not all his forays into the confessional were successful. In one TV interview Bowie enlightened the public with the knowledge that 'the problem with life [is that] it's got more than two sides'. Elsewhere, he dwelt on the changes wrought by his marriage: 'These days I'm analytical,' he told the *Sunday Times*. 'I used to not want to reveal myself too much because I wasn't sure what was in there.' To another reporter he added, 'I've become more gregarious . . . I've just found this new aspect of myself that enjoys conversation, to an extent I've never really realized before. It's great. It's really cool. It gives life a whole new dimension.' He praised Iman.

At the same time as Bowie boasted, 'Now I am compulsively heterosexual', his ex-wife was telling a gay-rights magazine of her concern for Aids victims. Angela's feelings about her old life were tested to the core by Joe's continuing refusal to see her. It was thirteen years since she had last spoken to Bowie.

In enthusing to David Wild about his New York sessions, Bowie had insisted he had nothing to prove. As he said, he had made a lot of money over the years; but he concealed the extent to which he drew on his deposit account. With EMI funds no longer reaching him, Bowie had to rely more heavily than ever on the income from his back catalogue. Neither of the last Tin Machine albums had sold, *Buddha of Suburbia* flopped, and Savage Records crashed in June 1993, making Bowie's new album near-invisible in America. He began to contribute regular journalism, but that, too, was not enough to finance his four homes. As in the late seventies, Bowie found himself more of an inspiration than a commercial prospect. His influence reached both extremes. At one end of the market there was Philip Glass, whose *Low Symphony* saddled Bowie's glacial *tour de force* with a perversely jaunty score. His Ziggy persona and record of thirty-four hits in the Top Thirty wooed the seventies retro-groups like Primal Scream and Erasure, while 'Boys Keep Swinging' could be relied on to raise interest in Brett Anderson, singer with Suede. That spring Bowie, wearing a grey suit, white shirt and fedora* played host to Anderson, to whom he offered a wry perspective on his career. In Britain at large, there was growing nostalgia for the lost world of flapping loon pants, horizontal lapels and bouffant hair. Other bands began shamelessly to take leaves from a style-book almost entirely invented by the *Diamond Dogs/Young Americans* albums. In a twist of fate, Bowie found his old, Ziggy-era hits being rediscovered just as he retired them. Truly it seemed, as the revival geared up with repeats of *Top of the Pops* episodes with classic glam regalia, that the seventies, in *Rolling Stone*'s words, were 'suddenly hip'. No one benefited from this renaissance more than Bowie.

As time went on, Bowie not only gathered a cult following among his peers but also excited new fans. Although he was always reluctant to join the music-business élite, he was eager to consolidate his reputation as a celebrity, a rock star. A self-styled outsider, he was also a sharp bargainer with record companies. He knew when to accept and when to reject a new deal. For a whole year – the longest single session of his life – Bowie had been at work in New York and Montreux on a project described as his 'wedding album'. This evolved, by April 1993, into *Black Tie White Noise*. Not only was it Bowie's first solo set in six years, it was his first studio collaboration with Ronson in two decades. After the Spiders disbanded in 1973, an army of Bowiephiles had first gone into mourning, and then passed the next twenty years wondering what kind of music the group would have made in their forties. *Black Tie White Noise* was the answer: in 1993, Bowie and Ronson were still singing about sex.

Black Tie White Noise was actually Bowie's fourth album of the nineties, but for most listeners it came as his first, the sequel to 1983's platinum *Let's Dance*. The music addressed such subjects as his marriage, Terry Burns' death and the Los Angeles riots, topics, he said, that were 'too personal' for a four-way democratic band. Lyrically, *Black Tie* dealt with the events of April 1992 in cahoots with Bowie's cover versions of Cream, Scott Walker and

---

*The same look, coincidentally, that William Burroughs had chosen for his lunch with Bowie twenty years earlier.

Morrissey. There were the usual in-jokes and nods to his past, as when he sang 'You've changed me ... Ch-ch-ch-ch-ch-ch-changed me' and reprised the piano part from 'Aladdin Sane'. Musically, the album contained enough of Bowie's stylized vocals to jerk nostalgic tears, but there were deft swings of direction: from Lester Bowie's gaudy trumpet, to the electronic treatments, through to the Barry White-like orchestration that threatened to break out on half the tracks. Keith Christmas insists at least one of his guitar hooks worked its way onto the album. Although the words were dark and the music leant towards the sparse techno-rock of *Low* and *'Heroes'*, there were light touches. 'I Know It's Gonna Happen Someday' was Bowie's imitation of Morrissey imitating him. 'I Feel Free' showed Bowie and Ronson not only accompanying each other with fraternal glee, but completely reworking the tune in the Euro-funk mould of *Station to Station*. There were also lapses of judgement. Reprising 'The Wedding' might have made perfect sense in the church in Florence, but here it came across as clunky and self-indulgent. Bowie's spoken lines in 'Miracle Tonight' were an embarrassment of would-be rapping. But, generally, underneath the affectations and Rodgers' tinkerings, melody reigned supreme.

The album's most arresting track was, logically, the first single, 'Jump They Say'. It neatly demonstrated Bowie's weird and much-copied ability to freight exuberant dance music with dark wordplay. The arrangement was all up-tempo funk and honks of Lester Bowie's trumpet. The lyrics dealt with madness and suicide. It had taken Bowie eight years to publicly come to terms with his half-brother's death. That the song had special meaning for him was shown by the frenzy of the promotional blitz. 'Jump' was worked to the radio with no fewer than four mixes. A CD-ROM version allowed users to create their own videos for the song. Typically, Bowie embraced the new technology with missionary zeal. Unlike most other music-oriented CD-ROMs, he said, his would not be archival, biographical or even based on an album release. Rather, he meant them to be fully interactive, and have a non-linear storyline, allowing the fan to 'approach the thing again and again and never go through the same experience'. Savage puffed 'Jump They Say' with TV, radio and print advertising, special promotions and a press release sent to 600 titles. Point-of-purchase materials and posters were also pushed. Although the song itself seldom strayed beyond the safe realm of radio-friendly pop-rock, it failed to clear six figures.

For the most part, the cuts on *Black Tie White Noise* followed one of two formulas. Bowie's and Rodgers' most compelling trick was to take a simple tune and tease the material in complex but unshowy arrangements. Thus 'The Wedding' veered, via church bells and a thumping bass line, into a squall of Middle Eastern riffing. The Tin Machine reject 'You've Been Around' and 'I Feel Free' were both transformed in the mix. 'Looking For Lester', otherwise a virtual echo of 'Chasing the Train', was revamped by way of Garson's *Aladdin Sane*-type tinklings and a horn part lifted from Steely Dan.

Elsewhere, Bowie toyed with the material with his thin but affecting voice. *Black Tie*'s title track recalled the lyrics on *Young Americans* – all soul harmony and choppy, danceable choruses. 'I Know It's Gonna Happen Someday' was in the dramatic vein of 'Rock 'n' Roll Suicide'. The delivery on 'Don't Let Me Down & Down' easily satisfied Lennon's definitive pop criteria: say what you mean, make it rhyme and keep it simple. 'Night Flights' was a neat example of Bowie's way with most of the tracks on *Black Tie*: he sang them like he meant them.

On 8 May 1993 Bowie was filmed by David Mallet at Hollywood Center Studios performing six songs from the album. Over the years the two men had produced some of *the* visual art of their day: videos like 'D.J.', 'Ashes to Ashes' and 'Let's Dance' epitomized their eras almost as much as the songs did. Much of Mallet's work, even when illustrating run-of-the-mill music, had become a new creative frontier, and a huge influence on mainstream directors. *Black Tie White Noise* was not one of these moments. One reviewer referred to the film as 'six cheesy, lip-synched performances ... a bare-bones set with slightly different, but consistently awful, lighting and direction ... Looks as if [Mallet] did this stuff on the cheap ... For years, each of his transformations pushed pop music in unpredictable new directions – now Bowie can barely keep up with everybody else.'

Black Tie was released just as the seventies revival swung to its gaudy peak. As Bowie's first solo outing in years, it could hardly fail. But no one could have predicted the commercial triumph. No one, in fact, did. The album went to number one in the home market. It did less well in America. Early in 1993 Savage's chairman David Mimran had predicted that Bowie would 'absolutely be the artist to break the label wide open … He's everything that I would use to describe us.' Six months later, the album dashed such hopes with weak sales. The company went bust. For the first time in twenty-five years, Bowie was temporarily without a record label. He forfeited a substantial American royalty. Even so, for most fans, his life was one of steady improvement. The general verdict on *Black Tie* was positive: the album was evidently less problematic than Tin Machine had been, and Bowie found himself being praised for having returned to type. He enjoyed a creative Indian summer.

Early that April, as *Black Tie White Noise* was released, Bowie took the time to phone his old drummer John Cambridge. They discussed Ronson's failing health. Bowie's reaction was complex. Cambridge remembers him saying, 'The silly sod won't stop smoking' and carping in similar vein, though with underlying affection. Three weeks later, on 29 April, the phone rang again. This time, Bowie told Cambridge that Ronson had died.

Bowie owed Ronson the real start of his career as well as the arrangements for some of his best songs, but their break-up had been marked by mutual bickering. The guitarist's solo bid finished the friendship in a single (and widely panned) album. Over ten years they barely spoke. The thaw began when Ronson guested at Bowie's Toronto concert in September 1983. In the main the next decade had been amicable. The friendship was fraught with the meaning Bowie projected into any lasting relationship with anyone who had been like a brother to him, and towards whom he therefore felt a mixture of love and rivalry. He praised Ronson's production of Morrissey's *Your Arsenal* and referred to him as 'my dear thing' in the studio. Only towards the end did he allow himself a touch of intimacy. Cambridge confirms that 'David was gutted' on the night of 29 April. According to David Sinclair, 'mention of [Ronson's appearance at the Concert for Life] almost brought tears to Bowie's eyes'. One of Mallet's assistants at the Hollywood shoot speaks of Bowie struggling to compose himself after listening to the guitar-heavy studio version of 'Moonage Daydream'. He referred to Ronson on the *Black Tie White Noise* video.

In a different context, however, Bowie still showed his ambivalent feelings about his past. He contributed to *Heaven 'N Hull*, the Ronson tribute album released in 1994. His other public comment suggested his feelings only in his peculiarly mixed response. 'I loved him,' Bowie said supportively. His support did not, however, extend to appearing at the memorial concert for Ronson at the Hammersmith Apollo. This resulted in a fiery outburst from a musician who had known Ronson immediately after his defection from the Spiders.

Bowie had planned to make good on the hit of *Black Tie* by reactivating Tin Machine. 'A dreadful commercial failure, but an artistic success' was his 1993 verdict on the group. Instead he was forced to start searching for a new label (he had five offers) and evade, as best he could, the fallout from Savage's collapse. By early autumn Bowie was interested not in booking studio time and touring, but in looking after his garden in Mustique. The year turned on a more and more quiet time for him, with Iman taking on some of the decisions and some of the hasty movements from place to place that once marked her husband's life. A woman who met them later that winter in Lausanne remembers Iman 'sending David on errands so that she could get on with business'. Often this tactic was not necessary because Bowie would walk off and disappear all day.

While Bowie was certainly suffering a decline in global sales – he had no US label – in other respects the early nineties were not wholly without value, nor that different from other periods. Crisis had always been a theme of Bowie's work, his most trusty material. The years 1990–3 were also years during which his reputation was refurbished. A second generation could watch his seminal early TV appearances, while new bands everywhere were tapping into the Ziggy saga and wearing clothes spun from the glam yarn. But the most substantial boost to Bowie's morale came late in 1993, when Nirvana chose to cover 'The Man Who Sold the World' on *Unplugged*. It would be hard to exaggerate the shove to his career. Reversing the premise of its title, *Unplugged* was ruthlessly sold in America. Kurt Cobain, not one to overpraise, spoke of 'the debt we all owe David'. In what seemed like a moment, Bowie had made a breakthrough, vaulting from the archives into the contemporary world of screwed-up nihilism, turned-around baseball caps and loud guitars. That one gesture led him to contact Eno and confirm plans for a new album. Bowie even spoke of touring again.

Ten years earlier, Bowie had enthused wildly over Nagisa Oshima's direction of *Merry Christmas, Mr Lawrence*. He admired him chiefly for his speed: 'I've spent more time making movies just sitting on my arse ... Oshima cancelled that out for me. Two takes and it was done, then he'd take the film out of the camera and send it, literally in brown paper, back to Japan where his editor put it all together. It was like real life. You only get one shot at it.' Some of the same spontaneity came through on Bowie's new album. He met Eno at Mountain studios early in March 1994. Bowie later spoke of the reunion as 'easy ... almost as though no time had been wedged in, like we were carrying on from the third album together'. Other than a mutual love of promiscuously mingling low and high art, the two shared a strong affinity for situationist behaviour. Thus, when the band arrived Bowie and Eno chose to welcome them not with the traditional greeting, but by handing them overalls. Gabrels, Alomar and the rest were then made to paint the studio. That done, each was given a character part – what Eno called an oblique strategy. Mike Garson was told, 'You are the pianist in a South African band. Play all the notes you weren't allowed to.' At other times the producers drew cards from a Tarot deck and attempted to translate the symbols into music. Bowie himself set to shuffling his lyrics electronically, with some suitably random results.

The basic tracks for *Outside* were recorded in ten days. The production and haggling over a record deal lasted eighteen months. By July 1994 Bowie was able to tell the *New York Times* that he and Eno 'don't feel part of what's going on at all now ... We feel totally distanced from everything, and that's kind of exciting. It kind of feels a bit dangerous because you're not sure if anybody's going to relate to what you're doing. People might dismiss it, which is fine – we're used to being dismissed.' As well as their 'album of so-called songs', the two were at work on a new CD-ROM, music for the La La La Human Steps, and a snatch of film soundtrack. The pendulum swing between need and fear of rejection now coloured all Bowie's interviews. His pose was evident when he turned down one label on the grounds that with his 'yob genes' he 'hardly fitted in a boardroom'. A new set of terms settled into Bowie's vocabulary: he was a bum, a vagabond, a footloose wanderer. This pose formed a neat contrast to the theme of marriage and home.

Bowie's double-act, the insider-outsider, checked and balanced both his work and his life. For all the oblique strategies and haphazard lyrics there were still pop tunes in search of a song. For relaxation, Bowie still took long walks in the Swiss countryside. He often read a book a day. He liked to attend art lectures. Bowie himself spoke in many voices, with no focal point. One week he was lunching with Princess Margaret in Mustique. The next Bowie was in New York for an audience with the underground artist Ron Athey. Athey, an Aids patient, greeted his guests by jabbing a knitting needle into his forehead and making an impromptu exhibition of paper towels soaked with his blood. Bowie had an unerring sense for performance art. By being both radical and mainstream, he could appreciate cultural pranks like Athey's without slipping the moorings of his familiar world. After leaving Greenwich Village, then, the cutting-edge explorer gave way to the native whom everyone could recognize. The expensive meal at the Upper East Side restaurant was followed in turn by the limousine hop to the exclusive hotel. Here Bowie became just another rock star, of a piece with a Jagger or McCartney, more interested in reading his advance copy of the *New Yorker* than in tearing down the guard-rails of normal society.

Later that autumn, in London, Neil Conti was surprised to hear from Bowie after a gap of nine years:

> He rang one night and said, 'What are you doing tomorrow?' We might have been picking up a conversation after ten minutes, not nearly a decade. For some reason, I turned up in the studio late. Bowie was furious, beside himself . . . After Eno calmed him down we did the session, which was great. David gave me a look and said, 'I'm touring next year. Interested?' He never explained the silence.

Nor, in the end, did Bowie invite Conti to tour. Kevin Armstrong, another member of the *ad hoc* group at Live Aid, was summoned in similar fashion six months later. In the course of playing guitar on 'Thru' These Architects Eyes' he found Bowie, since his marriage, to be 'unexpectedly likeable' and 'a dream to work with'. (Again, Eno played a key intermediary role.) For Armstrong, Bowie was an archetype of the unashamedly happy husband, the patron saint of family life who had become friend and father to a coterie of loyal musicians. A third man involved in the session at West Side Studio speaks of 'David in corduroys and a polo-neck ... a relaxed guy who was, if anything, nostalgic and sentimental about London'. Bowie visited friends, roamed with them in the streets around Soho and dined in Langan's. As well as his walks, he bought exercise equipment and gave a matching set to Eno. When he finally finished production of *Outside*, his life seemed happier. Iman was with him part of the time and he enjoyed showing her the scenes of his youth. The twin character parts – the unflinching modernist and the homesick Englishman – continued to get equal attention.

With this flickering desire to be a Renaissance Man, Bowie exhibited his first paintings and waited for the mixed response. He took his role as an artist and art patron seriously. Late in 1993, Bowie paid £20,000 to keep the controversial Peter Howson painting, *Croatian and Muslim*, in Britain after the Imperial War Museum rejected it. Six months later he was among forty pop luminaries exhibiting their work in aid of the charity War Child. While other celebrities like Bryan Ferry were content to show off their etchings of each other, Bowie produced a portfolio of fourteen prints entitled *We Saw the Minotaur*, and an additional poster. ('I would describe them as flashy, faintly topical and vulgar,' he admitted, a view the critics gave him no reason to retract.) That same month, he interviewed Balthus, the last survivor of the 1930s École de Paris, for *Modern Painters*.

This was the raffish, bearded Bowie who became a fixture at the Gay Hussar and the Colony Club, exchanging notes with his friends Jeremy Isaacs and Bernard Jacobson, to whom he was 'a breath of fresh and very unpretentious air [with] strong and intelligent views on art ... You could let him loose on anyone.' Bowie's own tastes ran towards the abstract, the avant-garde and the futurist. His idea of a contemporary artist was Damien Hirst. Bowie also collected works by Graham Sutherland and William

Tillier and admired the modernist Peter Lanyon. To combine all this with his frequent forays into art journalism and non-executive directorship of a magazine was not just dabbling.

In the eighties, albums like *Tonight* and *Never Let Me Down* had been slated as designer music, no more than the aural equivalent of soft furnishings: tasteful, subdued and dull. The next bizarre incarnation of Bowie's art seemed to confirm his critics' worst fears. He launched his own wallpaper collection. The project had its evolution in a studio joke between Bowie and Eno, in which they adopted alter egos – Davide and Briani, Designers of Bathroom Accessories. By March 1995 fantasy had become fact. Bowie's wallpaper, produced in tandem with Laura Ashley, featured two designs: British Conflicts, a portrait of Lucian Freud inside a Damien Hirst-type box; and The Crouch, with one of Bowie's charcoal drawings of a minotaur. (He had to suffer seeing the animal be castrated.) Critics wondered whether Bowie, having recanted on his past life, had over-compensated. One uncharitable reviewer spoke of 'getting a few rolls to do the downstairs loo, as a constant and poignant reminder of what became of one of my all-time heroes'. Another asked whether the wallpaper was in fact 'an artistic suicide note'. Unsurprisingly, that was not how Bowie himself saw it. 'I chose wallpaper because of its status as something extremely incongruous ... I haven't completely lost my sense of irony,' he told the *Sunday Times*. Bowie went on: 'I'm midway between high art and low art – I'm a mid-art populist and postmodernist Buddhist who is casually surfing his way through the chaos of the late twentieth century.'

Having already shown his *Minotaur* prints at War Child, Bowie held his first solo exhibition at the Kate Chertavian Gallery in London in April 1995. The retrospective of portraits, sculpture and computer-generated images drew the expected reviews. One critic described the work as 'post-A-Level, pre-art-school'. Another left with a terse 'Embarrassing.' Two paintings were, however, purchased by the reclusive Charles Saatchi, and three more by what Chertavian calls 'very important British collectors': a respectable tally for a first exhibition.

Bowie himself was on hand at the gallery on 19 April. He cut a genial figure, strolling arm-in-arm with Iman and speaking of his artistic debt to Owen Frampton. At some stage a woman named Margaret Cooper was able to tug at his sleeve. She wanted to know if, as part of an art project of her own, Bowie and his wife would allow her to paint and then photograph their nude bodies. They both, she recalls, 'looked startled'. Bowie promised Cooper that someone from his office would contact her. He then quickly walked out the door and into his waiting car. Just as the Mercedes drove off down Cork Street, Ken Pitt pulled up at the gallery.

'With me,' Bowie said, 'making a commitment to share your life is an epic decision . . . it tempers and redefines your existence. Once you start sharing things, you open up in a much larger way yourself . . . I've become far more gregarious than I used to be.' When they saw the change, Bowie's friends began by congratulating him that he was human. Like Kevin Armstrong, they applauded the unexpectedly warm soul emerging in the nineties. Marriage intensified Bowie's struggle to overcome self-consciousness in the two areas where it was a major factor: his music and the public aspect of his fame. He was careful to record in his journal those interviews where he managed to forget himself and those in which he was all too self-aware. At the same time, his volume of fan mail, after dipping in the late eighties, had soared again, and each letter brought him more news of Bowie the rock demagogue.*

Nowhere was the public and private man in greater conflict than in his marriage. In true show-business fashion, Bowie insisted this was off limits. Huge effort went into shielding the couple on their excursions into the nightlife of London, Los Angeles and New York. Yet Bowie knew exactly how to use the media when it suited him. In spring 1995 he and Iman set off for a private sightseeing tour of Africa, accompanied by just two reporters and a *Vogue* photographer. His particular desire to publicize conditions in Somalia expressed a mixture of idealism and cold-hearted pragmatism. Bowie's visit to Mogadishu won him more press than anything he had done since 1992. The principle was not lost on him: politicians and relief workers could

*He reported getting 'thousands of photographs' imitating the *Ziggy* album cover, and explanations of its meaning.

talk for months about the Somalian famine with barely a ripple of attention, but by being photographed there Bowie ensured global coverage. Nobody could accuse him of using the trip to his own ends. Nor is it certain that Bowie enjoyed being dogged by the press wherever he went. What is certain is that he was well aware of the advantage his place in rock history brought, as he admitted to a journalist: 'My celebrity status [is] something I don't ignore. I'm very much a product of the late twentieth century; the media is all. I can't buy into a new band who says, "You know we just do our music, and if somebody comes to our shows that's just a bonus." I think, "You fucking liar", that just isn't true . . . I'm far too experienced to buy into that crap.'

After Ziggy, Bowie was famous and determined to keep fame at arm's length. 'I want to go out like Vince Taylor.' Yet the attention of the pop pundits was deeply satisfying. He complained about the fuss that was made in Britain and America – all those photographers to avoid and soundbites to hoard against his next interview – but by these signs he knew he had made it. Twenty years later, like other reformed rock reprobates, Bowie had embraced the media as an ally. He knew they had a stake in his longevity. Unlike his peers, though, he was never going to accept the trade-off – the restraints on his other activities. 'Once you understand the tools,' he said, 'it's quite appropriate to move from medium to medium . . . As long as you apply those tools in a reasonable fashion, and with a certain degree of intelligence, you shouldn't screw up the project.' Thus Bowie exhibited his prints in London and New York; went into business with Laura Ashley; and produced part of the soundtrack to BBC 2's *History of British Art*. He continued acting.

Bowie had praised the rough, two-take tradition of *Merry Christmas, Mr Lawrence*. Unfortunately, few modern directors shared Oshima's exhilarating speed. Bowie continually carped at the long delays of most mainstream film-making. He denied having ambitions as an actor ('I don't particularly enjoy the process') and disparaged his own technique ('I can look left, I can look right and I can look straight ahead . . . Which do you want?'). His forte was the cameo. Bowie's roles tended to be laconic, often self-consciously quirky character parts, like the gangster he played in *Into the Night*. In 1995 he appeared briefly in an episode of HBO's *Dream On.* He was said to be considering a part in *Mystery Train,* a film life of Elvis co-produced by Mick Jagger. The theatrical world's attention was hardly riveted by Bowie's ten-minute vignettes. But its axes were still ground. His acting became a rallying point for those who saw an epidemic among VIPs – with their breezy confidence in their inabilities – of thinking that being famous for one thing qualified them to do anything else; and others who admired the prodigious range of his work.

Later in 1995 Bowie accepted a part he might have been born to play: Andy Warhol in Julian Schnabel's film *Basquiat, Build a Fort, Set It On Fire.* This was inspired casting, particularly in light of Warhol's quip, 'If you want to know all about me, just look at the surface of my paintings and films, and there I am. There's nothing behind it.' He was all front, something Bowie conveyed in a brilliant impersonation. For ten days on set, with the aid of a blond fright wig and corpse-coloured make-up, he *became* the dead artist. He arranged to borrow Warhol's clothes from a museum. 'They still smelt of him,' said Bowie. 'I even had his little handbag – a very sad little bag with all kinds of devices to make you better.' He was thrilled with the results. 'It was almost a workshop situation . . . I enjoyed the hell out of it,' Bowie told Paul Gorman. He announced elsewhere that it was a 'thoroughly good little movie'. The lesson Bowie drew from the last decade was that if he took on only those scripts he wanted, crowds would come. 'It's a matter of keeping your nerve. Do that and everything will follow.'

It did. After years of unfortunate films and anaemic albums, Bowie found himself in the thick of a style renaissance. His pinched, cadaverous look was copied on catwalks and advertising billboards; thanks to Rykodisc, his greatest hits were back on the chart; Suede and a host of other bands paid their own disingenuous tributes. Bowie again took the throne of British pop. He dealt with his various subjects with even-handed care. The Sunday supplements and lifestyle magazines were on side. Bowie established cordial relations with smaller titles like *Dazed and Confused* and *Ikon.* He answered questions on the Prodigy bulletin board. His *Black Tie* video was aired on TV. Bowie gave radio interviews and continued to explore his past by taking journalists on personal tours of London. He visited Bromley and Beckenham. In short, he enjoyed all the trappings of a revival. Sales of *The Singles 1969–1993* went to wild highs on a rising graph. Bowie's paintings achieved national coverage. As always, he spread himself thin: his mix of film and TV acting, journalism, art and rock led one critic to accuse him of 'try[ing] carpet bombing in place of precision bombing'. However, he admitted, Bowie normally hit his mark.

The self-confident and 'smug' man a partner met for dinner was at least as much the real Bowie as the nervy character of old. He still understood the ethics of fame, that the public expects arrogance in its rock stars. It was expected more than most in Bowie, whose ego could only have been boosted by the fact that, while a flop overseas, *Black Tie* had been touted as one of Britain's best albums of the year – some thought *the* best. In an indication of which way the rock *Zeitgeist* was going, Bowie's record even knocked Suede off the top of the charts. Perhaps the commonplace 'rediscovered' would do as a précis as far as his work was concerned. It meant something far more in Bowie's private life. With a few rare exceptions, the musicians and artists who met him in the early nineties spoke of a new composure and a willingness to forget the past – what Bowie now called 'all that shit'.

Bowie knew very well that life on the scale he lived it would not have been possible on recent sales. Tin Machine had not made him rich. The group were a token success: their albums sold a few hundreds of thousands and earned them a modest royalty. Meanwhile, Bowie's catalogue was soaring to new heights and climbed more steeply still when Rykodisc re-released seventeen titles. From mid-1995 fans could again buy his RCA albums alongside the three-hour *Sound + Vision* set, a full and at times exhilarating survey of his career. Only the back royalty flow made it possible for Bowie to live and travel as he did. He was 'hardly a goldmine', he told an artist friend. 'That fucking Ziggy *still* pays my hotel bills.' Bowie lived to exercise mastery over his own future. He was not afraid the money would run out, but that it rooted him to the past. In 1990, Bowie had determined never to play his old hits again. No such policy, it seemed, had been adopted by his record company. Rykodisc continued to issue box sets, bizarre 'bonus tracks', rarities and outtakes, all of which put flesh on the bones of the Bowie revival. With an alchemist's touch, he had turned himself from comfortable to fabulously rich, worth an estimated £45–50 million. Bowie was not exactly mean with money, but nor did he give it away. His problems with managers had left him with a healthy interest in his own assets. By 1995 Bowie was a director of half a dozen firms. His nostalgic streak showed even in his business dealings. When Bowie went to Companies House to register his marketing and publishing offshoots he gave them the names Stenton and Jones Music, proof of his lingering affection for his roots.

Finally, in June 1995, Bowie signed a deal with a new record company. According to industry sources, the contract with Virgin America,* if not on the epic scale of EMI, would earn him over a million dollars annually. As part of the buy-out, Virgin purchased the rights to *Let's Dance, Tonight, Never Let Me Down, Tin Machine, Black Tie White Noise* and *The Buddha of Suburbia*; all six were promptly reissued. Bowie found it hard to admit his delight, but it was evident to friends. Visitors to Lausanne over the next few weeks found him as happy as they had ever seen him. Apart from the money, Bowie had a specific passion. He had become obsessed about the countdown to the year 2000. He spoke of his once-in-a-lifetime chance to chronicle the millennium by releasing an annual album until, as he put it, 'Doomsday'. Bowie's ambition to live out the plot of 'Five Years' was not matched by any personal fatalism. He told a journalist that he and Iman planned a large family. For someone with Bowie's temperament, the idea that he was nearly fifty worked its own spell, and he may have been reminded of the recent deaths of several friends. Stronger still was the feeling that if he were going to accomplish his goals, especially in work, he would have to hurry. Late that summer, Bowie finished production on *Outside*. He shot a video for the album's first single, wrote the convoluted sleeve notes and donated a self-portrait for the cover. As if not a big enough contribution, he then gave two weeks of interviews.

---

*Bowie entered into a new agreement with the BMG Company in Britain.

Marriage, as he often admitted, had changed Bowie: the reins had slipped a little. He was more effusive, less wary, but just as dogmatic. He had views on literally everyone, himself included – a thoroughly confused, confusing product of late-century dissolution of reason, yet vindicated by artistic genius. He was turning this image into flesh and blood on *Outside*.

Bowie *had* changed. But beneath the surface amiability to people who hardly knew him, he was impenetrable to those who tried to get close. He still acted out the habits of the last twenty-five years and generally came on as the rock demigod. Would-be interviewers were vetted, some approved, many others aggressively rejected. The few were then flown to Los Angeles, where an assistant led them to Bowie's bungalow at the Château Marmont. A second staffer sat in the room with a tape-recorder while two make-up artists, Teddy and Paul, hovered nearby. Each journalist was allowed a strictly enforced forty minutes; should any exceed his welcome, Bowie's bodyguard would terminate the audience. With those few conditions, the interviews were affable enough. Bowie greeted each guest with a warm handshake and a charm that seemed genuine. For *Esquire*, he retained a 'certain core Englishness' which remained constant behind all the masks. To another reporter he had a 'dry, insistent voice' and an 'encyclopaedic mind' which he used, in a conversational *tour de force*, to dominate the meeting. Monologue was a place where Bowie felt very much at home. He could pour forth for hours on philosophy, music, art, the nature of God, on love, marriage, education and mental illness. Even experienced journalists sat silent, except when murmuring at intervals, 'Really! Yep!', until the heavy tap on the shoulder and the long walk outside to Sunset Strip.

Bowie may have 'run out of charisma', as he told a friend, but he could still command front covers when he chose to. In September 1995 alone his face loomed under the mastheads of *Vox*, *Ikon*, *Us*, *Interview* and *Musician*. He expounded on his chaos theory to Ian Penman: 'I see no way we can go back, philosophically, to a world of absolutes. Which I feel very comfortable with and I always have. The idea of juxtaposition has seemed quite relevant in the late twentieth century. I feel that we can distinguish as much *output* from the combination of seemingly irreconcilable information, as we can by abiding by the rule of some rather tenuous absolutism.' Bowie saw no moral certainties. He did, however, see the chance of personal salvation through love. 'I think that's really an epic and adventurous thing to do – to commit to a relationship which in all sincerity you see as lasting for the rest of your life.' He stumbled on from there, and the piece Penman wrote captured perfectly the characteristic qualities of a David Bowie interview: an avalanche of ideas, odd digressions, breezy evasions and the tendency to declaim from a great height. Bowie also spoke of his rejuvenating interest in technology. From the electronic treatments of *Black Tie* and *Outside* through to his infatuation with CD-ROMs, he was, as he put it, 'frequently confused, but consistently fascinated' by his computer. From his address on the Prodigy bulletin board – actually his study in Lausanne – Bowie answered questions on his albums, gave a bare account of his life, and admitted, 'My career was more about style ... I wouldn't give up any one aspect of what I do. One isn't more important than the others ... I find them all reciprocating mediums.'

Bowie was a success no one could have predicted a few years before, after the Glass Spider fiasco. Even *Time Out* treated him like a prodigal son (and then ran into flak from its own letters page, where a reader accused the magazine of a 'sycophantic' interview). Anyone poring over the tens of thousands of words being written about Bowie would have come away thinking him to be a civilized and rational adult with a refreshing attitude to fame and a wry slant on his past; it was a marvellous performance. For every cryptic oration ('It is almost as if history is ceasing to exist ... Then one presumes, metaphorically, that there is no future either'), there was an engaging quip, as when he called himself 'a born librarian with a sex drive', or told the *Evening Standard*, 'I'm a bit of a hybrid. On the other hand, Eno is more minimalist. He only wears black corduroy trousers.' If Bowie had a guiding philosophy, it was that nothing was simple any more. 'Our lives aren't tidy, and we don't have tidy beginnings and endings.' The counterpart to his apocalyptical take on life was the happiness he knew with his wife, son and stepdaughter. Deep into the brandy one night in London, Bowie, in tears, told a friend: 'Depression, always depression ... Without Iman, I'd have put my head in the oven by now.'

*

There are nostalgia merchants whose last albums are very like
the first. Having learned their trade, they practise it with little
variation to the end. They can be highly successful, unblushingly
working a formula and tirelessly burlesquing themselves on
stage. Bowie was not one of these musicians. In *Outside*, released
that September, he aimed to emulate the free-floating sense of
being on drugs – living outside oneself. Bowie gnomically
described the album as 'like Houston', a random array of styles
thrown up to Eno's design. When the two men had met in
Montreux eighteen months before, they worked on an improvisational piece in which Bowie took the job of a griot, or narrator.
The musicians were each given their own oblique strategy.
Gradually the twenty-two hours of tape were whittled down to
seventy-five minutes (though even then, *Outside* could have done
with a few days' more polishing in the production department)
and welded to the diary of one Nathan Adler, art detective, in
what Bowie called 'a non-linear Gothic Drama Hyper-cycle'. It
was all a long way from the days of 'The Laughing Gnome'.

Reluctance to reveal himself in interviews should be measured
against the astonishing candour of Bowie's confessions on record.
Those who saw the man exposed on *Outside* knew how clearly he
recognized his own deep flaws. For all his recent appearances in
Hello! and self-portrayal as a contented husband and father,
Bowie still had no straightforward way of enjoying himself. The
dark side was not destroyed. *Outside*'s theme was madness, which
guaranteed the album yards of coverage, as well as fatuous claims
from certain quarters that Bowie was tackling a serious subject
for the first time. Yet concept albums like this were hardly news.
Their faintly tedious models had been seventies acts like Deep
Purple, Pink Floyd and Yes, and nothing could more vividly
illustrate their special horrors than the overdesigned liner notes
that turned *Outside* into a small book. With the help of the
owner's manual, the album became 'an ultimately damning
portrait of an increasingly dysfunctional society ... a bleak,
extreme hypothesis on a potential future, sublimely presented'.
Somewhere beneath the jargon, there was a subplot about Bowie
himself. No matter how cheerful he was on the piste or
sunbathing in Mustique, depression kept threatening to break

out. There were times he seemed to be a man at war, the victim of a battle always going on within himself. Bowie was a romantic who believed in the redemptive power of love, but he was also a cynic, having been constantly disappointed by those he loved. At its worst, *Outside* wallowed in his own misery. The Cassandra-like storyline steered a course between dogged realism and high-flown expressionism: self-indulgent, and well suited to its time.

Lyrically, the album followed in the joyless scenario of *Diamond Dogs*. Musically, it pillaged the faux-jazz stylings of *Aladdin Sane*, a record Mike Garson described at the time as 'dissonant, rebellious, atonal, and very outside'. Bowie fashioned his tunes from punk, metal and art-rock; forever quoting, distorting, ironizing; turning it all to the melodic and sublime. He achieved musical transcendence by coating the morbid narrative conceit with enviably simple harmonies. Stripped of the bizarre background noises and tape loops, *Outside* was a dazzling album in need of an editor.

This was some of Bowie's most devastating music. The first single, 'The Heart's Filthy Lesson', blueprinted a sound that was 'dissonant, rebellious, atonal' yet with a hypnotic groove (as well as making good use of the piano part from 'Raw Power'). 'I Have Not Been to Oxford Town' may well have been the album's best cut, granting the dazed listener an infectiously catchy chorus. Elsewhere, *Outside* slyly pirated a number of Bowie's past glories. 'The Motel' began life as a ballad, then slowly revved into *Ziggy*-style crooning. 'Thru' These Architects Eyes' was a worthy follow-up to 'Golden Years'. 'Strangers When We Meet' (originally from *The Buddha of Suburbia*) came close to recapturing some of *Low*'s grandeur.

Highbrow critics, who snubbed Bowie for years, now rewarded him the moment he buckled toward seriousness. To them, *Outside* was a rite of passage, a metamorphosis of two seventies' survivors into *fin de siècle* artistes. Others, like Marcus Berkmann, saw Bowie and Eno as 'the grand old pseuds of British art-rock ... Overweening bilge is [their] very lifeblood. Without it they cannot function at all.' Certainly Bowie was not a man who thanked fans for his success, nor made life easy for his audience. Most of his new songs veered from self-accusation to a lurid catalogue of blood, guts, masochistic body-artists, hypodermics and mutilation. Among the facets of Bowie's character was a lifelong desire to shock, though his desire to be *seen* as shocking was probably even stronger. The same thing was at work in his manner as in his matter: he rarely wrote a lyric without feeling a pathological need to deconstruct it. Thus, after 'randomizing' in Bowie's computer, a verse emerged as 'Big deal Salaam/Be real deranged Salaam/Before we reel/I'm deranged' while even in the relatively lucid 'Strangers When We Meet' he felt obliged to render 'Head over heels' as 'Heels head over'. The words made no sense when trying to conjure a mood along with the music. They may have made more sense when scattering a few stray clues about Bowie himself. Since the narrator's year of birth was given as 1947, and the diary referred to both Berlin and New York, certain autobiographical procedures were clearly at work. Nathan Adler may not stand with Ziggy as one of Bowie's classic blinds, but it was a clever enough projection. For nearly thirty years he had written about madness, in part to preserve his own sanity. Bowie's 'art detective' was also his alter ego, the latest in a long series of therapeutic self-examinations, and a neat piece of transference.

Outside was generally well received, ecstatically so by those who saw it as a creative rebirth – Bowie at his volatile best. Memories were stirred in an effort to put the album in its context: 'I've never heard him sing better' (*Today*); 'his best in fifteen years' (The *Spectator*); 'his best for a decade' (*Arena*). To *Forum*, Bowie's mannered voice was the glue that held together the sprawling concept. He salvaged even the least accessible songs with his warbling vibrato. There was particular praise for the way he injected *Outside*'s densest material with infectious tunes. On the other hand, it was precisely for its lack of pop-melodic discipline that others slated the album: the two most frequently heard criticisms were that it was too long, and that it made no sense. It was a substantial hit.

Early in 1995 Bowie had said he felt no inclination ever to tour again. Six months later he was on the road. In late August, as the spate of cover stories hit the newsstands and the 'Heart's Filthy Lesson' video débuted in the MTV 'Buzz Bin', a seven-piece band featuring Garson, Alomar and Reeves Gabrels – but not the Sales brothers – rehearsed in New York. Virgin had lobbied for Bowie to support *Outside* and he agreed to play 'no more than six' dates alongside Nine Inch Nails, whose raw-edged *The Downward Spiral* updated *Low* for the mid-nineties. By late summer there were growing signs that the original itinerary was far too timid. Advance orders for *Outside* made it Bowie's fastest-selling album since *Tonight*. The reasonable assumption was that this was a major work by an artist for whom money would rain down at the box office. Early in September Bowie agreed to extend the tour, eventually settling on twenty-five concerts spread over five weeks. Opening night in Hartford was praised as 'dramatically imposing'. It was a portent of the next month.

The twin drama of a new solo album and American tour, Bowie's first in two and five years respectively, rebounded back to Europe. Radio 1 broadcast an hour-long interview taped by Mark Radcliffe in New York. French and German TV both aired documentaries. In Berlin 2,000 fans attended a preview of *Outside* at the David Bowie Club, which opened and closed its doors forever on the same night. Meanwhile, tickets were moving at a brisk pace in the major American cities – a modest $28.50 for the cheapest seats, most of which sold within hours. Around Seattle the black-market price was $150 or its equivalent in NFL football tickets.

Bowie's appearance was startling. Tall, elegant, showy – he took to wearing shiny black leather trousers and vests – he was voluptuously abandoned to recreating the bloody plot of *Outside*. He tuned up for the tour with a performance on *The Late Show With David Letterman*. At the words 'true rock visionary' Bowie strolled on, nodded to the crowd and dropped into his trademark crouch, knees ajar, tapping the floor with his polished dancer's shoes. The disparity showed between his dark clothes and the puce-red stage. After a perfunctory 'Heart's Filthy Lesson' – shorn of the studio effects, no more than a slab of bristling art-noise – he gave a wolflike leer and bared his teeth. Bowie looked seriously ill. The lights picked out the disconcerting colours of his eyes. For the first time in twenty years, he was physically reproaching his audience, turning his back even before the song ended. His grim 'Thanks' was an irony.

The tour took the same frequently antisocial line. On some nights concert-goers were confronted by a bare set, on others by a backdrop of torn drapes, a few chairs, a kitchen table and stark, operating-theatre lighting. Scrolls were rolled down to indicate changes of mood. The whole thing rested on Bowie's frozen presence, broken only by his ambling to the wings or slumping at the table. Meanwhile, the group ran through the cuts from *Outside* in panicky haste. Instead of the album's narrative theme, there was a jerky song-cycle that felt simply like a rehearsal. In some of the slower numbers, Garson's eccentric piano broke in as if from another world. It was fortunate Bowie was in good voice. Night after night, from Hartford to Los Angeles, he was *singing* – hitting the notes, finding new ones, phrasing carefully and often veering into mimickry. For years Bowie had been slipping in and out of cod cockney or a Southern black mammy drawl. On live versions of 'Bus Stop', from the first Tin Machine album, he let fly with a country twang. Now Bowie strafed fans in a nasally Brooklyn accent, rolling the word 'Warhol' around his mouth and reminding those with long memories of his vocal excursions on *Hunky Dory*. Bowie's live collaboration with Nine Inch Nails was the high-point of the show: his voice broke into rasping climaxes as no fewer than three drummers pounded away on 'Scary Monsters'. As the lights flared red and *Outside* welled up at bone-bruising volume, it was obvious that this was no happy-go-lucky *Let's Dance*-type revue. Not only was Bowie back; he was edgy again.

There was a reunion with Iggy Pop in New York. Bowie was heckled during a pair of acoustic numbers at a benefit in the Manhattan Ballroom. Now resolved to show his audience nothing but a calm, remote professional, he did not let this ruffle him. For most of the east-coast dates the crowds seized the new songs from *Outside* and applauded Bowie's tough-minded approach; elsewhere there were cries for Ziggy. He was on TV again in late October, warbling 'Strangers When We Meet' on *The Tonight Show* and then stooping to an interview with the host Jay Leno. Leno surprised him. Instead of the usual dip in the PR jacuzzi, he subjected his guest to a long and eventually comic harangue about Tony Mascia, the self-styled 'wheelman' and, for years, a hulking presence outside Bowie's hotel rooms. The next day the tour ended in Los Angeles. There was a party in a hastily converted warehouse. The guests, including Brad Pitt and Johnny

Rotten, drank champagne and acted out, with varying degrees of success, the designated theme of paganism. Bowie's double-breasted blue suit and silver crucifix made a striking contrast with the more vivid costumes. He was suffering from insomnia and the sense of jadedness this left him with the next day. A guest who spoke to him remembers the extraordinary grooves in Bowie's cheeks and the milk-pale tint of his skin. 'He really did have a ghostly quality. You noticed that, especially in a room full of Beautiful People dressed up like vampires.' Sedated for the long flight, Bowie then returned to London.

A fortnight later he was on stage at Wembley Arena. A sold-out house and a VIP box including Bill Wyman and Bob Geldof saw Morrissey meet the fate of all support acts. Just as Bowie was now well into his middle age, so were many of his home fans. Men in suits were to be seen in the Arena's hospitality suites, treating their business clients to a drink while, on the far side of a glass partition, the poet of misery went through his downbeat act. Bowie came on to mild applause. There were puzzled glances when he used the words 'Gothic' and 'fractal' in one of the few pauses between songs. Then Bowie screamed a hoarse 'Boys Keep Swinging', still perversely rooted to the spot. He kept up the same pose in 'The Man Who Sold the World'. 'My Death' followed. Bowie had always been a master of stage movement, but now, evidently, he was just going through the motions. To *The Times*, 'It looked like being an uphill slog ... as Bowie appeared from behind the drumkit, singing and walking as if in his sleep.' For the *NME* critic, saddled with the stifling desire to write flip, it was a night of low expectations:

El Bowza's latest lurch away from reality is entitled 'Out-side', which is kind of about 'outsiders' and involves all these strange neo-futuristic characters running around El Bow-za's head and it's a sort of concept album blah blah bollocks blah blah ...

It was a more convivial scene backstage. Ken Pitt, now seventy-three, mingled benignly with Glen Matlock, the once and future Sex Pistols bassist. A teenage girl burst through a door, screaming at Bowie, 'Forget me! You and all you queens!' before being led away. There was a party later in a West End hotel. Bowie's social façade did not always suppress his nature. At one point a woman sidled up to him. 'I made these for you, Davy,' she said, handing him a pair of red plastic clogs. With the woman out of earshot, Bowie turned to a friend: 'That's the kind of shit I have to put up with.'

On the whole, the eleven-city tour followed down routine lines: well-heeled fans, seamless PR and security, celebrity scenesters in the dressing room (including Tony Blair) and the general air of an army on the move. Bowie turned down the offer of a Lear jet and travelled between venues by private bus. There was drama in Aberdeen when Morrissey was taken to hospital suffering from 'exhaustion' – denying rumours of a backstage rift – and replaced by Alanis Morissette and Echobelly. In Birmingham the package was billed as 'the greatest music party in the world', and nearly lived up to the hype. There were fulsome reviews in Dublin and Belfast.

Meeting Tony Blair again begged the question of where Bowie stood politically. For years he had crashed from one pose to another: Buddhist, hippie, Nazi romantic, minority activist and, most recently, champion of Somalian rights. He had certain fixed views. Bowie saw America's hand behind most international crises; he condemned South Africa as a police state; he was a good European. For at least a decade he had moved one pound's width to the left with every pound he made. In 1989 the transformation of this private conservative into a public radical began with the violent harangue of *Tin Machine*. By the time he remarried, Bowie was unrecognizable from the man who said, 'I'd love to enter politics. I will one day. I'd adore to be Prime Minister. And, yes, I believe very strongly in fascism.' Nor did he see it as a betrayal of his Jones past to take a stand on social issues. He claimed the 'unprecedented neglect' of Britain's minorities was not part of his family's experience. 'My father spent his whole life helping people.' Terry Burns' harrowing end had also 'softened David overnight', according to a friend.

As Bowie became repulsed by 'white trash picking up Nazi flags', his old political flirtations were turned on their heads. Twenty years earlier, he had had 'this morbid obsession with the so-called mysticism of the Third Reich ... The stories about the SS coming over to England in search of the Holy Grail ... that aspect really appealed to me.' Now Bowie went on a 'wonderful Arthurian trip' around the sites of Glastonbury and Tintagel with his wife. Iman's influence was forcefully at work on matters of race. As a teenager, and later in the seventies, Bowie had followed the British post-war tradition with which he grew up. He giggled and made 'coon' jokes in private. Now Bowie told *NME*, 'There's this denial in America that slavery ever took place. I think there should be a confrontation and there should be a museum of Black America.' He grew alarmed, startled and then bitterly angry as he learnt more about conditions in his wife's homeland. Both Bowie and Iman spoke out against Somalia's leader, Osman Atto, and called for renewed foreign intervention in the country's affairs. Eventually the couple received death threats because of their stance. Sources told the *Evening Standard* that the Bowies' New York home had 'elaborate security precautions' including personal bodyguards, a reinforced front door and a hot-line to the police.

At the heart of Bowie's politics there was not a philosophy but a temperament. Essentially, it was the same as his art theory: he wanted bustle, activity, trial and error, anything that would convey a sense of shock and novelty. He was not a natural Tory. Although still in nominal tax exile in 1994, Bowie began to speak warmly of the Labour Party. With his customary quickness, he was among the first celebrities to embrace Tony Blair. Blair responded by telling Chris Evans that he thought Iman was 'stunningly beautiful'. The Labour leader met both Bowies at a *Q* awards lunch in London in November 1995. Later that week he was backstage at Wembley. 'I really like Tony a lot,' said Bowie, above disruptive bursts of Alomar's guitar. 'It seemed ironic that a major priority on both our minds was the challenge of how to present new ideas.' The admiration was mutual. Blair, who played in a band called Ugly Rumour in his youth, informed the *Daily Mirror*, 'I have always liked David. It was great to meet him.' Both men were amused by Blair's radio remark about Iman. They also shared a sense of concern about the fate of racial minorities. Bowie's outspoken views, which he fancied to have weight and importance and which actually had some influence, were not only shaped by his inquisitive mind, but, for all his worldliness, strangely English and banal. He wanted, for example, 'a better education for all kids'. Despite having released an album loosely based on the murder and dismemberment of a teenage girl, he was 'sick about violence'. Adolescents he pitied because they seemed not to enjoy themselves: 'They go through a *grimly* day-to-day existence. There doesn't seem to be the bounce that I remember when I was the same age.' The role in which Bowie fancied himself was that of the moralist, and the real need in British life, he told a friend, was 'the fight for good against evil'. His chief contribution to the struggle had been his lyrics, and until the early nineties nothing had been further from his mind than to translate his moral code into action. But after meeting Blair, Bowie began to quietly endorse Labour policies. By 1996 his political convictions were evolving from Swiss isolationism to an international social-democratic point of view. He spoke of returning to live in Britain under a Blair government. Rumours that Bowie had hopes of an honour, if not a role in the Heritage Department, were obviously wide of the mark. 'Total crap,' he told a reporter. But, whether in his songs or his periodic tirades in the media, he intended to 'explore the dynamic'; to be a thorn in the side of complacency. There was no higher office, Bowie felt, than exercising the moral imagination necessary to kick-start the next forward jump of history. 'My antennae have always been up for contradiction, for two or three bits of information converging at one central point and another thing coming out of that.'

Bowie was back on the road early in 1996. He turned forty-nine that January. As he approached his half-century he was still hopscotching across Europe, a twitchy figure in black, making good on his promise, despite the screams, not to resuscitate his greatest hits. Bowie still moved, when he moved at all, with agility; he was perversely fit. He never thought of himself as old, and preferred people twenty or thirty years younger for social friends. He found them anarchic and funny, a musician recalls, in contrast to his contemporaries, especially those rapt with what Bowie once called the Big Easy: money. 'If he sat next to someone at dinner who talked about stocks, it bored him shitless.' If Bowie was in revolt against the fans who shouted out for Ziggy, it wasn't from the standpoint of someone maturing unduly. 'I can remember clearly what my sensibility was like at 19,' he told *Us*. Bowie in his late forties was a man on the move, cruising in the slipstream of a revival, still raging against materialism and convention. The boyish demand for excitement was as strong as ever.

Bowie himself was by no means unaware of the nostalgic pull of his name. A hero-worshipper in his youth, he could spontaneously see things from the perspective of the typical fan who wanted to hear 'Changes' and 'Let's Dance'. To them, Bowie was less a *fin de siècle* artiste than a cherished character in a long-running soap. As the seventies party revved up with a second wave of new groups and unlikely reunions of old ones, the industry rushed to toast a true original. On 17 January Bowie was inducted into the Rock and Roll Hall of Fame and Museum in Cleveland. The city had 'special – sentimental' memories for him, as the scene of his first-ever American show. Bowie's sentimentality did not, however, extend to his either visiting the museum or attending the gala dinner in New York. Instead David Byrne accepted on his friend's behalf. After listening to a long list of reasons why Bowie was being honoured ('He was kind of a shrink and a priest, a sex object and a prophet of doom . . . He was kind of the welcome to the brave new world') an impatient Madonna broke in: 'Excuse me, it's also about how fucking gorgeous he is.' There were laughs and shrieks of agreement.

Bowie's induction was only part of a full-blown resurgence. There were no Grammy nominations for *Outside*. But elsewhere the critics and music chiefs were lavish with praise. When European rock writers came to decide on their favourite son, there were not many entries, and the verdict was quickly reached. Bowie was named artist of the year in both Holland and Germany. On 19 February he flew in to London after giving a concert in France. At a chaotic Brit Awards ceremony at Earls Court, Bowie and Eno were jointly recognized for their production of *Outside*. (There was an overnight surge in the album's sales worldwide.) Then Tony Blair took the stage to give Bowie the prestigious Lifetime Achievement Award. This was the third time the two had met in three months. A mark of Bowie's regard for Blair was the removal of the cigarette he otherwise kept in his mouth when not actually singing. The new friends clapped each other and linked arms for the cameras. Even the Brits could have produced no odder scene than this, the leader of the Opposition and the leering *enfant terrible* with the S-E-X earring and the Katharine Hamnett high-heel shoes. Bowie then sang 'Hallo Spaceboy', hastily collected his award, and left. He was in Paris by midnight.

The whole evening, particularly Bowie's decision to fly in and out for a few hours, was proof of his mutual respect for Blair; that and his arrival on the same list of approved entertainers as the likes of Elton and Phil Collins. There was an irresistible footnote to it. First Noel Gallagher accepted his own Brit from Michael Hutchence by telling him, 'Has-beens shouldn't present awards to going-to-bes.' (The off-camera remarks were more colourful.) Later in the show Michael Jackson launched into 'Earth Song', dressed as an incandescent Christ-figure with his arms out-stretched in a crucifixion pose. At that Pulp's Jarvis Cocker jumped on stage and attempted to seize a mike in order to make a statement about the 'sick shite' of the performance. He was dragged off and arrested for allegedly assaulting three children dancing with Jackson. By the time Cocker was released, and the charges dropped, Bowie was again heading to Lausanne. A woman who visited was surprised to see a man who had almost all he could expect from life still pitting himself against the world. Bowie was caustic about being 'shoved in a museum'. He dreaded becoming an institution. 'Saint Dave', he said, was not on his wish-list of appellations. Bowie told her that if he lost his 'edge' he would also lose his 'gift', and he was not prepared to make the trade. He repeated this theme again and again. Bowie chafed under the fear that he was being recognized as much for having endured as for the unrivalled quality of his recent work. He fretted out the months until his next album.

By 1996 the chief struggle of Bowie's life had faded but not vanished. It was a battle with a kind of self-consciousness that could be agonizing under certain conditions. Bowie's nerve showed itself in the fact that he chose to meet the struggle on two fronts: in his approach to his music, and in the private side of his fame. On his albums, especially *Outside*, he sought the ground of the agitator, the restless cynic single-mindedly concerned with a stark, brutal pseudo-realism. Elsewhere he sought to be a responsible husband and role model.

Outside of his music, and outside interviews, he often gave off an easy charm. He was not self-conscious in the company of the friends he made at the Gay Hussar. He was not married to misery. To those who met him in galleries and restaurants, who visited Lausanne and Mustique, Bowie was a convivial host, whose haircut and glasses befitted a man fast approaching, in professional terms, real antiquity. Memories of his own youthful looks perhaps made the contrast more poignant, but Bowie had aged. His skin was drawn. A sparse new beard was flecked with grey. With his haggard face, fossil eyes and shock of cropped blonde hair, Bowie still closely resembled a film star. In fact he took after one particular star, a favourite of his, and one whom Ronson could never see without noting the happy likeness – Vanessa Redgrave. Bowie did make small concessions to middle-aged vanity. He finally had his teeth straightened. For a visit to the Saatchi Gallery, both he and Iman dyed their hair red. He lost the 'mouldy, wilted' smell much noted in the seventies, though he could still give off a powerful reek of stale smoke. After kicking Gitanes he went through sixty to seventy Marlboro Lights a day, burning them right down to the knuckle, with another lit before the first was out. He tried frequently to quit. He read Allen Carr's *The Easy Way to Stop Smoking*. He listened to several tapes. When those failed he went to a hypnotist. The only thing he got from the couch, he later admitted, was a 'sore arse'.

He divided his time between his five homes and a boat in the Mediterranean. Twenty years earlier, Bowie had said his ambiguous goodbyes to an England he thought he would never see again, however often he went back in his lyrics, his hallucinations and his dreams. The trip there in May 1976 had been something of a nightmare return. Bowie took voluntary exile in Switzerland and Berlin. In his two decades' wandering around Europe and America he came over as endlessly curious but essentially home-loving, surprisingly sentimental and an Englishman to the marrow. Early in 1996 he began to speak about returning to Britain, enthused, apparently, by the prospect of a Labour government. He said as much to Tony Blair. Bowie also informed the *Sunday Times* that he found the fine artists working in London of more interest than the New York set. He confessed to an 'aesthetic nostalgia' for the Tate Gallery and English country churches. He enjoyed cricket.

Bowie wanted nothing to do with most religion. Paradoxically, he spoke of God playing 'an important role in my life . . . Every day I put my life in His hands.' It was difficult, for some Christians, not to see a double standard. Bowie failed to grasp the full contradiction because he defined the difference between their beliefs and his own in terms of honesty, wisdom and bitter experience. In his view, true faith came from a 'long, stubborn, painful trek' such as his mid-seventies odyssey. 'What was it somebody said?' Bowie asked *Esquire*. 'A wonderful analogy: "Religion is for people who believe in hell; spirituality is for people who've been there." That for me makes a lot of sense.'

Like a large number of artists, Bowie had become enthralled with the twenty-first century. He referred to the millennium as 'a symbolic sacrificial rite' and, bafflingly, 'the next Berlin Wall'. This, too – surviving to 2000 – he saw as a spiritual experience. All flowed from suffering; knowledge, as he once sang, came with death's release. For Bowie, illumination went with pain, and the oppressed found truth through hardship. Behind this train of thought lay a broad streak of self-pity, but it directed his compassion – in his lyrics and his film roles – on to those he saw as fellow outsiders. Bowie's identification with life's misfits stopped just short of paranoia. 'The last thing, the very last thing I could ever think of myself as being would be as a victim of anything or anybody.'

It was not always so. Until his late thirties Bowie's elastic music and brittle personality set new standards in risking chaos and succumbing to it. With Live Aid and marriage, sobriety and *Modern Painters*, he was no longer in hand-to-hand combat with the world. Bowie still laid down the law in the studio, but elsewhere he was a more genial, even satirically normal Englishman. Where once there was gay sex, now there were books. Instead of drugs, he was hooked on the Internet. Bowie's online postings became almost as much part of his mammoth PR machine as his live interviews. He used his computer to generate both his wallpaper prints and his lyrics. Bowie got up between five and six in the morning, an hour at which he had once been known to be starting dinner, in order to write. He still worked on his eternal screenplay. He painted, of course, and sculpted. For all the implied pain of the outsider's role he repeatedly championed, Bowie was a happy enough artist, someone who loved to test things, to try out new techniques and, above all, to make a virtue of a fresh creative stance. Formal ingenuity and the pride of a professional finish: these, he said, were 'bound up in who I am'.

Who was he? To John Landis, 'one of the first rock and rollers to consciously approach music as art'. For a director of the Warwick Group, Bowie's limousine firm, 'a down-to-earth guy from Brixton'. Bowie himself relished the ambiguity, and stressed his reformed, fun-loving character. 'I'm the most childlike person I know.' He admitted to craving the idea of 'one more time developing a character' but added, 'For the time being I'm *quite* happy being me.' As well as liking himself, Bowie became increasingly partial to the outside world. Until his second marriage, he rarely allowed himself the luxury of a normal social life. Thereafter his relationships became of supreme importance to Bowie. But his reserved charm fell shy of intimacy. Since the friendships were chiefly pursued over dinner tables or mixing boards, rather than in circumstances of prolonged physical and emotional closeness, they still resembled those struck up, casually and temporarily, with fellow passengers on the cruises he loved.

As his music made its latest bolt for the outside, Bowie himself became more accessible. He had been famously cool, and now he became afraid of his coldness. Of all the failings he saw within himself, this was the one he was most determined to conquer. He never did. Bowie certainly became warmer than in the past. It became common to see him, alone or with Iman, on the streets of Soho or walking in the door of the Gore Hotel. Bowie sanctioned a new fan club and communicated with subscribers on Prodigy. There was truth in his claim to 'enjoy going out for dinner and seeing silly movies and shoot[ing] the breeze for all hours'. But twenty-five years in the limelight had given Bowie reason to protect what space was left. Under the skin there was a part of him, inside and out of reach, as tightly coiled as ever. He still refused to give most information. Bowie's management company, his publicist and his London solicitors acted as a rampart against intrusions. He met unwelcome questions, even by friends, with a well-honed display of truculence or sarcasm. A close colleague calls him 'the man in the irony mask'. When an old friend sat down with Bowie in 1992 he came away impressed at how 'tight' he still was. It was the same with John Cambridge and the other Haddon Hall graduates: there was mutual affection, but always with the hint that 'David was in a different dimension'. Another man thought that Bowie, in his magpie fashion, 'basically used people for ideas'. Thus a guitar riff or a scrap of lyric would work its way on to an album years after he heard it. Bowie still clung to Lindsay Kemp's great maxim: 'You nick a touch of this, you nick a touch of that. Then you do it better simply by using Scotch tape, sawdust and a little imagination. And everyone will do it for you because they love you.'

The press still put him among the top half-dozen stars. They attributed this, in Robert Sandall's words, to his being rock's 'most visible link with the world of high(er) art ... For those old enough to have given up buying Bowie's records, as well as for those too young to remember the 1970s hits, he squares a circle.' There was endless fascination, and gossip, about his marriage. By 1996 the Style pages had discovered Bowie's four homes and his yacht (he sold his Mustique property, for £2 million, to a businessman named Felix Dennis); the arts titles were talking up his solo exhibitions, while the gossip columns embroidered his film projects like *Basquiat*. There was talk that he would publish a novel. Early that summer the *Mirror* reported that Bowie had been approached by the Austrian Cultural Chamber to take part in the opera *Der Freischütz*, an offer the singer said 'thrilled' him. Another paper spoke of his adapting the Ziggy saga for the stage. A third had him in cahoots with the composer Robert Wilson. For the first time in years there was a worldwide upsurge in Bowie stories.

His new work proved to be among his richest and his most involved. A lifelong chaos buff, Bowie continued to give elliptical interviews promoting *Outside*. 'I have always been drawn to the Bill Burroughs of this world, who produce a vocabulary that is not necessarily a personal one, but something that is made up of ciphers and signifiers which are regurgitated, reformed and re-accumulated ... I didn't impose a concept, it grew in parallel with the improvisations, the thematic device or idea, however non-linear it might be.' In spring 1996 he released 'Hallo Spaceboy' as the album's third single, radically remixed by Neil Tennant and backed with live versions of 'Moonage Daydream' and 'Under Pressure'. He still had a grand plan to record a series of concept albums until 2000. Bowie called this a 'Swiftian idea, using [the music] as a signpost to what is happening now'. According to this reading, his whole life-work had been a long drumroll leading to the *Outside* cycle. Bowie's resumption of his solo career convinced some that his devotion to Tin Machine had been no more than tactical. In July 1996 he headlined at the Phoenix Festival in England, where he resurrected both the Ziggy copper-shock haircut and a rabble-rousing 'Heroes'. Later that summer he was hard at work in Montreux, songwriting, rehearsing and poring through his back catalogue in search of ideas. *Diamond Dogs* was obviously the model of models. Orwell's theories fascinated Bowie. Another apocalyptical title, *Scary Monsters*, was also promising, but the *Ziggy* and *Let's Dance* eras proved sterile.

Bowie's greatest inspiration, and his first 'pure' success was the oracular and dynamic Berlin trilogy. Nowhere was he able to turn his world view into more productive means of hitting his goals. The equation was an old one: an unhappy life made for great art. Bowie spoke of his inquisitive, restless mind as a positive asset. 'I've always questioned dictums. I've always questioned what I've been told are the things I've got to live by or that this is the way things are done.' There was an almost demented wilfulness that linked 'Space Oddity' to 'Young Americans', *Hunky Dory* to 'Heroes'. Bowie was not just broad-based, he was staggeringly eclectic, a master of paradox and incongruity. As early as the mid sixties, he got used to the idea of subtly varying his voice with each new record. The vocal changeling had ever since become a central theme in Bowie's wardrobe. His susceptibility to Anthony Newley, Dylan, Bolan, Iggy, the Velvet Underground and latterly James Brown and Barry White was bound up with his stock self-image as a copyist, somehow able to blend ingredients and come up with a formula. This survived a critical backlash which would have made a lesser man blush. Despite the early flops, *Low*, the mid-eighties slump and the farcical about-turn on Tin Machine, the beguiling self-confidence endured. 'I deserve to be here,' Bowie told *Life*. 'I'm a very good writer. I've gone my own way and been very stubborn. That's the only reason for my existence ... That's always given me the friction I've needed.'

Bowie, in short, made a virtue of his defects. At its worst, his vision degenerated into fortune-cookie quips like 'It's not a simple world any more' and the wisdom that life has more than two sides. Sometimes the myth of Bowie as the thinking man's rocker needed careful burnishing. At his best, he was capable of ingratiating flashes of real insight. 'What I'm really confident doing is juxtaposing contradictory pieces of information together. I do that very successfully, because I've always been fascinated by it ... That's why I like Damien [Hirst] so much, because his visual contradictions, I find, set off reverberations ... within me, as a viewer. *That's* successful.'

Insecurity had been the theme that ran through Bowie's early work. He had seen himself as a freak: as a bisexual loner, from an incurably 'odd' family. 'I want to be a Superman. I guess I realized very early that man isn't a very clever mechanism. I wanted to make myself better ... I always thought that I should change all the time.' Bowie had used the words to promote *Station to Station*. Twenty years later they could have served just as well for *Outside*. Bowie never quite lost the taint of self-consciousness. With success, though, came confidence. Full of nervy brooding one moment, macho swagger the next, he faithfully reflected the upward track of his career. In the seventies Bowie had reeled through Europe as he dabbled in junior-school Nazism; in the nineties he made a friend of Tony Blair. Then he practised exotic sexual combinations. Now his only *ménage à trois* was a casual golf threesome with Iggy and Alice Cooper. This was happiness. Was this what he wanted?

Some critics thought that, with his wallpaper and then his portrayal of Warhol, Bowie had finally reverted to type – a clever parodist who was all surface. To them, *Basquiat* was a watershed. The childhood dislocation had become an inherited adult strength. After the obligatory decadence of his youth, Bowie in his thirties and forties lurched toward the mainstream. He followed the precedent of his own father. John Jones had collected a legacy on his twenty-first birthday, opened a club called Boop-

A-Doop and eventually become a gambler and alcoholic. After a life-saving operation he swore off drink and took a job he held for thirty-four years. Seen in this genetic context, there were numerous performances in Bowie's career but virtually no acting. 'I've always felt like a vehicle for something else,' he said, 'but then I've never really sorted out what that was.' What was most impressive was not so much Bowie's outrageousness as the brilliant inventiveness with which he filled the vacuum of his life.

At midnight on 7 January 1947 the clock above Lambeth Town Hall struck thirteen. The flukish event, caused by arctic cold, seemed to herald the birth a few hours later at Stansfield Road. Even as a boy, David Jones appeared, at best, only half in touch with reality, torn between warring parents, and a fugitive in his own fantasy world. Bowie's destiny to be always the outsider was thus blazed early on. It was greatly to his credit that he converted the youthful flaws into mature virtues. The result has been some of the most dramatic music to emerge from rock's first half-century, and some of the most thrilling images. 'There's a feeling that we are here for another purpose,' Bowie once said. 'And in me it's very strong.' It might have been the motto of a whole generation of seekers who badly wanted a god, and found him.

11
EARTHLING

David Bowie turned fifty on 8 January 1997.

In the weeks before and after, the music and trade press became a giant band playing just one tune, with the heavyweight papers singing along. Bowie was profiled in *The Times*, the *Independent*, the *Daily Mail* and the *Evening Standard*; MTV and VH-1 aired specials; ITV and the BBC weighed in with their own po-faced tributes. To no one's surprise, Bowie himself spent the day recording and rehearsing in New York. He had, he said, 'big work to do'. Bowie was, just as he once predicted, 'refus[ing] to opt out of life' on his half-century. His birthday marked a new high point for our acceptance of the idea that pop stars get older.

The next night, Bowie celebrated quietly with a few friends and 20,000 fans at a sold-out show at Madison Square Garden. Apart from an appearance by Lou Reed, the star-studded event looked like modern rock on parade: Billy Corgan of Smashing Pumpkins, Foo Fighters, Sonic Youth, Frank Black and the Cure's Robert Smith – all were trotted out to sing duets with Bowie on old songs as well as on cuts from his new album, *Earthling*. The two-hour show was as stagey as the Sound + Vision tour, if not quite on the scale of the Glass Spider farce. A forty-by-sixty-foot backdrop projected giant black-and-white video images of Bowie dancing with a beautiful blonde; tiny puppets with moving faces scowled and twitched around the set; giant rubber eyeballs rained down from the rafters; unmanned cameras zoomed in and out like baby robots; and even the roadies wore masks. The headliner came on in a lacy frock coat, again with his Ziggy cockade, his heavy mascara and milk-pale face making him look uneasily like Archie Rice of *The Entertainer*.

After generous slices from *Earthling* and *Outside*, Bowie looted the archives for a melodramatic 'Scary Monsters' and a perverse 'Fashion'. The 300-pound Frank Black, crooning the chorus dressed in jeans and a polyester short-sleeve shirt, duly provided the night's most surreal moment. Robert Smith joined in for an acoustic duet on 'Quicksand', a dark gem from *Hunky Dory*. The high spot of the performance came when Bowie traded verses with Lou Reed on 'Queen Bitch' and the Velvet Underground classics 'Waiting For The Man' and 'White Light, White Heat'. The band – for whom the bald look was apparently in – then struck up the power chords of 'Moonage Daydream'. Bowie sang along with Billy Corgan (also bald) on 'All the Young Dudes' and a bluesy 'Jean Genie', held up a cake, assured the crowd 'I don't know where I'm going from here, but I promise I won't bore you' and slid into 'Space Oddity' (a song he once promised never to play again), gamely standing alone with an acoustic guitar while pictures of his young self flickered across the screen.

Seeing Bowie in concert, one critic perceptively said, is like receiving an unmarked parcel in the post: you never know what you're going to get. Depending on his mood, Bowie might perform heart-rending folk-rock or ear-grating punk. He might even deliver a bomb. The arrangements and staging at Madison Square Garden caught Bowie midway between the pure pop of *Ziggy Stardust* and Tin Machine's grungy deconstruction. Most of the cuts from *Earthling* and *Outside* were played fast and furious, with no discernible melody. Bowie gave embarrassing, cockney readings of old chestnuts like 'Under Pressure'. 'All the Young Dudes', on the other hand, could have been lifted straight from the original LP. Reeves Gabrels brought off a note-by-note replay of the hoary 'Moonage Daydream'. 'The Man Who Sold the World' was genuinely haunting.

Backstage in New York, you could measure the status of the stars by the trail of handlers behind them. Frank Black came alone. Lou Reed arrived with a gang of four. And Bowie himself was all but swamped by his entourage. As well as Schwab, there were two bodyguards, a make-up girl and a hairdresser, sundry Isolar staffers and a full-scale TV crew. Iman brought up the rear. *Le tout* New York was at the party afterwards: fringe artists like Ron Athey mingled with supermodels and refugees from

Warhol's Factory. Originally, Bowie says, the concert's organizers had wanted to fluff up the show with 'safe choices' – family favourites like Mick Jagger and Tina Turner. He vetoed the idea. Nor, with the exception of Reed, were any of Bowie's long-time cronies invited to the party.

It says something for Bowie at fifty that, despite not having a real hit for years, his birthday found him firmly in the 'cool' column. There were lavish tributes from the likes of Sonic Youth and Smashing Pumpkins. 'It's the chameleon aspect,' says Dave Grohl. 'He can do anything well. He can look like a bum, he can look like a model.' Bowie's fashion makeovers continued to dazzle after thirty years. Early in 1997 he stamped his own brand of ironic cool on the Britpop phenomenon by appearing in a full-length Union Jack coat, suitably burnt, ripped, dipped in wax and dunked in tea and coffee so as to resemble a vintage war flag. Bowie's live-wire hair once again brought its mimics, if not in their previous numbers. That February he stopped the show merely by appearing at the Council of Fashion Designers gala in New York. Exploding flashbulbs almost rivalled Bowie's gleaming new smile. Even in a room full of beautiful people, he was the best, the most chic, the ones the roped-off fans cheered loudest. Bowie used what style gurus call 'the treatment' to deal with the press. One writer describes it as 'supplication, exuberance, scorn, glamour, the hint of decadence . . . Bowie moved in close, his face a scant millimetre from you, his weird eyes widening and narrowing, his voice a fey Brixton put-on.' Mimicry, humour and sheer presence made 'the treatment' an almost hypnotic experience and left the target stunned and helpless.

On those terms, Bowie was quite happy to be candid. He told one interviewer that his own favourite albums were *Station to Station* and *Low*. *Tonight* and *Never Let Me Down* were 'just awful . . . I shouldn't have gone into the studio and done them when I felt as I did. I'd totally fallen out of love with music.' Elsewhere, Bowie presented himself as a quinquagenarian of satirically normal habits, yet a man on the move, never happy to do the same thing twice. The only addictions he owned up to were cigarettes and coffee. He neither drank nor took drugs, and rarely watched television. 'I think the last ten years have been the most rewarding period of my life,' he told the writer Pete Clark. 'I like where I'm at and I feel very comfortable. I like being who I am, who I'm with, and what I'm doing ... I seem to have found an equilibrium in my life ... enjoy every day as it comes ... feel really quite enervated, er, no, energized, by waking up in the morning.' He viewed his career with an expected modesty, but also certainty that it was a great one. A friend of Bowie's says that 'nothing gives him a bigger kick than being "relevant". He was delirious when Nirvana covered one of his songs.' Later in 1997, Philip Glass released his *'Heroes' Symphony*, a homage Bowie found 'fab'.

Perversely, Bowie refuses to go gently into his golden years. 'I'm not a nostalgic person,' he told *Entertainment Weekly*. When Madonna inducted him into the Rock and Roll Hall of Fame, Bowie failed to show up (though he enjoyed watching a video of the night). Despite record company pleas for 'another *Let's Dance*', his 1997 album took a dense, hyperkinetic music – variously known as jungle or drum-and-bass – as its source. Judging from his excitement, *Earthling*, Bowie's twentieth solo studio outing, could easily have been his first.

The new, affable Bowie dabbled in some seriously pretentious hype. *Earthling*, he explained, was a 'sonic photograph' of his band. 'The arrangements and the structure of it was between [Gabrels] and myself, but the group's individual responses to it were cosmic.' At one point during the recording of *Outside*, Bowie had told Mike Garson, 'You're in a South African band. Play all the notes you weren't allowed to.' For *Earthling*, the pianist's brief was blunter, 'More anguish. Less virtuosity.' The results were songs like 'Seven Years in Tibet,' where Bowie wanted to 'conjure up a young Tibetan monk who had just been shot, his last experiences in the snow as the Chinese helicopters fly over'. 'Looking For Satellites', in which Bowie repeatedly chanted the words 'Shampoo/TV/Boyzone', was 'as near to a spiritual song as I've ever written: it's measuring the distance between the crucifixion and flying saucers'.

Bowie's eyes were still skyward, but the good news was that his feet were planted firmly on the dance-floor.

Earthling's starting point was a clubland hybrid of recycled reggae, disco technology and implausibly fast beats. The first cut, 'Little Wonder', was Bowie's most exciting and upbeat single since 'Blue Jean'. Freed from *Outside*'s spoken interludes and messy avant-garde flourishes, the music was free, fluid and full of hooks. From 'Little Wonder', Bowie upped the voltage on tracks like 'Battle For Britain' and 'I'm Afraid of Americans', both fuelled by turbo-charged guitars, bass-driven grooves and Bowie's own baritone croon. As usual, his stabs at rapping – heard here on 'Law' – were an embarrassment of cockney affect, but for the most part vocals and lyrics both meshed with the melodies.

Borrowing came easily to Bowie (who in turn was the most plagiarized artist of his day). *Earthling* nodded to all the usual suspects. The piano break from 'Battle For Britain' was lifted from John Cage; the bass on 'Little Wonder' from the O'Jays; and the voice on 'Looking For Satellites' mimicked Bowie's old hero and collaborator John Lennon. Elsewhere, he neatly cannibalized his own past, notably the 'plastic soul' noodlings of *Young Americans* that filled out half the tracks. Bowie's discreet pirating, a feature of his music for thirty years, would have been less forgivable without the fresh creative spark of his best work.

Earthling was a critical and popular hit, making the charts on both sides of the Atlantic. Optimistic fans praised it as the back-to-form album awaited annually since *Scary Monsters*. At worst, there was grudging respect for Bowie's enduring relish for new musical ventures. *Earthling* may not have broken new ground, but it was a creditable enough bid for relevance by any fifty-year-old.

As well as an album and concert, the birthday brought a spate of recycled quotes and present-day pronouncements on everything from Aids to UFOs. Bowie hit his sixth decade feeling 'strong and enthusiastic and fiery', he told the *Daily Mirror*. 'If people hadn't been asking me how I felt being fifty, it wouldn't have really occurred to me that I was.' He held forth on drugs. 'It's a dangerous thing to say, but I'm glad I took cocaine. I crawled out of it all and got away with it.' During the mid-seventies, he confirmed, 'I was so out of my gourd that it was nigh-on impossible for me to function in any rational way.' And on reincarnation: 'I believe in a continuation, a kind of a dream-state, but without the dreams.' Elsewhere, Bowie qualified his fixation on space travel. 'I think there's quite enough "otherness" here on our planet,' he told Pete Clark. 'There's enough looniness and weird conflicts on earth for me.'

Among the terrestrial strife in Bowie's own life was, of course, his ex-wife. Angela, now 47, still had a radically different take on the fall-out from their divorce. She spoke bitterly of losing touch with their son. According to her reading, sometime in the early eighties 'David chose to wipe me completely from his life. When Joe stayed with me all the arrangements were made through Joe's nanny, who travelled with him. When David phoned he wouldn't speak to me.' In 1984 contact between mother and son stopped altogether. 'It's as though I never existed,' says Angela. 'When we split up [Bowie] was seriously depressed and taking a lot of medication. He was paranoid he would go the same way as his half-brother . . . One reason I was happy to let David have custody was that I knew Joe would give him a reason for living. But instead of thanking me, they pretend I don't exist.' Bowie retaliated in a rare public outburst on his past. 'Living with Angie was like living with a blowtorch. She has as much insight into the human condition as a walnut and a self-interest that would make Narcissus green with envy.'

The truth of their marriage was different.

From the very start, Angela had developed a maternal as well as a wifely relationship with the lonely misfit with little experience of a mother's care and a settled home, and he soon became chronically dependent on her. Bowie, who wanted and needed a sacrificial wife and surrogate mother, left most of his day-to-day arrangements to Angela, as he later would to Schwab. Their way of addressing each other, in public and in private, reinforced the nursery theme. He was 'Nama-Nama'; she, 'ma' or 'mother'. And Bowie sometimes affectionately greeted her as Peg. His letters to her were solicitous and oddly puerile, as if he were writing to an older relative rather than a partner. Even later in the seventies he tenderly wrote to her as 'dearest' and 'darling', dedicated songs and albums to her, and defined her as charming, precious, fun, delightful and 'my life'. Though well aware of her limitations, Bowie was deeply attached to his wife.

By 1997, Angela belonged to an earlier, lost world, the era of 'Space Oddity' and Haddon Hall and sexual adventuring. It was doubtless as a human relic of his past that she most irked him. Others could vouch for Bowie's habit of erasing not just events, but whole lives which no longer fitted into reality as he saw it.

There was something admirable in the way he reinvented himself musically, never basking in past glories at the expense of a fresh creative pose. But Bowie went too far in rewriting his personal history. It was true that many of his friends had found Angela overbearing and could offer her little more than polite respect. Her own ambitions as a singer-actress were, bluntly, a joke. Yet Ronson and the other musicians agreed about Angela's solicitude toward Bowie. Though self-centred, she was always concerned for his success. She gave serious thought to his career, was at least part of the vision behind Ziggy, had a touching faith in his genius and never stood a breath of criticism against him. Her later behaviour did little for her image, and Bowie was right to carp that 'I haven't seen her for years, but she won't let go. She's either suing me or writing about my private life.' But that was to deny past affinities.

One friend's plausible theory for the wrangling is that both Bowie and Angela 'feel the classic guilt of irresponsible brats who spent their lives putting their own enjoyment first . . . Years later, self-justification sets in.' Whatever their defects as parents, their son (still Bowie's only child) shows perverse signs of normality. Joe celebrated his twenty-sixth birthday in May 1997. He is in the third year of a Ph.D. course at Vanderbilt University, Nashville, and has plans to become a philosophy professor. According to most estimates, Joe is well-grounded, shy, with a quiet pride in his father's fame but no wish to follow it. He expressed surprise when a newspaper contacted him with news of his mother. 'I can understand why she's looking for me, but it's a lot to take in,' he said. 'Please give me a chance to think about this. It all happened a long time ago and I need time to consider it.'

According to Angela, part of the reason she waived custody of her son in the first place was that 'I knew David had far more money, and could give Joe a better life'. Even that was to underestimate the global Bowie industry, with its song royalties, residuals, licensing, merchandising and performance fees, all consolidated by his new business manager, Bill Zysblat of the New York-based Rascoff Zysblat Organization – a man whose mission was to 'make David *Croesus* rich'.

Over the years, Bowie had never been afraid to try something new. His fashion metamorphoses and stage personae had converted into visual and musical thrills, from the Kon-rads to *Earthling*. Now, in 1997, he became the first major artist to turn himself into a share issue, payable over ten years at 7.9 per cent.

The asset-backed bond – the financial instrument that put an estimated $55 million in Bowie's well-tailored pocket – had long since helped banks turn home-loan payments and credit-card receivables into chunks of cash. But, until Zysblat, no one had dared think the annual income from hits like 'Rebel Rebel' or 'Let's Dance' might appeal to grey-suited executives looking for stable investments. Yet again, Bowie had left his rivals at the gate.

The key to the deal lay in Bowie's vast back catalogue, the subject of bitter wrangling with Defries and the other ex-managers, whose retention now became the single biggest coup of his career. In market jargon, the 'reliability of the revenue stream to pay off bondholders' enabled Bowie to get a triple-A credit rating – normally reserved for well-run governments or corporations like Microsoft – and a favourable interest rate. Investors each took a stake in an average two million album sales a year, as well as the revenue from 250 songs turned into sheet music, commercials and background for elevators, supermarkets and voice mail. Bowie himself signed a new $30 million contract with EMI for future work not covered by the bonds.

When Bowie decided to go with the deal Zysblat was 'terrified ... and it isn't over yet,' he says. 'The backers still have to be paid off.' But his fear that the privately-offered securities might not attract enough interest eased when *Fortune* reported the financial equivalent of what Zysblat calls 'a line round the block'. In short order, other stars like Elton John, George Michael and Sting were said to be set to follow Bowie's lead. Even Mick Jagger, one of the most financially savvy men in rock, was 'bowled over'. It just went to show, says Jagger, 'Dave's job is to be number one', rarely boring, never static, yet always bankable.

It was hardly surprising Bowie would seek financial security. As he said, he 'hadn't always been in the dosh', and there were some notably low moments even as *Diamond Dogs* and *Young Americans* scored hits on both sides of the Atlantic. Even so, Bowie went too far when he claimed 'I went to Switzerland in the first place because I was extremely broke – that's broke as in *no money whatsoever.* I wasn't very good at business, so I had very bad dealings with it.' In fact, in terms of assets and property, he was a millionaire before his thirtieth birthday. His grumble that 'Mick has all the bread – I'm skint' may have been true, relatively speaking, in 1977; but Bowie effortlessly upstaged his old friend twenty years later. With the bond issue he was no longer a cult, or a crusade, but a full-blown investment opportunity, and Wall Street took to him just as the Bowie boys had in London and the provinces.

In the past, ex-friends and colleagues had called Bowie a clever plagiarist, someone whose art lay in 'using Scotch tape, sawdust and a little imagination'. He told *Ray Gun* in April 1997, 'There's nothing purist about what I do. I'm a hybridist ... Much of what I do is a collection of odds and sods that life throws at me ... I tend to stitch up this kind of rag-bag of sounds.' As usual, Bowie was focused on the job at hand, stretching his interests beyond the scope of any other pop star. In 1997 alone, he created a piece called 'Where Do They Come From? Where Do They Go?' for the renowned Biennale di Firenze art show; wrote snatches of film score; reviewed art in *The Times*; contributed an essay to a book called *Ray Gun Out of Control*, in which he interviewed Yoko Ono and Roy Lichtenstein; and collaborated with Brian Eno and the composer Robert Wilson on an avant-garde work for the Salzburg Festival. Between times, Bowie wrote and recorded a new album, patronized bands like Photek, Prodigy and Underworld, toured the world, visited a Zen monastery in Japan, kept up his painting and sculpture and seemingly appeared at every hip gathering in London and New York. This was not the lifestyle of a man pondering retirement.

Bowie had long channeled some of his mental problems into a brooding self-containment Angela once called his 'ice man' persona. He was certainly shy. But Bowie's need to perform and make drama of his life outweighed his fears. The way he went back on the road, time and again, reflected his lifelong addiction to the stage. John Jones had once taken his son to watch a pantomime at a Brixton theatre. But instead of sitting in his seat in the stalls, David got 'right out among the ropes and scene-shifters' backstage, where a floor manager intercepted him. 'He was standing behind the curtain,' says the man, now in his eighties, who found him there. 'He wanted to see how it was done.'

Bowie relished the limelight. However coy offstage – as late as 1983, one journalist called him 'a ringer for the dormouse in *Alice in Wonderland*' – he came alive the very second he trod the boards. He was a master of self-promotion and loved the attention he won so quickly in 1971–2. Yet at the same time, he was not as confident about his future as the explosion of Bowiemania made out. For all the swagger of his live act, he remained unsure about his career, dreading, as late as 1975, that 'I'd end up on the shitheap'. It was presumably this fear that led Bowie to speak of having 'no money whatsoever' at the time he moved to Switzerland. Financial comfort, in the form of a $20 million advance, came in 1983 with his EMI deal and the multi-platinum triumph of *Let's Dance*. From then on, Bowie was never seriously in danger of going broke. That he continued to tour and record on a timetable that would have jaded a teenager said much for his nagging insecurity. It may have plagued Bowie to never think he was well-off, and that 'the shitheap' loomed, just as it had for so many of his maternal family; but it also made for great art, and a relentless work schedule that accelerated with each pound he earned.

In May 1997 Bowie began yet another world tour, the most lavish in enterprise and scale in a decade. As well as the familiar round of auditoriums and football stadia, he hit the European festival circuit that summer. Bowie said it 'brought out the sense of competition in me' to headline in rotation with other bands, with most of whom he musically wiped the floor. He even began playing at raves, blurting out six or seven of his hits to audiences younger – one wag put it – than many of his stage clothes.

Somehow, Bowie also found time for the studio. He had always written and recorded at wild speed, rushing over the rhythm tracks and then belting his vocals in a single take. Later in 1997 he was due to release another album (his third in less than two years), at a time when other rock dinosaurs like the Rolling Stones had taken creative semi-retirement. Bowie at fifty was still on the go, wrong-footing the critics, outshining all the competition. However small or large the stakes – whether hamming it up at a rave or headlining at Wembley – the premium was on novelty, shock, drama, all anchored by his steely professionalism. His longevity was still not all that odd compared to old-timers like Iggy Pop or Lou Reed. What set him apart from others, however, was his flair or genius for 'putting a song across'. When Bowie conjured a new look, redesigned his set or came up with props like the rubber eyeballs, it was always just a bit more, a little larger than others were ready to do.

Bowie was, and is, one of the most fickle rock stars working the stage. But without him one can hardly imagine the last thirty years; in part because, without Ziggy and all the rest, we can hardly imagine ourselves. Bowie is the story of his times.

Appendix 1
CHRONOLOGY

8 January 1947 David Robert Jones born at 40 Stansfield Road, London SW9.

November 1951 Enters Stockwell Infants School.

1955 The Joneses move to suburbia. The small cottage at 4 Plaistow Grove, Bromley, will be David's address for the next twelve years.

June 1955 Enrols at Burnt Ash Junior School in Bromley.

1958 After failing the eleven-plus and thus missing the local grammar school, he enters Bromley Tech that autumn.

1959–60 Discovers the world of free-form jazz, Italian bistros and Beat 'happenings' in frequent excursions to London with his half-brother Terry.

1962 David's friend George Underwood punches him in the face in a fight over a girl. His left pupil is permanently damaged. In later years, fans will seize on his different-coloured eyes as proof that their hero is an alien.

July 1963   David leaves school, announcing his inten-
                         tion to be a pop star. He takes a job as office-
                         boy in an advertising agency.

3 November 1963 David is present as a UK tour comprising
                         Little Richard, the Everly Brothers, Bo Didd-
                         ley and the Rolling Stones winds itself up at
                         the Hammersmith Odeon.

5 June 1964   The King Bees, with David Jones on vocals,
                         release their first single, 'Liza Jane'. Despite
                         being played on *Juke Box Jury*, it vanishes
                         without trace.

1965–6   As a member of the Manish Boys and then of
                         the Lower Third, David releases a number of
                         singles. They all flop.

Late 1965   In a search for a truism about 'cutting
                         through the lies', and to avoid confusion
                         with another young singer-actor, he chan-
                         ges his name to David Bowie.

17 April 1966   Ken Pitt, an experienced showbusiness fig-
                         ure and ex-manager of Manfred Mann,
                         watches Bowie's performance at the Mar-
                         quee Club. He is transfixed.

9 March 1967   Bowie, soon to be managed by Pitt, joins the
                         Performing Rights Society. He lists a total of
                         29 self-written songs, including a novelty
                         item called 'The Laughing Gnome', his next
                         single.

June 1967   Bowie's first, eponymous album is released
                         on Deram. It, too, flops.

1967   Bowie develops an interest in both Bud-
                         dhism and mime, and appears in a revue

with Lindsay Kemp called *Pierrot in Tur-quoise*.

1968   Bowie plays a cameo in BBC TV's *The Pistol Shot*, where he meets Hermione Farthingale. They become lovers. Bowie will also appear in *The Virgin Soldiers* and a commercial for 'LUV' ice cream.

2 February 1969 Bowie records his first-ever hit, 'Space Odd-ity', initially as part of a promotional film called *Love You Till Tuesday*.

9 April 1969   Bowie, at the Speakeasy Club to see King Crimson, is introduced to a 19-year-old exotic named Angela Barnett. The couple marry within a year.

20 June 1969   Bowie signs a new contract with Mercury Records, represented in Britain by Philips, for an advance of £1,250.

November 1969 'Space Oddity' peaks at number 5 on the UK chart. Bowie's second album (confusingly, also called *David Bowie* in the UK) is released.

20 March 1970 Bowie marries Angela at Bromley Register Office. In a not unrelated move, he defects from Pitt and joins forces with a 26-year-old litigation clerk called Tony Defries. The two men will enjoy spectacular success until they, too, fall out.

April 1971   *The Man Who Sold the World* is released.
                   The album comes with a sleeve showing Bowie lying on a chaise-longue, listlessly staring at the camera and dropping playing cards on the floor. He is wearing a dress.

30 May 1971   Duncan Zowie Haywood Jones is born in
                       Bromley. The baby is named not after his
                       father, but as an Anglicized version of the
                       Greek word 'zoë', or life. Bowie himself adds
                       'Duncan Haywood' in case, as a grown-up,
                       'Zowie object[ed] to his kooky name'. He
                       does.
                           Armed with an acetate of *Hunky Dory*,
                       Defries signs Bowie to a deal with RCA.

December 1971   The new album is released. Though not an
                       immediate hit, *Hunky Dory* is later dis-
                       covered as a classic.

January 1972   Bowie admits 'I'm gay' in *Melody Maker*.

February 1972   Bowie unleashes a new persona, the 'Wool-
                       worth's meets Nijinsky' icon Ziggy Stardust,
                       on an extensive UK tour. The *Ziggy* album
                       follows in June.

September–   The tour transfers to America. By the time
December 1972   he reaches the Beverly Hills Hilton on 16
                       October, Bowie has a travelling crew of 46.
                       His performance at Carnegie Hall wins rave
                       reviews from Andy Warhol, Truman Capote
                       and the arts correspondent of the *New York
                       Times*. Elsewhere, notices are mixed.

17 January 1973   Bowie tells a giggling Russell Harty, 'My
                       next role will be a person called Aladdin
                       Sane.' A week later he returns to New York
                       for a second, shorter tour.

April 1973   Over 100,000 British fans place advance
                       orders for *Aladdin Sane*, making it the fastest-
                       selling album since the Beatles. It goes
                       straight to number one.

3 July 1973   On the final night of a triumphant UK tour, Bowie tells a shocked Hammersmith Odeon, 'This is the last show we'll ever do.' He takes the boat-train to Paris to record an oldies album, *Pin-Ups*. It, too, hits number one.

April 1974   Bowie washes the red dye out of his hair, releases the futuristic album *Diamond Dogs*, and moves to America. A cost-to-coast tour, unprecedented in scale and theatricality, opens in Montreal on 14 June.

29 January 1975   A cocaine addict and virtually broke, Bowie appears at RCA's office in New York to ask for a cash advance. The next morning he starts proceedings against Defries. His new album, *Young Americans*, is a worldwide hit.

Later in 1975, Bowie moves to Los Angeles, begins dabbling in black magic and takes a lurch to the extreme, neo-Nazi right. Somehow during this lost year he also stars in his first feature film, *The Man Who Fell to Earth*, and records a new album.

January 1976   *Station To Station* released; yet another hit.

2 February 1976   Bowie begins a world tour that will end in Paris in May. He moves into homes in Switzerland and Berlin.

2 May 1976   Bowie appears at Victoria Station, standing in a black Mercedes convertible, apparently giving his fans a Nazi salute. *New Musical Express* runs its photograph over four columns, under the headline 'Heil and Farewell'.

8 January 1977   In Berlin, Bowie turns thirty. A week later, his album *Low* is released; it, too, is eventually discovered as a classic. Before the end of the year, Bowie follows it with the sublime *'Heroes'*.

29 March 1978   Bowie begins a year-long world tour.

May 1979   *Lodger* released.

31 December 1979   Bowie sees out the decade by appearing on TV simultaneously in three countries. Six days later he performs on *Saturday Night Live*, dressed first in a solid body suit and then in a Chinese airline hostess's uniform.

8 February 1980   The Bowies' divorce settlement gives Angela alimony of $750,000 spread over ten years; a gagging order prevents her from speaking about her marriage for the same period. Joe Bowie lives with his father.

1980   During the year, Bowie tops the charts with 'Ashes to Ashes' and his album *Scary Monsters*. He also appears in a Japanese saki commercial and stars in *The Elephant Man* on Broadway.

27 January 1983   EMI pay Bowie a reported $20 million advance against five albums. The first, *Let's Dance*, is a massive international hit. It yields three top-thirty singles and sells six million copies. EMI describe it as their fastest-selling release since *Sergeant Pepper*.

18 May 1983   Bowie begins the Serious Moonlight tour. The 98 concerts, spread over seven months, are seen by $2\frac{1}{2}$ million fans. On the last night, 8 December, Bowie sings 'Imagine' as a tribute to John Lennon.

16 January 1985   Bowie's half-brother, Terry Burns, walks onto the line at Coulsdon South station, lies down with his neck on the rail and waits for the London express. He is killed instantly by the passing train. He was 47.

June 1985   A group of musicians in Abbey Road Studios, London, receive a letter saying they have been hired to work with 'Mr X'. They collaborate on Bowie's 'Absolute Beginners' session and later back him in front of 70,000 fans and a TV audience of a billion.

13 July 1985   Live Aid.

1986   Bowie is seen in two feature films, *Absolute Beginners* and *Labyrinth*. London Weekend Television pays him the ultimate compliment of including him on *Spitting Image*. In June, Bowie performs 'Dancing in the Street' at the Prince's Trust concert in London.

April 1987   Bowie emerges from Swiss exile with a new album, *Never Let Me Down*, and a lavish and bizarre tour. Both are widely panned – and later disowned by Bowie.

1988   After contemplating retirement, Bowie meets the guitarist Reeves Gabrels and recruits the rhythm section Tony and Hunt Sales. The result is Tin Machine, a middle-aged garage band that brings down howls of rage from the fans, but that Bowie loves.

February 1990   Bowie launches the Sound + Vision tour, playing his greatest hits for the last time. The musical arrangements are adequate. The special effects are immaculate. Bowie plays to full houses everywhere.

14 October 1990   Bowie meets Iman Abdul Majid, a 34-year-old Somalian-born actress-model, in Los Angeles. She will become his second wife.

20 April 1992   Bowie performs at the Freddie Mercury tribute, the Concert for Life, at Wembley. After the anthemic 'Heroes', he drops to his knees and recites the Lord's Prayer.

24 April 1992   Bowie and Iman marry in Lausanne. A church service takes place later in the spring in Florence.

April 1993   *Black Tie White Noise* released. A British number one, it slumps in the US after Bowie's record label folds.

March 1995   Bowie designs his own wallpaper collection, produced in tandem with Laura Ashley. A month later he holds his first solo art exhibition at the Kate Chertavian Gallery.

September 1995   *Outside* released. Bowie supports the album on tour in the US and Europe.

January 1996   Bowie is inducted into the Rock and Roll Hall of Fame. A month later he wins the prestigious Lifetime Achievement Award at the Brits in London.

18 July 1996   Headlines at the three-day Phoenix Festival at Stratford-upon-Avon.

Summer 1996   Promising a *fin de siècle* album cycle, Bowie returns to the studio.

8 January 1997   Bowie turns fifty in New York. The next night, he celebrates with a few friends and 20,000 fans at Madison Square Garden.

January 1997   *Earthling* released.

February 1997   Bowie becomes the first major artist to turn
                     himself into a share issue, payable over ten
                     years at 7.9 per cent. Bondholders each take
                     a stake in an average 2 million worldwide
                     album sales a year, as well as revenue from
                     spin-offs. Bowie himself pockets an esti-
                     mated $55 million from the deal, and signs
                     a new $30 million contract with EMI.

May 1997   Bowie again tours the world.

August 1997   Back to the studio.

Appendix 2
BIBLIOGRAPHY

Bowie, Angela, with Patrick Carr, *Backstage Passes* (Orion, 1993)

Carr, Roy, and Charles Shaar Murray, *David Bowie: An Illustrated Record* (Eel Pie Publishing, 1981)

Claire, Vivian, *David Bowie* (Putnam, 1977)

Currie, David, *David Bowie: Glass Idol* (Omnibus, 1987)

Edwards, Henry, and Tony Zanetta, *Stardust: The David Bowie Story* (McGraw-Hill, 1986)

Gillman, Peter, and Leni Gillman, *Alias David Bowie* (Hodder & Stoughton, 1986)

Hopkins, Jerry, *Bowie* (Macmillan, 1985)

Miles, *Bowie In His Own Words* (Omnibus, 1980)

O'Regan, Denis, and Chet Flippo, *David Bowie's Serious Moonlight* (Doubleday, 1984)

Pitt, Kenneth, *The Pitt Report* (Omnibus, 1983)

Rock, Mick, *Ziggy Stardust* (St Martin's Press, 1984)

Thompson, Dave, *David Bowie: Moonage Daydream* (Plexus, 1987)

Thomson, Elizabeth, and David Gutman (eds.), *The Bowie Companion* (Sidgwick & Jackson, 1993)

Tremlett, George, *The David Bowie Story* (Futura, 1974)

SOURCES AND CHAPTER NOTES

The author has a great many debts. The following notes indicate the principal sources used in writing each chapter of the book. Formal interviews (many conducted by phone) and on-the-record conversations are listed by name. Inevitably, friends requested that their comments remain anonymous and therefore no acknowledgement appears of the enormous help, encouragement and kindness I received from a number of quarters. Where David Bowie himself is quoted, the sources are his own published interviews or the memory of those who spoke to him. In this context, I should particularly mention *Bowie In His Own Words* by Miles.

Chapter 1

A full account of Bowie's 'farewell' performance is available in books, magazines and on film. For all its rough edges, *Ziggy Stardust, The Motion Picture*, produced and directed by D.A. Pennebaker, is the best documentary. Personal comment was supplied by John Hutchinson and Julie Anne Paull. For the account of Bowie in late 1995, newspaper reports and my own memory are entirely responsible.

Chapter 2

Various accounts of Bowie's childhood have been previously published, most notably in Peter and Leni Gillman's *Alias David*

Bowie; I acknowledge, as any Bowie author should, the deep debt owed to the Gillmans' research. My own travels took me to Stansfield Road, Brixton, to Bromley and to Beckenham. I am grateful to Burnt Ash Primary School and its headmaster Nigel Green, as well as to the staff of the General Register Office and of the British Newspaper Library, Colindale. Other sources included: Edith Baldry, Lesley Buzan, Chris Farlowe, Trevor Gaar, John Hutchinson, Edith Kohl, the late Steve Marriott, Phil May, Eric Myren, Tony Newman, Peter Perchard, Kenneth Pitt, Len Price, Don Short, Eric Smith and Dick Taylor. Dudley Chapman's quote first appeared in *Alias David Bowie*. Other published sources included *The Bowie Companion*, edited by Elizabeth Thomson and David Gutman, and Henry Edwards and Tony Zanetta's *Stardust: The David Bowie Story*. Robert Sandall's description of Bowie first appeared in the *Sunday Times*.

Chapter 3

Sources for the period 1967–70 included: John Cambridge, Keith Christmas, Terry Cox, Jeff Griffin, John Hutchinson, Tom Keylock, Mary Parr, John Peel, Kenneth Pitt and the late Mick Ronson. I owe a special debt to Ken Pitt's *The Pitt Report*, as well as to his *Love You Till Tuesday*, the thirty-minute film shot in 1969 and released on video fifteen years later. Thanks also to the two former friends of Bowie, both of whom prefer anonymity, who steered me through Beckenham. Returns for MainMan and Tony Defries' other financial holdings can be seen at Companies House. The previously referred-to published sources, as well as Angela Bowie's *Backstage Passes* and Dave Thompson's *David Bowie: Moonage Daydream*, were all consulted. I should also thank the tenants of the former Trident Studio.

Chapter 4

Bowie's life as Ziggy Stardust is vividly recalled by Peter and Leni Gillman's *Alias David Bowie*. It is a pleasure to again acknowledge this book, as well as Angela Bowie's *Backstage Passes*, Roy Carr and Charles Shaar Murray's *David Bowie: An Illustrated Record*, Henry Edwards and Tony Zanetta's *Stardust: The David Bowie*

Story, Jerry Hopkins' *Bowie*, David Thompson's *David Bowie: Moonage Daydream* and Elizabeth Thomson and David Gutman's *The Bowie Companion*. I should particularly mention interviews with and profiles of Bowie previously published in *Creem*, *Melody Maker*, *New Musical Express*, *Newsweek*, *Rolling Stone* and *Sounds*.

Primary sources included: Edith Cearns, Brian James, Phil May, Alan Motz, Julie Anne Paull, Andy Peebles, Kenneth Pitt, the late Mick Ronson, Dick Taylor and the late Andy Warhol.

Further research was carried out in the General Register Office and Companies House, London, and the Paramount Theatre, Seattle.

'Life On Mars?' (Bowie) © EMI Music Publishing/Tintoretto Music/Chrysalis Songs

'Time' (Bowie) © EMI Music Publishing/Tintoretto Music/Chrysalis Songs

Chapter 5

Comment on Bowie in mid career was provided by Keith Christmas, Alan Motz, Alan Parker, Kenneth Pitt, Ryan Ward and Willie Weeks. Herbie Flowers returned my phone call. Special thanks to Noel Chelberg for his technical help.

The previously named published sources were all consulted; I should especially mention Bowie's meeting with William Burroughs, as reported in *Rolling Stone*; and the account of Bowie onstage in 1976 by Patrick MacDonald in the *Seattle Times*.

Details on Bowie's finances were again supplied by Companies House.

The Man Who Fell to Earth (British Lion Films, 1976) is probably as good a view of Bowie at the time as any; *Cracked Actor*, Alan Yentob's BBC documentary, is also valuable.

Among the sources in Berlin, I should single out Fred and Cindy Smith; without them I could never have retraced Bowie's steps through the city.

'Life On Mars?' (Bowie) © EMI Music Publishing/Tintoretto Music/Chrysalis Songs

'Word On a Wing' (Bowie) © Jones Music America/Chrysalis Songs/Fleur Music

Chapter 6

Major sources in Berlin included Milan and Nicole Drdoš, Gitta Fuchs, Uwe Herz, Stuart Mackenzie and Fred and Cindy Smith. Maggie Riepl of the *Berliner Morgenpost* and Horst Wendt at Deutschland Radio were invaluable, as was a source at the Brücke Museum.

Angela Bowie's decline and eventual disappearance from Bowie's life is charted with painful honesty, in her own books *Free Spirit* and *Backstage Passes*, as well as in back issues of the *Daily* and *Sunday Mirror*.

Other sources included the *Daily Mail*, *Melody Maker*, *New Musical Express*, *Rolling Stone*, the *Sun* and *The Times*. William Burroughs, his secretary James Grauerholz and Phil May all kindly made themselves available.

I watched *Just a Gigolo*.

'Sound and Vision' (Bowie) © EMI Music Publishing/Tintoretto Music/Chrysalis Songs

'China Girl' (Bowie, Iggy Pop) © Tintoretto Music/EMI Music Publishing/James Osterberg Music

'It's No Game (Part 2)' (Bowie) © Tintoretto Music/Fleur Music

'Blackout' (Bowie) © Bewlay Bros Music/Fleur Music

Chapter 7

Sources included Terry Cox, John Hutchinson, Andy Peebles, Kenneth Pitt, Tim Rice, Keith Richards and Willie Weeks. Among the books consulted were *Backstage Passes*, *Stardust: The David Bowie Story*, *Alias David Bowie*, *David Bowie: Moonage Daydream* and *The Bowie Companion*; among newspapers and periodicals, the *Daily Express*, the *Daily Mirror*, *Newsweek*, the *New York Times*, the *Observer*, the *People*, *Rolling Stone*, *Time* and *The Times*.

The Hunger (MGM, 1983) and *Merry Christmas, Mr Lawrence* (Palace Pictures, 1983) can both be found on video.

William Burroughs and Jane Spalding kindly provided their comments on Bowie in *The Elephant Man*.

Documentary material was again obtained from Companies House and the Performing Rights Society.

'Ashes to Ashes' (Bowie) © Tintoretto Music/Fleur Music
'Cat People (Putting Out Fire)' (Bowie, Giorgio Moroder) ©
MCA Music Publishing/Music Corporation of America
'Modern Love' (Bowie) © Jones Music America

Chapter 8

Invaluable help was given by three musicians who backed Bowie
at Live Aid: Kevin Armstrong, Neil Conti and Matthew Seligman.
Other material was supplied by Edith Cearns, Jeff Griffin, Nick
Miles, Andy Peebles and Roy Wendt. I should acknowledge the
David Bowie Information Service.

Published sources included the previously named books, most
notably *Alias David Bowie* and David Currie's *David Bowie: Glass
Idol*. *Architectural Digest*, *Bild*, the *Guardian* and *Rolling Stone* were
all consulted.

Into the Night, *Absolute Beginners* and *The Last Temptation* of
Christ are all available on video.

Chapter 9

Various accounts of Bowie's marriage to Iman have been
previously published, most obviously in *Hello!*. The *New York
Times* also provided details.

Personal comment was supplied by Kevin Armstrong, John
Cambridge, Jeff Griffin, Phil May and Bela Molnar. Periodicals
included the *Christian Science Monitor*, the *Independent*, *Melody
Maker*, *New Musical Express*, *Rolling Stone* and *Us*. Gus Dudgeon's
quote first appeared in *The Bowie Companion*.

The Linguini Incident and *The Concert For Life* (the Freddie
Mercury tribute) are both on video.

'Video Crime' (Bowie, Tony Sales, Hunt Sales) © Jones Music
America/RZO Music Ltd

'Tin Machine' (Bowie, Tony Sales, Hunt Sales, Reeves Gabrels)
© Jones Music America/RZO Music Ltd

'Space Oddity' (Bowie) © Essex Music International

'Young Americans' (Bowie) © EMI Music Publishing/
Tintoretto Music/Chrysalis Music

Chapter 10

Final comment and summaries were provided by Kevin Armstrong, John Cambridge, Keith Christmas, Neil Conti, Margaret Cooper and Kenneth Pitt. Published sources included *The Bowie Companion*, the *Daily Mirror* and *Life*; the long interview with Bowie by David Sinclair appeared in *Rolling Stone*.

Bowie's return to the charts and the stage in late 1995 was heralded by an explosion of media coverage: *Dazed and Confused*, *Esquire*, *New Musical Express*, the *Sunday Times*, *Time Out*, *The Times* and *Vox* were among titles consulted.

Thanks to Joan Lambert, Terry Lambert and Emma Lynch for their cuttings.

Bowie's *Black Tie White Noise*, directed by David Mallet, is available on video.

INDEX

Lovecraft, H.P., 78
Lovin' Spoonful, 26
Low, 51, 85, 149, 150, 154, 165–8,
172, 174, 176, 181, 182, 187,
188, 191, 193, 194, 201, 203,
208, 215, 229, 243, 296, 323,
325, 337, 342
The Lower Third, 34–7, 51
Lucas, George, 252, 254
Lulu, 114, 169, 201, 208
Lust For Life, 172, 233
Lynn, Viv, 179

McCann, Elizabeth, 205
McCartney, Paul, 26, 249, 250
MacInnes, Colin, 238
Mack, John, 300
McKenzie, Scott, 26
Mackenzie, Stuart, 184–5, 199–200
MacKinnon, Angus, 158
McLaren, Malcolm, 101, 171
Madonna, 271, 282, 286, 331, 343
Magician's Workshop, Falmouth, 49
MainMan, 68, 83–4, 94–5, 98, 103,
112, 113, 121, 122, 123, 127–8,
134–6, 218
Major, Tom, 52
Mallet, David, 186, 192, 204, 220,
223, 224, 230, 246, 304, 308
Malta, 55–6
Man of Words, Man of Music, 59–60
The Man Who Fell to Earth, 147–9,
153, 155, 165, 167, 179, 205,
213, 253
The Man Who Sold the World, 72, 73,
74–5, 84, 115, 156, 186, 203,
229
Mann, Manfred, 38
Manish Boys, 30–1, 32–3, 69
Margaret, Princess, 260, 312
Marquee Club, London, 31, 33, 35,
38, 62
Marriott, Steve, 34, 58
Martha and the Vandellas, 242
Marvin, Hank, 31
Marziale, Rev. Mario, 301

Mascia, Tony, 180, 194, 212, 267,
287, 326
Maslin, Harry, 146
Matlock, Glen, 327
May, Phil, 33–4, 115, 192, 216–17,
293
Mayersberg, Paul, 213–14
Melody Maker, 33, 36, 44, 62, 86, 89,
92, 100, 104, 112, 126, 136–7,
140, 153, 157, 166, 168, 176,
182, 184, 207, 211, 222, 253,
276, 284, 292–3
Mendelssohn, John, 73
Mercury, Freddie, 181, 209, 210,
215, 219, 298
Mercury Records, 51, 52, 55, 64, 68,
73, 79, 81
Merrick, John, 205, 206
Merry Christmas, Mr Lawrence, 186,
213–14, 215, 311, 316
MGM, 213
Michelmore, Cliff, 31
Mico, Ted, 253
Midler, Bette, 110, 133
Miles, Nick, 261
Mimran, David, 309
Mingus, Charlie, 26, 104
Minnelli, Liza, 110, 299
Minnie Bell Music, 83
Miracle Jack, 216
Modern Painters, 165, 295, 313, 334
Molnar, Belar, 295
The Monkees, 36, 294
Monroe, Marilyn, 135
Montez, Chris, 238
Moody Blues, 35
Morgan Studios, Willesden, 50
Morissette, Alanis, 328
Moroder, Giorgio, 212
Morrissey, Paul, 81, 172, 307, 309,
327, 328
Mosley, Oswald, 10
Most, Mickie, 72
Mott the Hoople, 93–4, 113
Motta, Stanley, 25
Motz, Alan, 116, 124

Other titles of interest

**THE ACCIDENTAL
EVOLUTION OF
ROCK'N'ROLL
A Misguided Tour Through
Popular Music**
Chuck Eddy
430 pp., 101 illus.
80741-6 $15.95

**ARE YOU EXPERIENCED?
The Inside Story of the
Jimi Hendrix Experience**
Noel Redding and Carol Appleby
258 pp., 28 photos
80681-9 $14.95

**AWOPBOPALOOBOP
ALOPBAMBOOM
The Golden Age of Rock**
Nik Cohn
New preface by the author
272 pp., 12 pp. of photos
80709-2 $13.95

**BLACKBIRD
The Life and Times of
Paul McCartney
Updated Edition**
Geoffrey Giuliano
488 pp., 128 photos
80781-5 $15.95

**BOB DYLAN: THE EARLY
YEARS
A Retrospective**
Edited by Craig McGregor
New preface by Nat Hentoff
424 pp., 15 illus.
80416-6 $13.95

THE BOWIE COMPANION
Edited by Elizabeth Thomson and
David Gutman
304 pp., 15 illus.
80707-6 $14.95

**BRIAN ENO
His Music and the
Vertical Color of Sound**
Eric Tamm
242 pp.
80649-5 $14.95

**CHRISTGAU'S RECORD GUIDE
The '80s**
Robert Christgau
525 pp.
80582-0 $17.95

**COUNTRY
The Twisted Roots of
Rock 'n' Roll**
Nick Tosches
New preface and appendix
290 pp., 54 illus.
80713-0 $14.95

**THE DA CAPO COMPANION
TO 20th-CENTURY
POPULAR MUSIC**
Phil Hardy and Dave Laing
1,168 pp.
80640-1 $29.50

**DARK HORSE
The Life and Art of
George Harrison
Updated Edition**
Geoffrey Giuliano
395 pp., 105 photos and illus.
80747-5 $14.95

**THE DARK STUFF
Selected Writings on Rock Music,
1972–1995**
Nick Kent
Foreword by Iggy Pop
365 pp.
80646-0 $14.95

A DREAMER OF PICTURES
Neil Young: The Man and His Music
David Downing
272 pp., 22 illus., 18 in full color
80611-8 $14.95

ERIC CLAPTON
Lost in the Blues
Updated Edition
Harry Shapiro
256 pp., 50 photos
80480-8 $14.95

HEROES AND VILLAINS
The True Story of the Beach Boys
Steven Gaines
432 pp., 66 photos
80647-9 $14.95

THE LIFE AND TIMES OF LITTLE RICHARD
Updated Edition
Charles White
337 pp., 70 photos
80552-9 $13.95

NO COMMERCIAL POTENTIAL
The Saga of Frank Zappa
Updated Edition
David Walley
240 pp., 28 photos
80710-6 $13.95

PIECE OF MY HEART
A Portrait of Janis Joplin
David Dalton
287 pp., 91 illus.
80446-8 $14.95

PINK FLOYD
through the eyes of . . . the band, its fans, friends and foes
Edited by Bruno MacDonald
400 pp., 32 photos
80780-7 $14.95

REMEMBERING BUDDY
The Definitive Biography of Buddy Holly
John Goldrosen and John Beecher
210 pp., 160 illustrations, including 4 pp. in color
80715-7 $18.95

SONGWRITERS ON SONGWRITING
Expanded Edition
Paul Zollo
656 pp., 52 illus.
80777-7 $18.95

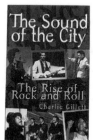